# Dear Courier

# Dear Courier

## The Civil War Correspondence of Editor Melvin Dwinell

*Edited by Ford Risley*

Voices of the Civil War • Michael P. Gray, Series Editor

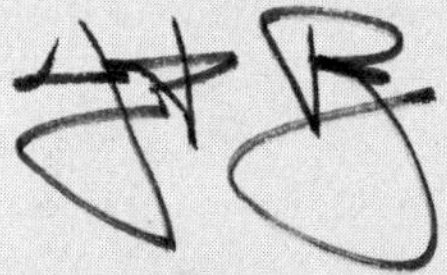

The University of Tennessee Press / Knoxville

First Edition.

The Voices of the Civil War series makes available a variety of primary source materials that illuminate issues on the battlefield, the home front, and the western front, as well as other aspects of this historic era. The series contextualizes the personal accounts within the framework of the latest scholarship and expands established knowledge by offering new perspectives, new materials, and new voices.

LIBRARY OF CONGRESS CATALOGING-IN-PUBLICATION DATA

NAMES: Dwinell, M. (Melvin), 1825–1887, author. | Risley, Ford, editor.
Title: Dear Courier : the Civil War correspondence of editor Melvin Dwinell / edited by Ford Risley.

DESCRIPTION: First edition. | Knoxville : The University of Tennessee Press, [2018] | Series: Voices of the civil war |

IDENTIFIERS: LCCN 2018019699 (print) | LCCN 2018029213 (ebook) | ISBN 9781621902942 (pdf) | ISBN 9781621902935 (hardcover)

SUBJECTS: LCSH: Dwinell, M. (Melvin), 1825–1887—Correspondence. | Newspaper editors—Georgia—Rome—Correspondence. | United States—History—Civil War, 1861–1865—Personal narratives, Confederate.

CLASSIFICATION: LCC E605 (ebook) | LCC E605 .D95 2018 (print) | DDC 973.7/82092 [B] —dc23

LC record available at https://lccn.loc.gov/2018019699

# Contents

# Illustrations

# Foreword

In the spring of 1864, Union forces under the direction of Gen. William T. Sherman plunged from Tennessee into Georgia in hopes of taking Atlanta, but his troopers stopped about seventy miles northwest, in the foothills of the Appalachians. There, the community of Rome held a strategic position. It was at the confluence of two rivers, the Oostanaula and Etowah, which converge to form the more lengthy Coosa, running deep into Alabama and joining a river system that leads all the way to Mobile Bay. Sherman knew strategic points on the map, and this was certainly one of them. Readers of other volumes in the Voices of the Civil War series might have familiarity with the Union's use of vital waterways both inland and in saltwater, detailed particularly in the recent work *Sailing with Farragut: The Civil War Recollections of Bartholomew Diggins* (2016). In addition to being close to important waterways, Rome was situated on a railroad nexus that linked a line that stretched from Chattanooga to Atlanta. The importance of railroads—their building, protection, and repair—is also a topic addressed in an earlier Voices volume: *Confederate Engineer: Training and Campaigning with John Morris Wampler* (2000). With such an operational opportunity, and also rumors that the city housed iron furnaces for cannon production, Union troops prepared to take Rome. Rome was eventually captured, and stores and shops in the "Hill City" were either requisitioned or ransacked. As the soldiers marched onto Broad Street, they found a newspaper with a small printing press: the *Rome Courier*. That establishment was seized, too, and Yankee printers used the press to publish a new publication for the inhabitants in blue.

It may have come as a surprise to the Union troops that the newspaper's editor had also been a Northerner, who moved from New England to the South. Leaving the Green Mountains of Vermont, as well as his teaching job and principalship, Melvin Dwinell headed for the rolling hills of northwest Georgia in the early 1850s, eventually settling down as an editor until the Civil War broke out. There were many other circumstances in which men originally from one region enlisted on the "other side," as *A Confederate Yankee: The Journal of Edmund*

*William Drummond, a Confederate Soldier from Maine* (2004), another volume in this series, showed so well. Unlike Drummond, Dwinell did not find love and marry into the South, but he did eventually adopt the Southern cause. Although Dwinell did not own slaves, under his supervision the *Rome Courier* was a moderate Democratic newspaper that supported the institution. After the surrender of Fort Sumter, Dwinell swelled with war fever and decided to enlist in the Rome Light Guards, which became part of the 8th Georgia Infantry. He continued to write prolifically.

Contemporaries noted that in Rome crowds would gather at the railroad depot, waiting in anticipation to find the latest news from the front. Any information from the war was highly desired, especially since there were few telegraph lines and frequent disruption in transportation. Dwinell slaked their thirst for news, sometimes penciling his letters to the *Courier* as often as three times a week. An experienced journalist, he was on top of the latest information, including the names of soldiers injured or killed, which provided relief for some, and perhaps the beginning of closure for others. He also provided the community with the 8th Georgia's whereabouts, their successes and their failures—revealing some information that, in retrospect, may have gotten him reprimanded by superiors.

More than a century and a half later, it has taken the skillful eye of Ford Risley, a former newspaperman turned academic, to bring Dwinell's "written voice" back from the Civil War, saved from the obscurity of microfilm shelves. The result is this volume. Risley painstakingly pieces together about two hundred of Dwinell's letters, providing context and clarity, and bringing to life his experiences during the two and a half years he served in the 8th Georgia. Risley's research was conducted extensively, while the narrative spans the antebellum era through the postwar period. The inverted careers of editor Dwinell and editor Risley makes for a collaboration in one of the best newspaper correspondent accounts that come from the Civil War, and as series editor, I am proud the press is bringing this important work to light.

*Dear Courier: The Civil War Correspondence of Editor Melvin Dwinell* fills a void in the historiography on a variety of levels. Among the more than fifty volumes of the Voices of the Civil War collection, this is the first that has been told through the viewpoint of a newspaper correspondent. This affords the reader not only an inside perspective, but also an evolving evaluation of his exposure to army life—shifting views, from perceptions of generals and the enlisted men (which he became an advocate for), to introspection on the hardships of war. For example, Dwinell wrote after First Manassas, "One of the most remarkable mental phenomena, was the sudden strange drying up of sympathetic feeling for the suffering of the wounded and dying. I could never before look even upon small operations, or persons in extreme pain from any cause, especially when blood was freely flowing. . . ." Dwinell explained how he might faint at such sights heretofore, but after his soldiering experiences, witnessing "the most terrible mutilations, the most horrid and ghastly expression of men in a death struggle . . . heads shot through and brains lying about," he "viewed all of this with far less feeling."

The letters begin in spring of 1861 at a training camp outside of Atlanta and conclude in the fall of 1863, while the 8th Georgia was camped outside of Chattanooga. Their scope covers battlefronts to behind the lines, including picket duty, social events, religion, desertion, and military punishment. Guided by Risley, who adds illuminating chapter introductions, extensive annotations, and an enlightening Epilogue, Dwinell conveys the excitement of being a member of the Army of Northern Virginia and the drama of the major battles in the Eastern theater. There are also descriptions of important locales, such as Harpers Ferry, "a wild and romantic place," through the South Mountains and into Chambersburg. Dwinell chronicled the unit's participation in larger campaigns at Bull Run, the Peninsula, Seven Days, and finally Gettysburg, where the editor was wounded.

The book will appeal to a host of audiences. Environmental historians will find rich insight in Dwinell's description of the rising floods in Richmond, while economic historians can follow the changing market conditions in the city. Medical historians will be interested in how the officer chronicles small pox quarantines in camp, as well his explanation of the growing fears that the spread of deadly disease would take over Southern society. Students of memory will appreciate his descriptive dedication of a monument to a fallen brigadier general, while demographers will find Dwinell's meticulous death and injury records invaluable. Scholars of society and culture will see viewpoints on abolitionism and slavery, as well as illuminating remarks on recreation and religion. In one amusing letter, Dwinell gives a detailed description of the differences among Southern troops, segregated by regions and social order—a kind of cultural genealogy. Political historians will find value in a rare wartime account of Georgia soldiers engaged in the state's gubernatorial race. There is even mention of highest-ranking political leaders, as Dwinell describes a visit by Confederate President Jefferson Davis to the 8th Georgia's camp. Davis was temporarily detained from entering by an unknowing and overzealous sergeant of the guard, R. F. Hutchings. After the proper credentials were doled out and the president recognized, a good laugh was had—at the expense of Hutchings, of course.

After being wounded at Gettysburg, Dwinell was furloughed and returned home to Rome. While there, a group of residents nominated him to run for the Georgia House of Representatives and he was elected. His superior officers, including James Longstreet and George Anderson, refused to accept the resignation because they held service record in high regard. Anderson argued that they could not afford to lose "so valuable an officer" as Dwinell. However, they were overruled and the editor began his brief stint in the legislature. But it was his duty-in-arms, with pencil and notebook in hand, that made for a service record that would reach far and wide 150 years later. Before he went into his first major engagement, Dwinell wrote what he thought might be his final letter. He looked home to Rome, and declared, "Good Bye readers of the *Courier*. I hope you will hear from me again in a few days. If all-wise Providence orders otherwise, then a long farewell." Thanks to Providence, he did write a few days later, and thanks to the efforts of Ford Risley, you have one of the finest volumes by a Civil War correspondent.

Michael P. Gray
East Stroudsburg University of Pennsylvania

# Acknowledgments

Thanks to my daughter, Emily, and to Cary Dillard, who transcribed many of Melvin Dwinell's letters in the *Rome Courier*. As always, the staff of Penn State's interlibrary loan office was unfailingly helpful with my numerous requests for microfilm and other materials. I am grateful to the staff of the Rome-Floyd County Public Library who, during several visits, helped me locate information about Dwinell and the *Courier*. Annie Aupperle checked sources, found illustrations, and helped with other tasks. Virginia Harrison assisted with the index. Keith Bohannon and Russell McClendon read the manuscript, corrected errors, and offered valuable suggestions. For their encouragement along the way, I want to thank two fine Georgians, John Inscoe and Wally Eberhard. I also appreciate the support of Michael Gray, editor of the Voices of the Civil War series, and Scot Danforth, director of the University of Tennessee Press. Finally, I owe a special debt to my family, who have listened to me talk about Melvin Dwinell for far, far too long.

# Prologue

Melvin Dwinell supplied readers of the *Rome Courier* with news of the Civil War from a hometown perspective. During his two-and-a-half years as an officer in the Confederate army, the editor wrote approximately two hundred "Dear Courier" letters that were published in his newspaper. With a reporter's eye and a writer's touch, he provided an insightful and valuable picture of life in the Eighth Georgia Infantry, a regiment that participated in several of the war's major campaigns.[1]

Dwinell described the terror of being in a battle for the first time, the excitement of seeing a Union spy balloon, and the sadness of witnessing a soldier executed for killing another soldier. He told readers about the danger and tedium of picket duty, the inspiration of religious services, the joys of camp recreation, and the devotion of a local woman who wanted to bring her wounded brother home. He also wrote about the problems of crime and desertion, the inadequate shoes and clothing with which Confederate troops were forced to endure, and the problem of some men shirking their duties.

The editor's tireless dedication to writing letters regularly to the *Courier* made him one of the most prolific Southern correspondents during the war. Although numerous Confederate editors, including several from Georgia, left their newspapers behind to fight for the South, most carried on only an occasional correspondence, if they wrote at all. Dwinell, on the other hand, wrote weekly and usually more often. In fact, the sheer quantity of his war correspondence is comparable to that of some of the Confederacy's full-time journalists.[2]

Dwinell was born in East Calais, Vermont, on July 9, 1825, one of ten children of Israel and Phila Dwinell. The fifth child, he was "fitted for college" at nearby Montpelier Academy and then attended the University of Vermont. After graduating in 1849, he served briefly as a schoolteacher and principal in Morrisville, Vermont. For reasons never made clear, he moved south in 1853 to teach school, first in Harris County, Georgia, and later in Macon County,

Alabama. On January 1, 1855, he purchased a half interest in the *Rome Courier*. A year later, he bought the remaining shares of the newspaper, becoming editor and sole owner.[3]

Situated in the foothills of the Appalachian Mountains, Rome had been established in 1835 in what was then known as "Cherokee Country." Four years earlier, Georgia's General Assembly had claimed all Cherokee land in northwest Georgia. Founders built Rome on bluffs overlooking the Etowah and Oostanaula Rivers, where they joined to form the Coosa River. Known locally as the "Hill City," Rome developed into an important trading and transportation center for frontier northwest Georgia. It also became the seat of government for Floyd County. Floyd County grew swiftly in the 1850s and by the end of the decade had a population of 15,915 residents, including 5,913 slaves. As the county's commercial center, Rome boasted numerous small businesses, including one bank, two hotels, one dry goods store, two hardware stores, two book and stationery stores, and a jewelry shop. Among the manufacturers were four sawmills, two iron foundries, two furniture factories, one gunsmith, and one tobacco processor. Rome also had two other valuable assets: a railroad spur that connected it with the Western & Atlantic Railroad running between Atlanta and Chattanooga, and steamboat service to Greensport, Alabama.[4]

View of Rome. Ballou's Pictorial (November 1, 1856).

Farmers in Floyd County produced a variety of cash and subsistence crops. They also reared livestock for market and their own consumption. Corn, wheat, and tobacco, as well as hogs, cattle, and sheep, were the main sources of income for most farmers. The area's climate was only marginally suitable for cotton; most farmers found there was less profit in it than other crops. Even so, slaves were the backbone of the county's agricultural economy. More slaves lived in Floyd County than any other county in northwest Georgia. However, the majority of residents owned no slaves, and only ten owned more than fifty. The largest slaveholder in the county owned ninety-three slaves, many of whom were hired out.[5]

* * * * *

The *Rome Courier* had been founded in 1843 as the *Coosa River Journal*. In 1849 the name was changed to the *Courier* when A. M. Eddleman and S. M. Jack purchased it. The antebellum era was a lively period for partisan journalism in the South, and it was not unusual even for small towns to have two or more party newspapers. In the decade leading up to the war, Rome supported three other newspapers at various times: the *Rome Southerner & Advertiser*, the *Rome Observer*, and the *True Flag*. Despite the competition for readers and advertisers, Dwinell guided the *Courier* successfully from its small office on Rome's main thoroughfare, Broad Street. In 1860, the *Courier* began publishing three times a week, appearing on Tuesday, Thursday, and Saturday. It also maintained a weekly edition.[6]

Under Dwinell's direction, the *Courier* was a moderate Democratic publication. In its editorial columns the newspaper supported slavery, arguing that it was in the best interests of the region and the entire country. Mindful of his northern upbringing, and no doubt hopeful that the Union could be saved, Dwinell supported Constitutional Union candidate John Bell in the pivotal 1860 presidential election. After Republican candidate Abraham Lincoln's victory, the *Courier* urged readers to "beware of rash counsels" and added, "If revolution must come, let us go into it *deliberately*." Residents of the area should "hope for the best but at the same time be making preparations for the worst." Moreover, any preparations should be "*constitutional* and *lawful* in their character."[7]

Dwinell, who did not own slaves, eventually supported Georgia's decision to become the fifth Southern state to secede. The *Courier* declared that with "a spirit of self-sacrificing patriotism . . . a great a glorious Confederacy" would arise from the ashes of the United States. Dwinell traveled to Montgomery, Alabama, in February and reported on the opening session of the Confederate

Congress. He described the inauguration of Jefferson Davis as president, calling it "the grandest pageant ever witnessed in the South." The *Courier* proposed Rome as the permanent capital of the Confederacy, saying, "[t]here is more propriety in the suggestion than many would at first sight suppose." It also reported on the excitement of residents when the new flag of the Confederacy was raised over a local livery stable.[8]

When Confederate forces captured Fort Sumter on April 12, 1861, the *Courier* proclaimed: "The War Gloriously Begun." Rome celebrated news of the fort's fall with a "torchlight procession, illuminations, pyrotechnics and . . . enthusiastic displays generally." In an editorial, the *Courier* confidently boasted of Confederate prospects: "[T]he high way to glory, with duty and patriotism as our guides, stretches out distinctly before us."[9]

Even before Fort Sumter's fall, men had begun joining Floyd County's three existing volunteer companies—the Rome Light Guards, Cherokee Artillery, and Floyd Cavalry. The companies had been stepping up their training for months. The Light Guards drilled on Rome's Broad Street and, during inclement weather, in city hall. One member, physician George S. Barnsley, wrote that he felt disgusted at the idea of "men shooting each other about questions" that should be settled politically. However, he also admitted, "marching in the streets filled our bosoms to overflowing with patriotism; and especially as the pretty girls threw flowers and kisses to us."[10]

The Light Guards and Cherokee Artillery soon tendered their service to the Fourth Georgia Volunteer Brigade. Among the members of the Light Guards was Dwinell, who had been elected second lieutenant. Edward J. Magruder, a graduate of the Virginia Military Institute, commanded the unit. On April 23, officers from the Floyd companies departed for training outside Atlanta at Camp Smyrna, which had been renamed Camp Brown. A week later, Dwinell wrote his first letter to the newspaper, beginning with the salutation that would become well known to readers, "Dear Courier."[11]

After four weeks of instruction the officers returned to Rome, where the troops had been drilling outside of town at Sheibley's School House. By that time, other companies from the county had been organized. The Floyd Cavalry had disbanded and turned into an infantry company renamed the Miller Rifles, in honor of local physician, Dr. H. V. M. Miller. The Floyd Infantry was also organized. While the men drilled, commanders busily tried to equip their companies with canteens, blankets, knapsacks, and, most importantly, rifles. The men were using their own firearms, mostly outdated hunting rifles.[12]

The three infantry companies from the county left for Virginia in the span of a week at the end of May. The first to depart was the Floyd Infantry, with the

Light Guards and Miller Rifles marching along to see them off from the Rome train depot. The Light Guards left on May 27, with much of the town turning out to say good-bye. Most of the men carried a trunk or two with their possessions, and a few even took young slaves as personal servants. Two days later, the Miller Rifles departed. The three units eventually became part of the Eighth Georgia Infantry Regiment (known as companies A, E, and H respectively.)[13]

Before he left, Dwinell turned over the publishing duties of the *Courier* to his assistant editor, B. G. Salvage. Soon Salvage was forced to defend Dwinell from an editorial attack by one of his home-state newspapers. The editor of the *Burlington Free Press* apparently had read an editorial by Dwinell supporting slavery and criticizing the policies of President Lincoln. The *Free Press* editor declared that Dwinell "shames the land of his birth, the mother who nursed him, and teachers who taught him, by praising slavery, which he knows to be a curse, repeating slanders about the free North, which he knows to be false, and advocating treason, which he knows to be crime." Salvage promptly replied that Dwinell believed slavery to be "a blessing, not only to the black and white race of the South, but *pre-eminently a blessing* to the Yankees of New England, who have hitherto enjoyed the monopoly of manufacturing . . . goods out of *slave grown* cotton." He declared, "If this be 'treason' let his Vermont friends make the most of it!" Moreover, continued Salvage, "If the editor of the Free Press and hundreds of thousands of other dupes of Northern fanaticism, had pursued the course of friend Dwinell in coming South, and learning from actual observation the true state of affairs . . . we would still be united, prosperous and happy people."[14]

Dwinell was not the only resident of Floyd County originally from the North. In a letter published in the *Courier* with the title "Our Citizens of Northern Birth," an unidentified writer said that natives of the North now living in the county were too sensitive to criticism of the region. The condemnation of the North understandably was "the indignant outbursts of a wronged and persecuted people." Moreover, the writer declared, "It is the duty of every citizen to show by actions, as well as by words, that he is with us, and we have a right to know the true position of all who are in our midst, whether they be of Northern or Southern birth, and whether they have relatives in the North or not." The writer further stated, "[While a man] can never forget, and should never cease to love the land of his birth . . . we can see no place for sympathy with the North, as a people in their unholy and abominable designs upon the rights and security of the Southern States."[15]

* * * * *

Dwinell's "Dear Courier" letters began in April 1861, when he was training with other officers outside Atlanta. They ended in October 1863, when the Eighth Georgia was outside Chattanooga, Tennessee. During the years the editor served in the regiment, he took part in several major battles and campaigns, including First Manassas, Peninsula, Seven Days, and Gettysburg. He became seriously ill in 1862 and was not with the Eighth Georgia when it fought at Second Manassas and Sharpsburg. Dwinell was wounded during the second day of fighting at Gettysburg, and he left the army later that year after being elected to the Georgia legislature. Before the Federal army captured Rome in the spring of 1864, he joined the exodus of residents who fled. The *Courier's* office was briefly used by Union troops to publish a soldier newspaper and then was wrecked when the Federal army left. Dwinell returned to Rome after the war ended and rebuilt the *Courier.*

Dwinell wrote his letters to the *Courier* using a pencil and memorandum book that he carried in his pocket. Because the letters were sent via the mail—and the Confederate postal system was notoriously slow—they usually did not appear in the newspaper for at least a week and, frequently, longer. This could pose problems during a major campaign because letters describing the events leading up to the battle were sometimes published after the outcome of the fighting already was known. The *Courier* regularly published two, and occasionally three, letters from Dwinell in a single issue, either because of delays in the mail or because the newspaper was published only three times a week.[16]

Dwinell penned his letters whenever and wherever he had the time. While in camp, he would often write a few paragraphs, put away his pencil, and resume the letter again when he had the time. Much of his correspondence that appeared in the *Courier* was written over the course of a day or two, with the times noted in the letter. Following the journalistic practice of the day, Dwinell did not include his name on his correspondence and simply identified himself as "M. D." His letters did not have a headline when they were published in the *Courier.* They were identified with the simple heading, "Editorial Correspondence."[17]

Readers of the *Courier* awaited Dwinell's letters with great anticipation. "I would not miss our friend Lt. Dwinell's letters for twice the subscription," one reader wrote. "He has never received his due for his labor." Residents found news of the war difficult to come by, especially during the first year, when the town had no telegraph line connecting it to nearby cities such as Atlanta and Chattanooga. With no other source of news, residents eagerly looked forward to the arrival of the train from Kingston that carried the mail. The train conductor often found a large crowd waiting at the Rome depot. As he carried the mail to the post office, townspeople stopped him repeatedly to ask if he had any news.[18]

The honest and compelling quality of Dwinell's correspondence, combined with his clear, straightforward writing style, put him in the same league with the most talented Southern war correspondents. As an officer, he generally avoided the sort of critical examination of the Confederate army and administration that could be found in the writing of some full-time journalists. Still, Dwinell did not entirely avoid sensitive subjects. He pointed out the problems of crime and desertion among soldiers. He described the inadequate clothing and equipment that the troops were forced to endure. And he wrote about the heavy drinking that many Southern troops—both enlisted men and officers—regularly engaged in.

In some of his early correspondence, Dwinell revealed military information that might have been useful if it had fallen into enemy hands. However, he soon became more careful about what he told readers. Generally, he avoided the kind of atrocity stories about the Union army found in the writings of less talented soldier correspondents. Still, he regularly used disparaging terms like "cunning devils" and "vile wretches" to describe enemy troops. To his credit, Dwinell did not often give estimates of casualties because they were usually exaggerated. The few times he did, he was sometimes right but more often wrong.

Like the good newsman he was, Dwinell recognized that what readers back home wanted more than anything was news about family, friends, and neighbors serving in the army. He rarely sent correspondence that did not mention the health of soldiers from northwest Georgia, especially the "Floyd Boys," as he called residents of the county. Soldiers from the area who were promoted, transferred, or killed or wounded in the fighting received special mention in his letters.

As journalism written on the spot, Dwinell's letters to the *Courier* have strengths and limitations. As a group, they provide a valuable narrative account of the Eighth Georgia, a unit that took part in many of the significant campaigns and battles of the war in the East. They also have a richness and forthrightness that a skilled and observant journalist can provide. However, because they were usually written in haste, the correspondence often suffers from a lack of context. And because the letters were published for a wide audience, Dwinell sometimes had to be guarded about what he wrote. His personal letters to his family in Vermont give insight into his reasons for fighting, as well as his unbridled devotion to the South.

The 1862 Confederate Conscription Act would have exempted Dwinell from serving in the army. The law excused from military service members of the Confederate Congress and state legislatures, government clerks, postmen, telegraph operators, newspaper editors and printers, ministers, teachers, and others with jobs considered of importance to the war effort and the maintenance of the country. Nonetheless, hundreds of newspaper employees chose to serve anyway, many in the regular army and others in state militias. In late 1864, President Jefferson Davis called for changes to the exemptions in the conscription law that would have required newspaper editors and others to serve. However, the Confederate Congress never seriously considered the proposal.[19]

The vast majority of Dwinell's correspondence in this book is taken from the *Courier*. During the war, the newspaper published two editions, the *Weekly Courier* and the *Tri-Weekly Courier*. All of his correspondence collected here was taken from the *Tri-Weekly Courier*. The few private letters to his family that exist came from the Melvin Dwinell Papers at the Georgia Department of Archives and History. In general, the grammar and spelling of Dwinell's letters to the *Courier* and his family have been retained. As a newspaperman, he was an experienced writer and his grammar was sound. However, he occasionally misspelled words, including the names of people and places. They are corrected in the notes. Like many writers of the era, Dwinell often used extemporaneous punctuation in his letters. In the interest of readability, any unnecessary punctuation has been removed. Finally, it should be noted that Confederate names for battles are used. In several instances, the North and South gave different names to battles. Because this is a collection of letters from a Confederate correspondent, the Southern names are used.

# I

# "The Men Look as Bright as Their Own New Buttons"

## *April–July 1861*

After arriving at Camp Brown, Melvin Dwinell wasted no time in writing his first letter to the *Courier*. He described the old church meeting ground, renamed for Governor Joseph E. Brown, and the efforts of the men to set up camp. The editor also told readers how the officers of the Light Guards sewed their own battle flag, and how the company was proud to be the first one to raise its flag in camp. Just a few days after the Floyd County troops arrived, Brown visited the camp. In a surprising speech, he announced that the men training there would remain in the state as home guards because they were not yet "sufficiently skilled in the science of war." The speech caused "great disaffection" among the officers, Dwinell wrote, and the next day the governor reversed course. He declared that "all would get service as soon as they could reasonably desire."

The orders to depart for Virginia soon came, and at the end of May, the Floyd troops arrived at Camp Howard Grove outside Richmond. Located on the Mechanicsville Turnpike, it became a rendezvous for companies from across the state and soon was known as Camp Georgia. In several letters, Dwinell described how the men were settling into camp life. With an eye for an entertaining anecdote, he told the story of how President Jefferson Davis, upon arriving at the camp for a visit, was ordered by the dutiful sergeant of the guard to wait until his identity could be confirmed. The sergeant was the Light Guards' own Fred Hutchings.

Jefferson Davis. Library of Congress.

The next week the Eighth Georgia was on the move to Harpers Ferry, and in a series of letters Dwinell described the long, grueling trip. The regiment initially piled into two trains for the first leg of the trip to Gordonsville, then transferred to another train to reach Manassas Junction. The regiment subsequently traveled over the Blue Ridge Mountains and into the Shenandoah Valley town of Strasburg. The troops marched the eighteen miles to Winchester and then took another train for the final leg of the trip to Harpers Ferry. Yet the Eighth Georgia did not stay long and soon was marching back to Winchester, which Gen. Joseph E. Johnston believed was a better spot to meet Union forces. In case the *Courier's* readers might misconstrue the move as a retreat, Dwinell wrote, "We do not flee from the enemy, but go to meet them."

When the soldiers finally arrived in Winchester, they camped at a tranquil spot known as Hollingsworth Grove. Dwinell described the pleasant times spent there, including evenings in which the men often sang together. In one letter, he included the verses of a popular song, "Georgia," with words written by a member of the Light Guards. Soon, however, a measles outbreak spread through the camp with devastating consequences. Several of the Floyd men became ill, but none died; other soldiers were not as fortunate. In all, twenty-one members of the regiment perished, and forty-four were mustered out of service.

Throughout the early months of the war, Dwinell described the comings and goings of the Floyd troops. Some of them were assigned new duties, and others were mustered out of the army for various reasons. He also made sure to inform readers about the condition of the men from the county, identifying those who were ill and updating their conditions. In July, Dwinell told his parents in Vermont, "this rough life agrees with me finely." The now die-hard Confederate boasted that the South would never be defeated on the battlefield.

CAMP BROWN, near Marietta. Ga.,
April 24th, 1861

**DEAR COURIER:** This is the second day of our corps in camps, and matters begin to assume a sort of mater-of-course air—a home like feeling of contentment and good nature is now seen upon the countenances of "the soldier men," instead of the uneasy state and disagreeable strangeness of yesterday.

*Camp Brown* is five miles below Marietta, and has hitherto been known as the Smyrna Camp Meeting Ground. It is a beautiful grove, now neatly cleared off, and, in all respects, is a really delightful place. There are fourteen of the old camp meeting tents still standing and in tolerable condition. These are

Harpers Ferry. Library of Congress.

occupied—two by the commissary department—(one for provisions for the men, the other for forage for horses,) and the other twelve make very comfortable quarters for the men—the five officers of one company to a tent. Besides these there are twelve canvass tents—each affording pleasant quarters for one company.[1]

Most of the day yesterday was spent in the, to novices, rather disagreeable duties of pitching camps, providing camp equipage and furniture and the labors of setting up for house keeping generally.

It was the writer's fortune, in company with Lieut. Hall, to be the first detached for guard duty.[2] We were posted to guard the commissaries quarters from 11 ½ A.M. to 12 ½ P.M., and it was a weary pacing back and forth we had of it, in the hot sun.

The arrangements not being complete, most of the messes had a sort of picked up dinner yesterday, but since then our meals have been wholesome and good enough. The regular daily rations for a mess of five, is: 6 lbs. 4 oz. beef, or 3 lbs. 6 oz. bacon; 5 lbs. 10 oz. light bread; ½ lb. rice; 5 oz. coffee; 9 ½ oz. sugar; 1 gill [½ a cup] salt; ½ pint vinegar; 2 oz. soap and 2 candles. Those provisions and the camp furniture are all furnished at the expense of the State. Butter, eggs, vegetables, &c., if had at all, are at the expense of the respective messes.

Gen. Phillips made a speech yesterday evening, in which he stated that the reason the Governor had ordered this encampment was, to prepare as soon as possible, the Company officers of the Brigade for actual service, and through them their respective Companies; and he expressed the belief, founded upon assurances from the Governor, that his command would be called into the field as soon as it, or any companies of it, were sufficiently well drilled to render it expedient to do so. He said the 4th Brigade was no "Home Guard," but was organized for the purpose of doing service for the Confederate States, in Georgia or out of it, wherever they might be needed.

Camp Brown, near Marietta
Saturday, April 27th, 1861.

**Dear Courier:** The noise, confusion and hubbub generally about a Military camp of volunteers are plead in extenuation for the want of perspicuity and method in these letters. The one dated April 24th was retained and, by mistake, some sheets of blank paper sent instead.

There are now as reported twenty-eight companies represented in the encampment. The men are all in excellent health and spirits, and are learning the science of war as fast as possible. There probably never was an assemblage of men more eager to learn, than are the officers at Camp Brown. There is not in all the Camp a murmur of complaint, nor any grumbling about hard fare or the fatigues of duty. In fact it would be very ungracious for any one to find fault, for so far as the acts of our excellent officers, Gen. Phillips and Major Capers, are concerned, *fault* is a thing that cannot be *found*: and, beside, the men are not disposed to *forge* them.[3]

The tactics of camp are regular, system and order prevailing in all things, and business now moves on, not exactly "like clock work," but yet with as much precision as could be expected from a volunteer corps. We have a great many little interesting scenes and occurrences, and the general prevalence of good humor, wit and repartee, intermingled music and songs, prevent anything like dullness, when off from duty, and keep such as otherwise might be so disposed, from thinking too much of home. Last Wednesday the Rome Light Guards sent to Atlanta and got the necessary materials, and then set up until one o'clock at night making a Confederate Flag. Before retiring it was completed and raised. This was the first flag raised in the camp. The next morning at sunrise the balance of the Rifle Battalion were invited to join the "Guards," and the Flag was saluted by forming in circle and marching eight times round it in double quick time. As soon as the balance of the encampment learned the cause of this novel demonstration, the welkin was made to ring by the land huzzas from all the quarters.

On yesterday, Friday, Seaborn Jones, Jr., Capt. of the Polk county Rifles was elected Lieutenant colonel of the Rifle Battalion. He has resigned and another election is ordered on next Monday.

Yesterday was a very exciting day at Camp Brown. At eleven o'clock all turned out to escort Capt. Mays' company, the Toombs volunteers, of Calhoun, called into service. Gen. Phillips made a short but very patriotic farewell speech, which was appropriately responded to by Capt Mays. When at the train a report was received that the "Rome Light Guards" had been ordered out. Our boys huzzaed until they could hardly speak; they were congratulated by their friends and the excitement was kept up until late in the evening when it was learned that the report was false. It rained nearly all the forenoon, but this did not keep the men in their quarters. Several ladies have visited the camp from Marietta, and yesterday there were seven from Atlanta, and when they left were escorted to the cars by two companies from Atlanta, and the two from Rome.

The ladies of Marietta have tendered a complimentary dinner to the entire encampment, to be given on next Wednesday, May Day. There will probably be a crowd present on that occasion.

We have no time for further writing at this present. The members of the Rome companies send their compliments to all their friends. D.

Camp Brown, April 29, 1861.

**Dear Courier:** Nothing of particularly exciting interest occurred on the Sabbath. The day was properly observed, but as usual all hands turned out at reveille at 5 o'clock A.M.; to dress parade at 6 ½ P.M., and we had tattoo at the regular hour at 9 ½ and taps at 10 P.M. The drums beat for church call at 11 A.M., and most of the officers, in full dress uniform, in the encampment attended preaching at the stand. An excellent sermon was preached by the Rev. Mr. Graham, stationed preacher at Marietta. Another particularly interesting sermon was preached at 3 o'clock P.M., by President Rambeaut, of Cassville. It is highly gratifying to know that a large portion of the officers in this Brigade possess that highest style of bravery, which is fortified by christian faith, and a calm reliance in that "Divinity which shapes our ends, rough hew them as we will."

Capt. M. A. Stovall was highly complimented on Saturday by being appointed *pro tempore* commander of the Brigade during the absence of Gen. Phillips on Sunday.[4] Dr. Lawrence was also appointed substitute for the Adjutant General during two or three days last week. It cannot be otherwise than pleasant to the citizens of Rome and vicinity to know that their companies are thus flatteringly noticed.

Gen Phillips received a telegraphic dispatch on Saturday from Gov. Brown, urging him to hasten on the organization of the Brigade as rapidly as possible, because he expected the entire force would very soon be called into the field.

It is astonishing indeed to notice the rapidity with which the officers here improve in drilling. Most of the companies belonging to this Brigade have been organized during the last few weeks, and a large majority of the company officers, at the commencement of this encampment, were almost entirely ignorant of military tactics and discipline. But their hearts are in the work and they apply themselves with the utmost earnestness. This is a beautiful morning and the men look as bright as their own new buttons.

Saturday at 7 P.M., 110 troops from Alabama passed by here on their way to Richmond, Va. They are to rendezvous at Dalton for a short time. Last night at the same hour 450 more from Alabama passed up to join them.

The men here are all well, in excellent spirits and eager to go to the wars.

Capt. Mays, of Calhoun, with his company of 93 men, the Toombs Volunteers, passed down the road for Augusta, this morning, and we regret very much to learn that one of them, by the name of Beech, fell under the train at Calhoun and had both his legs cut off by being run over. They are a fine looking set of fellows and as they passed this camp they were greeted with the most enthusiastic cheering. M.

Camp Brown, near Marietta, Ga.,
May 2nd, 1861.

**Dear Courier:** The hour between breakfast and morning drill we snatch at "trying to catch the flying moment as they pass," and employ them in posting you in regard to matters "here and hereabouts."

On Monday night Gov. Brown visited the camp that honors *him* with its name. He was received by the Cavalry Corps and escorted to the Brigade parade ground where all the balance of the Companies were drawn up for a grand reception. He made very few remarks at the reception, but after supper he was called out, and made, what seemed to us, a most ill-timed and inappropriate speech. He said the 4th Brigade was organized for the defence of Georgia. He said the State might be invaded—he feared would be—and this corps was to be the "Home Guard." He presumed every man in the Brigade was eager for the fight, but discretion was at least as noble a virtue as valor, and inasmuch as we were not sufficiently skilled in the science of war to make our efforts correspond with the spirit of our intentions, in efficiency, it was his intention to keep this Brigade at home until it was well disciplined, or until there should be no reasonable apprehension of the invasion of the State. He said he did not intend to send off all the best companies of the State, so as to leave it in a comparatively defenceless condition—the dearest interest of all citizens—their homes, kindred and firesides. He said he might send other companies, younger and less disciplined than any in this camp into, immediate service, for the reason that the honor of the State was at stake in this organization. It would be his effort to get the Brigade into service as a whole, if that should be impracticable, then they should go as Regiments or Battalions, or finally as companies; but at all events they should go with their officers, and in the more extended organization practicable.

There was great disaffection throughout the encampment on account of this speech, and no little murmuring must have come to the ears of the Governor. A petition was drawn up and signed by all officers who had an opportunity, and presented to him, praying that he should change his policy and send to earliest service the oldest and best disciplined companies. The next morning he made another speech in which he somewhat modified the positions taken, and said there was no doubt but that all would get service as soon as they could reasonably desire it, in Georgia or elsewhere, in the Confederate States. He stated that some might be called upon to exercise the cardinal virtue of patience, but this would be to their own advantage, and also that of the State. If he had only made the second speech, much disaffection would have been prevented, and as it is, it went far towards effecting a reconciliation.[5]

Yesterday was a gala day in this camp. The ladies of Marietta provided one of the most sumptuous repasts it has ever been our pleasure to enjoy, and it was participated in by the "soldier men"—who have been deprived of delicacies, for past ten days—with a keen relish. There was a large assemblage of ladies present from Marietta, Atlanta and elsewhere, and everything passed off to the utmost apparent satisfaction and delight to all concerned. God bless the ladies, their presence make pleasant all occasions, endears all places, and they dispense the sweetest of earthly blessings.

CAMP BROWN, May 4th 1861.

**DEAR COURIER:** There has nothing of particularly exciting interest transpired here in the past two days. The Fourth Brigade is now completely organized except the Battalion of Artillery. The following is a list of the Brigades, Regimental and Battalion Officers, the names of the Companies and their Captains:

*Field Officers of the 4th Brigade of Georgia Volunteers*
Wm Phillips, Brigadier-General,
F. W. Capers, Adjut. Brig. Inspector,
S. E. Blakly, Aid-de-Camp,
Hugh Buchanan, Aid-de Camp
Field Officers of the 1st Regiment
W. T. Wofford, Col.
S. Z. Ruff, Lieutenant Col.
Jeff Johnson, Major,
Dr. V. J. Roach, Sergeant,
J. B. Brown, Asst. Sergeant
J. N. Williams, Serg. Major,
James Vaughan, Quarter Master,
J. R. Wickie, Commissary.
1st Company McDonald Guards,
J. M. Johnston, Capt.
2 Company Acworth Infantry,
J. B. O. Neal, Captain.
3 Company Ga. Volunteers,
Lieut. H. M. Johnston, in com.
4 Company Jackson Guards,
J. H. Neal, Captain.
5 Company Cass co. Volunteers,

John Landervilk, Capt.
6 Ga. Highlanders,
J. A. Crawford, Captain
7 Company Jackson co. Volunteers,
D. S. Jarrett, Captain.
8 Company Davis Guards,
J. C. Roper, Captain.
9 Company Stephens Guards,
J. E. Starr, Captain.
10 Company Gilmer co. Volunteers,
W. Jones, Captain.
Field Officers of 2nd Regiment.
W. W. Boyd, Col.
T. C. Johnson, Lieut. Col.
A. J. Hutchins, Major.
Dr. H. V. M. Miller, Surgeon.
Dr. G. L. Jones, Assistant Surgeon
Sam Shals, Master,
G. B. Butler, Pay Master,
A. J. Kendy, Sergt. Major,
J. P. Perkins, Commissary.
Adjuntant not yet elected.
Palmetto Guards,
Lieut. Bell, in command.
Milton Volunteers,
Lieut. F. M. Cowan.
Canty Lee Volunteers,
Kendrick, Captain.
Tugola Blues, Millican, Captain.
Decalb Infantry, Fowler, Captain.
Kingston Vol., John Hooper, Captain.
Carroll Vol., Curtis, Captain.
Hartwell In'try, Skellan, Captain.
Sonora, In'try, Hunter, Captain.
Rome Lt. Guards, Magruder, Captain.
Field Offices of Battallion of Cavalry.
W. W. Rich, Major.
J. W. Arnold, (Acting) Adj.
Surgeon not yet elected.

W. S. Payton, Quarter Master,
Commissary not elected.
1st Company Coweta Rangers
J. W. Wilcoxton, Capt.
2nd Company Cherokee Cavalry
A. M. Franklin, Leiut. in command
3rd Company Cherokee Dragons,
W. B. C. Puckett, Capt.
4th Company Walton Guards,
Geo. Hillver, Captain.[6]
Artillery Battallion.
Field Officers not yet elected. Election to take place on Monday or Tuesday next.
1st Company Cherokee Artillery,
M. A. Stovall, Captain.
2nd Company, Murry co. Art'ry,

__________

3rd Company, Dixie Guards,
Guswald, Captain.
4th Company
name and Capt. not reported.

It is reported that Capt. M. A. Stovall will be elected to the command of this Battallion.

CAMP BROWN, near Marietta, Ga.,
May 7th, 1861.

**DEAR COURIER:** I have no time for writing this morning except to notice one or two changes that have been made in the Regimental officers as follows:

J. P. Perkins has been appointed Adjutant in the 2nd Regiment instead of Commissary, and A. J. Kennedy to the latter office, leaving the office of Sergeant Major to be supplied.

The Field Officers of Artillery Battalion are to be elected to-day.

This Camp is to break on Thursday morning unless different orders are previously received from the Governor. The following is a list of the officers of the Rifle Battalion, omitted by mistake in my last letter:

*Rifle Battalion—5 Companies.*
Lieut. Col. Seaborn Jones Jr.
Adjutant, Jas. H. Lawrence

Paymaster, A. M. Morris
Companies.
Cambell Rifles, Capt. T. C. Glover
Cass Rifles, Capt. R. C. Saxon
Polk Co. Rifles, Lieut. H. F. Wimberly in command.
Dalton Guards, Capt. R. T. Cook.
Habersham Vol., Capt. E. S. Barclay
M. A. Stovall was this day elected Colonel of the Artillery Battalion. D.

Camp Howard Grove
Richmond, Va., May 31, 1861.

**Dear Courier:** We arrived here at 8'clock yesterday evening. Our men all report themselves well, but there are some cases of slight indisposition occasioned by the fatigue, change of habits, &c.

We are about a mile from the center of the city, in a beautiful pine grove. Only six companies are yet arrived of Col. Bartow's Regiment, but the others are expected soon.[7] The Arkansas Regiment is camped about a half mile from us in full view. Andy Pitner and Henry Johnson called on us this morning. They are in excellent health and seem to be playing the soldier with much satisfaction.

Last night we lodged in a wood tent, formerly used by an Agricultural Society—the whole company in one room. The provisions provided for our journey have been of great service to us—in fact we must have suffered without them, for we have drawn no rations yet. The Light Guards realize the wisdom of the plan of having all our necessaries for service provided before coming to the place of rendezvous. Some companies that have been here several days are still without the comforts necessary for health, and are only satisfied with the assurance that their wants shall be supplied as soon as possible.

I have no very particular news to communicate in regard to general movements from this point. The number of troops at present rendezvoused at this place even is not known to me. We have probably passed in coming to our quarters from the city about 5,000. As fast as Regiments are fully organized they are sent forward, some to Manassas Junction some to Harper's Ferry and some to Norfolk.

Capt. Magruder left this morning to accompany his wife to the home of his father.[8] Mrs. M., by the way, received a great deal of attention on the journey, and seems to enjoy the trip very much. We were delayed in Lynchburg from 8 o'clock Wednesday morning to until 6 A.M. on Thursday. The citizens, and among them, Capt. Bohanna, M.D., deserves especial mention, showed the company many kind attentions, besides giving them a fine supper at the Piedmont Hotel. This favor was very highly appreciated, especially for the reason that we had been on cold victuals for the two days preceding. Our company—every man of them—behave themselves like gentlemen on the route, and received very high compliments for their genteel deportment, and soldier-line appearance.

It is probable that we will not be mustered into service until Monday. The expectation is, that as soon as our Regiment is fully organized, and all the companies are present, that we will be ordered *towards* Alexandria, and we hope to be able to march both *to* that city and *through* it.

President Davis was making speeches to the Ga. Regiment as we came into camp yesterday evening, but neither he, nor any other of the officers, give any intentions of their plans for prosecuting the war.

This is a bright warm day, and we have had a pleasant, yet busy time in pitching tents, arranging our "tricks and traps," and putting things generally to rights for regular camp life. M. D.

Camp Georgia, Howard Grove
Richmond, Va., June 3d

**Dear Courier:** The march of events here keeps step to the music of the times. There are now eleven Georgia companies in this encampment, averaging about 90 men each. I understand it is Col. Bartow's intention to get one more—the Athens Artillery. If he does, then the Regiment will be composed of ten companies of heavy Infantry, and Rifle company—the Rome Light Guard—and one Artillery. This would be an irregular number but it is thought it will admirably suit the place to which we are expected to go and the service we will have to encounter. The present belief is that the Regiment will be ordered to Manassas Junction on Wednesday the 5th inst.

The Arkansas Regiment that was encamped near us left yesterday for Acquia Creek near Fredericksburg. There are some twelve or fifteen regiments now encamped near this place. Some come and others go every day.

The Miller Rifles arrived here on Saturday night, all well and in good spirits. There was some dissatisfaction, however, yesterday, among some of the members, when they learned that they would be armed with Muskets. Fifteen of them were honorably discharged by Capt. Towers, in accordance with his pledge given them before leaving home, that if they could not get Rifles he would do so. He paid their expenses home.

The following are the names, viz: L. B. Arnold, R. B. Wright, J. R. and W. J. Leazer, Silas Embry, N. R. and W. B. Coleman, W. T. Whitehead, Thos. J. Self, David S. Teat, Jourdan Reese, W. M. Greer, Thos. E. Thornhill, Dr. Duane and M. L. Palmer. Their *pluck* was seriously questioned by other companies, and they left the camp amidst taunts, jeers and groans. Their *right* to go was not questioned, but they were believed to be entirely too fastidious in regard to the kind of arms to be furnished them. Dr. Duane and M. L. Palmer showed their willingness to do service by immediately joining our company.[9]

Capt. J. F. Cooper's Company were mustered into service several days since, Capt. Towers' and Magruder's this morning. From the Light Guards, Lother, Penny and Beasley were excused, and they will probably return home.

There are no men on the sick list from either the Miller Rifles or the Light Guards, though there are several slightly indisposed, but by no means seriously ill. There are three men from the Floyd Infantry in the hospital, but we learn that they are doing well.

All letters for our companies should be directed to the company, care of Col. F. S. Bartow, Richmond Va., and if not here they will be forwarded to us. M. D.

Camp Georgia, Howard Grove,
Richmond, Va., June 4th

**Dear Courier:** Important movements are on foot and the Georgia Regiment has been ordered to Harper's Ferry. After dark last night, President Davis, accompanied by Secretary of War, L. P. Walker, came into camp and ordered Col. Bartow to get his command in readiness for marching as soon as possible. A little after 10 o'clock a messenger came from the President bringing an order for the Regiment to march for Harper's Ferry at 6 this evening. It is understood that the Lincolnites are about attempting to establish a line of posts from Alexandria to that place and we are sent to cut them off.[10] The hum of preparedness this morning is quite intense, and you never saw the inmates of a bee hive more busy. Our men are eager for the fray, and if their discretion is proved to be half equal to their spirit they will do efficient service in the hour of trial.

We still have one or two men slightly indisposed, but not too ill to accompany us, Skidmore, who is the worst off, is able to be up, and the Doctor thinks is well enough to travel. Beasley, excused from our company, has joined the Floyd Infantry.

The following is a list of the Companies in this Regiment, viz:

Oglethorpe Light Infantry, of Savannah.
Macon Guards, of Macon.
Atlanta Grays, of Atlanta.
Oglethorpe Rifles, Oglethorpe co.
The Lechter Guards, of Augusta, are here but do not belong to the Regiment.
Echols Guards, of Merriwether county.
Rome Light Guards, of Rome.
Miller Rifles, of Rome.
Floyd Infantry, of Rome.
Pulaski Volunteers, of Pulaski county.
Beauregards, of Chattahoochee county.

All the companies from our place and most of the others go this evening; the balance as soon as transportation can be provided—probably to-morrow. We go by Gordonsville and Manassas Junction.

Letters should be directed to the Rome Light Guards, care of Col. F. S. Bartow, Ga. Regiment, Harper's Ferry, Va. M. D.

Camp Georgia, Howard Grove
Near Richmond, Va., June 4, 9 PM.

**Dear Courier:** Our Regiment failed to get off to Harper's Ferry this evening in accordance with the command issued this morning. The reason of this is that some of the arms and accoutrements could not be got in hand in time.

We have had an interesting time today in packing up and getting ready to meet the enemy. The order was to provide in our haver-sacks sufficient provisions for three days. This made an unusual amount of cooking necessary, and no small perplexity in deciding what, how much to take and how little would do. We expect to march on foot at least fifteen miles, and apprehend that the railroad track may be torn up at almost any point after reaching the vicinity of our mercenary vandal foes.

A Battalion of Flying Artillery, from New Orleans, numbering 310 men, arrived here to-day. They bring with them eight six-pound brass cannon, and the balance for a full outfit are being provided here, and are nearly ready.

An interesting incident occurred last night, at the time of the President's visit to the camp. Sergeant R. F. Hutchings, of our company, was acting sergeant of the guard, and he hailed the Chief Executive of the Confederate States, and compelled him to stand until satisfactory assurances were given of his right to pass the line. Of course Ferd did not know the President, but he made a good point by faithfully discharging his duty.[11]

We now have all our accoutrements and forty rounds of ball cartridges, and we shall cheerfully comply with the order to march for Harper's Ferry, at 8 o'clock to-morrow morning.

W. Frank Ayre, of Rome, has been appointed Quarter-master of this Regiment, Geo. C. Norton as his Sergeant, and Dr. H. V. M. Miller, Surgeon.[12]

A great many ladies visit this camp every evening at the time of dress parade, 6 ½ o'clock, and they and the citizens generally, have been very kind, generous and obliging.

Embankments are being thrown up in two or three places, for the fortification of this city. Nobody is frightened, but there is a busy earnestness of effort every where seen. M. D.

Strasburg, Va.,
Friday, June 7th, 7 o'clock A.M.

**Dear Courier:** Col. Bartow's Regiment left Richmond on Wednesday, at 1 o'clock P.M. It took two trains, one of 13 cars and the other 11, to carry us all, and we were much crowded at that. There are about 850 men in all. We arrived at Gordonsville at 6 P.M., at Manassas Junction at 3 Thursday morn. At this place are about 9000 troops, under the command of Gen. Beauregard, and more are every day coming.[13] They have commenced throwing up fortifications here, and a large number of negroes arrived for that purpose while we were there. Suspicious persons are taken almost daily near Manassas. They brought in five while we were there. They are tried by Court Martial, and if the evidence is sufficient of their unfaithfulness to the Confederate States government, they are sent to jail. It will be remembered that this place is only 27 miles from Alexandria, and shots are frequently exchanged between the scouts of the two armies.

We left Manassas at 1 o'clock P.M., on Thursday, and moved over the Manassas Gap Railroad to this place, a distance of 76 miles. Arrived here last night at 7 o'clock. We passed through a beautiful and picturesque country, rather wild and broken, but of good soil.

The corn is hardly large enough to work the first time yet. There are splendid large fields of wheat on the way, and these are the only crops except the luxuriant clover that has already made fat thousands of beeves. The wheat is about two weeks later than in our vicinity, and promises a very large yield.

There are many false rumors in regard to fights. In the last eight days there have been but two that are well authenticated, one at Acquia Creek, in which the enemy lost at least five men, and had a ship considerably injured; we had "nobody hurt;" the other was at Fairfax C.H., on the night of May 31st, in which the Lincolnites lost in killed 10 or 12, and 5 prisoners. We lost the brave and gallant Capt. Marr, and had two men slightly wounded.

It is thought by some that our Regiment will be sent forward from Harper's Ferry in a few days to Northwestern Va., perhaps to Grafton or Phillippi. The prospect of an immediate fight fades away as we approach the supposed battle field. Still the knowing ones are confident that it cannot be long postponed. M. D.

Camp Fair Ground, near
Winchester, Va., Saturday, June 8th

**Dear Courier:** Since leaving Richmond, the Ga. Regiment has, by almost continuous motion, so confused day and night, that I am really in doubt as to what day of the week or month this is. My own count makes this Friday, and I have an indistinct remembrance that the first day of this month was Saturday, but last night a news boy brought some papers into this camp which he positively asserted were that day's paper. These were dated Friday, June 7th, and, as newspaper dates have been my calendar for the last five years, this was received as "proof, strong as the confirmations of holy writ," and, as my honest convictions yielding, I have dated this letter as above.

Our own movements have fully verified the saying that "large bodies move slow." The *order* was to leave Richmond on Wednesday at 8 A.M.—we *did* leave at 1 ½ P.M.—the command was to be ready to march from Strasburg yesterday at 8 A.M., we left the camp at 10 and the town at 10 ½ A.M. the Light Guards, however, "wish it to be distinctly understood" that the delays were not their fault. Our camp, I am proud to state, has never been five minutes behind time in filling the order for any movement of the Regiment.

Yesterday came the "tug of war," not in deadly conflict with the enemy, but in overcoming the distance—18 miles—from Strasburg to this place. We learned early in the morning that all could not ride on account of inadequency in the means of conveyance provided, and the Light Guards were one of the first companies that offered to walk; the Oglethorpe Light Infantry and the Macon Guards made the same proposition, but all the other companies rode in large heavy wagons provided for the purpose, and to carry the baggage, Col. Bartow highly complimented the companies that so cheerfully volunteered to perform this severe duty. Our march was over a fine macademized road, in a direction a little West of North, and through one of the most delightful countries I have seen, and abounding in evidences of wealth and refinement. Strasburg is at the terminus of Manassas Gap, nearly surrounded by high mountains—the Blue Ridge—and more beautifully picturesque scenery I have not seen anywhere, and the exceeding loveliness of the scenery continues unbroken from that place to this. The Light Guards were honored by being thrown in front and thus led the way in the first heavy march of the Ga. Regiment. We all stood the march much better than was anticipated. Leaving Strasburg at 10 ½ A.M., we only stopped four times—once a half hour for dinner, and three other times, 15 minutes each, to rest and get water, and the balance of the time, until 6 o'clock in the evening, when we arrived at Winchester, we were continuously moving forward. We passed through only two towns—Middletown and New Town—on the way. Twelve of our men were detailed for guard duty, and on that account rode, and six others were too much indisposed to undertake to march, and six or eight more gave out on the way. Only about 40 marched into Winchester. Of these some seemed ready to dance a jig, but most of them looked quite sober and stepped very carefully. There are some sore feet this morning, but aside from that all who marched through are in excellent trim. Our invalids are all doing well and will probably soon report themselves ready to do duty. The Regiment are ordered to be ready to take the train for Harper's Ferry to morrow morning at 8 o'clock. M. D.

Camp Defiance
Near Harper's Ferry, Va.,
Tuesday, June 8.

**Dear Courier:** This has been a pleasant day, and good humor has generally prevailed. Of the nineteen regiments, in and near Harper's Ferry, only three are camped in sight, but these as well as our own are intensely busy in drilling, and in every way getting ready for a grand battle that is daily expected.

We have been much excited from false rumors until now nothing is believed, except by the over credulous, until it is either officially announced, or confirmed by the most undoubted authority.

The apprehension that there was a skirmish at the Maryland heights yesterday was without foundation. The firing was the old guard discharging their firelocks. We have official information that there were two skirmishes up the river, yesterday, in the direction of Martinsburg. In the first we had one man wounded and a horse killed, and the Federalists had four men killed; in the second we lost none, and the enemy had five men killed. Martinsburg is in Berkley county, which gave over 700 majority against ratifying the Ordinance of Secession, and it is probably that all these ten were Virginian submissionists. Our scouts in that direction, when they came in this morning, reported that considerable firing was heard last night in the vicinity where the skirmishes occurred in the day, but the occasion or result of it, I have not learned.

The Stephens Light Guards from Greensboro, Ga., Captain Oscar A. Dawson, arrived here yesterday and joined Col. Bartow's Regiment.[15] Col. Gartrell's Regiment also arrived on the same day and camped near us.[16]

There is now no immediate prospect either of our leaving Harper's Ferry, or of the place being evacuated. I am inclined to the opinion that Gen. Johnston, who is in command of the forces at this place, keeps his own counsel, and his plans may be quite different from the indications, as exhibited in unimportant movements.[17] There are many rumors that seem quite improbable. For instance, it is asserted that there is not a single cannon mounted on any of the many heights that command the place, and that there are no breast works or other means of defense. In the little town of Boliver, between our camp and the Ferry, I am informed that there was but one vote cast by the residents in favor of ratification, in the recent election, and beside there are doubtless many spies in our midst constantly. It may be that on this account, our commanders suffer even our own men to be deceived, in regard to the strength of the place against an immediate attack. Another rumor of the same class is that there is no ammunition here except what is in the cartridge boxes of the soldiers.

Mr. Goulding, who joined our company yesterday, reports several narrow escapes, in making his way from N. York to this place. He says he was knocked down once, shot at another time, and in Baltimore arrested and imprisoned fourteen days. He is a very spirited young man, and may have been indiscreet in strong expressions of Southern feeling.

We to-day heard from Skidmore and J. T. Moore, who are still at Gordonsville. They are both improving and expect to join the company again in a few pays.[18] Josiah Johnson has come up entirely recovered, and has been doing duty to-day. There is now no one here belonging to the Rome companies who is sick that I know of. Our camp is in a high healthy position, and I think that the abundance of exercise that we get regularly, the pure atmosphere we breathe, tolerable good water, and the bountiful supply of good wholesome rations given us, that we will all soon be as robust and hearty as could be desired. The middle of the days here are intensely hot, but the nights are quite cool and damp. M. D.

Harper's Ferry, Va.,
Sunday night, June 9th.

**Dear Courier:** The Georgia Regiment arrived here to-day at 1 ½ o'clock P.M. We did not get off from Winchester until 11 this morning, and as the train was a long one, it took us two hours and a half to make the distance of 32 miles. We passed through a tolerably pleasant and fertile country, but no means equal to that between Strasburg and Winchester. The wheat all the way—and there is a great abundance of it—looks finely and so does the clover, but the corn is miserably small—only from four to six inches high.

Before leaving Winchester, Colonel Bartow made a short speech to the corps, in which he reminded the men that this was the holy Sabbath, and, that, although the exigencies of war demanded that we should do service by traveling, yet he hoped all possible regard should be had for its sacred hours, so dear to christians. While on parade, we had prayer by Rev. Mr. Bell of Capt. Tower's company. It is worthy of note, that in all our Regiment, of over eight hundred men, I do not recollect of having heard of a single curse to-day, nor a secular song even, but many a sacred hymn, and now while I write at 9 P.M., there is a large number of the Light Guards singing familiar hymns.

Harper's Ferry is a wild romantic place, and the surrounding scenery is grand, almost to sublimity. The town is built upon a tongue of land running down between the Shenandoah and Potomac rivers, and high abrupt mountains come down to both rivers on the sides from the place. There are two or three splendid residences a little up on the Bluff, but most of the importance of the point is on account of the Armory buildings, some twenty or thirty good two and three story back buildings—situated on a very narrow bottom on the tongue, and the hitherto prevailing belief that it was the key to Northwestern Virginia. But the machinery is now nearly all moved to Richmond, and as a Military Post, it is now believed that it has been overestimated. An officer, high in command, has just said to me, that with the present force here, about 10,000 men, it is costing the Confederate States much more to hold it, in his opinion, than it is worth. It is rumored that the railroad bridge that crosses the two rivers just at their confluence, will be blown up and burned, perhaps, to-morrow, and the place abandoned. If we are forced to a choice between this place and Winchester, the latter is considered vastly more important, as with that gone, supplies are cut off from here.

Our troops took three canal boats today that came down the Chesapeake & Ohio canal, made prisoners of the men—some twenty or thirty—and burned the boat. They were still smoldering when we came.

It has been suggested that our Regiment ought to be named the "Georgia Hunters,"—hunting for a fight. While at Richmond, we were told that the first battle was expected to be at Manassas Junction. We petitioned to be sent there, but before the order was received, it was thought that Harper's Ferry was the point of danger, and so we were ordered here. Before reaching Winchester, it was thought that an attack might soon be made upon that place, and we were ordered to stop there until further orders, and after being there about 24 hours, we were ordered onto this place. Unless there is a prospect for an immediate conflict here, our corps will probably be ordered back to Manassas Junction or some where else. This flying style of service enables us to see a large extent of country, and will make our men experts in pitching and striking tents, but not very profitable to us as soldiers, or the country.

There are about 400 Confederate troops stationed at the Point of Bocks, twelve miles below here, and a fight is expected there to-night.[19] The fate of Harper's Ferry will probably be decided in some way in a day or two.

There are none of the Rome companies now seriously ill that I know of. Josiah Johnson and Mr. Wimpee, whom we left in Strasburg, we have just learned, are up. Geo. R. Lumkin and Geo. Sanford, we left at Winchester, the former not very sick, and the latter, by no means dangerous.[20] The men generally are getting accustomed to camp life, and it is to be hoped that the ill effects of "breaking in" are near over.

Monday Morning. Our camp is in a wheat field in rear of the town on a hill back of Boliver, about ¾ of a mile from the Armory. Mr. Goulding, a son of Rev. Goulding of Kingston, Ga., is just from Baltimore and says all Maryland is ready to rise as soon as we gain the first signal victory.

We have heard from the Point of Bocks this morning, and learn that our troops have all left that place, marched here, and burned all the bridges on the way. They arrived here at 9 o'clock this morning. There is probably a skirmish—10 o'clock, A.M.—going on, on the Maryland Heights opposite to us. We heard some 70 guns, but no messenger has yet arrived.

We were marched around on the hills about here yesterday to the distance of about five miles, in search of a camp ground, and had the biggest sweat in the hot sun we have had yet, and were all very much fatigued last night, but all hands came out as bright as new dollars this morning.

We are expecting orders every minute, but as yet know nothing of what will be required of our Regiment.

Our friends wishing to send letters can have a package made up at R. S. Norton's store every Saturday evening, and we will thus be more likely to get them than if sent single. M. D.

Camp Defiance,
Near Harper's Ferry, June 13th.

**Dear Courier:** We have news that there was a battle yesterday, Wednesday, at Bethel near New Port News in which rumor says 1,000 of the enemy were killed and a very small number of our men—how many not stated.[21] We have just received orders to get ready as soon as possible to march—we are not informed where—but probably to Winchester. Three Regiments before ours have just been ordered to that place. It is 32 miles, and we expect to march the entire distance—carrying our knapsacks. There is great haste now in our camp in making preparations to leave. I have just learned that we go to Winchester certain. Drs. Miller and Gregory arrived yesterday. Dr. Gregory takes his knapsack and marches as a private.[22]

We do not *flee from* the enemy, but *go to meet them*. May the God of battles go with us and prosper us. If we die we are determined to die like men at the post of danger and of duty—if we live, a glorious future awaits us. It is reported that a large Federal force—say 10,000—is on the way to Winchester, through Martinsburg.

Good bye readers of the Courier. I hope you will hear from me again in a few days. If an all-wise Providence orders otherwise, then a long farewell. M. D.

FRIDAY MORNING, 14th. It is now 7 o'clock, and we are still here. Bartow's Regiment is held back for the rear guard. The entire force here is moving forward to Winchester. Our Regiment will probably leave in less than one hour. We struck tents yesterday at 12 o'clock, and have had a very disagreeable time since. Slept last night in the open air, and have had nothing warm to eat since yesterday morning.

The bridge at Shepardstown, 12 miles up the river, was burned by our men at 2 o'clock this morning. It was a splendid sight from our camp. The fine Railroad and Carriages bridges were blown up and burned at 5 o'clock, this morning. Harper's Ferry will be entirely evacuated at noon to-day. It is a bright, warm morning, and we expect a very disagreeable and fatigueing march to-day.

Some of the Federal scouts came down the Maryland Heights yesterday evening, after our forces had left that position, to within 600 or 700 yards of the bridge—they were seen, fired upon and fled. M. D.

SUNDAY MORNING, June 16, 1861.

**DEAR COURIER:** I do not know the name of this camp, but it is 4 ½ miles South of Charlestown, and near the road leading to Winchester. We left Harper's Ferry yesterday at 11 o'clock A.M. It is 12 ½ miles from that place to this. The bridges, and all the shops and public buildings at Harper's Ferry were burned on Friday. The place is deserted and in complete ruins. Our regiment was the last of 10,000 troops quartered in that vicinity. There were more fortifications on the different heights about, than I had any idea of. These were all burned, and the smoke from them indicated their number and location. With the men we had there, and the fortifications, the place could have been held against an attacking force of 50,000 men. We are now on the march to meet the enemy, probably in the vicinity of Winchester. Our army now encamped here, is upwards of 10,000 strong, and we have no fear of the enemy, no matter how many they number. We have 450 cavalry, and one company of mounted artillery.

This does not seem much like Sunday morning, as all hands are busy packing up for the march. It is twenty miles to Winchester, and we are marched to that place; we expect to reach it to-day. It was exceedingly hot yesterday, and will probably be so to-day, and very dusty. We marched on a good McAdamized road. Our Regiment is in the rear, and the Light Guards the last company. Our men are all well and in good spirits. No one would mistrust, from seeing the men, that we expected a battle before night.

There are various rumors as to battles between Martinsburg and Winchester, but they are not well authenticated. It is also rumored that the Federalists burned Washington City, and evacuated it on yesterday.[23] M. D.

Camp Bunker's Hill,
Monday Morning, June 17.

**Dear Courier:** Yesterday, instead of marching to Winchester, we turned to the right from our camp of Saturday night, and marched in the direction of Martinsburg, 15 miles from this place, passing through Smithfield. The Division of the army to which we are attached is under the command of Gen. Joseph E. Johnston. Our force divided yesterday morning—2000 going directly towards Winchester, and the remainder—probably about 8000—took this direction. We are now 15 miles from Martinsburg. It is reported that 30,000 of the enemy are near that place, and marching in the direction of Winchester.

Once or twice yesterday I had a view of our entire division, and the spectacle was truly elegant. Just think of it; a half mile of baggage wagons, and another of living, earnest, patriotic *volunteers*—not a mercenary or constrained man in the entire ranks—the column moving in perfect order; in four ranks in silent grandeur.

Our movements are controlled entirely by those of the enemy. Reveille was beat at 3 ½ o'clock this morning, but we will probably not get in motion before 7, it takes so long to get so many ready. We encounter no serious difficulty in our forced march, except in getting cooked rations. Most of our cooking vessels were sent to Winchester, together with all our tents and other baggage that we were not willing to undertake to carry in our knapsacks. It has turned out that the knapsacks are carried on wagons. The nearness of the enemy, however, prevents much complaint.

I was most happily surprised at seeing such complete respect paid to the Sabbath yesterday. The day was as completely observed as possible, for an army on the march. We organized a Sunday School yesterday morning in the Light Guards, by electing G. T. Stovall Superintendent, M. Dwinell Secretary, and L. T. Mitchell, Chorister. Had reading of the Scriptures, and were singing when we were ordered to fall into line for marching. Most of our company will join the school. We expect a battle before night, but these things are very uncertain. M. D.

Camp of Gen. Johnston's Command
Three miles from Winchester,
Tuesday, June 18, 1861.

**Dear Courier:** I will commence this letter by correcting a mistake of yesterday. Bunker's Hill is 8 miles from Martinsburg instead of 18 as stated. We left camp yesterday at noon, and instead of marching in the direction of Martinsburg, turned to the left, and took the road for Winchester, and had the most fatiguing march yet, although we only traveled 9 miles. We have not had anything like regular meals since last Thursday morning, except a good warm supper given us the citizens of Charlestown, on Saturday. Besides being hungry, our company was in the rear, and instead of being allowed to step off at a smart walk, we were continually being stopped in the hot sun, from two to five minutes at a time, just a little too long to stand in such a situation, and not long enough to break ranks and sit.

This is very bad place to get news, even in regard to our own situation in reference to that of the enemy. According to the most reliable news that I can get, when at Bunker's Hill, we were within some 10 miles of 10,000 of the enemy, who were in the vicinity of Martinsburg.

When I wrote yesterday, the expectation was that we would be led immediately to our attack. But a council of war was held, and the facts that we had no cavalry, and had only one small company of artillery, with 4 guns and 20 rounds of cartridges, and also that our entire force had only our own average, 20 rounds, induced the decision, that we should advance and make our stand at or near Winchester.

We are resting this morning, after a very good breakfast, and have no idea as to what the next order to us will be. It is rumored that the Lincolnites are again advancing on Romney, about 40 miles in a northerly direction, and it would be just our luck to be ordered to meet them.

The Light Guards have only three men, too much indisposed for duty, and they are not very sick. Our men are all with us.

A Brigade was organized yesterday, composed of the 7th and 8th Georgia Regiments, and the 4th Alabama Regiment, and two Battalions of Kentucky troops, and Col. F. S. Bartow appointed Brevet Brigadier General. Lieut. Col. Montgomery Gardner of Augusta, Ga. now has command of our (the 8th Ga.) regiment, and Thos. L. Cooper is our Major.[24] Our boys were greatly nerved up yesterday with the expectation of an immediate engagement, but we now have no such excitement. M. D.

P.S. All communication should be sent to Winchester for the present.

In Camp, 4 Miles from Winchester,
June 19, 10 o'clock p.m.

**Dear Courier:** Our Brigade has been in this camp since Monday evening, and very little has occurred worthy of note in this time.

It is now very currently reported and generally believed that on Sunday night at Bunker Hill, we were encamped only about 8 or 9 miles from some 10,000 of the enemy, under the command of Gen. Patterson.[25] The intention of Gen. Johnston was to meet them, but while he was surveying the ground and before he had determined where to draw up his line of battle, a courier came in and informed him that Patterson's command had turned back towards Williamsburg, and, as it would be impossible for our army to come up with them, before reaching the Maryland line, and not wishing to become invaders, it was thought best to turn towards Winchester, and await another movement of the enemy. It is reported that Patterson's force has crossed back into Maryland, and that the Federal troops under Gen. McClelland, who were marching towards this point from the direction of Wheeling, have also turned back.[26]

Two Regiments of Virginia troops, under Cols. Gibbons and Hill, left this place yesterday, to meet Gen. McClelland at Romney. There is rumor in this camp to-day, that Lincoln has sent a messenger to President Davis, asking for a cessation of hostilities until after the 4th of July. This seems consistent with the reported movements of Patterson and McClelland, but there may be no truth in any of these rumors.

The two days rest and the full supplies of wholesome provisions that we have had here, has fully restored the buoyancy and blithesome spirits of the men, and we now eat our meat and bread with our fingers, and sleep in the open air with contentment. Orders were issued this evening, to be ready to march to Winchester to-morrow morning at 7 o'clock. Our tents and baggage are at W. and, as there is a probability of remaining there for several days, and perhaps weeks, we will probably be allowed to fix up regularly and comfortably for camp life. There is some talk about fortifying that place, and, if so, we will probably have a chance to try our strength and ability in the use of the pick axe and the spade.

There are now only a few cases of indisposition in any of the Floyd county companies, and those only slight.

Our Quartermaster, W. F. Ayre, with whose appointment his numerous friends are delighted, has not yet reported himself for duty. Geo. C. Norton has the promise of being promoted to the office of Commissary, with the rank of Captain. He has been most efficient and active in performing the triple duties of Commissary, Quartermaster and Sergeant, for the past two weeks, and I am sure no more competent or worthy, inexperienced man could have been appointed.[27]

At night the boys have a merry time in singing many familiar songs, and the following is quite a favorite:

GEORGIA.

*Parody on "New England," by a Member of the Light Guards.*

Georgia, old Georgia,
I'm far away from thee;
My heart as I wander,
Turns fondly to thee;
For bright rests the sun
On thy clear winding streams,
And soft o'er the mountains
The moon pours her beams.
CHORUS: Georgia, old Georgia
I'm far away from thee;
My heart as I wander,
Turns fondly to thee.
Thy breezes are healthful,
And clear are thy rills,
The harvest waves proudly,
And rich o'er thy hills.
Thy maidens are fair,

Thy yeoman are strong,
Thy rivers run blithely,
Thy vallies among.
CHORUS: Georgia, old Georgia, &c.
There's home in old Georgia.
Where dear once of mine,
And thinking of me,
And the days of "Lang Syne,"
Blest be the hours
When the war is all o'er,
I'll sit by the hearth-stone,
To leave it no more.
CHORUS: Georgia, old Georgia, &c.

Camp near Winchester,
Friday, June 21.

**Dear Courier:** Yesterday our brigade moved forward toward Winchester 2 ½ and camped 1 ½ miles from that place. All our tents and other baggage was brought up, tents were pitched, and the men very generally participated in the luxury of a change of clothing. When it is remembered that we had been deprived this enjoyment for a full week, and during three days of that time had been on the march over very dusty roads, it will be understood that this opportunity was improved with great eagerness and pleasure.

Nothing worthy of note came to my knowledge in our camp yesterday, except the visit of two prisoners, taken by five of our scouts, within three hundred yards of Gen. Patterson's camp near Williamsport, on Thursday morning. One is a Colonel, who refuses to give us his name, and the other Lieut. Chase, son of Gov. Chase, of Ohio, now a member of Lincoln's Cabinet.[28] Our brave scouts were in ambuscade and had ventured thus near the line of the enemy, with the determination, if possible, of learning the plan of Gen. Patterson's movements. The two officers above named, strolled outside the line, when our scouts rushed upon, arrested, and threatened them that if they said a word they would shoot them instantly. The prisoners submitted and were hurried off with the utmost speed. They were last night sent to Richmond.

Reliable information has been received that there was a skirmish at Westport, 17 miles from Romney, on Wednesday the 19th inst. The following are the particulars as reported. We had three Regiments at the latter place—the commands of Cols. Gibbons and Hill of this State, and one Tennessee Regiment. Two companies from each of the Virginia Regiments and one from the Tennessee Regiment, were detailed to make an attack on the enemy at Westport. A regiment of the Federalists had been encamped at the latter place but most of them had been detached to protect a railroad bridge not far from that place. Yet leaving a large guard to protect the ammunition, camp baggage, cannon, &c. The companies above named, marched up and fired upon them. The Lincolnites returned the fire and fled like wild horses. They left six of their number dead upon the field, four cannon and a large amount of baggage and ammunition. None of our men were killed, and only one slightly wounded. A just Providence seems to direct the flying bullets in all our conflicts with the hypocritical enemy, and fortune favors the brave in the holy cause of human liberty.

Only two men are now in the hospital from our county—Stinson and Drammell—and these are not very sick. M. D.

Camp near Winchester,
Saturday, 10 P.M., June 22, 1861.

**Dear Courier:** The Second Brigade to which the 8th Georgia Regiment is attached, has just received orders to be ready as soon as possible—by sunrise tomorrow morning at latest—to march toward Williamsport, with three days supply of cooked provisions in our haversacks. Williamsport is about 30 miles from here, and the cause of this command to march, is the report that the Federalists again are invading this State in large force at that point. Of course we will have a very busy time to-night, in cooking and making the necessary preparations for this sudden and unexpected march. Most of the men had "turned in" for the night when they were called up to hear the order, and they turned *out* in their undress *multiforms*, making quite a grotesque *appearance* but the *voices* were unanimous in loud shouts of exultation, at the prospect of meeting the demoniac enemies of our young Republic.

It seems to be the fate of our regiment, to be on the march on Sabbath days. Last Sabbath we marched 15 miles, the one before went on the cars, from this place to Harper's Ferry. Tomorrow we will probably march as far as we have strength to carry us. Five four-horse wagons are allowed to a regiment, and in these will be carried the knapsacks, and the least amount of camp furniture that will do us. We are to leave our tents standing with most of the baggage in them, and these will be guarded by such of the men as are not *sick*, yet too much indisposed to endure the fatigue of a long march, and the exposure incident thereto.

Frank Ayre, our Quartermaster, and seven recruits arrived this morning to join the Light Guards—Hal and Jos. Johnson, Pinson, McCullough, Greer,

Brodie and Payne. Z. B. Hargrove and George Demming have been appointed assistants in the Hospital.[29] M. D.

P.S. 7 ½ o'clock Sunday morning. I have just learned that our acting Brig. Gen. Bartow, will not order a march, until further news is received from Williamsport. It may be that the movement of the enemy at that place was only a feint, for the purpose of leading the Confederate forces astray. We were ready to march at sunrise, but I am afraid that we are to endure the same tedious hanging on that we suffered at Harper's Ferry. M. D.

2d P.S. It is now 10 ½ o'clock and a report is now current, that only twenty-five of enemy crossed the Potomac at Williamsport yesterday and thus our prospect for an immediate fight has again vanished. There is no predicting now, when we will leave here, perhaps not for weeks. M. D.

Camp near Winchester, Va.,
June 25, 1861

**Dear Courier:** There is no exciting news to communicate from this point, at this time. Appearances indicate that there will be no fighting in this vicinity, at least until after the meeting of the Federal Congress. The force of the Lincolnites that crossed the Potomac on the 16th inst., has returned and fallen back to Frederick, Md. The 2d Virginia Brigade is now encamped within four miles of Williamsport, on the identical ground occupied by the enemy on the 16th. It is now pretty generally believed that the two armies, and each without knowing the movements of the other, commenced the retreat on that day, at almost precisely the same time. *We* were short of ammunition, there is no doubt of that but what *their* excuse may be has not transpired.

We had as many rounds of cartridges on Monday, when we turned *from* the enemy as we had on Sunday, when we turned *towards* them. There is any amount of grumbling very generally expressed, by the men under Gen. Johnston's command, because of his change of direction at Bunker Hill, on that occasion. All now think that we then lost our only *immediate* and perhaps the only *remote* chance also for a fight. There, perhaps, never was an army more eager for the fray, than ours was on that occasion, and now that it is known that our force ceased the pursuit, before it was *certain* that the enemy had retreated, peculiar mortification is felt on account of it.

That Sunday morning was an exciting time. For over an hour we expected to either be immediately drawn up in line of battle on the ground we were on, or else to move forward, not exceeding three miles, and then meet the mercenary vandals in deadly conflict. Of course many of our men were excited, but I saw no exhibitions of craven hearted fear, and much less excitement than I had expected on such an occasion. Two or three shed tears in parting with their friends, before the expected battle, and I saw several give up their watches and purses to the Surgeon and others, who were not expected to be in the heat of the fight. Some read their Bibles; some tried to look very unconcerned, and whistled to keep their courage up, and some talked brave to conceal timid feelings; but the majority exhibited a degree of calm, stern determination that would have been creditable to veterans.

The command of Gen. Johnston is called the Shenandoah Division of the Army, and is composed, I believe, of four Brigades, or 12,000 men.[30]

W. F. Ayre was officially announced as Quartermaster of this Regiment yesterday, and Geo. C. Norton as Commissary. The health of the Floyd county companies is generally good. Two of Capt. Towers' men, Remer Diamond and Miller have the measles. They are at a private house and well cared for. Of the Light Guards there is only one—Jett Howard—unable to do military duty, and he is not confined to his room, but is in town.

It is getting to be quite dry in this section of country, there having been no rain in two weeks or more, of any considerable amount. The wheat crop is now nearly matured, and is tremendous. The days are hot and the nights cool. We have excellent water here and are in every way comfortably situated. M. D.

Camp near Winchester, Va.,
Wednesday, June 26th.

**Dear Courier:** It seems to be foreordained and predestined that our Brigade shall not continue long in one place. The foxes have holes and the birds of the air have nests, but we have not remained long enough in one place to dig the one or build the other. Today we moved only about two miles from the North to the East side of the town, and this was done for the purpose of securing a more pleasant camping ground. The move was a good one but the manner and time of it was outrageous. It would not be a source of very bitter complaint if it was the first occurrence of the kind. But the fact is, that nearly every time our Regiment has been called upon to move, we have been ordered to be in readiness from two hours to two and a half days before starting, and in every instance, except one, there has no *good* reason, and *no one at all* apparent, except *negligence.* Good sense would seem to indicate that the corps should move forward at the precise time they were ordered to do so, and, if some portion were not in readiness *they* should be the ones to suffer, and not those who had promptly done their duty. To-day we were ordered to be in readiness to leave camp at 7 A.M., but did not move until noon. In this instance the fault was surely with the Brigade officers, for it was ascertained just before starting that the delay was occasioned by the officers hunting a place to move to. We were thus kept in suspense after packing up all our things, until the cool of the morning had entirely passed away, and then without dinner, in the broiling hot sun, with heavy knapsacks and guns. Several of the Light Guards "gave out" on the way and two came very near fainting. It was intensely hot, and sun stroke was seriously apprehended by several. But we are here now, in a beautiful grove, with a splendid spring near by, and the indications are that we have very comfortable quarters, for, perhaps, several weeks.

Our camp is in sight of the house in which George Washington, then Colonel of a Virginia Regiment, had his headquarters in 1760, when fighting the Indians. It is a two story stone house of moderate size, and has neither an antique or ancient appearance. The house was erected, but not finished, in the year 1754 by Isaac Hollensworth. He was driven away from the property by the Indians, and the premises were not occupied in 1760 when Col. Washington was sent here to protect the frontier inhabitants against Indian depredations. He built a fort on the site where the town of Winchester now stands. The timber used in the construction of the breast works, was cut from the field that is now our parade ground. The estate was granted to Isaac Hollensworth by Lord Fairfax, it has continued in possession of the family ever since, and is now owned by two very interesting young ladies—his great grand daughters—who have in their possession the original grant. It is an incident quite remarkable, that Gen. Bartow now has his head quarters in the identical room occupied by Washington over a quarter century ago, but how different the circumstances. The savage children of the forest were then in their way, repelling invasion of "pale faces," and the encroachments made upon their hunting grounds, and for the protection of *their* "peculiar institutions;" and now we are trying to repel an enemy quite as bloody, more vicious and unreasonable than the Indians themselves, and as much more vile and wicked as their superior mental and educational advantages can make them.

On this same Hollensworth estate and near the residence, is a field in which the Hessian prisoners were encamped after the battle of Trenton, who settled in the Northwestern part of the State, and whose descendants are nearly all Federalists, and I wish we could get a few thousand of them encamped on the same field.

W. F. Ayre, has been promoted to Brigadier Quartermaster, and Dunlap Scott appointed Regimental Quartermaster. A man by the name of Camp, belonging to Col. Gartrell's Regiment, from Coweta county, Ga., was accidentally killed this morning, by the discharge of a pistol he dropped.

The first Prayer Meeting in camp, that has come to my knowledge, was held by the Light Guards last Sunday night. Arrangements have been made for three a week, Sunday, Tuesday and Wednesday nights.

Camp near Winchester, Va.,
Friday June 28, 1861.

**Dear Courier:** Time has dragged slowly with us here for the past two days, for the reason that we have nothing to do except our regular duties and these have ceased to be novel and exciting. Our customary routine for the day is reveille at 4 o'clock A.M.; breakfast at 5 ½; company drill at 7, for an hour and a half; squad drill from 9 ½ to 11 o'clock; rest and prepare dinner till noon; after dinner until 4 o'clock P.M., we have for washing, mending and ironing clothes, cleaning arms and accoutrements, and sleeping if we have time for it; at that hour there is a Battalion drill, continuing an hour and a half; at 6 dress parade; supper at 7; Tattoo at 9 ½, and taps at 10 o'clock. Some few men are *shirks*, and make themselves and messmates miserable, by trying to avoid their duties, especially those connected with the culinary departments; but most of them cheerfully perform their duties and show their good sense and breeding, by acting well their parts. Our rations are ample; beef and bacon alternately; flour, (and occasionally meal and rice,) sugar, coffee, soap, candles and salt. Butter, eggs, chickens and lard are luxuries that we can get occasionally by paying for them. The three former have advanced a hundred per cent since we were here before. Butter now command 25 cts., eggs 25 cts. per doz., and spring chickens 20 cts. each. We live quite as well as could be expected, and the apprehension is that unless we get some more marching to do soon, we will all get fat and lazy.

The citizens of Winchester are worthy of praise beyond the power of language to express, for their extensive and untiring exertions in providing quarters and nursing the sick. I went through the town yesterday, and nearly every house, whether large or small, with indications of wealth or poverty, seemed full of invalid soldiers. There is very little sickness except measles, and with the fine nursing thus provided, very few cases have proved fatal. Only some half dozen cases have as yet appeared in our Regiment. There are, as near as I can learn, about 7,500 troops encamped near this place, and it is not strange that there should be considerable illness among so many.

A portion of the 9th Georgia Regiment arrived here to-day, Col. E. R. Gaulding commanding. This is to take the place of the Alabama Regiment which has been transferred to a South Carolina Brigade.

The farmers in this section are now cutting hay and harvesting wheat. Labor, as one would suppose, is quite scarce, and cradlers cannot be had in sufficient number at three dollars a day. The crops of wheat and clover are excellent, but the corn is small and suffering for want of rain.

The first death in our Regiment, since its organization, occurred this morning in the decease of a man by the name of Williams, of the Stephens Rifles. He died of pneumonia. There is now very little sickness in our Regiment, and no cases of severe illness that I know of. There are only some five or six cases of slight indisposition in all the Floyd co. companies.

A Mississippi Regiment left here this morning at 2 o'clock for Harper's Ferry to prevent the reconstruction of the Railroad bridge at that place. It is rumored here this evening that they had encountered a portion of the enemy—had killed some thirty of them and lost seven of our men. This may or may not be true.

There is, of course, nothing certain about it, but it seems to me probable that we will be here for several weeks.

All communications for Gen. Bartow's Regiment should be directed to care of the Captain of the company—Winchester, Va. M. D.

Camp Near Winchester, Va., July 2d.

**Dear Courier**: This is a cold, bleak morning, with a strong North wind, and more like December than July. Nearly every man in the Brigade slept cold last night, and they all look sour and cross this morning, and move about more like stiff old wagon horses than like the buoyant youths with elastic steps on ordinary occasions. It is not improbable that this disagreeable change in the weather will be detrimental to the health of the encampment.

As usual last Sunday was a day of extra duties for the Regiment. Saturday night we were notified that there would be a Regimental Review and Inspection of Arms and Accoutrements next morning. Every man's arms and accoutrements were expected to be in perfect order, and this caused the men to be as busy as possible, until the hour of parade arrived. It commenced to rain just as we marched on the parade ground, and we were dismissed, but told to hold ourselves in readiness to re-assemble at the tap of the drum, and thus were kept in a State of expectancy until noon, when the Light Guards were ordered to be ready in 30 minutes to march to town, for the purpose of doing guard duty. We swallowed our dinners in haste, put on our rubber cloths, and soon were on our way, through the mud and rain, to the Guard House in the town. Our duties were to guard some twenty cannon, the ammunition stores, the hospital and some dozen prisoners, and at night, do the general police duties of the city.

We commenced duties on this post at 2 P.M. on Sunday and were not relieved until 8 P.M. on Monday. Sufficient meat and bread was sent to us from camp for supper Sunday night, and at 10 A.M. next morning we got *bread* enough for breakfast. This is all the provisions we received through the quarter master. Some of our men suffered from hunger, hot most of them went to the hotel and paid 50 *cts a meal.* This was rather hard, considering that their pay is only about 36 *cts a day.* Of course, our kind and obliging Quartermaster has some good reason for this treatment, but we have not as yet been informed what it is.

There was melancholy accident in one of the Mississippi Regiments last Friday, occasioned by the unexpected ignition of a canister of Powder, by which eight men were wounded—one mortally. The rumor referred to in my last letter about a fight at Harper's Ferry, was entirely without foundation. There have been no recent conflicts with the enemy in this section, that I have heard of, neither there is likely to be.

There are a few cases of measles in our Regiment, and quite a number are indisposed from inoculation for the Small Pox, but the general health of the command is good. There are but three or four cases of indisposition in the Light Guards, and these are by no means severe. It is rumored that we will draw pay for the first month's service to-day. This will be a happy time for the boys—if it comes–for most of them are getting short of funds.

W. Frank Ayre has been appointed Brigadier Quartermaster, and Dunlap Scott is acting Regimental Quartermaster.[31]

Our mails are very irregular, and it is rumored that there has been rascality on the part of the Post Master here, or some of his Assistants. I have written to the *Courier* regularly three times a week, since leaving Richmond. M. D.

Camp near Winchester,
3 ½ o'clock, P.M. July 2, 1861

Since writing this morning, the aspect of things about this camp has very much changed. At 2 o'clock this afternoon, we received orders to be in readiness as soon as possible to march, with one day's rations besides supper for to-night. We were notified to be equipped as light as possible, and be prepared for a forced march; to pack our knapsacks, which would be carried on wagons, and provide ourselves with forty rounds of catridges.

The occasion of this order—issued as I understand to Gen. J. E. Johnston's entire command—is, the report that the Federal enemy is crossing the Potomac at Williamsport, 26 miles from here, in large numbers, and it supposed that we are ordered to meet them. We have been disappointed so many times that this order produced no great sensation in our Regiment, and the men show some degree of reluctance, in the apparently forced haste of making preparations to march.

Later, 6 P.M. The wagons are now being packed and the companies falling in. I have no actual knowledge of Gen. Johnston's intentions—but presume it is as above intimated. M. D.

Camp near Darkesville,
*alias Bucklesville, alias Hardscrabble, Va.*
July 4th, 6 o'clock P.M.

**DEAR COURIER:** Since yesterday all has been quiet in and about our camp. There has not, so far as I have heard, been even a skirmish between the outposts. We suppose the Federalists are celebrating the day at Martinsburg. We could distinctly hear cannon about noon. In the skirmish of the 2d, near Martinsburg, 20 of our men are missing besides the two killed and seven wounded; they were probably taken prisoner. Seventy-four of the Lincolnites were taken prisoners and some *say* 200 of them killed.

We have done first rate eating and resting to-day, and will be in excellent condition for hard work to-morrow. I was quite sure yesterday there would be a fight to-day—it did not occur—what will happen to-morrow I will not attempt to predict, but to me a fight seems much less probable than yesterday. The enemy have full possession of Martinsburg—they number about 3000. Nearly every citizen except those of notorious Union sentiments were taken prisoners. M. D.

Camp near Darkesville,
7 ½ o'clock A.M. Saturday July 6.

Gen. J. E. Johnson's command is still here, and there are no apparent indications of an immediate fight. We hear much and believe little in regard to our next movements. It is rumored that a reinforcement of some eight or ten Regiments is on the way to join us from Winchester; if this is true we may make a stand here; but if this assistance does not come, then it is thought by many that we will be ordered to fall back to Winchester. Some 6 or 8 prisoners were taken yesterday by our men, and our pickets were once driven in, but "nobody hurt." I shall write every day if there is any way to send the letters. M. D.

# 2

# "I Was in Almost Constant Expectation of Being Killed"

## *July–September 1861*

In early July, the Union army crossed the Potomac River at Williamsport, Virginia, and skirmished with Confederate forces. Gen. Joseph E. Johnston ordered his army north to meet the Federal advance. As Melvin Dwinell told readers of the *Courier*, the Confederate troops deployed at the hamlet of Darkesville and prepared to face a larger force under the command of Gen. Robert Patterson. Although there was some skirmishing, the two armies never met, and after several days Johnston ordered his men to return to Winchester.

On July 18, Dwinell and the Light Guards marched out of camp. The men of Johnston's command soon learned their destination: Manassas Junction, where they would be joining Gen. Pierre G. T. Beauregard's army for what many expected would be the first major battle of the war. The troops marched the thirty-five miles to the Piedmont Station of the Manassas Gap Railroad and then took the train for the remainder of the trip. They arrived several miles from Manassas Junction on the morning of July 20, as the sun was rising in the sky, Dwinell wrote. The men rested briefly and heard accounts of skirmishing at Blackburn's Ford on Bull Run, a stream flowing just north of Manassas Junction. One force had already left for Manassas Junction, and Johnston's troops soon made the four-mile march to join them. The Eighth Georgia arrived at its campsite, located in a wooded spot not far from Bull Run and got some much-needed rest.

The next day, Sunday, July 21, the men awoke early and soon were making a circuitous march to the battlefield. Artillery units were already exchanging fire, and Dwinell wrote that the men of the Eighth Georgia were ordered to load their guns and lie down. After enduring cannon fire for some thirty minutes, the men were ordered into a thicket of woods that provided cover. They were expected to engage a battery of Union artillery from that location. However, the Georgians faced a far larger Union force that poured a murderous fire into them. "The balls whizzed about us like hail in a thick storm," Dwinell wrote. "Our men fell with fearful rapidity." By the time the fighting was over, the Eighth Georgia had suffered some of the heaviest punishment of the day. Even so, the Battle of First Manassas proved to be a major victory for the South.

In a brief letter to his parents soon afterward, Dwinell wrote that it was "a miracle" that he escaped unharmed. Five men around him fell dead, and others were wounded. Dwinell also recounted the casualties among the Floyd troops, including George T. Stovall, his former associate at the *Courier*. Several weeks after the battle, in one of his more reflective letters, Dwinell described the feeling of being in a battle for the first time: "[T]hough I was in almost constant expectation of being killed . . . there was no

Stone House. Battle of First Manassas. Library of Congress.

painful realization of fear, such as would make one hesitate to go wherever duty called. As the dangers really increased, and friends were seen falling thick upon either side the apprehension, or rather the fear, of them became strangely less, and without feeling secure there was a sort of forced resignation to calmly abide whatever consequences should come."

Several days after the battle, the Eighth Georgia moved to a more permanent spot, about four miles from Manassas Junction, where the troops spent the remainder of the summer. They spent most of their days resting and awaiting orders to move. In a letter to his parents, Dwinell declared that he was "ready to strike again for the just cause in which I am engaged." He added: "If I should meet any of my relatives on the battle field in Lincoln's army they will there be considered as my enemies and treated as such." As one of the first officers to fall at First Manassas, Col. Francis S. Bartow promptly became a symbol of bravery and dedication to the Southern cause. The Eighth Georgia decided to honor the place where their commander fell and held a dedication ceremony on September 4, which Dwinell described in a long letter to the *Courier*. It was the troops' first chance to revisit the battlefield, and Dwinell recounted how the men were movingly reminded of all that had happened there.

Camp Near Winchester, July 9th.

**Dear Courier:** Our Regiment arrived here at our old camp at 8 o'clock Sunday eve, and we were all delighted to get *home* again, for where our tents and baggage are is our home, and the only one we expect to see as long as the war lasts. Our march was a very severe and fatiguing one, it being of the hottest days of the season. The different regiments commenced leaving Darkesville about 6 A.M., but it was 9 o'clock before ours, which was to bring up the rear, left. A large number fell out of ranks in the course of the day, and my *guess* is that we passed nearly or quite a thousand men, who had thus failed to keep up with the various regiments before us.

This division of the Army were absent from their regular encampment on this excursion, five days, with no tents, very few cooking utensils or baggage of any kind, and whatever suffering there may have been, was endured as became brave men. Because there is no murmuring, but on the contrary a general prevalence of cheerfulness and good spirits, it must not be inferred that intense hardships are not endured by the Confederate soldiery, but that actuated by a lively sense of patriotic duty, they perform what would otherwise be the most irksome tasks with such a hearty good will as makes light the heaviest loads.

Yesterday was a day of rest, washing and mending. So far as I can hear, very few were made actually sick by our trip last week, and nearly all in our Regiment were at the 7 ½ o'clock drill this morning.

At dress parade last night, an order was read from Gen. Johnson, in which it was stated that he, at Darkesville, offered battle to the enemy for four days which was not accepted, and as they had so much the advantage in numbers, he did not deem it politic to hazard the sacrifice of attacking them in their strongly fortified position in the town of Martinsburg, and hence issued the order to fall back to this place. This seems to be the truth and the whole truth in this matter. The enemy having full possession of Martinsburg, could, by stationing themselves in the houses, have made sad havoc upon our forces attacking them, especially as we had but little artillery.

An order was given yesterday prohibiting newspaper correspondents from giving publicity to the number, movements, and position of the Confederate Army. For obvious reasons this is right, but before there was any restriction, I thought the readers of the *Courier* were as much entitled to this information as others, and so gave some few items.

There is now not severe illness in any of the Rome companies so far as I know; but the measles are getting quite plentiful: eighteen cases in Capt. Tower's, ten or twelve in Cooper's and one in Magruder's. They are well cared for in private houses in town, and are all doing well. There has, as yet, been but one death in our Regiment, since we entered the service; that was a member of the Greensboro company.

Let no one of our friends be troubled by extravagant rumors. If there should be any important movements on hand they will be informed of the *facts* at the earliest possible moment. M. D.

Camp Near Winchester,
Thursday, July 11th 1861.

**Dear Courier:** Nothing particularly exciting or interesting has occurred in our camp since my last. At seven yesterday morning, orders were issued to cook what provisions were on hand, pack up and be ready to march, at all events, by 12 o'clock. At 10 we were ordered to hasten preparations and be ready to march whenever the order should be given; at 12 o'clock another came, to cook provisions for one day more. There was some mistake about this last, for the rations had not been issued, neither were they in camp or within reach of the men. The efforts to fill the orders made a very busy fore noon for us all, and it was probably better for us to spend it thus than in idleness. When such orders are issued, it is really amusing to hear the thousand and one suggestions made by subordinate officers and privates, as to the propriety or impropriety of the command to move at all; and then to hear the certainty of *their* knowledge as to where we should move to, if at all, and what we should do. In this case, all of our guesses and surmises have been in vain, for we are still here, and it has not yet transpired where it was intended to move us. It is rumored that the order was occasioned by a report that the enemy were advancing.

As I have nothing in particular to write this morning, I will narrate a few incidents of camp life that may be interesting to our readers.

A soldier attempted to pass a sentinel's post one night, without having the countersign; he insisted upon his purpose, but was resolutely kept back and informed that no many could pass that post without saying "*Richmond*!"

The "Officer of the Day" not long since, in going his rounds of duty came to a sentinel on guard, from Kentucky, who failed to give the customary salute. The officer asked him why he did not salute him, he responded, *"salute, h—ll, that was played out long ago."*

When at Darkesville the other day, Ike Dunkle had himself arrested and put with the prisoners of war, for the purpose of drawing from a Pennsylvanian, we then held in durance vile, such knowledge as he might possess in regard to the enemy.

Ike played the trick well, and got from the fellow all he knew in regard to the number, position, &c., of the Lincolnites.

The sale of liquor to the soldiers, was long since prohibited in Winchester, but yet, by some hook or crook, some of them manage to get "a wee bit of the creeter."

We had a heavy shower yesterday and another the day before.

There is very little frivolous or unreasonable excitement in camp, but the general belief is that we are on the eve of important events. Gen. Johnston's forte is said to be to *conquer* battles without fighting them.

It is now 7 o'clock and we are awaiting orders not having any idea as to where we will go, or what to do; perhaps we will not move at all. The sick are doing well and the measles are still extending. It is rumored that 800 of the enemy crossed into Virginia at Hagerstown yesterday and that Patterson moved a portion of his command 2 ½ miles this way from Martinsburg. One of the Oglethorpe Light Infantry from Savannah, by the name of Strickland, died of Pneumonia, last Sunday morning. M. D.

In Camp near Winchester, Va. July 13.

**Dear Parents:** It is quite a long time since I have written you as these are exciting times it is not improbably that you are anxious to hear from me. Our company volunteered for the war and we left home on the 27 of May. The day before leaving I wrote to you and the same day sent my miniature taken in my military dress. I hope you received both. We came immediately on to Virginia. Stopt seven days I believe in Richmond, were mustered into service—I as 2nd Lieut. And then came on to Winchester. The last 18 miles we marched between 10 A.M. and 6 o'clock P.M.; the first real hard-ship was endured. I tell you there were many weary legs and sore feet that night in our Regiment—(the 8th Ga.). This was June 6th. On Sunday the 9th we took the cars for Harpers Ferry: remained at that place until Saturday the 21st and then commenced a march in this direction. We marched 12 miles the first day and slept in the open air as we had done the two nights previous. The next day Sunday we marched 18 miles in the direction of Martinsburg where we expected to encounter the enemy, camped that night at Bunkersville 8 miles from Martinsburg where Gen. Patterson with 8000 or 10,000 Federal troops was reported to be encamped. The next day Monday We were drawn up in line of battle and thought a fight was certain in less than two hours, But it seems that both armies turned from each other at about the same time. We then came to near this place where we have remained ever since except on July 2nd we started again to meet the enemy at Martinsburg where Patterson commanded about 10,000. I cannot tell you our number but this is certain, if here was any lack in numbers it was made up in "pluck." We offered them battle for four days which not being accepted we then returned. We marched to within a mile of M. where Pattersons force was, where we halted at noon on the 3rd, marched back on Sunday the 7th a distance of 18 miles. We are encamped in a beautiful grove one mile from Winchester, have good water, are well fed, well clothed, lodge in good canvass tents and are in every way as comfortable as possible under the circumstances. This rough life agrees with me finely and I am getting fat at it. If not prohibited I would like to give you some statistics of military strength and preparations in our new Republic. I will merely say this much which I fully believe, viz: It would be as easy for Abe Lincoln to reduce the White Mountains to the level of the ocean as to conquer these states and then it would do him quite as much good when accomplished.

We are in the valley of Va. the richest farming country I have ever seen. The wheat here is just harvested and is an excellent crop. Give my love to all relatives and enquiring friends and accept my hearts warmest affections for yourselves. If I have relatives in the Federal army please inform me. Your afft. Son Melvin

P.S. Please answer immediately, directing the letter to me "care Capt. Magruder 8th Ga. Regiment, Winchester, Va." then put in another envelope containing 20 cts in stamps and direct the outside one to "B Whitesides, Franklin Ky." If I get an answer to this I will write often.

Camp Near Winchester, Va., July 15

**Dear Courier:** It has been some days since I have written to our readers, simply for the reason that there has been no particular occasion for so doing. After the excitement of the first week in this month, there followed, as a natural sequence to the physical fatigue and mental exhilaration incident thereto, a state of general debility, that was unpleasant to experience and not gratifying to behold. But there was no undue or censurable relaxation, and if any evidence had been wanting, of the deep seated determination and fervency of spirit, in the Confederate Army, to sustain the holy cause in which we are engaged, it was here exhibited, under such circumstance as to convince the most skeptical.

There is now, so far as I have heard an expression of opinion, no doubt as to the wisdom of the order, to fall back to this place from Darkesville, on the 7th inst., and the confidence of the army in Gen. Johnston, has been increased rather than diminished by the movement.

Patterson is still at Martinsburg with his mercenary horde, and has made no advance in this direction, except to send a large picket guard out to Big Spring, 2 ½ miles this side. Our advanced pickets are quartered at Bunker Hill, 6 miles this side of him, a battalion of cavalry, under the command of Col. Stewart.[1] Frequent skirmishes occur between them, and Patterson complains that his out posts and reconoiters are hunted down like foxes.

There is, without doubt, great dissatisfaction in the Federal Army. The knapsacks of the 72 prisoners, (most of whom it would seem had been laborers) taken in the battle near Martinsburg on the 2nd inst., were searched, and many letters from their friends at home found. In these were found dolorous accounts of distress, and they all begged the soldiers to return as soon as their period of enlistment should expire. One of these persons was asked what he was fighting the South for. He said, *"for eleven dollars a month."* In his simplicity he told the truth, not only as concerns himself, but also for a large portion of the Northern Army.

It is currently reported here that the three Regiments of Patterson's command, whose time had expired, have already gone home, and it seems quite likely, that if their time is worth more than eleven dollars a month, most of the others will leave as soon as they can. There is an occasional exhibition among these hirelings of Yankee shrewdness. One is reported to have occurred near Romney a few days since, which, however, cost the fellow his life. He had been taken prisoner, and was placed, with his arms tied, on a horse behind a Tennessean. He managed to pick the cap from the gun of his guard, then jumped from the horse and ran. The Tennessean snapped at him two or three times, then capped his gun and shot him dead.

There is no truth in the report that a great battle was fought near Romney last week, in which it was said that sixty of the 1st Georgia Regiment, under Col. Ramsey were killed.

A private, belonging to the Kentucky Battalion, was shot dead in town last week by his Orderly Sergeant, for disobeying orders. Chas H. Smith, Esq., of Rome, has been appointed Commissary for this Brigade, with the rank of Major.[2]

James Earp, of Capt. Towers' Company, died last night at 10 o'clock. He went to sleep at sunset, and without a struggle or seeming to awake he breathed his last. He was at a private house in town, where he received all the kind attentions that could have been possible anywhere. He was greatly beloved by all who know him, and his loss is deeply deplored. His remains are to be buried by his company this afternoon, with military honors.

There is a large number of cases of measles in the Miller Rifles and Floyd Infantry—some thirty in each—but all are doing well and none are very sick. There are no cases of measles in the Light Guards, and only a few cases of indisposition. Wesley Rush, who has been unwell for two or three weeks, will start for home, on leave of absence to-day or to-morrow.

Luke Mitchell, and the corps with which he is connected arrived here yesterday. Our Regiment has received no pay yet. Papers from home are sought for with great eagerness. The *Courier* comes regularly. There is a general desire that *Jackson* would continue his interesting letters "To Our Boys."[3] M. D.

Camp Near Winchester,
4 o'clock P.M., July 15.

**Dear Courier:** Since writing this morning another sensation has been started. This morning a report has been current in town, that the advance guard of Gov. Wise's command, numbering 1,000 to 1,500, had been led into ambush, near Phillippi, were surrounded by some 5000 of the enemy, through whom they cut their way, with a loss of 150 men and retreated. This report needs confirmation, especially as to numbers. Couriers came in here at about 12 o'clock to-day, and report that Patterson, with an increased force, now amounting, as some say, to 36,000 is moving, in three columns, towards this place. His centre column is reported to be this side of Bunker Hill, which place is 11 miles from here.

Orders were issued at 1 o'clock to our Regiment, to cook, as quick as possible, three days rations, put them in our haver-sacks and strap up our blankets and oil-cloths in a convenient form to carry. All else is to be packed up and left in the tents. We are now as busy as bees, in making preparations to move, not knowing where we are to go.

6 o'clock P.M. The order has just been issued to strike tents, thus indicating a change in the programme.

7 o'clock. The Light Guards have orders to fall into line. 'Tis expected that we are to march out some two or three miles, for a picket guard. I shall write to-morrow if I have a chance.

TUESDAY MORNING, 6 o'clock. Our Brigade last night moved through town just to the outskirts, on the side toward Bunker Hill. I have had no news this morning, in regard to the movements of the enemy. We will probably remain in the field where we now are until their approach. M. D.

Camp Near Winchester,
Tuesday, July 16, 4 o'clock P.M.

**DEAR COURIER:** Last night we slept in an old field, about a mile North of town, near the road to Bunker Hill. We remained in that field until 2 ½ o'clock this afternoon, when we moved back some 300 or 400 yards towards town, and were ordered to send for our tents, all but two of which had remained at our camp on the East side of town.

A portion of the forces here were drawn up in line of battle, this morning, but Bartow's command was not. Patterson only made a *feint* of dividing his force into three columns, and they all—some say 17,000 and others 36,000—camped just this side of Bunker Hill last night, and remained there until near noon to-day. Our Adjutant has just informed us, that the news has been received at Headquarters, that the advanced guard of the enemy are advancing on us. If we had not been so many times mistaken we would now feel certain of a fight soon.

C. Wesley Rush, on account of ill health, received an honorable discharge, and started for home to-day.[4] The company all very much regret the necessity of his leaving us. The General positively refused to grant him a furlough as he desired.

4 ½ o'clock. Col. Stewart's Battalion of Cavalry, that had been stationed some 6 miles from here, have just come to town in haste. They report that when in ¾ of a mile of the advancing enemy, they were fired upon with shells,

by which one of their men was severely wounded. They retreated, and when they had come some two miles, came very near being cut off by one wing of the enemy, within 4 of this place Stewart's command have again gone out as skirmishers. If this all ends in less than *smoke* even, and an account of it constitutes a part in the history of our life in camp, and as such may be interesting to the readers of the *Courier.*

6 o'clock Wednesday Morning. All is quiet this morning, and there was no alarm last night. My own opinion is that we will not have a fight, at least for some days to come. Our men are all in excellent spirits, and if we are called into an engagement, I predict a good account from the Georgia Volunteers, and all the rest of the Shenandoah Division of the Confederate Army.

The sick are all doing well, and many who have been off from duty for some time, came out yesterday. We are now comfortably situated in our tents, with all our baggage with us. M. D.

Camp Near Winchester,
Wednesday July 17, 10 o'clock P.M.

**Dear Courier:** To-day has been quiet in this camp. This evening news came that some six thousand of the enemy were in Smithville, a town 6 miles East of Bunker Hill, while the balance of the force, now believed to be about 30,000, remain at the latter place. The presumption is, that they intend to attempt to flank us here, by coming up to the East of the direct road with one column of their army. They will find Gen Johnson ready for them, whatevmaneouvring may be, unless I greatly misjudge.

Since five o'clock we have thrown down probably six miles of fence, for the purpose of opening a battle-field, and I never imagined men, on the eve of an expected fight, could be in such excellent spirits, and so enthusiastic.

It may be that this movement of Patterson is only a sham, but it really looks like there would a fight here before long.

Most of the sick are doing well, though one of the Chattooga county boys died to-day, of Pneumonia, his name was Allen. Of the Light Guards all but four were on duty to-day.

7 o'clock Thursday Morning. Orders have just been issued to pack up baggage, strike tents, cook two days rations and be ready to march immediately, we know not where, but expect only two or three miles towards Smithvile. No news from the enemy this morning. The 11th Georgia Regiment arrived yesterday.

Manassas Junction, Saturday,
July 20th, 7 1/2 o'clock A.M.

**Dear Courier:** About one half of the force that left Winchester on Thursday, and arrived at Piedmont Station yesterday morning, came to this place on the cars yesterday and last night. Our Regiment left Piedmont at 7 P.M., yesterday, and did not arrive here until near 2 o'clock this morning. We were very much crowded on the cars, and of course the chance to sleep was a slim one. The reason of so much delay I do not know. The distance is only 35 miles. We had some coffee this morning, and are now scattered round on the ground, trying to get what rest we can, before marching to Bull's Run—some four miles from here.

The particulars of the fight there on Thursday, you have probably received before this.[5] The belief prevails here that the enemy lost in killed about 900. We had ten killed and some 30 or 40 wounded. This statement is as I receive it, and I cannot vouch for its accuracy. We expect to remain here until the balance of Johnston's force, that we left at Piedmont Station, to come up, probably this evening, and then go to Bull's Run. The expectation yesterday was, that there would be a big battle to-day. Yesterday the enemy under a flag of truce, were allowed to collect their dead and bury them. Beauregard, as reported, has possession of the battle-ground.

Our men stand up wonderfully well, under the fatigues of she past two days and nights. Most of our baggage and all the tents, were left at Winchester. I hear it said that these will be sent to us in a day or two.

The entire force that was here previous to yesterday morning, has gone to Bull's Run.

Battle Ground on Lewis's Farm,
Tuesday July 23, 1861.

**Dear Courier:** The present is the first opportunity I have had to write, since the awfully glorious and momentous events of Sunday, the 21st inst. And even now, I can give but a meagre, hasty, and very imperfect account of a small part of the important transactions, because we have already received orders to move.

Our Regiment left our place of bivouac, of the night previous, at 6 o'clock on Sunday morning. The cannonading commenced some half hour before this, two reports being heard once in about five minutes, in the direction of Bull's Run, and seeming to be about two miles distant.

We marched round by a circuitous and zigzag course to the left, with the intention of flanking the right wing of the enemy, and attacking them. We marched at quick time, and a part of the time double-quick until ten o'clock, when opposite our place of destination, we were drawn up in a line extending back from a battery of four guns of Virginia Artillery, commanded by———.[6] The cannon balls from the celebrated Sherman's Battery, soon began to fly about five or ten yards over our heads, with a whiz that was surprisingly loud. Directly bomb shells began to burst over our heads and on either side. We were ordered to lie flat down on our faces. The cannonading became very brisk. There must have been some ten or fifteen cannon playing on the 8th Regiment, and the battery we were placed to guard. At about 11 o'clock we were ordered to leave here. This order was promptly obeyed, although by rising to our feet we were in full view of the enemy's battery, from which we had been partially protested by the brow of the hill, on which we were. We were intended to support Gen. Bee in a charge, but were led to the extreme right of the attacking force, going under the cover of woods, between us and the enemy's artillery.[7] We were led up and deployed in a pine thicket, and ordered to fire. The enemy were about 100 yards, and many of them protected by stables and stacks of straw and hay, and all by a fence. The balls whizzed about us like hail in a thick storm. There were probably six thousand men firing upon our force of six hundred. Most of Col. Gardner's command loaded lying down and rose up to fire. Our men fell with fearful rapidity. After about twenty minutes, we were ordered to fall back, to a place where the intervening ground would protect us from the enemy's fire.

After falling back about 200 yards we halted, faced about, loaded, and again rallied upon the enemy, at the same place as the first charge. After firing one or two rounds, we discovered a large, heavy column on our right, that we had supposed to be a portion of Gen. Bee's command, were enemies, and were carrying the stars and stripes; just then they opened fire upon us, and we were obliged to fall back again, out of this cross fire. In these fearful charges sad havoc was made in the Regiment. We then fell back, firing in retreat, and formed under Major Cooper, some 600 yards back of the pine thicket. We could then rally only about 150 men, and this remnant retired in good order from the battle-field, and as a Regiment did not return, although many individuals did, under other commands.

Col. Bartow, acting as Brigadier General, was killed.[8] A more intrepid, brave, and gallant man never lived. Col. Gardner had his leg broken in the first charge, and was left on the field, because he would not suffer the men to stop in that fearful place to carry him off. He was taken prisoner, but afterwards released by the enemy when they retreated, upon condition that he would have six or eight wounded Yankees properly cared for, and sent home with their arms.[9]

Adjutant Branch of our Regiment was killed.[10]

The following is the loss in the Rome Light Guards: C. B. Norton, G. T. Stovall, James B. Clarke, Dr. Duane and D. C. Hargrove killed.[11]

Anderson, Stevenson, McOsker and Howard severely wounded.[12] Capt. Magruder wounded in the left arm.

The following are slightly wounded: A. J. Bearden, R. W. Boggs, J. D. Jones, G. L. Aycock and J. T. Shackelford.[13]

The missing are John Black, Wm. Barron, T. McGrath, M. A. Ross and J. R. Payne. It is supposed that most or perhaps all of these were taken prisoners.[14]

Of the Miller Rifles Thos. Mobley and Frank Lathrop were killed.[15]

Thos. Hills was wounded probably fatally, and O. B. Eve severely, W. A. King had his right arm shot off about the elbow, Louis Yarbrough is probably fatally wounded.[16] Ben Price and Wm. Ware are slightly wounded.[17]

In the Floyd Infantry, Aaron Harshaw, F. M. Madrey, Wammack and Chastain are killed.[18] Capt. Cooper, Geo. Martin, O. M. Porter, H. Burns and Holbrook severely wounded.[19]

Who are missing from the Rifles or Infantry I have not learned.

I have to close this hasty letter.

Notwithstanding the great loss a most glorious victory was won by the Confederate forces. The field is ours. We have taken forty two cannon, including Sherman's Battery, over a hundred baggage wagons, and any amount of Baggage, and pursued the enemy to Fairfax Court House.

We spent yesterday—a very rainy day in hunting up the dead and burying them. They were decently intered and the funeral service read.

The loss in killed and wounded in the 8th Ga. Regiment is probably about 200, or one-third the men engaged in the Battle. The entire Confederate loss is believed to be about twelve or fifteen hundred in killed and wounded.[20]

The enemies loss between two and three thousand. We took a large number of prisoners say 500 or 600.

Gen. Bee was killed, as also Col. Fisher, of one of the Virginia Regiments, and Capt. Howard of the Echols Guards Merriwether county Georgia.

The general estimates I have made of the losses on both sides are quite vague and unsatisfactory to myself even.

If our readers knew the circumstances under which this letter is written they would be more disposed than otherwise to excuse its want of systematic order.

Clarke, Duane and Hargrove were buried on the field near where they fell. Norton and Stovall were carried to Manassas Junction, some six miles from the battle field, and will be buried there or sent home.[21]

Our entire force marched out for this battle was said to be about thirty thousand. That the enemy is variously stated from fifty to one hundred thousand. Most of our army has already moved forward and the balance will go soon towards Washington City. M. D.

Camp Near Battle Ground,
8 o'clock P.M., Tuesday, July 23.

**Dear Courier:** Since writing this morning, I have gathered some further particulars in regard to the glorious victory of the 21st. As the facts are made known, the complete route of the enemy, and utter confusion into which they were thrown, becomes more and more evident. Instead of getting *forty-two* of their cannon, *sixty-four* have already been brought in, and there is reason to suppose that still more may be found, provided this number does not include all they had. Our troops, detailed for that purpose, have been finding them all day, run off, in concealed places, by the roadside. In addition to the cannon, it is reported that the road leading to Alexandria, is literally lined with muskets, rifles, Minnie muskets, &c, &c. This morning twenty-seven of Lincoln's commissioned officers, including several of the Staff, were sent to Richmond as prisoners of war.[22]

The sneaking, cunning, and perfidious meanness of our enemies was exhibited on the day of the battle, by their using a flag, one side of which, represented the colors of the Confederate States, and the other those of the United States. It was by the use of this that our Regiment was so badly cut up. The column that flanked us showed the Confederate Flag until they got to the position where they could do us the greatest possible injury, then turned to us the Federal side and fired. For doing this when they sent a flag of truce to Gen. Beauregard asking for the privilege of gathering up and burying their dead, it was denied. How can they expect any courtesy when they thus set at defiance all rules of civilized warfare? The low spirit that governs them and their miscreancy was also exhibited on the 19th, when having leave to bury their dead of the 18th, they made use of the truce in throwing up barricades and breast works.

A. J. Bearden was taken prisoner and carried some four miles from the battle ground. This was after our Regiment had fallen back. He was carried to the headquarters of the enemy, and there saw a large number of gentlemen from Washington City, New York and other places, eating, drinking and carousing over *their* victory. Not long after, news came that their army was retreating, and our cavalry was in hot pursuit. Then ensured a scene of indescribable confusion among this white kid gentry in their efforts to secure their personal safety by flight. When our cavalry came up, Bearden claimed his own freedom, and took captive the Captain who had been guarding him. Chas. Harper, of the Miller Rifles, was taken prisoner, and with two or three others, was guarded by six of the Hessians. After a while, more prisoners were put in the care of the same guard, so that their number exceeded that of the hirelings holding them, our boys watched their opportunity, snatched their guardians guns and took them all prisoners. Another instance in which the tables were turned on them occurred with a member of our company, Robert DeJournett. He was on the retreat when a mounted officer, supposed to be a Colonel, rode up to within 15 or 20 paces, and cried out, "your life! your life! you young rebel." DeJournett turned, raised his gun and shot him through, while the officer was attempting to draw his pistol, and DeJournett made a hasty retreat in safety, though a volley of muskets were fired at him.

It is now certain that John Black, Marcus Ross and John Payne were taken prisoners and carried off. McGrath came in to-day unharmed. This accounts for all the Light Guards. No prisoners were carried off from the Miller Rifles. Several of the Federal prisoners have told us that they had expected to be hung as soon as the battle was over. They have been taught to believe that the Southerners are a set of complete barbarians.

Wm. Martin, of the Floyd Infantry, died last night. Howard, McOaker and Anderson, of our company, have been sent to Gordonsville. They were doing well.

Our Regiment has not yet re-organized, and we did not move to-day, as was anticipated. We were all very glad to see Rev. John Jones when he came into camp today.[23]

It is said that the Lincolnites *have taken Washington City*. They certainly by report, hold no place this side of Alexandria. M. D.

Battle Ground near Manassus Junction July 24 1861

**Dear Parents**—On last Sunday I was in the midst of one of the hardest fought battles that has ever occurred in America—I am without a scratch or even a bullet hole in my clothes—Five of our men fell dead by my side—four were mortally wounded—and six or eight more severely—It seems a miracle that I escaped unharmed. The Confederate Army was victorious and completely routed Lincoln's forces—We took 64 cannon of the best kind, 100

heavy baggage wagons—about 600 Prisoners and drove the enemy back some 12 or 15 miles and would have persued them to Washington but our men gave out from sheer exhaustion.
Your aft. Son Melvin

Near the Battle Field, 6 miles from
Manassas Junction, July 25.

**Dear Courier:** The events of the bloody 21st still continue, as they become known, to amaze even us who are here. If any previously doubted the righteousness of our case, or that a just God smiled upon and blessed our patriotic efforts, t˜o repel the wicked invaders, they now see such overwhelming evidence of these facts as to convince the most skeptical.

It is perfectly astonishing that the last man in the 8th Georgia Regiment was not killed in the most brave and gallant charge made in the pine ˜thicket, in the early part of the battle. The saplings, all about where we stood, are literally pealed and shot to pieces. We numbered five hundred and fifty-nine men in ranks. There were at least three thousand of the foe—and most of them regulars—in front of us, and about as many on the right. Our Regiment deployed here—entirely without support, sustained in the first charge a most deadly fire for thirty minutes, while with cool courage and accurate aim, our men poured the missiles of death into the ranks of the enemy. At the command we fell back in good order, and again at the order rallied to the same place. This would *seem* to be wanton sacrifice of our men, but it was *really* one of the wisest movements of the day, and it is believed to have turned the tide of battle.

The enemy, as prisoners now tell us, believed they were contending against at least six thousand men, and we thus held them in check fo˜r an hour and a half, and until our reinforcements could be brought on the field. Thus, although we did not have the pleasure the most despicable and hated enemy, that e˜ver contended on the battlefield, we have yet the gratifying satisfaction of knowing that the 8th Georgia Regiment performed a most important part in the most memorable events of this glorious day.

Geo. T. Stovall and Chas B. Norton fell in the first charge, within five steps of each other, and at almost the same instant. They were most bravely and gallantly fighting in the front rank, and two more heroic or better men never fell on the field of honor. Their many virtues and excellent traits of character, are now so distinctly present to the minds of their numerous friends and acquaintances, as to beggar any eulogy that I might attempt in this hasty letter. They were two gentlemen of such transcendant good qualities, of head and heart, as we are not likely "to look upon their like again." James B. Clark fell in the second charge, equally the bravest of the brave in the deadly fight. He was a noble youth, and much beloved by all who knew him. Near the same time and place of the two first, D. C. Hargrove was killed. No braver man fell that day, nor one who was more manfully contending. Dr. Duane was killed by a shot after the second charge.

Col. Bartow was killed some time after the second charge of the 8th Regiment, after two horses had been killed under him, and while he was bearing the colors and leading on the 7th Regiment. It would be impossible for a man to show more indifference to danger than he did on this bloody field.

Col. Gardner had his right leg broken below the knee, in the second charge. He is a most excellent officer, very much beloved and highly respected by all his command. It will be very hard to satisfy the Regiment with any other man in his place, and probably it will only be supplied temporarily; that at least is our hope.

The evidences of the great extent of the victory still continue to accumulate. It is now currently reported that we have taken 360 heavily loaded wagons, beside a complete village of ambulances, carriages and other vehicles. President Davis is reported to have said in a speech since the battle, that of the men *actually engaged in the fight*, we had only fifteen thousand, and the enemy thirty-five thousand men. He also said we had taken more baggage wagons, baggage and provisions, than all that there was previously, for the entire army, at Manassas Junction.

I learned yesterday that there were 237 wounded enemies—now prisoners—at Stone Church, six miles from here, all found there, together with 60 of them dead. They had tried, probably, to carry these off, but their retreat was too hasty to allow it. Ex.-Gov. Manning of S.C., now one of Gen. Beauregard's Staff, said yesterday that our loss is estimated at one thousand, and that of the enemy, in killed and wounded at between eight and ten thousand.

Among other things taken were two or three wagon loads of demijohns of fine liquors and baskets of champaign and other fixtures for a jubilee, in honor of their expected victory. Seward, Greeley, Gen. Scott and many other distinguished Lincolnites, are reported to have been near the battlefield and watching the movements with telescopes.

In writing these hasty letters I am obliged to record facts and incidents as they occur to me or not at all—but hope the absence of order will not entirely deprive them of interest. I have just heard of the valliant conduct of Billy Barron when he was taken prisoner. He, with one or two others were with Col.

Gardner, and trying to protect him after being wounded. A squad of ten or fifteen of the enemy charged down upon them, and ordered them to surrender, but Barron fought, striking with his gun, until completely overpowered, and was then carried off as a prisoner.

Lewis Yarborough, of the Miller Rifles, died of his wounds last night. Jas. W. Langston with ten other recruits for the Light Guards, and Alec Harper with some fifteen or twenty for the Miller Rifles, arrived. The boxes of eatables and luxuries were opened with the greatest pleasure, and I am sure such things were never better or more fully enjoyed. The "goodies" were shared by all, and many hearty thanks and cordial good wishes were expressed for the loved ones who sent them.

The 2d Brigade will hereafter be under the command of Gen. Jones, an old Army Officer.

The spirit of Virginia ladies was exhibited in the conduct of Mrs. Thornton on Sunday evening. She lives on the road taken by the retreating enemy, and there was no white man about the place. A Yankee, exhausted from running, rushed into her kitchen and fell fainting. She applied restoratives, gave him some fine brandy, and when he was sufficiently recovered to receive it, supper. She then ordered a serveant to take his gun and telling him he was her prisoner, sent for one of our officers and had him marched off. A few moments after one of Mrs. T's servants coaxed one of these same Hessians into the kitchen, and they took *him* prisoner.

The Fire Zouaves, Lincoln's "pet Lambs," were slain like sheep—out of 950 is said that only 200 escaped. Many of their bodies are still unburied.

It is amazing to see the completeness and excellence of the arms and accoutrements of the Federal troops. A better equipped army probably never entered the field.

Since writing the above John Black and Marcus Ross have come into camp. They tell us that they escaped from the enemy on Sunday evening during the confusion of the general stampede. They marched several miles with them until their Guard got separated from them, and then calling themselves Federal troops from Wisconsin, they managed to edge themselves off until they finally broke for the woods and escaped. They traveled nearly all night not knowing where they were. Ross had a painful wound in his hand, and when they were certain that they were among friends they stopped about 22 miles from here. Black is unhurt. John Berry had two fingers on his left hand shot off and is otherwise injured.

Camp of 8th Regiment Ga. Volunteers
near Manassas, July 30, 1861.

**Dear Courier:** Through other sources you have doubtless received, before this time, most of the important particulars of the great and glorious, though dearly bought, victory of the 21st. In my other letters, I have noticed very little except the movements of our own Regiment, for the reason that I desired to chronicle my own observations rather than the doubtful rumors that came to my ears, and I have even yet, not had opportunities to get facts in regard to the general plan and movements of the battle from reliable sources. The only satisfactory report of the memorable deeds of that day will be the *official* one, which will probably soon be forthcoming.

The following facts and incidents will be interesting to most readers. There is probably not an officer in the Confederate army, more beloved by his command, and for whom there exists a more confiding respect for his military character and attainments, than is enjoyed by Col. Montgomery Gardner. He is familiar with his men, yet commands their full and high respect. The following speech made to the Regiment just before we were led into battle is accurately illustrative of one of his peculiarities, viz: that he is a man for *fighting* rather than *talking*. I quote from memory, yet am sure the report is full and *verbatim*: "Fellow Soldiers: I shall soon lead you into battle; I cannot make a speech, and havn't *time* now if I could. Keep cool, obey orders—follow me, and we will whip them, egad." Every movement and command, until he fell from his wound, evidenced the utmost calmness and discreet bravery. It is the earnest wish of all, that he may speedily recover and again take his post at the head of our Regiment.

Other Captains may have done just as well, but I *know* that Captain Magruder was cool and discreet in his commands. He was wounded in the left arm in the very first of the fight, by a buck-shot, but continued during the fight, at the head of his company, with his arm in a sling. Late in the evening, and after the fight had ceased in that part of the field, he took a prisoner in the following manner: He had gone some little distance to a spring for water, while there a man with a musket approached. He drew his pistol and demanded "who comes there." The man answered "a member of the Wisconsin Regiment." The Captain said "throw down your gun and surrender, or I will blow your brains out." The man threw his gun forward so that it stuck up on the bayonet. The Captain then marched him off to where other prisoners were, and had him put under guard.

Where all were so brave and so well acted their part in the awful tragedy, it may seem invideous to particularize, but I cannot refrain from referring to the self-sacrificing devotion to comfort of our wounded, who had been left on the battle-field, exhibited by Geo. S. Barnsley.[24] There were none of our Regiment known to be left on the field, yet, he, with two or three others, spent the time from 5 P.M. until 3 o'clock the next morning in searching out and bringing in such as could be found. Considering the extreme fatigue and exhaustion of all, this peculiar kindness of heroism is worthy of high commendation.

We are now resting, getting ready for a re-organization of the Regiment and Brigade.

John Dunn, of the Floyd Infantry, died from his wounds last Saturday.[25]

Tommy Hills, of the Miller Rifles, one of the bravest and best young men in the army, died from his wounds on Sunday.

McOsker, of the Guards, is very bad off. The balance of the Floyd county boys are doing well, so far as I have learned.

Several of our men have recognized acquaintances among the prisoners, large numbers of which continue to be found.

Some of the Oglethorpe Light Infantry boys, a few days since, while hunting for eggs, under a barn in the neighborhood, found three Yankees and took them prisoners. M. D.

Camp Bartow, near Manassas,
August 5, 1861.

**Dear Courier:** It has been several days since I have written to you mainly for the reason that I have quite fully experienced the wonderful state of exhaustion and debility—amounting to almost complete prostration—consequent to the great and indescribable exertions, both physical and mental, of the glorious 21st. Every person has experienced to some extent a sense of vacuity after extraordinary excitements. By multiplying this a thousand fold, some idea may be formed of the prostrate condition of our Regiment since the memorable battle of Manassas. With resolute men, the ability to endure increases to a marvelous extent, with the accumulation of exciting causes; but after these causes are removed, the natural depression, that follows, is as much below the ordinary equilibrium as it had been carried above. Since that "day so foul and fair," until the past few days, when the men had began to brighten up, the ordinary routine of camp duties have seemed idle formalities, altogether frivolous, and they were reluctantly performed with feelings of repugnance that amount to almost disgust.

As the little glowing description of the march of Gen. Johnston's command from Winchester to this place, seems, from its non-publication, to have been lost, and in order that our condition upon the day of battle may be better understood, I will now give a few of the leading facts: On Thursday July 18th, five Regiments, including the 2d, had orders to march from Winchester. Our Regiment left camp at 1 o'clock P.M., without dinner, and only food enough in our haversacks for one meal. When a half mile out of town, we were told that the march was to Manassas. Arrived at Millwood at 6 o'clock, and to the Shannandoah River, thirteen miles from Winchester, at 9 o'clock. Four hours were consumed by the army, in fording the river. Passed the Blue Ridge through the Paris Gap, and arrived at that town distant from the river, five miles, at 3 o'clock A.M., on Friday; here lay down on the ground, without blankets, and rested three hours, then resumed the march to Piedmont Station, on the Manassas Gap Railroad—distance five miles—where we arrived at 9 o'clock. Our wagons came up about noon and we got a very good dinner, ready at three o'clock. From 7 P.M., till 2 A.M. Saturday, we were on the cars between Piedmont and Manassas—detained by the rascality of the conductor, who was believed to have been bribed by the enemy, and who has since been shot.

My letter published in the Courier of the 30th ult., gives an account of our movements of Saturday. We marched not less than ten miles on the morning of the battle.

From breakfast Thursday morning, until after the battle on Sunday, the men of this Regiment received about sufficient food for two full meals. In this time they marched 35 miles—fording the Shannandoah, and crossing the Blue Ridge—and were for several hours, crowded in the most uncomfortable manner in the cars.

I have been thus particular in reporting our movements, because it has been intimated by some few who did not know the facts, that the survivors in the 8th Georgia Regiment broke down very soon after the bloody charge.

I saw a statement a few days since in a communication in the *Richmond Dispatch*, that the Oglethorpe Light Infantry occupied the right of the Regiment in the charge in the pine thicket. The falsity of this statement is only equaled by the presumption of the writer.

Below is an accurate statement of the numbers entering the battle of the 21st, from the various companies of the 8th Georgia Regiment, and of the killed, wounded and prisoners:

| | | No. | K'd | W'd | Pr's |
|---|---|---|---|---|---|
| A. | Rome Light Guards | 56 | 5 | 14 | 2 |
| B. | Oglethorpe L't In'ry | 83 | 5 | 25 | 3 |
| C. | Macon Guards | 62 | 4 | 16 | 2 |
| D. | Echols Guards | 42 | 2 | 11 | 1 |

| | | | | | |
|---|---|---|---|---|---|
| E. | Miller Rifles | 37 | 2 | 15 | 0 |
| F. | Atlanta Grays | 76 | 3 | 20 | 7 |
| G. | Pulaski Volunteers | 36 | 4 | 14 | 0 |
| H. | Floyd Infantry | 40 | 4 | 12 | 0 |
| I. | Stephens L't Guards | 78 | 7 | 13 | 1 |
| K. | Oglethorpe Rifles | 33 | 0 | 16 | 0 |
| Total | | 543 | 36 | 156 | 16 |

Gen. Samuel Jones, who has been appointed to command our Brigade for a few months, had charge of the Institute at Marietta, Ga. We, as yet, have no Lieutenant Colonel. A. R. Harper is acting Adjutant, and Lieutenant Reese is acting Quartermaster of the Regiment. Our Brigade—the 7th, 8th, and 9th Georgia Regiments and Ky. Batallion—is now encamped 2 miles N.E. from Manassas. Our regular drills were resumed three days since.

Lieut. Gen. R. Lumpkin has resigned on account of ill health. He was an excellent officer and much beloved by the company. Z. B. Hargrove and Marion Ezzel have applied for, and will doubtless receive honorable discharges, on the ground of chronic ill health; also, McOsker, on account of his wounds. Howard, Anderson, and Stephenson, will probably get furloughs for 60 days on account of their wounds, and Ross for 30 days.

Several applications for discharges and furloughs will be made by members of the Miller Rifles and Floyd Infantry, but I have not time to go around and learn their names.

Rev. John Jones preached to us yesterday an excellent sermon. He will hold prayer meetings every evening, at eight o'clock, as long as he remains in camp.

There is considerable sickness in the Floyd county companies, but none are considered dangerous.

Of the general movements of our Army, you can learn more at your various homes than we can here in camp. M. D.

Camp Bartow near Manassas, Va. Aug 6th

**Dear Parents:** I have only time to write a few lines and no paper to write on. My health is perfect. We are now awaiting the reorganization of our Regiment and Brigade. Our troops never were so confident of success, and there are enough now in the field to repell <u>any</u> force that may invade Confederate soil. I did not expect to come out of the battle of the 21st inst. Alive but thank God I am still well and ready to strike again for the just cause in which I am engaged. If I should meet any of my relatives on the battle field in Lincoln's army they will there be considered as my enemies and treated as such. My whole heart is with the South—Several Brothers have already met in opposing armies—The scenes are affecting but the Southerners have never to my knowledge flinched from their patriotic duty—

Give my love to such of my relatives as care for the regards of a "rebel" if there be such—accept my warmest love for yourselves and Brothers & Sisters nephews and Neice.

Your son Melvin

Camp Near Manassas,
August 7, 1861.

**Dear Courier:** I have no particular news to communicate, except the joyous relief we experienced yesterday, from the painful anxiety felt, in regard to the fate of Wm. A. Barron and John R. Payne. They are prisoners in Washington. We had feared that our unscrupulous enemies had murdered them, more particularly because Barron did not surrender but was overpowered when taken.

The following is a copy of a letter received by James T. Moore from Barron:

Washington, July 30th

**Dear Uncle:** I have an opportunity of writing a few lines, to say that I am well, have plenty to eat, good quarters, kind attendants, and in fact everything to render my situation as easy as possible. I think Capt. Magruder and Col. Gardner can and will give an account of how I was taken. I could have escaped with ease, and with less danger than I experienced by staying by the side of the Colonel. I must close. I remain, Yours truly, W. A. Barron
P.S. John R. Payne is here and well.

To-day A. J. Bearden was elected fourth Sergeant in place of Ike Donkle, resigned.[26] Mr. Donkle has been ordered to Richmond, by the Secretary of War, as is presumed, for the purpose of sending him to Rome, to work on the rifled cannon being manufactured by Messrs. Noble.[27] He will be much missed by the company, on account of his jolly disposition, kind heartedness and entire apparent disregard for danger. We regret to loose him, but his services many be more important to the country in his new sphere of action.

These days are exceedingly hot and the nights warm. M. D.

Camp Bartow, near Manassas,
August 13, 1861.

**Dear Courier:** As everything in the way of news, incidents, accidents, &c., pertaining to the great battle of the 21st, is eagerly sought for by all who have relatives or friends in the Confederate Army, and as this includes nearly every family in the country, the writer of this is so presumptious as to undertake "*a description of one's feelings in the battle of Manassas—it being his first experience.*"

Though at different times and places our Regiment had been, some six or eight times, drawn up in line of battle, and we had gone through all the little heart sinkings, trepidations and fearful apprehensions, which most men experience, upon the eve of entering the life and death contest, yet, when we *knew* that a great battle was about to be commenced, yet there was such a deep and thrilling earnestness in the cannon's first booming, as convinced us of the certainty of the fearful work about to be done, and a deep seated apprehension of danger—though not generally shown by palid cheeks or trembling limbs—was experienced. The certainty of danger became still more apparent, when coming near the range of one of the enemy's batteries, we heard the whizzing of the death dealing missiles, as they passed with a horrid significance of what we might expect from better aim.

The "pomp and circumstance of glorious war," suddenly dwindled down to the severest kind of plain, common sense, and it very soon became apparent, that common sense rules must be the basis of all discreet actions. At the first sight of the enemy, all the bug bear delusions that may have existed in the fancy of any one, as to their appearance, were suddenly dispelled, and they looked at the distance of three hundred or four hundred yards, precisely like so many of our men.

Quite different from all my fancies of great battles; this was not fought in a broad open field, where the two grand armies could be drawn up in long, unbroken lines, and approach each other in heavy columns. There is no considerable extent of right level ground on this memorable field, but is completely broken with hills and dales, meandering branches and protecting groves. And in extent, the hottest part of the battle field was about one miles by three quarters in width. On such a field, of course, the awful grandeur of appearance of the approaching armies was lost. Then when the firing commenced, that wonderful, indefinite and superhuman grandeur of movements, that my imagination had painted, all faded out, and in its place I had an ugly, dusty, fatiguing and laborious realization of the *actual* in battle. I experienced most fear when the first cannon ball passed over, with a tremendous whizzing, about twenty yards off; and felt the most dread apprehension, when ordered immediately after, to take a position on a little eminence, in fearful proximity to the place the ball had just passed. After our Regiment had moved forward some 200 or 300 yards, we again came both in range and sight of Sherman's celebrated Battery, about three-fourths of a mile from us. Their shell and balls came fearfully near, and as one passed through an apple tree just over my head, a cold chill ran over me, and I suffered from agonizing fear, for probably, three or four seconds, but after this, during the entire battle, though I was in almost constant expectation of being killed, yet there was no painful realization of fear, such as would make one hesitate to go wherever duty called, or prevented a full and free exercise of all the faculties of body and mind. As the dangers really increased, and friends were seen falling thick upon either side, the *apprehension*, or rather the *fear*, of them became strangely less, and without feeling secure there was a sort of forced resignation to calmly abide whatever consequences should come.

At no time did I experience any feeling of anger, or discover any exhibition of it in others. A stern determination and inflexible purpose, was the predominant expression of countenance of all, so far as my observation extended, and any sudden exhibition of passion would have seemed ridiculous.

One of the most remarkable mental phenomena, was the sudden and strange drying up of sympathetic feeling for the suffering of the wounded and dying. I could never before look upon even small operations, or persons in extreme pain from any cause, especially when blood was freely flowing, without intense pain and generally more or less faintness. But on this occasion I beheld the most terrible mutilations, the most horrid and ghastly expression of men in the death struggle, men with one arm or a leg, shot off, others with the face horridly mutilated, heads shot through and brains lying about, bodies half torn into, and at the hospital, some 50 men with legs or arms just amputated and a half cord of legs and arms, and men in all degrees of pain, from the slight flesh wound to those producing death in a few moments, and viewed all this with far less feeling than I would ordinarily have seen brutes thus mutilated. This obduracy I am truly glad, was only temporary. Only two days after the battle I caught myself avoiding the sight of the amputation of an arm.

I have written thus much of my own feelings, not because they were peculiar, but according to my best knowledge and belief, were nearly the same as those shared by a great majority of all those who were in the heat of the battle, for first time, on the glorious 21st.

Our Regiment is now having an easy time. There is considerable slight sickness, but none dangerous that I know of. Dr. Miller has been appointed

General Director of the Medical Board for our Brigade—the 2nd—but he still retains the office of Surgeon of the 8th Regiment. Capt. Carr has been temporarily assigned to assist Maj. Cooper in commanding the Regiment. M. D.

Camp Bartow, near Manassas,
August 19, 1861.

**Dear Courier:** For the past two weeks we have had rather a gloomy, disagreeable time of it, with no exciting incidents to rouse our ambition, or break the wearisome monotony of military duties, mechanically performed. But amidst the lowering gloom of this outward world we had a glorious flood of warm, glowing sunshine upon our hearts on last Saturday, when Mr. Sam. Johnson arrived, with five recruits for the Light Guards, and the same number for the Miller Rifles, and a most rich and abundant supply of eatibles and drinkables, the very sight of which made our "mouths water" and excited a joyous shout of exultation at the prospect of the "good time a coming." In regard to any small matter, perhaps there never was seen a more anxious crowd of eager expectants, than the one that assembled around the boxes to see them opened, and for each to get his share in the general distribution. If the ladies, who so kindly send these luxuries to the soldiers, could see and hear the expressions of joyousness exhibited on their reception, and know how proud the boys are at being thus remembered, it would half repay them for their pains-taking in these labors of love.

For such lady friends as the Floyd county companies have at home, even *cowards* would fight, and surely "our boys" will contend with a fervency that knows no yielding, for the fair and lovely who make their homes so dear.

The very considerable supply of clothing sent by the ladies of the 859 District G. M., was also received with feelings of unfeigned gratitude. Quite a number of the articles sent were actually needed, for immediate use, and it will all doubtless come in play in a short time. While at home most of the men in the various companies used to get under clothing, they hardly knew how, by a sort of matter-of-course way, as it seemed, the tattered and old always seemed to be replaced by new and wholesome articles. But in camp when one's unmentionables, for instance, become worn out, he is sure to have a *feeling* realization of this *significant* or it may be *insignificant* fact, and the discomfort thus arising is perhaps far more than can be conjectured. As these boxes were opened, one could almost read the *words* "God bless the ladies," from the countenances of the brave and hearty men who stood around.

A proper distribution of the various articles was made, in accordance with the wishes of the fair donors.

Donations. When here some three weeks since, Mr. R. S. Norton very generously and kindly promised to give the Light Guards fifty dollars, towards paying Dr. J. M. Gregory, our most excellent company Physician and Surgeon.

Mr. Robt. H. Johnson, who for some years did business in New York, but returned to his native Georgia last spring, has, with a degree of generosity only suited to such noble natures, unconditionally pledged two hundred and fifty dollars for winter clothing, for the company, to be paid next January, and he proposes to double the amount, if it is needed. If our lady friends should see fit to send any more articles, underclothing, such as shirts, under-shirts, and drawers would be most acceptable, as it is desired to have the outside clothing uniform. It will soon be quite cool in this latitude, and woolen socks on the damp, cold ground, will greatly conduce to the comfort of the soldiers.

Lieut. Lumkin's resignation has been accepted, and McOsker has been discharged. Z. B. Hargrove has caused the application for his discharge to be withdrawn, and patriotically declares that he will not quit the army so long as he has strength to shoot a gun, or the enemy still lingers upon Confederate soil. The other applicants for discharges or furloughs have, to wait until they are able to go before the Medical Board for examination. M. D.

Camp Bartow, near Manassas,
August 28th, 1861.

**Dear Courier:** Even in time of actual and active war, there must necessarily be days and weeks, of dulls and comparatively uninteresting duties, incident to and naturally following great conflicts, and many tedious delays and irksome labors, in preparation for the bloody strife expected on some indefinite, but ever apprehended, future day. This has been the condition of our Regiment, since the ever memorable and glorious battle of Manassas. Our duties have been light, but, paradoxical as it may seem, all the more irksome and "grievous to be borne," on account of their very ease, and the little time required in their performance. It seems to be a natural sequence to the commendable submission that good soldiers yield to their commanders, that they carry this feeling of subordination too far, and, because, for instance, they sometimes are compelled, in obedience to orders, to undergo prolonged and severe labors and privations; when they have the opportunity they indulge too freely both appetite and love of ease, and thus glide into a state wherein minor duties become unpleasant, and slight deprivations are complained of.

If our organization is not soon perfected, and the Regiment put to some more active duties, a loss of some portion of the hardihood previously acquired, may be feared, and even sickness will be more prevalent than it otherwise would be.

Fevers, mostly Billious, Typhoid and Intermittent, are now much more abundant than at any previous date, and except Measles, there is now more sickness in this regiment than at any other time, since we have been in service. Of the Light Guards there are now sick with fevers: Capt. Magruder, W. S. Booton, convalescent; Geo. King, A. R. Johnson, T. W. Swank, these three are quite ill; Dan'l Miller and George Milam.[28] Lewis Bell has the Measles, Barrett is nearly well, but has not yet reported for duty; Henry Smith has been indisposed for several days, but is now nearly well.[29] All these except Smith and Miller are at Gordonsville. The present sick of the Miller Rifles are Willis Rice, T. J. Ellis, John Hill, Wm. Gear and Harvey Brice—are all recovering from the Measles; T. W. Asbury has been quite sick with fever, but is recovering; Charlie Harper is quite low from the effects of Measles and disease of the lungs; A. G. Bobo and Pyles are both recovering from Measles.[30] Of the wounded Funderberk is not expected to recover; Fain and King are doing well.[31]

Of the Floyd Infantry there are none in camp too ill to be up and about; Drummond is still at Winchester. The following have been sent off sick and not since heard from, viz: James Calahan, L. J. Farmer, Joel Bagwell, W. Henderson.[32] Capt. Cooper, at last accounts, was quite ill, and not expected to live, W. R. Hidle died from the effect of his wounds last week. Martin Burns and Thos. Wright are very low from the effects of their wounds.[33]

Of Oswell Bones Eve, Orderly Sergeant of the Miller Rifles, who died on the 20th inst., I cannot speak too highly. Loved and respected by his own Company, and highly esteemed by all who knew him, his loss is greatly deplored by all his companions in arms. He endured the most agonizing sufferings with a soldier's fortitude and Christian resignation, and finally with calm and buoyant hope yielded up his spirit to the Savior, whom he loved. "After life's fitful fever he sleeps well."

The Light Guards send their sick to Gordonsville, where they are under the care of our most excellent company physician, Dr. J. M. Gregory. Other companies provide for their's in the best manner in their power.

The statement in the *Courier* of the 18th, that Dr. Miller was, with his own private means, purchasing comforts for the sick is a mistake. He has, as I am informed, some hundred and fifty dollars or more placed in his hands for this purpose, but the difficulty has been in getting such things as butter, eggs, chickens, vegetables, etc., as there is no one appointed for this purpose, who has the power to go where they are to be had.

It is understood that Dr. McFarland, a young physician of Savannah, has been appointed assistant Surgeon, and will have charge of this Regiment.

It is reported that Maj. Thomas L. Cooper has been promoted to Lieutenant Colonel, and Capt. J. F. Cooper to Major.

An effort is being made to get assigned to the command of this Regiment, an officer of experience and Military Education, until Col. Gardner is sufficiently recovered to resume his post. He is doing well, but it will probably be at least three months before he can do military duty.

Within the past few days two instances of patriotic generosity and affectionate regard for the soldiers, have come to my knowledge, that are so remarkable as to deserve to be chronicled in the history of these interesting times. They both occurred in Floyd Co., Ga. One was the act of Mrs. Brice an old Lady of Cave Spring whose son and main support is a member of the Miller Rifles. When her neighbors were recently sending on packages to *their* relatives and friends, *she*, by strenuous exertions and actually depriving herself of some of the comforts of life, made up a larger one than any of them, for her son, and had inscribed upon it the motto "Liberty or Death." The other instance was the act of Mrs. Nancy Hamilton, a poor widow lady who lives near Floyd Springs, and supports herself by taking in weaving and other work for her neighbors. She sent "For the Soldiers" two pair of one serviceable Pants and of Socks. I am told that she purchased the raw material—the cotton and wool but every particle of the work on these articles was done by her own aged and patriotic hands. When the christian Matrons of our country, by such acts of self-denial and energy, cast into the treasury of our cause, as it were their "widow's mites," surely there can be no such word as fail in the final account of this war. There may be many who have given more and with greater ostentation, but none in the Biblical and real, sacrifiding sense of *giving*, have done more than these noble hearted Ladies. May they long live and enjoy the full tide of prosperity that will follow an early peace.

It is currently reported in camp today and generally believed, that there was a skirmish at Falls Church yesterday, between 300 Federalists and 75 of our men. The loss of the enemy is reported to be ten killed, seven prisoners and a large number wounded. Our loss was two killed, a few slightly wounded and no prisoners. As usual the Lincolnites ran, leaving their dead and wounded. It is further rumored that a small fight is going on to-day near the same place.    M. D.

Camp Bartow, near Manassas, Va.,
September 5, 1861.

**Dear Courier:** The events of yesterday were exceedingly interesting to the second Brigade of this Division of the Confederate Army, and their memory, tinged with sacred tenderness, will be ever cherished, by the brave hearts who witnessed them, with feelings of hallowed joy.

The occasion was that of marking, in a proper way, and with suitable ceremonies, *the place where Bartow fell.*[34] At the instance of some of their officers, the members of the 8th Georgia Regiment, had procured a small marble shaft for this purpose, and the other Regiments of the Brigade—the 7th, 9th and 11th Georgia, and the Kentucky Regiments—had been invited to join them in this act of respect and commemoration. Accordingly, these commands left their respective encampments at about 8 o'clock, yesterday morning, and marched separately to the battle-ground—a distance of seven miles—where they arrived between 10 ½ and 11 o'clock. After stacking arms, the various Regiments were dismissed until the necessary arrangements could be completed for raising the shaft, or, perhaps, it would be more properly be called a post.

Only the 7th and 8th Regiments of this Brigade were in the battle of July the 21st, and to the members of these corps, this re-visiting the place of their strife and glory, was one of deep and strange interest, with commingling emotions of joy and sorrow. As they walked over the field, the sight of nearly every point in it would, by association, bring to vivid remembrance, some exciting scene in the awful tragedies of that eventful day. Here one stood when he heard the first cannon ball pass in fearful nearness to himself; there he saw such a friend fall—and, O, how distinctly, he now sees him with his mind's eye—his imploring look, and outstretched arms; yonder was the enemy's battery, and how their angry mouthes belched forth the livid streams; what a shout there was when such a Regiment advanced to that point; how the heart sunk when our forces fell back there, how the enemies balls made the dirt fly around us as we passed along here; how good the muddy water in this little branch looked when we double-quicked across it; what horrid anxiety there was to know whether the Regiment yonder were friends or foes; here a cannon ball was dodged; there a bursting shell avoided; there was seen A leading off B, who dragged one leg; here came C, supported between D and E, and so awful bloody in face; yonder laid F with his hand significantly on his breast, and at various points round about, were friends and strangers, lying fearfully still, some on their faces, some on their backs, some with folded arms and legs drawn up, and others with outstretched limbs. Still, we pass on, finding distances, strangely different from what they seemed on that fearful day, seeing several houses, not many hundred yards distant, that were not then noticed, and finding many natural objects strangely out of place. Each one, naturally, seeks the place where his own Regiment had its severestt struggle. Arrived there, he sees and hears one again, the indescribable scenes of bloody carnage, and fearful horror, which his memory now presents with most painful distinctness. He imagines that he again hears the whiz-z-z-z of the cannon ball—the zip—zip-zip-p-p-p of the musketry charge, and the quick whist, whist of the rifles. He sees where this and that friend *stood*, and where the other *fell*.

But the roll of the drum reminds us of our wandering, both physical and mental, and we're returned to the place where the gallant Bartow fell, to witness the interesting ceremonies that was about to be performed. It was 2 o'clock P.M., on the ever memorable 21st, when this gallant and much beloved commander, breathed his last, and his noble spirit took its flight from a field of bloodiest strife to realms of eternal peace and rest. He fell about 300 or 400 yards of the South-west corner of the battle-field, and within 100 yards of where his Regiment was first exposed to the enemy; just at the very crisis of the battle, after our forces had been compelled to give way again and again and was just there regaining some of their lost ground. But a moment before he was killed, he had taken the colors of the 7th Georgia Regiment in his own hands, advanced some distance toward the enemy, and in the face of their fire, planted them, and rallied the men forward to this new line, which he told them Beauregard had commanded that they should hold at all hazards. In this immediate vicinity and at that time, was the last desperate struggle before the final route of the enemy. Gen. Bee was killed about 150 yards to the right of where Bartow fell, and Col. Fisher, of one of the North Carolina Regiments, about 250 yards in front after the Lincolnites had commenced retreating. Those three brave officers all fell in a short space of time.

The preliminaries being arranged, a hollow square was formed around the place where the stone was to be erected, by the four regiments composing the 9th Brigade, commanded by Col. Bartow, with the staff officers in the centre. The officers were ordered in front and the Brigade brought to parade rest. The sight here presented, was duly impressive, grand and patriotic. There was something really exhilarating in the idea of these thousands of sun-burnt and hearty soldiers, who have endured the hardships and privations of a campaign already long; who have resolutely performed long, forced marches and murmured not at the attendant hunger and fatigue; and who, with unblanched cheeks have met the most unplacable of foes in the storm of battle, and, even against great odds, and put them to inglorious flight—for such brave men, whose very appearance gives incontestable evidence of long and severe service, to assemble for the enobling and patriotic purpose, of honoring the memory and perpetuating the good deeds of their commander, is a fit crowning act of their many virtues. When those ranks stood, apparently, in seriously contemplative mood, their sorrow was sweetened by heaven-born music with its soft and mellow strains. The band played a beautiful funeral march, and the time and its fine execution were so completely in harmony with, and so tenderly touching to the finder feelings, that the "pearly drops were seen to course each other" down many a bronzed cheek.

The ceremonies were then continued in the following order:

2d—Prayers by Rev. John Jones, Chaplain of 8th Georgia Regiment.

3d–Music—"Camping at Grenada."

4th—Address by Hon. Mr. Semmes, Attorney General of the State of Louisiana.

5th–Music—"Let me kiss him for his mother."

6th—Address by Maj. J. L. Cooper, of 8th Georgia Regiment.

7th–Music—"The Marseillais Hymn."

8th—The putting of the Post in its place by Brig. Gen. Jones, assisted by the commanders and portion of the Staff Officers of the different Regiments.

The Music by the band, belonging to the 1st Regiment Georgia Regulars, was most excellent—by far better than that of any other band we have been in the habit of hearing in the service. The prayer was peculiarly appropriate, and offered in that chaste and pathetic style, so characteristic of our faithful and most beloved Chaplain. Of the speech by Mr. Semmes, I cannot give even a synopsis, without prolonging this letter to an unreadable length. He was pleased at having an opportunity to express the sympathy of Louisiana with Georgia, and all the other Confederate States, in their present troubles, and to assure the hearty co-operation of his own State, in all the necessary sacrifices, struggles and labors to secure our independence. He said our independence had been virtually achieved, by the bloody victory of July 21st, but we must maintain the prestige then gained, suffer no defeats but continue our onward march. He said England and France would not interfere in our behalf, until it should be known that we needed none of their help. He compared our privations and sufferings with those of our revolutionary ancestors, and showed how comparatively insignificant they are, while the independence we shall obtain will be almost transcendently more important, and prospectively glorious. The heroes of '76 relieved themselves of the yoke of a single King, held in check by our enlightened christianity, and wholesome constitutional constraints. But we will be released from the tyrannies of a fanatical, pagan, skeptical mob of abolitionists. He closed by paying a beautiful tribute to Col.

Bartow, and said that in his death was particularly realized the beautiful saying of the Latin poet, *"dulce et decora pro patria mori,"* it is sweet and honorable to die for ones country. He said he need not exhort Confederate soldiers not to prove recreant, but in times of severe struggle it be well to remember the dying words of their gallant commander and "never give up the fight."

Maj. Cooper's speech was short but full of pathos. He had not intended to speak, but thought some Georgian ought to raise his voice on this interesting occasion, in commemoration of the virtues of one of her most brave and gallant sons. He made a most interesting allusion to the dying words of our lamented commander, uttered, as they were, as the tide of battle was turning in our favor, and he exhorted the men, that however severe their hardships might be, or however desperate the struggle, to remember the dying words of our late, lamented and much beloved commander, and "never give up the fight."

The Shaft is plain white marble, six feet long, four feet above ground and about eight inches in diameter at the top. The inscription on it is,

Francis S. Bartow
*"They have killed me boys,*
*But never give up the fight!"*

After lowering the stone into its place, each one of the Staff Officers, threw a few spades full of dirt around it. When they were through, a beautiful young lad, Miss Barber, living in the vicinity, stepped forward, and taking up a handful of dirt, threw it in. This tribute, thus beautifully paid, was heartily cheered by the soldiers. Mrs. Branch, of Savannah, the mother of our lamented Adjutant, being present showed her appreciation of the departed hero in the same way.

These ceremonies being over, we soon took up our line of march for Camp Bartow, where we arrived about sundown, much fatigued, but well pleased with the manner in which the day had been spent.

Sept. 6. For the past two weeks our forces have been gradually moving on towards Washington. Adjutant Harper has gone out this morning with Gen. Jones to look for a camping ground in the vicinity of Centreville, some 8 miles from here, a little west of North and due North from Manassas. Centreville is 26 miles from Alexandria. There is more or less skirmishing every day, in the vicinity of Alexandria. A grand battle is expected soon. M. D.

Camp Bartow, near Manassas,
September 9th, 1861.

**Dear Courier:** It is sometimes a satisfaction to hear from one's friends, even if they have nothing of exciting interest to communicate. I presume upon that fact in the present writing. Our Regiment continues in about the same state of health, that it has been for the past three weeks. Some have recovered and others became indisposed. There are now no cases of dangerous illness in this camp, or of members of it in other places that I know of. Measles still prevail to a large extent, nearly every new recruit taking this disease, when he first comes into camp. It is believed that some are having it the second time. Charley Harper is just recovering from the Measles, and he is sure he had the disease several years since. The assurance that it is proof of his good looks, did not seem to be much satisfaction to him, when the fever was on, and he could taste nothing else. Sanford Williamson has got them "good," broke out as full as can be. He is a little too sick to joke, but yet is doing well. There are a few cases of Mumps. The victims of this disease are laughed at for their consolation, and have nothing to do but "grin and bear it."

There was rather a singular surgical operation performed last Saturday, on A. J. Bearden, of our company. It will be remembered that he received a slight wound in the head, in the battle of the 21st. It soon healed over and he thought no more of it, except occasionally an unpleasant sensation in the vicinity of the wound, and there was a small rising. He went to our assistant Surgeon, Dr. McFarland, who told him there was some foreign substance between the skin and skull. Mr. Bearden consented to the operation, and the Dr. soon cut out a buck-shot, that had flattened on the skull, until its thickness was about one third the diameter. It was located above the left ear and on the oval part of the skull. It is singular that this shot should have been there forty eight days and he not know it.

Capt. J. F. Cooper is reported to have died last Thursday night. His commission as Major, I understand, was received to-day. His sufferings must have been of the most excrutiating kind. He was a man of great energy and determination, and served his country with a zeal surpassed by few. "Peace to his ashes."

We distinctly hear cannonading nearly every day, in the direction of Alexandria, and Washington. Yesterday 253 prisoners passed down here, on their way to Richmond, taken some where up there. We will probably move soon, but until further notice, our mail matter should be directed to Manassas.

The sick of the Light Guards, except a few yet in camp, are in Gordonsville, and doing well. They miss Dr. Gregory very much, and it is to be hoped that he will hasten back. Send him along. Doubtless the Romans would like to keep him there, but we *must have him here*. The sick of the Miller Rifles and Floyd Infantry are scattered at various places, and even the officers of those companies do not know where they all are. But so far as they can learn there are none very sick. It is really wonderful that there should be so much sickness in this Regiment, and so few deaths—there having been but three since the battle. This is probably due to the great care of the company officers, and the excellent and skillful treatment of the Surgeons.

There has been considerable excitement in regard to our Regimental Officers. The War Department has decided that all vacancies in this Regiment, will be filled by regular proclamation. This makes Maj. Thos. L. Cooper Lieutenant Colonel—he received his commission this morning—and throws him in command, until Col. Gardner recovers. Col. Cooper is a fine, accomplished gentleman, and with study and experience will doubtless make an excellent commander; but there is a very strong desire to have a regular army officer to command us. This is not likely to be gratified.[35] M. D.

September 10th, 1861.

**Dear Courier:** Our camp just now is quite lively, and the men are as busy as bees, in packing up their "duds" and getting ready to leave. The order was issued at 9 ½ o'clock this morning, to get ready to move as quick as possible, and as there was nothing said about cooked rations, it is presumed the march will be a short one—most likely to the vicinity of Centreville. We are allowed but one wagon, with four horses, to the company, to carry three days rations, tents and all other baggage, and it will be perceived that there is great perplexity in deciding what shall be taken, and what shall be left with a strong possibility of being lost.

George Demming and Z. B. Hargrove were both honorably discharged on account of chronic illness, and yesterday left for home. Zack's "pluck" is good, but his health won't endure the privation and hardships of camp life. Demming very reluctantly received his discharge, but the Surgeon insisted that his health required it. Leonidas T. (Coon) Mitchell has received the commission of 2d Lieutenant in a Cass county company, of which Jett Howard is Captain, and has been transferred to that command. Coon is every inch a good fellow, one of the best of good singers, and on account of his ever prevailing good humor, splendid singing, and generous feelings, he will be much missed from the company. Howard is a fine fellow and possesses excellent accomplishments, of both head and heart, and will doubtless make an excellent Captain. We confidently hope that these men, both formerly members of the Light Guards, and with us on the glorious 21st, may win unfading laurels in their new sphere and association.

Barna and Wade both arrived here last week, and the boys enjoyed keenly the literary feast that they brought, in the epistolary form.[36] Wade, by some mishap, left the boxes entrusted to his care in Lynchburg, and has now gone back after them. The sick, so far as I can learn, are doing well—none in the Floyd companies very sick.

All communications for the present, should be directed to Manassas, and they will be forwarded to us if we leave the vicinity.

P.S.—2 o'clock P.M.—We have not moved yet, and it is now probable that we will not move until to-morrow morning.

# 3

# "Matters Are Jogging along Here"

## *September–December 1861*

A week after the ceremony honoring Col. Francis Bartow, the Eighth Georgia broke camp and marched to a new location outside Fairfax Court House. Washington, DC, was just fifteen miles to the north, and Melvin Dwinell told readers how the men could see the city and even the US Capitol, which was still under construction. With the two armies so close to one another, regiments performed picket duty regularly. He explained how the opposing pickets sometimes held informal truces to visit and swap needed items. But other soldiers on picket duty sometimes traded fire with one another, and the results could be deadly.

At the end of September, Dwinell put together a chart listing the number of deaths in each company in the Eighth Georgia. He noted that the regiment had suffered numerous casualties at the Battle of Manassas, and that many other men had died from disease. On a brighter note, in another letter, Dwinell described the great joy of the troops in getting packages from home. "[A] happier set of men have seldom been seen," he wrote. On October 1, President Jefferson Davis visited camp to discuss strategy with his commanders. The Georgians had just left for another stint on picket duty, and so the men missed the opportunity to see their commander in chief. However, the troops did see one of the Federal army's curious spy balloons operated by Professor Thaddeus Lowe. The balloons, which could rise one thousand feet above the ground, conducted aerial reconnaissance in areas with little topography. In a clever bit of writing Dwinell noted, "Lincoln's overseer sees over a vast country." A few nights later, some men

Spy Balloon. Library of Congress.

thought they saw the balloon again, but it turned out to be just a bright star. Everybody enjoyed a good laugh over the mistake.

The *Courier's* editor also explained how, with coffee in short supply, the Confederate Commissary had begun issuing each man a half gill of whiskey every morning and evening. To avoid any problems, the soldiers had to drink their allotment at the time it was given. The whiskey was especially welcomed on the cold, damp mornings they were increasingly enduring. In mid-October, Dwinell became sick with what he called "camp fever" and left to receive medical attention in nearby Gordonsville, Virginia. He was treated in a local hospital and then recovered at the home of Col. James Magruder, the father of the Light Guards' captain. While he was sick and recuperating, Dwinell's correspondence stopped for three weeks.

When he returned, Dwinell continued keeping readers updated on the troops and volunteers from Floyd County. Dr. Robert Battey, a Rome resident and surgeon with another regiment, was "looking well" but tired from the exhaustion of his job. Thomas Hooper, another resident, had earned a series of promotions and now was major of his regiment. Still, the task of writing to the *Courier* regularly could be a chore, Dwinell acknowledged. In one letter, he told readers, "I am not in a mood to write, to-night, and am just doing it from a sort of sense of necessity." But as he had done for the past six months, the editor provided interesting news. In one letter, he wrote of how the men amused themselves watching the opposing artillery engage in target practice. Some men also were playing a new game that was becoming popular in camp: "base ball."

On another occasion, Dwinell described the punishments handed out to lawbreakers in the Confederate army. For example, he wrote: "A private, found guilty of drunkenness, when on post as sentinel, was sentenced to hard labor for thirty days, and to be put in the stocks four hours a day, every third day of this time." Also, "A private, found guilty of stealing, was sentenced to forfeit two thirds of the pay that is, or may be due him, and to be confined for the period of three months to hard labor, with a weight of twelve pounds attached to his leg by a chain, and then to be drummed out of service." In another letter, he described in detail the melancholy sight of two soldiers being executed for a more serious crime.

Throughout the fall, there was an expectation that fighting would resume: something the Floyd troops were eager and ready for, Dwinell told readers. Like all the companies, the Light Guards took regular turns doing picket duty but saw no action. By early December the realization had set in that, in fact, there would be no immediate battle, and the army at Centreville began making plans to build winter quarters for the first time. On Christmas Eve, Lt. Col. Thomas L. Cooper and the regimental quartermaster rode out to look at possible sites for the quarters. As Dwinell explained, Cooper's horse became spooked and unexpectedly galloped into the woods. The quartermaster lost sight of Cooper, and when he finally found him, the lieutenant colonel was lying on the ground "nearly senseless." Cooper had been "dashed against a tree," Dwinell wrote, and was gravely injured. He never regained consciousness and died the next day. Then on Christmas Day, Pvt. M. L. Sanders of the Light Guards died at the regimental hospital after being seriously ill with typhoid fever for more than two weeks. Sanders was a beloved member of the company, Dwinell told readers, and the Light Guards grieved the loss of their comrade. The deaths made for a sad Christmas for the Eighth Georgia.

In Camp, (not yet named,)
Thursday, Sept. 12, 1861.

Yesterday the 2d Brigade, including the 7th, 8th, 9th and 11th Georgia, and one Kentucky, Regiments, left their old camps and marched in the direction of Fairfax Court House, about eight miles. They all encamped near each other. The Eighth is now on a Military Road, made by Gen. Braddox, and running between Fairfax Court House and Centreville, and at this point, about a mile south of the turnpike between these places. We are four miles from each of these places, and the same distance from Fairfax Station, and some 10 or 12 miles from Manassas.

Our new camp ground is only tolerably pleasant. It is in an old field, in the midst of a poor country, never thickly inhabited, and now nearly depopulated, except the presence of numerous military camps. The devastation, almost necessarily incident to the presence of large armies, here, perhaps, produces as little damage as in any other section of the South, of the same extent, that is inhabited at all, as could be found. It is a poor, old, worn-out country. Between the scarcity of fencing material, and the unproductiveness of the land, as few enclosures are made, as possible, and many of the roads are not fenced out at all. In this vicinity, the country is rolling, but there are no high hills. A large portion of the timber is second growth. The soil is a greyish brown, with an admixture of sand, and in places, is clammy.

We heard cannonading yesterday, probably, skirmishing, in the vicinity of Alexandria: which place is 18 miles from our present camp. There is a constant expectation of a grand battle. Last night—which, by the way, was very rainy, and, pouring down in torrents a part of the time—the 9th and 11th Georgia Regiments, received orders at about 10 o'clock, to march forward, in the direction of Alexandria. The alarm, however, turned out to be a false one, and they passed back, by our camp to their own, this morning, at about 9 o'clock.

This is a beautiful, bright morning, with genial warmth and a delightful breeze. The tents are all struck to dry off the ground, the blankets and clothes, many, of which, got thoroughly soked last night—are spread out to dry, and the men, all busy in cleaning their guns, and the good natured hum of voices that everywhere prevails—all combine to render the scene now lying out before me, both pleasing and satisfactory.

The fact that Mr. James H. Johnston, of the Light Guards, had received an honorable discharge, was inadvertantly omitted in my last letter.[1] He performed well his part in the company and for the country, and we regretted very much to part with him. He returned home to prosecute the tanning and shoemaking business—branches of manufacturing now greatly needed in the Confederate States.

Willis Rice, of the Miller Rifles, is reported to have died a few days since, probably, at Richmond.[2] In the Courier of September 5th, there is a statement in my letter of the ill-health of Charley *Harper*, it should have read *Charley Hooper*. The former has been ill, but is now about camp, and the latter, I understand, is doing well.[3] There is no material alteration in the other sick that I have heard of. Sanford Williamson is having the measels very hard.

Our men were paid off up to the 1st of July last week. They received, including twenty one dollars commutations for clothing, some thirty-seven dollars each. It is expected that the balance due, up to the 1st of the month will be paid in a few days.

Our Post Office address will, for the present, continue to be Manassas Junction. M. D.

Camp of the 8th Ga. Regiment,
(Four miles West of Fairfax, C. H.)
Sunday, Sept. 15, 1861.

**Dear Courier:** It is now 6 o'clock, a.m., and orders have just been issued to cook one days rations, and be ready to march at 9 o'clock. We are ordered to Anandale, a little town ten miles from here, in the direction of Alexandria. It is understood that our Regiment and the Kentucky Battalion are all that are ordered to that place, and that we are sent there for picket duty. Anandale is between Alexandria and Fairfax Court House, eight miles from the former and six from the latter place.

This camp, with the tents standing, and the sick who are here, will be left in charge of the convalescent. There are none here who are much sick, that I know of. I have not heard from the sick left behind since arriving at this camp. Capt. Magruder was still sick in bed, on last Thursday. Lieut. Hall, of the Light Guards, is not well enough to march. He is suffering from Rheumatism.

Col. A. Shorter came into camp yesterday. I don't know that he brought anything, except his own cheering presence, but the Floyd boys were all very glad to see him.

'Tis not expected that there will be a grand battle at Anandale soon, but lively times are anticipated somewhere, not many days hence. M. D.

Camp Mason's Hill,
Monday, Sept. 16.

**Dear Courier:** The 8th Georgia Regiment left their camp four miles the other side of Fairfax Court House yesterday morning at 9 o'clock. The day was excessively hot—the heat being probably more intense than on any other day in the last six weeks. From our last camp, by Fairfax Court House, the distance to this place is eleven and a half miles. The march was very fatiguing, and we arrived at this Hill, recently became quite noted, on account of its military importance, at 4 o'clock, P.M.

This is a place, at this time, of exceeding interest and tremendous importance, in a military point of view. It is our out post in the direction of Alexandria, which is almost due East and seven miles distant, and concealed from view by intervening highlands. As the observer standing on Mason's Hill casts his eye along towards the North, he sees, the following objects of interest: first, the high towering spire of the Theological Seminary, two miles North-East from Alexandria; second, Fort Ellsworth, on Shuter's Hill, only about two and a half miles from this place, and where we can clearly see the "Stars and Stripes," floating in the breeze; where yesterday, saw the glimmering of the enemy's bayonets when on their evening parade, and this morning heard their reveille drums; third, and in about a North-East direction is Fort Corcoran, a strong defence for Washington City; fourth, the Federal Capitol itself is in full view, and probably seven or eight miles off; fifth, the "soldiers home"—an Asylum for the homeless of the Federal army, who are no longer fit for duty—is seen in the dim distance; sixth, and only about a mile off is Munson's Hill, in full view, and now very strongly fortified by our men; seventh, is another hill, about a half mile North of the last, with a small breast work upon it, also in our possession. The Maryland Heights are in the distance, and beyond all the above-named places. The Potomac is visible for about a mile just below the direction of Alexandria. The Natural scenery, as viewed from this Hill, is among the loveliest this writer has ever seen, yet the *awful interest* that now pervades it all, forbids its full and unalloyed enjoyment. The statements made above are probably not altogether accurate in regard to *distances*, but are given according to the most reliable information that could be obtained *here at this time,* and, *as* they *seem.*

We go out on picket at 2 ½ P.M, to-day. There is now nothing before us but the foe, and we are again at the post of danger and of honor. By a mutual understanding between the forces, the firing at pickets is now nearly abandoned, so far as pertains to those who are posted at this Hill and their opponents.

There was heavy firing this morning, in the direction of Chain Bridge—both cannon and musketry—I have not heard *where,* nor the result.

A distressing accident occurred last night to Mr. Stinson, of the Light Guards. We were lying on our arms with loaded guns, and by some unaccountable means, his gun was discharged and the ball passed through his left foot, between his little toe and the next and about one inch back of where they join. No bones were broken, and it is hoped that the wound will not prove very serious.[4]

We were aroused at midnight by the firing of the pickets in the vicinity of Munson's Hill. The Regiment was in line in two minutes. Our services were not called for and we were all soon again asleep, whereto our hard day's march strongly invited us.

It is expected that we will remain here but four days, unless *extra excitement* detains us longer.

The Post Office for the command still continues at Manassas, from whence our mail matter will be forwarded. M. D.

Mason's Hill, Sept. 18, 1861.

**Dear Courier:** Nothing of startling interest has yet occurred in this vicinity. The 8th Ga. Regiment went out on picket guard on Monday, at 4 o'clock P.M., and returned yesterday, Tuesday, at the same hour. Our watch was distinguished by no remarkable occurrence. The centre of our posts and thence running to right and left, is in a direct line, between here and Fort Elzey, about ¾ of a mile from here, and 1 ½ miles from that stronghold of the enemy. The enemy's picket line is within from 250 to 400 yard's of our's, and the foes frequently see each other. There is an understanding among the pickets on both sides, that they will not shoot each other, so long as they remain within their recognized bounds, and that they will respect flags of truce. With this understanding men on either side, wishing to converse with their enemies, wave a white handkerchief, and after seeing it recognized by the same signal from those opposite, they start on both sides and meet in the middle ground, between their respective lines. This friendly intercourse, though it is against positive orders, is not unfrequently indulged in. Yesterday Adjutant Harper, Commissary Norton, and Capt. Lewis, together with several privates of the Atlanta Grays, met the enemy's pickets, some twenty in number, shook hands, and conversed with them for half an hour or more. True to their characteristics, the Yankees all wanted to *swap* something, and so several of the party exchanged knives and some trinkets with them. One of these Federals was Capt. Danforth, son of the celebrated engine manufacturer of N. Jersey, and he said his Regiment came for the war, and "*they expected to fight it out.*"

This friendly intercourse does not exist at all among the pickets about Munson's Hill and their opponents, but on the contrary they there shoot at each other on every opportunity, and some are killed nearly every day. Some three days since there was a very remarkable *duel* between one of our pickets near Munson's Hill, a German belonging to the 19th Va. Regiment, and a Yankee, on a post opposite, some 500 yards distant. When they first commenced firing at each other, the Lincolnite was concealed behind a house, and our man covered by a tree. Each was on the watch, and when the other exposed himself he would crack away at him. They soon got to shooting at the same time and then to stopping out in full view while shooting and then retiring to their covers to load. They thus continued loading and firing as rapidly as convenient, until the thirteenth round, when the abolitionist was made to bite the dust.

We hear cannonading every day, more or less, the most of which is said to be target practice by the Federals at Arlington Heights. These Heights cannot be seen from here, but we can see the flag staff there with a tolerable glass.

There now seems to be little probability of a general fight in this vicinity within the next few days.

Our tents are left at the old camp, and we are bivouacking, and expecting to return to the former camp next Friday. There are no new cases of sickness in the Floyd companies. Wm. Greer, of the Miller Rifles is reported to have died at Richmond a few days since. This makes fifteen in all, lost from that company. M. D.

Camp of the 8th Ga. Regiment,
September 20, 1861.

**Dear Courier:** This Regiment left Mason's Hill yesterday, at 3 ½ o'clock P.M., after marching about a mile a courier came up, and said it was the order of Gen. Longstreet, who has command in the vicinity of our frontier fortifications, that we should halt, and await further orders. Cannonading was distinctly heard, and seemingly nearer than that we had been hearing for the past four days. It was said that the enemy were advancing on the Turnpike South of us, the road leading direct from Alexandria to Fairfax Court House; and that they were throwing shell at our pickets, on the very posts that we had left. It seems that our force was not needed, for, after remaining stationary until 7 o'clock, we were ordered to continue our march, on to the camp occupied previous to the 15th inst. The companies were suffered to become mixed up with each other, and the members scattered from their respective commanders; not from any apprehension of danger, but from the *supposition* that it would relieve the men and lessen the fatigue. Several men wandered from their commanders and fired their guns, not, it is to be hoped, with a malicious intentions, but, as they had been in heavy rain Tuesday, in order to clean them. This created an alarm, and the Regiments encamped in the neighborhood of

Fairfax Court House, doubled their pickets, and sent out scouts through the woods, supposing that the enemy were advancing upon them. When within a mile of our camp, the Regiment was halted, and commanders of companies ordered to collect their men, and prohibit the firing; but the several companies were however, then, too much scattered, to be easily brought together, and the same irregular firing was continued, until we got to the camp.

By this time several Regiments near by, had become thoroughly alarmed, and we heard the *long roll* beating at two or three of them. Of course there is considerable excitement this morning about the matter, and efforts are being made to find out the guilty parties. As might be expected, the corps, thus necessarily alarmed, are not in very good humor about it. I have stated these facts, not for the purpose, as might seem, of reflecting upon any one, but for the sake of letting our friends, at home, know what are matters of interest and excitement with us here.

We left our halting place in the woods at 7 o'clock. The full moon already risen, and pouring its soft, silvery rays in lovely profusion through the rich green foliage, the beautiful azure of the star gemmed canopy, and the soft, balmy breeze, peculiar to early autumn, combined to render the night exceedingly lovely and pleasant. Except that mentioned above, our march was marked by no incidents worthy of note.

As we passed through the old and rather pretty village of Fairfax Court House, I was disposed to compare the place to Ben Thornton's proposed company, which was to be composed of *all captains* for nearly all the tolerably tall buildings, on the main street, looked like hotels. We arrived *home* at 11 ½ o'clock, tired, hungry and sleepy, but less worsted from our excursion, picket duty and five days bivouacking, than we had anticipated.

Yesterday, we heard of the death of three of the Miller Rifles, Wm. Skinner, B. F. Price and Corp. McNutt, the two former at Warrenton and the latter at Richmond, and Pledger died there a few days previous.[5] This company has now lost in all nineteen men. Eight either killed in battle or died from their wounds, and eleven from disease. These were all good and true men, who nobly did their duty, and ought to be chronicled as martyrs to our just and holy cause, just as much as if they had fallen by the hands of the enemy, on the field of bloody conflict. The amount of suffering endured by the brave sons of the South in the tented field, can never be known, but the fearful mortality gives some indication.

I have heard of no new cases of sickness in the last few days. We are ordered to move camp tomorrow, on to the road between Fairfax Station and the Court House—2 miles distant from here.

P.S. Dr. Robt. Word made us a short visit this morning and Col. J. W. H. Underwood on Monday. We are always glad to see our friends from home. M. D.

Camp of the 8th Ga. Regiment,
Wednesday Sept. 25, 1861.

**Dear Courier:** The names of Camps seems to be "played out," and now they are only designated by the numbers of the respective Regiments. We moved to this camp on the 21st inst., and its location is a little South of a line from Fairfax Station to the Court House, about one and a half miles from the former, and two miles from the latter place. Nothing of exciting interest has occurred since our arrival here. Since Monday we have heard no cannonading in the direction of the Potomac, and it is said that the war between the pickets in the neighborhood of Mason's and Munson's Hills has ceased. This has been done, and very properly too, by mutual agreement. Surely the war can never be ended, or its results materially affected by picket skirmishing.

Not only in this Regiment but in this entire division of the Confederate Army so far as reported, the amount of sickness is rapidly on the decrease. There are now very few new cases, and the old ones are nearly all convalescent.

The mortality in this Regiment has been great, and all the deaths, with two or three exceptions have occurred since the battle of July 21st. The following is a statement of the losses of the companies respectively. In the column of killed, is included those who have died of their wounds since the battle:

| | Killed. | Died of Dis. |
|---|---|---|
| Rome Lt. Guards, | 5 | 1 |
| Oglethorpe Lt. In'fty, | 6 | 2 |
| Macon Guards, | 5 | 0 |
| Echols Guards, | 4 | 6 |
| Miller Rifles, | 8 | 11 |
| Atlanta Grays, | 6 | 0 |
| Pulaski Volunteers, | 8 | 7 |
| Floyd Infantry, | 8 | 1 |
| Stephens Lt. Guards, | 7 | 2 |
| Oglethorpe Rifles, | 1 | 1 |
| Total. | 58 | 31 |

It will be remembered, that in proportion to its size, the 8th Ga. Regiment suffered in the great battle, more than any other, and yet, even in this, over half as many have already died of disease, as were killed, including those who have since died of their wounds.

The following members of the Miller Rifles were yesterday honorably discharged, on account of chronic ill health: Chas. W. Hooper, John Oswalt, W. J. Cannon, R. S. Wimpey and M. M. Wright.[6] Capt. Towers is one of the kindest of commanders, and most attentive to the wants of his men, and this great fatality is altogether unaccountable.[7]

Of the Rome Light Guards, Miller, Young, Aycock, and Dolph Johnson returned, well, to camp to-day, and report that the others, who have been sick at Gordonsville, will return with Capt. Magruder, probably Saturday.

Messrs. Barrett and Skidmore have been detailed for special service.[8] The former to act as Post Quarter Master, at a new Station 3 miles west of Fairfax Station, called Sangster's Station, and the latter to be Secretary to Gen. Jones. The statement that V. A. Stewart was at home on furlough is probably erroneous. He left camp on sick leave for the Hospital.[9]

We are now having a wonderfully quiet time, and we seem rather to be in a camp of instruction than in the very teeth of the enemy. But this very calm may be portentous, and dark threatening clouds may be gathering just over the hills to the east of us.

8 o'clock P.M. Intimation has just been given of the storm brewing by an order issued, to cook three days rations, and be ready to march at a moments warning. It is said that the enemy have crossed the Potomac, in force at Lewinsville, occupied that place and driven our men back.

We have only one day's rations on hand. The men will cook this, and then, if no more arrives, they will go to rest.

Lewinsville is probably 10 or 12 miles from here. It is, as I am told, on the river, a little above Georgetown.

Thursday Morning, 7 o'clock. Have received no orders to march yet. No news. M. D.

Camp of 8th Ga. Regiment,
Near Fairfax Station,
September 27, 1861.

**Dear Courier:** There is now going on a regular, old fashioned equinoctial storm, a real South-easter, and the way the tents flutter and pop in the gale, makes it quite lively for the inmates. It commenced raining last night, and has continued, off and on, ever since, and the wind rose this morning about ten o'clock. It is now eight o'clock P.M. and the wind has partially lulled. If some of Old Abe's fleets on the coast don't catch their deserts in this storm, it will almost shake my belief in the doctrine of special Providence. It may not be right to pray that they should all be "in the deep bosom of the ocean buried," but one surely might wish that they should all be wrecked, the wicked invaders taken prisoners, and their vast amounts of arms and provisions fall into the innocent hands of our persecuted young Republic. But the ways of providence are mysterious and past finding out," and whether our enemies are swallowed up in the sea, like the hosts of Pharaoh of old, or are spared to try the faith and strength of hearts and arms, there are abundant reasons for believing that the Lord of Hosts is with us, and will, in His own good time, deliver us, if with the proper spirit we put our trust in him.

On the morning of 26th we learned that the Regiments in this vicinity were not needed in Lawrenceville, as our forces already there had driven the mercenary dogs that made the attack, back to their dirty kennels. Our loss is reported at one killed and some few wounded; that of the enemy very considerable, but how many is not known.

Orders were issued to our regiment to-day, that hereafter we should keep constantly on hand cooked rations for three days. Doubtless an advance movement is contemplated, but the *precise time and place* is left to *conjecture*, so far as we underlings are concerned, and probably to *circumstances* in the plans of our commanders.

James T. Moore was, on yesterday elected Third Lieutenant in the Rome Light Guards, to fill the vacancy occasioned by the resignation of Geo. R. Lumpkin. Today John C. Reese, previously 2d Lieutenant in the Floyd Infantry, was elected captain of that company, Dr. C. S. Jones of the Atlanta Grays 2d Lieutenant and H. M. Langston 2d Lieut.

We now have two Battalion Drills a day, and the Regiment begins to appear like itself again. On Tuesday were reviewed by Gen. Jones, of our Brigade, and on yesterday, Thursday, by Gen. Joseph E. Johnston. The boys are rapidly recovering their health, strength and spirits, and a good report may be looked from them in the next battle.

The dews are exceedingly heavy, the nights are cold and require a fire to make us any ways comfortable. M. D.

Sept. 28. The much looked for cars arrived last night.

Camp of 8th Ga. Regiment,
Near Fairfax Station,
September 30th, 1861.

**Dear Courier:** The past two days have been delightful weather, and busy, joyous and good natured set of men you never saw than were the Floyd county boys on last Saturday. Mr. Thos. Price showed his honest face—now shadowed by dark clouds of sorrow; on account of the death of his gallant son, the news of which he had not heard until his arrival in camp on Friday night, and from that time until noon the next day, when the boxes commenced coming in, the men were as impatient as children to see their christmas gifts, to learn what had been sent to each. Cicero was most warmly and heartedly greeted. When the boxes had all arrived, none, so far as I can learn, were disappointed in a share, and a happier set of men have seldom been seen. No poor word painting of mine can give expression to the evident feelings of gratitude and thankfulness, and the tender glow of affection that lighted the countenances of all, and suffused the eyes of many, as they looked upon these affectionate tokens of considerate esteem and regard, from the "loved ones at home." These contributions to their comfort and happiness, gladden the hearts and strengthen the arms of the "soldier men," and by making them, the scriptural injunction, "bear ye one anothers burden," is most happily fulfilled by the lovely fair, and such cannot go upon the tented filed. If the donors realized that "it is more blessed to give than to receive," they will be abundantly happy in the bestowment of these presents. God bless the ladies, and enable the soldiers to so discharge their perilous duties, as to be worthy of their esteem and affectionate regard.

During the last four or five days, the rumors of war have been sufficiently abundant to keep a fair degree of excitement. On last Thursday evening our forces were withdrawn from Falls Church, Munsons, Mason's and Padgetts Hills, and all other frontier posts, and brought back to within two or three miles of Fairfax Court House. The entire of our line of advanced pickets is on the turnpike about 4 ½ miles from that place, and the line extends to the right and left of this point at about right angles with the road. It is rumored that the enemy is occupying Mason's Hill, and those other places for which the Confederate troops were withdrawn, and that they are cautiously advancing in three columns. At 10 o'clock this morning we heard the "long roll" in several Regiments, between our camp and the Court House, and learned that they were drawn up in line of battle. The cause of this is not yet known.

8 ½ o'clock p.m. There has been no fight within hearing to-day. Our Regiment has just received orders to be ready to march to-morrow morning at

7 o'clock. We go out as an advanced guard with five day's rations, one being cooked to-night. Our precise post is not yet known. If anything of exciting interest occurs I shall write on the very first opportunity. There is not certainty of a general fight soon, but no knowing when it may come. M. D.

Bivouac of 8th Georgia Reg.
Oct. 2, 1861

**Dear Courier:** Our Regiment, together with the 11th and 15th Georgia, and 33rd Virginia, are now bivouacing at Mills' Cross Roads, a place on the road from Fairfax Court House to Falls Church, 5 ½ miles from the former and 2 ½ from the latter place. We left camp yesterday morning at 7 o'clock, and, coming by a circuitous route, did not arrive at our place of destination until past one, having marched fully ten miles.

Several circumstances combined to produce the impression that there would be a great battle yesterday or today. The forces at all our out-posts had fallen back to the vicinity of the Court House, and President Davis had come up from Richmond, and he and Generals Johnston and Beauregard all reported to have taken quarters together at that place. But all is quiet as yet. Our scouts go down on this road to within a mile of Falls Church, and report no movement in that direction. We are now about four miles from Mason's and Munson's Hills, and eleven from Washington City, and if there had been heavy firing at those places, or between any of them on Manassas, it certainly would have been heard here

We saw Lincoln's grand vidette machine, yesterday, in which Prof. *Lowe* gets tolerably *high*, and, by this *Lowe*-flung game. Lincoln's overseer sees over a vast country, and can doubtless discover any large encampments or movements of our army. The Balloon was judged to be about seven miles distant from where we were at the time, and 1,000 or 1,500 feet high. It was in the direction of Mason's Hill, and was believed to be sent up from that place.

There are three or four Regiments bivouaced at this place. There is nothing of particularly exciting interest here. Two men of the 11th Georgia Regiment while out on picket duty were mistaken for the enemy, and fired upon by a portion of the 15th Georgia Regiment. One of them was severely wounded in the left arm, the other was slightly hurt. Two Lieuts. of the same, (11th Regiment,) each dropped his pistol, which discharged and inflicted severe wounds.

Our company have just come in from picket duty—went out yesterday at 3 o'clock, p.m., and returned at the same hour to-day. We had no excitement, whatever, beyond what is necessarily incident to this duty, but of course, we are all very much fatigued by the watching and I am altogether indisposed to long letter writing.

Thursday Morning, 7 o'clock. All quiet as yet, and no indications of an immediate forward movement from this quarter. Capt. Magruder, after an absence of five weeks, on account of sickness, returned to our company yesterday. He received a hearty welcome from all. M. D.

Bivouac of 8th Ga. REgiment,
Mills X Roads,
Friday, October 4, 1861.

**Dear Courier:** Rather for the purpose of informing you that nothing of exciting interest has transpired, than of communicating absorbing news, I drop you a few lines this morning. We lay about our place of rendezvous, yesterday, until one o'clock, when the Light Guards were ordered to go out as a scouting party, to scour through certain woods, in advance of our outposts, where the enemy's scouts had been seen in the morning. We went to the place indicated, deployed as skirmishers, and went "scooting" about through the woods for a hour or two without discerning any trace of the enemy, except in their distant camp on Taylor's Hill. This is a new stronghold just behind Fall's Church, and the trees were not cut down until yesterday, so as to expose it to view from this direction. We could see them putting up tents just outside the breast works, and a large number were pitched there in the course of the evening. Our company went down to within a mile of Fall's Church, and Capt. Magruder, with a scout by the name Carm, went forward in sight of the Federal pickets, and so near to them that they undertook to cut them off, but were distanced by a little smart double-quicking.

We are now satisfied that the enemy's pickets are very near Fall's Church, which place they are strongly fortifying but whether it is for the mere purpose of holding, or to have it as a strong hold, to fall back upon in an advance movement, we know not. At all events they are very busy there, and show no signs of immediately advancing.

With the exceptions of a little rain on Wednesday, we have had a delightful time for being out without our tents. The nights have not been so cool, nor the dews so heavy as they had been before.

There was a nice little sensation, about half past seven last night, when it was reported that Lincoln's balloon was again visible. The object pointed out as being the veriable thing, very much resembled a star of the first magnitude, was a little North of East, and about five degrees above the horizon. The men could see it "dance about," "jump up and down," "grow dim," "flash up," and produce various other evidences of being a moveable body, at no great distance. One person got some rather tart words, for his obtuseness, because *he* could not see these giratory [*sic*] movements. But when the *stars* had risen a little higher, it became evident, to some one who knew, that the "hobgoblin" was neither more or less than the beautiful star *Capella*, in the constellation of Auriga. Of course there was a good laugh over the *sell*, and all hands retired to their *downy* couches, that is to say, flat down upon the ground.

We are required to put out all the fires and keep no lights after dark, that our position may be as much concealed as possible.

The Floyd boys are all getting along very well. The Miller Rifles were out on picket yesterday. Our company goes out again at one o'clock to-day. M. D.

Bivouac of 8th Georgia Reg.,
Mill's Cross Roads,
Sunday, Oct. 6, 1861.

**Dear Courier:** This is a beautiful pleasant Sabbath morning, and a sort of Sunday quiet and serene placidity pervades the rude tabernacles of our temporary abode. It would, probably, be an interesting sight to our friends at home, if they could see us, the very personification of half rested weariness, in our present situation, under and about our extemporized shelters. The place of bivouac is in the skirt of a pine thicket, on the margin of an old field. The different messes, composed of from four to six men each, have all built little bough houses, by sticking two crotches about six feet high in the ground, laying a pole in these, and then placing others with one end on this and the other on the ground, at an angle of about 45 degrees, and making a sort of thatched roof of pine boughs, with bushes stood up at the sides. This description seems to be the idea of formation, but it has not been realized, in the same way, in any two instances; each mess taking advantage of the ground, adjacent trees and convenient materials. The men are more in groups, many reclining on their blankets in their shantes, rehearsing past incidents and acts, and discussing the probabilities of future movements. A sort of good natured, thoughtful quiet prevails, and many a low sigh and fervent prayer has been breathed for the loved ones at home. It's a sweet thought that we are remembered there, and that at this very hour, the united prayers of assembled thousands, are ascending to the Throne of Grace, for the protection and preservation of the Confederate army, and the success of our glorious cause.

This duty the Regiment is now on, that of advanced guard, is decidedly the most unpleasant, in the service. In the first place, it is necessary to leave the regular camp without tents, and with just as few incumbrances to a rapid and forced march as possible. Not too much provisions, a sparce allowance of blankets, camp chests and cooking utensils, and no spare clothing at all are to be taken. The result is, that after the second or third day, various articles, such as salt, pepper, vinegar, coffee, soap, clean towels, tobacco, &c., either from loss or imprudent use, give out, and then commences a general system of borrowing and begging, greatly to the annoyance of those who have these little comforts. Then, picket duty is particularly unpleasant. A regiment fills a line about two miles long, and two or three companies are detailed at a time to occupy it. The line of pickets is about half a mile in advance of the regiment. The posts are from two to four hundred yards apart, from three to six men are stationed at each, and here they are to remain, keeping up the most vigilant look-out and *hear-out* for twenty four hours. At least two, at each post, are required to be on the watch all the time. The general instructions are to see and not be seen, hear and not be heard, to shoot down or take as prisoners any small number of the enemy approaching, for men on adjacent posts to rally on one attacked, and if overcome, then all, to rally at the place agreed upon for the company; if the enemy should be seen in too large number to attack, then the men are to fire off their guns as a signal, and rally at once on the company ground.

These lines of pickets, it will be remembered, are placed close up—sometimes within three or four hundred yards to where the enemies lines are known to be occupied. Every reader may guess for himself what his feelings would be while acting as sentinel on such a post. Of course all do not experience the same; but all, if they are faithful to their duty, are obliged to be in a state of constant apprehension and expectation, that at the next instant he may see the Hessians, either prowling about or approaching. This state of horrid suspense and anxiety produce all the unpleasant sensations incident to going into battle, and yet is entirely devoid of the stimulating excitements of such an occasion. Beside all these, every good soldier is jealous of his fame, and he thinks if he should be killed, wounded, or taken prisoner while on picket, there would be no glory attached to the affair, and he would only receive a passing notice, that it occurred in a little skirmish, and he would soon pass out of mind. But though these duties are unpleasant to many, yet there is no apparent skiruking back from them, and each regiment willingly, so far as is known, performs its part.

Yesterday evening a little before sundown, we had a little extra excitement, just enough to break the monotony of the regular routine of duties. A portion of the Washington Artillery, with one cannon, were ordered to advance to within about a mile and a half of Taylor's Hill—a large encampment of the enemy, and fire upon it. Four companies were detailed as a guard to accompany them, two of Col. W. D. Smith's Regiment, the Atlanta Grays and Miller Rifles. The Light Guards coming in from picket duty, met, and volunteered to accompany them. We took a concealed way round through the woods, arrived at the desired point and opened upon the Lincolnites. The Artillery fired five times with their six pound rifled cannon, as rapidly as they could load, but the shots all fell short. They then limbered up and immediately started back, and we all followed. When the firing commenced, the enemies pickets ran in, and some confusion was noticed in their camp. We saw them forming in line of battle, and when we were fairly under way returning, they opened with their cannon upon us, as we *suppose*, but none of their *balls* were seen or heard of. The firing was just about sunset. We returned without accident.

2 o'clock, P.M. Our Regiment is now falling into march back into our old camp near Fairfax Station. M. D.

Camp of 8th Ga. Regiment,
Near Fairfax Station,
Oct. 12, 1861.

**Dear Courier:** Nothing of special interest has transpired since my last letter. There was a Brigade drill under Gen. Jones, our Brigadier, on yesterday and the day before. On the first day, the 8th and 11th Georgia and Kentucky Regiments only were present—on the second, these and the 9th Georgia. Gen. Jones showed that he was entirely familiar with the drill, and made a good impression in regard to his skill and ability as an officer. These Regiments are now all small inefficient force—averaging, probably, less than 450 men each.

The 7th Georgia is doing picket duty at Mill's Cross Roads, and there was rumor yesterday that six of their men were taken prisoners the night before. The report states that they were sitting around a fire, and that the enemy closed around and took them, almost without resistance. Surely men would not be that careless under such circumstances.

Geo. R. Sanford returned to camp on Thursday. We were glad to see him back in such perfect apparent health. He very narrowly escaped with his life at Withville, on his way here. In changing his baggage from one car to another on a bridge some 30 feet high, he fell to the water below and between bruising and drowning, made a very narrow escape, but was only slightly injured.[10]

The supply of coffee having given out, our Commissary commenced on the 10th inst. to issue whiskey instead. The order to commanders of companies, is to deal out to each man one-half gill every morning and evening. It is understood that unless each man drinks his portion at the time it is offered, he looses it otherwise. If this plan is strictly adhered to, there can be no excesses from this source, and the whiskey rations may be beneficial these cold, damp mornings.

No signs of a grand, immediate movement are discernable.

In a little affray between Williford and Hagie, of the Atlanta Grays, the former had his left leg badly broken. M. D.

Gordonsville, Saturday, Nov. 2, 1861.

**Dear Courier:** Perhaps a sufficient apology for my long silence, in addressing you, is found in the fact of my having been "under the weather" from indisposition, with which I was attacked three weeks since—at first quite severe, but which soon gave way under good medical treatment and excellent nursing. I am now fully restored to health, and shall return to camp next Monday.

During the past week I have enjoyed the hospitality of Col. James Magruder, the father of our gallant and much beloved Captain. He is a fine specimen of the highest type of the *Virginia gentlemen*, and, at his house, the high reputation of this noble State, for generous hospitality, is more than realized. All of four sons, and his son-in-law, Col. Warren, are in the army, and are doing all, that valor and bravery can do, to assist in expelling the hordes of despicable hirelings from our soil, who, *for the present*, destroy our peace, and *threaten* our subjugation. He has one son now at home, who was dangerously wounded on the 10th of September, in a skirmish. One or more invalid members of our company have partaken of his hospitality, and enjoyed the kind attentions of himself and interesting family, nearly all the time since our first arrival in old Virginia. Capt. Magruder has hosts of friends in this vicinity, and as fast as the sick, at our Hospital here, becomes convalescent, these "Good Samaritans" send in their carriages and take them to their own homes, where their tender nursing clinches down the skillful medical treatment they had previously received from our excellent physician, Dr. Gregory, and secures a full restoration to health and vigor. Our company is indeed fortunate in having such a Captain so circumstanced.

As for news in camp, I can communicate nothing of recent date, except, that as was stated by passengers yesterday, all was quiet and there was no apparent prospect of an immediate general engagement. McClellan is reported to have withdrawn all his force, except his pickets—who are still near Fairfax Court House—to Alexandria and Arlington Heights.

Wm. Moore, son of "Coosa River John," returned home some three weeks since. He has been an invalid ever since he came into the camp, and was not mustered into service. He expressed much regret that he could not serve his country as he would like to. Barrett, A. J. Bearden and Shockley,[11] were all honorably discharged from service, on account of chronic ill health, about a week since. We regret, exceedingly, to loose such capital good fellows from the company. Two of them are the "highest in the nation," in more senses than one—all of good "grit," and men who, if they had the physical ability, would gladly be where the battle rages fiercest.

You may have heard that R. F. Hutchings has been elected Orderly of the Light Guards, in place of J. T. Moore, promoted to the Lieutenancy; and Charley Harper elected Lieutenant in the Miller Rifles.[12] They are both worthy and well qualified, and will do credit to themselves and honor to their respective companies.

The general health of this division of the army is rapidly improving. Hundreds of soldiers pass this place daily, who have been sick, but are now returning to camp for duty. M. D.

Camp of 8th Ga. Regiment,
Centreville, Va., Nov. 7, 1861.

**Dear Courier:** The writer returned to camp, after an absence of three weeks, on sick leave, last Tuesday. This place is seven miles from Manassa and on account of the recent heavy rains, and the immense amount of wagoning over this road—all the supplies of this division of the army coming over it—this highway is exceedingly rough, and, in some places, almost impassable.[13] A bridge, a half mile below, having been washed away, the present crossing of Bull Run is at Mitchell's Ford, about a mile above the battle ground of July 18th. At this ford are breast works extending at least a quarter of a mile both up and down the Run, on the Manassa side, thrown up by our troops for defence at the time of that battle. The numerous scars upon the trees show that there has been a fight here also.

Shortly after crossing Bull Run, which is about four miles from Manassa one begins to see scattering encampments—perhaps a half dozen Regiments—but coming on a mile or so farther, and getting upon an eminence, he sees not a "tented field" merely, but a whole country full of groups of tents, and appearing, at a distance, not unlike numerous flocks of clean white sheep, all lying in calm repose and chewing their "cuds" in the full enjoyment of peace and plenty. But as one approaches nearer, the *wrinkles* upon the front of "grim visaged war" begin to disclose themselves, and the scene changes from one of mere beauty to the stern reality, which has a majesty and eloquence in its appeal to the feelings, that arouses ones patriotism, fires the blood, while at the same time there may be a tinge of horror at the sight of the death-dealing engines and instruments.

Of the exact, or even approximate number of troops, now stationed at Centreville, it would not, perhaps, be discreet to speak, or what the extent may be of the preparations that are being made to close, to the enemy, this main avenue to Manassa. There are doubtless men enough here to whip any amount of *sheep stealing sneaks* that will attack them, and Massa Abe's slaves will probably find this "is a hard road to travel."

In the general movement to this place, which took place on the 15th ult., and included all the Regiments in this vicinity, there was, according to all accounts, a very interesting time. The 8th Georgia Regiment received orders at 10 o'clock P.M., to strike tents, pack mess chests, baggage, &c., and be ready to march immediately. Many of the men were already asleep, and being thus aroused, by such an order, unexplained, except that our army was falling back, it had rather a startling effect. The Regiment was ready and moved from the encampment at one o'clock A.M.; marched to the headquarters of the Brigadier General, where they were halted until three, when they took up the line of march for this place, distant six miles. The whole country was alive with moving troops, and soon the road became almost completely blockaded with wagons, which formed train over a mile long. Being thus obstructed the corps did not arrive at Centreville until 8 o'clock Wednesday morning, the men having spent a most disagreeable and fatiguing night. At first the tents of the different Regiments and Brigades were pitched as "close as they could stick" to each other. Since then, for health and convenience in getting wood, water, &c., the different commands have been somewhat scattered. The first week after arriving here, the excitement was pretty well kept up, by the constant expectation of a grand battle. This gradually died away, and nothing has *actually occurred* more interesting than a great storm, last Friday night and Saturday morning, that blew down several tents, and from the incident exposure, of which many men are now suffering with bad colds, slight pneumonia, &c.

On Tuesday I had the pleasure of meeting Dr. Robt. Battey, of Rome, and Surgeon of the 19th Ga. Regiment. He is looking well but shows signs of severe and long protracted labor. His success in the Regimental practice is probably without a parallel in the Confederate army. The *average* number reported on the sick list, and actually under treatment, for the past three months, was *two hundred and thirty three*, and yet, out of this large number, only *two* have died. It is a great pleasure to record such an exhibition of scientific skill and untiring industry, by one of our most worthy and respected citizens.

It will be gratifying to the numerous friends of Thos. W. Hooper, to learn of his popularity and rapid promotion. He resigned his office in the C. S. Navy and came on to Richmond, about the time Col. Mercer's Regiment—then a Battalion—was being organized. He was requested to act as Adjutant; but before he could receive his commission for that office it was necessary for him to be commissioned as Lieutenant. The latter the Staff offices procured for him, and was then commissioned Adjutant, which office he filled with so much credit, that when they came to make up the full organization for a Regiment, he was recommended by the commissioned officers, and commissioned Major of the Regiment. This is stepping up pretty fast for a young man in his twenty second year, and, I believe, make the *seventh*, ranking as Major, in the Confederate Army from Rome, besides two Colonels, two Lieut. Colonels, and another Colonel, still, from the county.

The first killing frost here, was about two weeks since, but now the foliage is nearly all killed, and the weather is cold and disagreeable.

Dr. McFarland has resigned and Dr. Miller is now acting as our Regimental Surgeon. There are but two members of Company A, that are much sick at this time. W. F. Booton, who is at Mountain Top, and John J. Black, who left here this morning for Gordonsville. Both have fevers, but neither was considered dangerously ill at latest accounts. The general health of the Regiment continues to improve.

Car No. 2 is now daily expected and anxiously looked for. M. D.

Camp of 8th Ga. Regiment,
Centreville, Va. Nov. 11th, 1861.

**Dear Courier:** Although matters are moving along quietly here, and there is no great bluster, or particular incidents of thrilling interest, yet this division of the Confederate Army, is neither idle nor engaged in unimportant exercises. The work of throwing up fortifications and breastworks continues with unabated fervor, and that already accomplished has quite a formidable appearance. Our *ordinary* duties, except roll call and dress parade, are always dispensed with on the Sabbath but yesterday the regular details were made for working on the fortifications, and the men were not allowed "to divide Sunday from the week." All this work is being done, not for the defence of Centreville, a little old place of about a dozen houses, but—as it is conjectured—because it is hoped thereby to be enabled to stop Lincoln's "grand army," if they should undertake the "on to Richmond" movement again, with a comparatively small force, and thus allow a considerable past of the force now here to be removed, either to other fields of active operations, or to winter quarters, convenient to the great central supply depots. These works are in an open field, on the highest land anywhere in this vicinity, and it is by no means improbable that McClellan, through his balloon agency or otherwise, has full knowledge of their progress.

The Regiments all seem to be "looking up." Not only are those who have been sick returning, but all are becoming more robust and hearty. Although there is such a vast number of men here, the burial salute has been heard but once in the past three days. The sable clouds of mourning, however, passed over our Regiment on last Saturday, on learning that Capt. Hamilton Cooper, of Company B, died the night previous. He was a brave officer, who well understood his duties, an accomplished gentleman, a good man, and much admired and esteemed by his companions in arms, and all who knew him,

"He sleeps his last sleep; he has fought his last battle;

"No sound can awake him to glory again."

There are at least two hundred more men reported for duty, now, in our Regiment, than there was six weeks since, and there are less complaining ones now. But if the intensity of cold increases much more, and we are no better protected from it than by our present clothing and tents, it is to be feared that the winter diseases will be quite as bad as those of the summer have been.

Speaking of the 8th Georgia Regiment, reminds me that it has received a very high compliment from each of the three most noted men of the day. On the evening of the 21st of July, Gen. Beauregard was passing by a portion of this corps, and enquired what Regiment it was, and on being told that it was what there was left of the 8th Georgia, he raised his cap, saying, "I salute the 8th Georgia Regiment." The second was from Gen. A. S. Johnston, who is reported to have said to our Surgeon, a few days after the battle of Manassa that "the 8th Ga. Regiment there made the most gallant charge I ever saw."[14] Lastly, President Davis, a few weeks since, in a conversation with Capt. Magruder, said with emphasis, "*the 8th Georgia Regiment is known.*"

There is not much excitement here now. Occasionally we have an interesting little incident; as, for instance last Friday seven Federal prisoners were brought in, *five* of them, while in a house near Fall's Church, had been taken by *three* of our cavalry, and the other two were taken while on picket post.

Our present line of infantry pickets is from Fairfax Station to the Court House thence on the main road to Leesburg. The cavalry pickets are, in some places, several miles in advance of this line. Skirmishers are sent on from time to time, who sometimes go nearly to Mason's Hill and Fall's Church. The enemy, in force, are, at least, eight or ten miles from here. No general engagement is expected at this place very soon; although if the Lincolnites should make anything like a successful attack on Savannah, there is no telling what acts of desperation it might excite them to up in this direction. Our principal anxiety now is concerning winter quarters.

The Car No. 2 has not yet arrived. M. D.

Camp of 8th Ga Regiment,
Centreville, Va., Nov. 17th, 1861.

**Dear Courier:** It is sometimes difficult to know how to commence, and, perhaps, still more so, to carry on a letter, in an interesting manner. Now that is just my fix. With only a meager supply of news items to communicate, that are likely to prove entertaining, and neither time, taste nor disposition to weave a "fancy tale," I have sat with paper spread out and *pencil* in hand, full five minutes, (in the mean time taking a chew of that vile weed, that ought rather to be *eschewed*) and still, "like a man to double business bound, I stand in pause, where first to begin, and both neglect." The truth is, I am not in a mood to write, to-night, and am just doing it from a sort of sense of necessity, which goes very much against the "grain," for, like Jack Fallstaff, I hate to do any thing "on compulsion."

But without running round Robin Hood's barn any more, I will plunge "*in medias res*;" and so here it goes for the first grand fact—interesting, mostly to the recipients of a most acceptable supply of clothing, shoes, eatables, drinkables and table condiments, received by Car No. 2. Fact No. 1 is that the aforesaid Car No. 2 arrived last Wednesday, and most of the boxes were brought into camp on Friday. I am sure Colonel—I should say *General Stewart*; but it is so hard to keep the *run* of these military titles—and Mr. Till Dozier, never met friends more glad to see them than were the Floyd county boys on this occasion. The boxes were opened with great eagerness, and the deep emotions of heartfelt thanks and gratitude, found silent expression in moistened eyes, in not a few instances. Not that the men were actually suffering, to any considerable extent, for the want of necessary clothing or other things, to make them comfortable, but because it is so sweet to receive tokens of affectionate remembrance from those we love, that the heart speaks through its own legitimate channel.

The soldiers from Floyd county have *never suffered for clothing*, nor for *food*, except on a few forced marches, and the same is true, so far as the writer's knowledge extends, of the entire Confederate Army. There has been some *grumbling* against the Commissariat of our army, but to a considerate man it is perfectly surprising that it has been so perfect. The fact that our new Government, without any preparation, threw suddenly into the field two hundred thousand men or more with hardly an experienced man to fill all the offices in the Quarter Master's and Commissary's Departments, ought to be more than sufficient reason for any allowances, in their behalf, that the facts require. In this division of the army, at least, the men have always had an abundance of wholesome food, and there has been plenty of forage until recently, and even now there is no great scarcity.

But before getting too tedious to be readable it may be best to sprinkle in another news item. Item No. 2. On yesterday the 16th inst., a company of our cavalry about fifty in number, took thirty-two Hessian prisoners, five wagons loaded with corn, and four horse teams attached to each, beside thirteen extra horses. It seems that these Lincolnites were out foraging near Falls church, when the Cavalry came up on them. Our men charged on them, killing two or three, and they—though armed with their brag guns and quite equal in number to our force—ran like frightened hares. After taking thirty-two of them prisoners, the balance of them some twenty or thirty more, had got so far off, that our men would risk loosing the horses and wagons if they pursued the cowardly scamps, and so they let them go. The thirty-two brought into camp, among them two or three commissioned officers, are mostly fine looking men, splendidly dressed, and say they belong to the 30th N.Y. Reg. They are quite chatty, and seem disposed to make light of their imprisonment, joking and talking freely. One of them said, when they came in sight of our breastworks and fortifications, that he had a d—d sight rather approach them with his present escort, than under the command of this own General. He no doubt spoke the truth and showed quite as much self-respect and patriotism, as most of these hirelings seem to possess.

The principal "small talk" about camp is concerning winter quarters, cold weather, army movements, &c., &c. As to winter quarters, no one, not even our Major Generals, know unconditionally and with certainty, anything at all. Still every man has a right to *conjecture*, *hope*, talk and exercise his guessing faculties to an indefinite extent. As for the cold there is no sort of doubt about that, and the whole army are unanimous in a s*ensible* conclusion. The cold has really been in tense for the past three or four days, with plenty of ice, and on Friday morning it was discernable that the far off mountains had "clapt a white cap on their mantles blue." The soldiers generally have only a moderate supply of clothing to protect them from the winter's cold; but most of them have built in their tents a sort of rock and turf stove with flues, so as, with good wood, to make them quite pleasant, when inside and thus protected from the North winds chilling blasts.

Almost every day rumors are rife of McClelland's advance, but so far they have all proved false. The belief is general here, supported by refugees and deserters, that the Federal larder is getting quite lean at Washington, and that the "grand army" will soon be *compelled* to move either forward or backward, or starve where it is. In the meantime our works, here, are being pushed rapidly on to a great state of perfection and the completeness of the fortifications, combined with the very superior natural advantages of the place, make it a complete Gibraltar.

Swilling, of the Floyd Infantry, died last Thursday.[15] The sick of the Light Guards, are at latest accounts recovering. None very sick of the Miller Rifles, that I have heard of. M. D.

Camp of 8th Ga. REgiment,
Centreville, Va., Nov. 21st, 1861.

**Dear Courier:** There is nothing of special interest that has occurred here since my last letter. The weather, (that much abused introductory topic) has been, for the past three days, remarkably pleasant for "November when fine days are few," and, as it is such an important element in determining the comfort or discomfort of people, and so directly influencing their health, it may properly be regarded as an important item of news in communicating to distant friends. Is it not quite a gratification to their numerous friends at home, to know that the great majority of Georgia Soldiers in the Eastern part of Virginia have been *comfortable* for some days last past? If so, then it is surely a part of the legitimate business of one communicating, to mention such an important source of comfort and consequent health and happiness. The temperature is not that of June, nor is the almost constantly blowing breeze a "gently sighing zephyr," but yet it has been what is expressed by that good old English word *comfortable*; but as it is now growing cold, perhaps enough has been said upon this subject, important as it is.

The daily routine of duties here have not been materially changed of late. Throughout this entire encampment, from each Regiment, about seventy five men are daily detailed to work on the breast-works. These are divided into two reliefs, each being on duty one hour then off for the same time, for eight hours, making four hours work for each relief during the day. Most of the boys handle *spades* and *picks* rather awkwardly, and probably could not be induced to labor with these tools, except for the furtherance of that glorious cause in which their lives are pledged. But as it is, they tug away through "muck and mire," not only without *grumbling* but even *cheerfully*. Two men are detailed from each company every day, to cut fire wood. This is taken from a forest nearly a mile and a half distant, and twelve loads, or about six cords, constitutes the daily supply for this Regiment. Our post guard has recently been reduced from *thirty-nine* to *fifteen* men, beside one Lieutenant, commanding the Guard, one Sergeant and two Corporals. Beside these about twenty men from each Regiment are constantly detailed for making and repairing roads and bridges in this vicinity. After taking out all these, and excusing three or four more, from each company, for various *reasons* and *pretences*, the Captains have left for their daily drills, from fifteen to thirty men each; rather a small "turn out," but drilling is getting to be such a bore to the men, that it is, at least, satisfactory to them.

Our Calvary pickets and scouting parties bring in prisoners almost daily. It has become such a common occurrence, that it excites little interest, in camp, unless there is a large number, or something peculiar in their mode of capture. On last Tuesday I chanced to see ten of these mercinary rascals—a Lieutenant and nine men, two of whom were wounded. They belonged to the 14th N. Y., from Brooklyn, and are said to be the "pets" of Henry Ward Beecher.[16] The Lieutenant is a good looking man, the balance "scrub" stock, but all were well dressed, and had good overcoats. As they were marched off towards Manassas, between two files of soldiers, the crest fallen officer's expressive face indicated a strange commingling of emotions—a compound of disappointment, dread and mortification, with a little lurking sediment of anger discernable.

We hear heavy firing almost every day in the direction of Dumphries and Evansport, but what it all amounts to we have no idea, until two or three days after, when we hear through the *Richmond papers*. So far as getting any thing like reliable news from these interesting places is concerned, we might as well be 500 miles distant, instead of 25. Of course we hear plenty of *rumors*, but none but fresh recruits *even think* of believing them.

Capt. Magruder has been quite ill for several days. He left for Gordonsville yesterday on sick leave. The sick generally are doing well and recovering.

The numerous friends of Col. Printup were rejoiced to see him in camp a few days since. He left for Richmond to-day. M. D.

Camp of 8th Ga. Reg. near
Centreville, Va., Nov. 24, 1861.

**Dear Courier:** All is yet quiet here and nothing has occurred to interrupt the usual rounds of duties regularly performed during the past thirty days. The latest sensation, here in regard to McClellan's grand "onward to Richmond," was a report that, three days since, he reviewed a force of seventy-five thousand troops, all ready for this undertaking. Rumor gives quite a diversity of feeling to the Lincolnites in reference to this movement. This ancient dame asserts that some of them say they *will* go, others say they *will not*. It is the writer's opinion that if they do not all *have* their "wills," they had better make them before they start. Their very quietness for the last three or four days may be significant; none have been taken prisoners in this time, nor even have either marauding parties been seen by our pickets.

All the Batteries of Artillery encamped in this vicinity, are practicing daily at the various redoubts, where each will be stationed in case of an attack here, and are getting the range of their guns and strength of their powder, by shooting at targets placed at those points where the enemy will be likely to appear. It is quite interesting to witness this target practice, and watch the cannon balls as they whiz through the air. It is *fun* to see them flying *from* one, while it is anything *but* that to see them coming towards him. The ball from a six or twelve pounder can be easily seen by any one standing near the gun, and looks nearly as large as a crow with its wings closed. Large crowds frequently gather round the redoubts while this practice is going on. This exhibition of "fire works," and playing "base ball" are the principal amusements at the present time, in camp. Up to a week ago ball playing was quite in vogue, but it is now a little too cold for this kind of recreation. It is snowing now, and if it continues, the boys will probably have a bout with snow balls in the morning.

The cold weather and the rains are beginning to tell sadly upon the condition of the horses in camp. There is no shelter whatever provided for them, and after working all day, perhaps on muddy roads, they are hitched to the wagon wheel, about half fed, and thus left to shiver through the cold night. It is indeed pitiable to see these poor dumb brutes on a cold morning, all drawn up, as if they had attempted to shrink within themselves, trembling with cold, and looking almost beseechingly at passers by. Many wagoners do not half do their duty to these noble animals, and they would not stand acquitted if tried by the test, "The merciful man is merciful unto his beast."

No intimation has yet been given as to "winter quarters." It is highly probable though, that if there is no battle here in the next ten days, that very soon after that, a considerable portion of this army will either go into winter quarters near some railroad, or else be sent to some distant point to meet the enemy. If McClellan is determined to have a winter campaign, then let him come on; our troops can at least stand the exposure as well as his. The glowing enthusiasm of Southrons would keep them warm while his mercenaries would be freezing.

Private Milligan, of Capt. Jonas' Company, from Chattooga co., is reported to have died here in camp, on Saturday, 23rd inst. M. D.

Camp of 8th Ga. Regiment,
Centreville, Va., Wed. Nov. 29th, 1861.

**Dear Courier:** Our Regiment came in this evening from picket duty. It has been a regular thing with this Brigade, for each Regiment to go out on picket once in fifteen days, and remain out three days each time. Our last tour was a regular pleasant one. The first two days were regular cold, but we had plenty of wood for that portion of the Bivouac, and at some of the picket posts even, fires were kept. The last day was quite mild. Three companies went on posts at a time, and remained out 24 hours. It is now quite warm and it commenced raining at about sunset to-night, and it looks like very much a long, slow rain.

Yesterday forty-four Federal prisoners were marched off to Richmond. They belonged to a Regiment of Cavalry and together with their horses, were taken by a party of our scouts the day before. Their horses are said to be very poor. A Captain and one or two Lieutenants were in the party, and they are all represented as being very well dressed. They seemed to very sanguine of the entire success of the movement. McClellan is believed to be about commencing, and which they positively assert. One of them said that the Federals would start for Richmond with two hundred and fifty thousand men. Of course no one here believes they have more than about a third of that number for this purpose.

The expectation of a great battle somewhere on this western bank of the Potomac, or this side of there, is both general and very strong. It is deemed in fact, by many, to be inevitable. Last night couriers came in from Leesburg and Evansport and reported that the enemy was advancing in force, in the vicinity of both those places. It is hardly expected that they will have the temerity to make the attack *here* first, if they can possibly avoid it. Our troops are in good heart, and to all human appearances are much better prepared in every way, than they were on the 21st of July.

An order was issued this evening that the baggage of every man must be reduced to one suit, a change of under clothes, and over coat and one blanket; or in case a man had no over coat, he could keep two blankets. This looks very much like we are expected to make a march soon. But in what direction of course we have no knowledge, and it will doubtless depend upon circumstances.

It may be that some circumstance, or combination of circumstances will deter the *braggarts* from crushing the *rebellion* at "one full swoop" in the next few days. It is said that "all signs fail in a dry time," and there has certainly been a great derth of battles in this vicinity—considering that over 200,000 hostile troops have been menacing each other, for over four months, and never separated during this time, by a greater distance than twelve or fifteen miles. But now, if we are correctly informed, there is something more than mere signs, for the advance has actually commenced.

Extensive and most careful preparations have been made on both sides, for it is believed by many, that upon approaching the great conflict, will turn the fate of the present war. What will be the result no human tongue can tell. Our cause is just, and with faith let the unanimous voice of prayer ascend to the Lord of Hosts, for his guidance on our army movements, and for success to our arms.

Choice, Clayton and Milam, returned well to camp last Tuesday.[17] Owens is still at Gordonsville and very sick. Marion Payne is quite sick in camp and will probably leave for Gordonsville tomorrow. Dr. Gregory is now here for a few days.    M. D.

Camp of 8th Ga. Reg., near
Centreville, Va., Dec. 2, 1861.

**Dear Courier:** No fight yet, and even the brilliant prospect for one, has nearly faded out. All campaigns are liable to such disappointments, and this being by no means the first, to this army, the men do not "take it to heart" so much as might be conjectured. It has been remarkably quiet in this camp for the past three days, and no incidents of exciting interest have come to the knowledge of the writer.

It could certainly not be reasonably expected that in an army of over 100,000 men, there would be no misdemeanors of offences committed, that are punishable by military law. Many of the companies from the larger towns and cities, contain not a few of the men whose exploits have been made public through the Police reports of their own city papers, and their disposition to indulge in unlawful diversions, even here, where they have devoted their lives to the cause of patriotism, has not departed from them. It is not to be inferred that *all* who have been Court Martialed, belong to the class above alluded to, but that very many of them do. As it may be a matter of interest to the readers of the *Courier* to know the *kinds of punishment*, inflicted under military law, I give below a synopsis of General Orders No. 64, read a few evenings since, at the dress parades of all the regiments in the Army of the Potomac. Nearly all of the culprits, the result of whose trial was published, are from New Orleans, and are Members of Wheat's Battalion; one company of which, the "Tiger Rifles," have become quite notorious. They are said to be regular "wharf rats." The charges and findings are noted in their order:

No. 1. A private charged with assaulting a sentinel, is sentenced to ten days confinement in guard house; and to be put in the public stocks two hours each day of that time.

No. 2. A private, found guilty of drunkenness, when on post as sentinel, was sentenced to hard labor for thirty days, and to be put in the stocks four hours a day, every third day of this time.

No. 3. A Lieutenant, found guilty of disobedience to orders, was sentenced to be reprimanded in the Brigade General Orders.

No. 4. A private found guilty of assault upon the Officer of the Day, and mutinous conduct, ordered to be put to hard labor for six months, having an iron weight of twenty pounds attached by a chain to his leg, and at the end of that time, to have his head shaved and to be drummed out of the service.

No. 5. A Sergeant, found guilty of joining in a mutiny, was reduced to ranks, confined to hard labor for 30 days, and wear a ball and chain during that period.

No. 6. A Sergeant, charged with drunkenness on duty, was found not guilty.

No. 7. A private, found guilty of stealing, was sentenced to forfeit two thirds of the pay that is, or may be due him, and to be confined for the period of three months to hard labor, with a weight of twelve pounds attached to his leg by a chain, and then to be drummed out of service.

No. 8. A private, found guilty of refusing to obey orders, and joining in a riot, was sentenced to forfeit one half of his monthly pay for six months, to have a twelve pound ball attached to his leg during that time, and then be drummed out of the service.

No. 9. A private, found guilty of joining in a riot, coming to a charge bayonet and cocking his gun, with intent to do bodily harm to the officer in command, was sentenced to be confined to hard labor for twelve months, with a twelve pound weight attached to his leg and forfeit all pay which now is or may be due him, and then have his head shaved and to be drummed out of service.

No. 10. Same charge and finding as case No. 9.

No. 11. A private found guilty of stealing money, was sentenced to forfeit all the pay that is or may be due, to be confined to hard labor, with a twelve pound weight attached to his leg for three months, and then have his head shaved and be drummed out of service.

From the above the reader will get a pretty good idea of the crimes and punishments most common, that come before a Federal Court Martial. Crimes of a lower grade are tried by Regimental or Battalion Courts. A few weeks since in the publication of an order of a similar kind to the one of which the above is a synopsis, it was announced that two Lieutenants had been dismissed the service, and two others deprived of their swords, and ordered to remain in camp for 30 days without pay—guilty of charges not now remembered by the writer. But one sentence of death has as yet been published to this army. That was a private in the Virginia Cavalry, found guilty of shooting his Captain with intent to kill. He was ordered to be shot.

Virgil A. Stewart, of the Light Guards was discharged the service some weeks since, because he had a commission in John C. Eve's company. He has the good wishes of the company, and it is to be hoped that he will find his new sphere of action both useful and agreeable. Henry L. Johnson was discharged last week, for the reason that he had obtained, as a substitute Joel S. Mann.

"Hal" will be much missed by the company because of his fine social qualities, and it was a matter of much regret that he should leave. He expresses a determination to return to the wars again, as soon as the interest of his family have been properly attended to. It is expected that F. M. Ezzell will receive his discharge to-morrow, because of ill health.[18] He is a good fellow and we are sorry to loose him. M. D.

Camp of 8th Ga. Regiment near
Centreville, Va., Dec. 5, 1861.

**Dear Courier:** To the great majority of soldiers in this camp the prospect of an early fight here ebbs and flows like the tide of the sea, and with approximately, as much regularity. It must not, however, be inferred that this *seeming*, to the men, has any thing at all to do with the *real* and *actual* movements of the enemy. The most of us are apt to *infer*, from this or that order of our Generals, that there *is* or *is not* to be great battle in a few days. Thus men become very confident in an opinion, based, it may be, upon one or two insignificant facts, and two or three orders, the reasons for which are not comprehended; and, as is generally the case with persons who come to conclusions, after having considered only a small part of the facts in the case, their certainty of correctness, in their own estimation, is increased in proportion as their knowledge of the relative facts has been limited. In looking back for the month, one can discover nothing, in the conduct of the commanders, inconsistent with their firm conviction that there would be a great battle fought, about this time, either here or at Evansport, most likely at both places. Just now the opinion seems to prevail that the fight will, at least, be first commenced at the latter place.

Last Tuesday, the 3d inst, there was a Review by Gens. Beauregard, Johnston, and Smith, of the Brigades of Gen. Jones, (ours) Gen. Toombs,' and a Regiment of Calvary. It was a bitter cold day, with a cutting north wind, and the ground frozen, yet it was a most eloquent exhibition of real sterling worth and undying patriotism. This display could hardly be called *brilliant*—a word so frequently used in describing mere "military shows"—for while the great majority of the men had on overcoats, very many did not, and of those who did have this comfortable garment, hardly a single company—except the Regiment of Georgia Regulars—had all those of the same style or even color. But, thanks for the general appreciation of our holy cause, there are not many men in the Confederate Army merely for the purpose of making a "pretty show." The *Yankees* pride themselves on their military *appearance*, but the Southern boys on their warlike *acts*.

The review was in the highest degree creditable. It would have done any Southern patriot's heart good to see these 5000 or 6000 men, marching in review before the Generals whom they love and respect, and every man proud, not of mere gewgaws and the trappings of war, but his eyes glistening with deep seated and burning patriotism, and proud in the hope that he is soon to be in the great battle that will perhaps, decide the fate of our beloved country.

An order from Gen. Johnston, was read to each Regiment, concerning the "Battle Flag" that had been presented to them some three weeks since. In this order it was stated that the enemy are now advancing upon us, and that if this Flag should be borne triumphantly through the expected great contest, it would then be adopted as the Banner of the Southern Confederacy. Those furnished the Army, are about four feet square, and entirely red, except a cross of blue about five inches wide, and running obliquely from corner to corner. On this cross, representing that brilliant cluster of stars, known as the Southern cross, and white stars in number equal to that of the States. The flag was greeted with three hearty cheers from each Regiment. It is thought by many, to be a prettier flag than the "Stars and Bars," but what is more and better, it is entirely distinct from, and cannot be mistaken for the "Stars and Stripes."

There was quite a little sensation in camp this morning, occasioned by a report that six of the Georgia Huzzahs had been killed in a skirmish last night. It is now ascertained that more were certainly killed, and only one missing. The facts, as I am reliably informed, are these. Capt. Warring with one Lieutenant and twenty-four men started some time after night had set in, for Buck's Station—a Depot between Fairfax Station and Alexandria. It seems that the enemy knew our men were accustomed to go to this place in the night, and so they had set a "trick" for them. At a place well suited to their purpose, they stretched a rope across the road and concealed themselves—eighty in number as one of their men taken prisoner reported—in the bushes on either side. Two of our men were riding a little in advance of the balance of the party, and, when the horse of one of them stumbled against the rope, he hallooed back to his comrades that they were entrapped. This seemed to be the signal for the Hessians to fire. The fight was short, but desperate. Capt. Warring ordered his men to charge upon the foe, but the bushes were so thick, and the ground so boggy that it was not practical, and so they made a hasty retreat, but not until they had discharged their double-barrelled shot guns at their cowardly assailants. Capt. W. was slightly wounded in the face. Privates Heidt, Clemons and McIntosh, each received flesh wounds—none of them dangerous. Orderly Sergeant Thos. Dunham is missing, and his horse has been found, it is feared that he was either killed or taken prisoner. We lost four horses killed. The enemy's loss is not known further than that one was certainly killed and one taken prisoner. I have written the full particulars of this little skirmish because, although they frequently occur, yet it is very seldom that our forces retreat or come out second best.

It is by no means uncommon to kill four or five Lincolnites, and take 20 or 30 of them prisoners, but it goes quite hard with us to loose a single man. M. D.

Camp of 8th Ga. Regiment,
Centreville, Va., Dec. 9th, 1861.

**Dear Courier:** It has been a beautiful day of painful and sad interest, to a large portion of this army. For the first time in their lives, thousands of volunteers have witnessed a military execution. The carnage of the battle field, and the bloody deck, in no wise prepares one to behold with indifference or without deep, heart sickening emotions of pain and melancholy, the cool and long deliberated execution, of even culprits, deserving of death, according to law and military custom, with all the formalities and parade attending a lawful tragedy, so sad and gloomy. Like the last three, to-day has been remarkably pleasant and the bright sun and soft bland atmosphere seemed rather indicative of May, than of December. At 9 ½ o'clock several regiments, all without arms except the commissioned officers, and some thousands of men strolling at will, might be seen wending their way towards the encampment of Wheat's (La.) Battalion.

An order had been read last evening at dress parade, to the effect that two men of this corps, having been found guilty, by a General Court Martial, of mutiny and a murderous attack upon the Officer of the Guard, when in the discharge of his duty, would, as a merited punishment for their crime, be "shot until they were dead," this cast concourse had started out, for the sad purpose of witnessing the execution. A melancholy expression marked the countenances of all, they spoke with hushed voices, and the merry joke and hearty laugh, were not heard in this vast throng, and to any, entirely unacquainted with the facts, it would have been evident that some important event of painful interest, was about to transpire. A large crowd gathered around the tent where the prisoners were confined, to get a glimpse of these pilgrims, about to start to "that country from whose bourne no traveler returns."

When they came out, in order to be carried to the place of execution, one of them stepped forward, with a buoyant, elastic step, and, placing his hands upon the hind end, jumped into the wagon, with great sprightliness and agility. It was a common covered road wagon, and he walked to the forward end, placed his hands upon the fore board, and, while drumming with his fingers and whistling a tune, danced a short jig. He then said to the driver, "Come old man, hurry up your team and let's be off." The other gave evidence of a more full and rational realization of his situation. He seemed to make no effort to "dis game," but with the contrite spirit of a higher manhood, not attempting to counterfeit the sacred feelings, natural and becoming to his awful situation, he deported himself with gravity and commendable solemnity. A guard of two companies with fixed bayonets, one marching before and the other behind the wagon, accompanied them, besides a special guard of eight men, immediately around the vehicle. When they arrived at the place of execution, just to the south of this general encampment, the Battalions and Regiments had all been drawn up, so as to form three sides of a hollow square, and they were carried to the fourth side, which had been left open. The graves had been dug, and the coffins setting near them, must have been painful sights to these unfortunate men. When the Romish Priest, who had been very attentive all the morning, had administered to them the last rites of their Church, with their hands pinioned behind them, their feet tied to posts, and their eyes blindfolded, they kneeled down to await their awful fate. Twenty-four men of their own company, the Tiger Rifles, were to be their executioners. These were drawn up within about twenty steps in front of them, one half of each squad were loaded with balls, and the rest with blank cartridges. At the word of command, these squads advanced about five paces, came to the "ready," "aim," "fire," and the poor fellows fell dead, riddled with four or five balls each. The colonel of the Battalion, the Priest, and two or three others, stepped to them, to see if they were indeed dead. Then the Priest took a position a few steps in advance of the dead bodies, and addressed the multitude. He said *whiskey* had brought these men to that awful situation in which they were then seen, and he faithfully and feelingly warned the soldiers of the Confederate Army, to beware of its use.

The whole ceremonies attending the execution, were conducted with the utmost propriety, were very imposing, and seemed to have a salutary influence upon some ten thousand men, who witnessed them.

There is no news here of special interest. No indications of Federal troops advancing, and some, at least, of their advanced pickets have been withdrawn. As long as this warm weather continues, we are as comfortable as would be possible anywhere, and, consequently, just now, there is not much uneasiness about winter quarters. M. D.

Camp of 8th Ga. Reg., near
Centreville, Va., Dec, 16, 1861.

**Dear Courier:** The scenes that are really becoming quite momentous here, have not undergone any exciting changes in the past five days. Even the picket duty, on which the first five companies of our Regiment were from Wednesday to Saturday night last week, has ceased to interest as it formerly did. The principal inconvenience experienced, is the extreme cold of the nights and the disaccomodations arising from being out without tents, and a large portion of cooking utensils. For over two weeks we have not had a drop of rain, nearly every day has been bright and pleasant at midday, with keen, cold nights, and frosty mornings. When on picket, the bivouack is in the woods, and the men quickly make crude booths, that, to some extent, protect them from the cold, and then they build huge fires in front, which are kept up through the night, and thus make themselves comparatively comfortable. Our present line of Infantry Pickets, is eight miles from the enemy's line, and as our cavalry videttes are stationed on all the conspicuous points, three or four miles in advance of the Infantry, there is not danger enough on Picket Post to make it interesting.

Companies A and C, had a little excursion on Saturday, that, by way or variety, was rather interesting. They went to fill on order to two companies from our picket, to escort some forage wagons, some miles into neutral territory, that is into the country lying between the two lines of pickets, of the two hostile armies. The two companies went eight miles and a half beyond our Infantry Pickets, where Company C, with a portion of the wagons, stopped for hay, corn &c., but Company A, with the rest of them, went a mile and a half further, and halted within a mile of the Potomac, upon the opposite bank of which, is a large encampment of Hessians. We were concealed from this camp, by an intervening grove, but our very close proximity to the enemy, and the great probability that we might be discovered, made our situation quite an interesting one. It was highly gratifying to see how cool, and completely self-possessed the men were while here. There was not the least exhibition of that little nervousness, that some men would have shown, in a like situation, six months ago, but they had all the unconcern and nonchalance of veterans. To be sure there was no enemy *in sight*, but the best place to try a man's courage, is not when he is actually in a fight, because it may then be impossible for him to back out, but when the danger of it is imminent, and particularly if there is reasonable apprehension that the enemy may make an attack, with unknown odds. Our wagons, eight or ten in number, were soon loaded with corn and oats, and we marched quietly back to the balance of the escort, without seeing anything of the enemy, except a balloon, evidently eyeing us, and a distant camp, and hearing nothing from them, besides some excellent music, from one of their brass bands. We rode from our picket posts out to the place of the forage, in the wagons, but had to march back to our camp in Centreville that night, a distance of 14 miles. We got *home* at 10 o'clock, well pleased with our trip, but very much fatigued.

Dr. Gregory left for home last week, and very sorry indeed were we to part with him. Besides the agreeable gentleman, we have ever found him to be, his professional services have been invaluable to our company. This fact will be appreciated, when it is known that out of some sixty who have died from disease from this Regiment, only one, the lamented Gibbons, was from our company, and he was not visited by Dr. G in his last sickness, for the reason that he was carried to a relative, some twelve miles from where we were then encamped. The Dr. has endered himself much to all the company, but especially, and in a very peculiar manner, to those who received his tender care and kind treatment in sickness.

The prospect of a fight here is now extremely dim, and arrangements are being made for moving back, preparatory to going into winter quarters. I am reliably informed that this corps of the army will quarter for the winter, forming a line from Sudley's Church, on by, the battle ground of July 21st and Manassas, and thence on to the Oceaquan. The movement is expected to be made this week.

There are not new cases of sickness among the Floyd county boys, that I have heard of, and those previously reported are all doing well. Ezell, Phillips and Owens of the Light Guards have all been discharged on account of chronic ill health.

There will probably be a great rush for furloughs, as soon as we get into winter quarters, but it is not likely that many will be granted at first. M. D.

Camp of 8th Ga. Regiment, near
Centreville, Dec. 18, '61.

**Dear Courier:** Matters are jogging along here after about the same style as have been their want for the last four weeks. The weather still continues fine, and the regular recurrence of eating, sleeping, roll calls and drilling, continues with as much regularity as the rising and setting of the sun.

In the 7th Georgia Regiment, which is our nearest neighbors on the right, they have had quite an interesting time during the past week, in re-enlisting. They are coming up to the "scratch" right nicely. Their twelve months' enlistment does not expire until May or June, yet, since the passage of the new law, giving a bounty of fifty dollars and a furlough to all twelve months' volunteers who re-enlist for the war, Capt. Wilson, of Atlanta, Commissary of the Regiment, who, by the way, is a capital good fellow and quite popular, has, with patriotic zeal, stired up the boys, and out of seven hundred and twenty, now in camp, five hundred and eighty-nine have already re-enlisted.[19] When the absentees all return, Capt. W. says he hopes to increase the number so as to bring it up to at least seven hundred. This is quite right in spirit and action, and if all other Regiments of twelve months' volunteers do as well, it not only will save lots of *drafting*, but will keep up a *well drilled* army of *hardened* men—considerations of no small importance. The army now in the field have pretty well got through with measles, mumps, and the general breaking into camp life and habits, so necessary in order to endure its hardships.

The 21st Georgia Regiment, Colonel Mercer, have encamped within a half mile of us. The Regiment is now moving back some five or six miles, preparatory to going into winter quarters. The "Sharp Shooters" are getting along finely, and the general health of the company is good. Geo. N. Yarborough, was yesterday, elected Capt. of the Floyd Infantry, and Joe Nichols, 2d Lieut., Jr., of the same company. James Verdery is now Adjutant of that Regiment. The Polk co, boys are in good health and getting along admirably. H. T. Battle has risen rapidly in his company. He was mustered into service as a private, was first elected 2d Lieut., Jr., and afterwards Captain. It is said that he both pleases his men, and makes an efficient and good commanding officer.

There are none of the Floyd boys much sick, except M. L. Sanders; he has been quite ill since last Saturday. He is still in camp.

We expect to go into winter quarters in a few days. M. D.

A Fearful Battle at Drainesville!
Camp of 8th Ga. Reg. near
Centreville, Va., Dec. 20, 1861.

**Dear Courier:** Our arms have today met with one of the saddest disasters of the whole campaign in this section of the country. The particulars of the battle have not yet been, in full, heard at this place, but enough has been learned to make it certain that five Regiments of our forces have been taken in and sadly cut up by the enemy. The particulars are as follows: This morning at about 3 o'clock, four Regiments of Infantry—the 6th S.C., 11th Va., 10th Ala., and 1st Ky., with Cutts' Battery of four guns and a Regiment of Cavalry, went out towards Drainesville—a little town fifteen miles from here—for the purpose of reconnoitering and clearing the way, and then to guard two hundred and thirty wagons, that were to be sent to the vicinity of that place for forage. Shortly after the Regiments this long train of wagons started. Nothing of interest occurred until the wagons had arrived nearly to Hearndon, some three miles this side of Drainesville. There they were ordered to turn about as quick as possible and return to this camp. Before the train had got under headway to return, the firing commenced. It seems that the enemy had, last night, moved a large force, some 10,000 or 12,000 men and thirty pieces of Artillery to Drainesville, unknown to Gen. Stuart—the famous Cavalry commander—who had charge of this expedition. Our forces and the wagon train were so near upon them when their number and position were made known, that Gen. Stuart deemed it necessary to give them battle, more especially for the purpose of securing the retreat of the wagons. The fight commenced a little before 2 o'clock, P.M., and lasted two hours. The Ky. Regiment, by mistake, fired upon the South Carolina and killed five. Our men are represented to have behaved most gallantly, and fought with desperation against these overwhelming numbers, until ordered to retreat, and then they fell back in perfect order. The extent of the casualties is not exactly known. Gen. Stuart's estimate of the number killed is between forty and fifty. It is supposed that we had some sixty or seventy seriously wounded, besides quite a large number slightly. Of course there is as yet quite a large number missing, most of whom will probably come up tomorrow.

Col. Forney, of the 10th Alabama Regiment was severely wounded in the arm—some say it was shot off, others that it was completely shattered. Lieut. Col. Martin, of the same Regiment, was killed dead while in front of his command, waving his sword and bravely encouraging his men on. Col. Taylor of the Kentucky Regiment was wounded in the face, and is missing; Capt. Cutts, of the Sumter (Ga.) Artillery, is said to have behaved most gallantly, and immortalized himself by his bravery and untiring activity. His men were badly cut to pieces, and he acted as Capt., gunner, and all. One of his caissons was exploded, killing six horses. After most of his men were disabled at one gun, he is said to have loaded the piece, by himself, and after getting a good aim fired it at the enemy. He left some of his caissons, but brought off all his guns.

Capt. E. A. Wilcox, Quartermaster of our Regiment, has just now, (11 o'clock, P.M.) came from the battleground, and reports that the enemy had not advanced at all, and that he left our men bringing the wounded and dead off the field. His estimate is, that our loss in killed and wounded will not exceed seventy-five. He states that our forces had moved back to Herndon, and that most of them would be back to this camp by to-morrow morning.

There seems to be some uncertainty as to what course Gen. Johnston will pursue. Three Regiments have already left, since the news of the battle, to join our forces at Herndon, and the 8th Georgia has orders to be ready to march at a moment's warning. But if it is true that the other Regiments already on the ground, are coming back, others will hardly be ordered to their support. At the earliest opportunity I will give further particulars.

Our Regiment has subscribed about two thousand five hundred dollars for the relief of the Charleston sufferers in the late fire, to be taken out of the next pay received from the Government. Pretty liberal, is it not? If all the Regiments in the army of the Potomac do as well, the Charlestonians will be relieved from immediate want, at last.

Saturday Morning, 8 o'clock. No further news—all quiet here. It is now probable that no further demonstration will be made by either side. M. D.

Camp of the 8th Ga. Reg., near
Centreville, Dec. 21, 1861.

**Dear Courier:** It is with the utmost pleasure that I am enabled to announce that our loss at Drainesville was not as great as was believed last night. Our dead have been buried to-day, and all told, amount to only thirty-six, and our entire loss, as now estimated, in killed, wounded and missing does not exceed one hundred and seventy-five. Col. Taylor of the Kentucky Regiment, came in late last night, and was only very slightly wounded in the arm, not serious enough to prevent his doing duty. Nine of the 10th Alabama Regiment were killed, but I have not been able to learn their name, except that of Lieut. Col. Martin.

It is now ascertained that the enemy retreated about the same time as our forces, and that their loss was probably much greater. The people of Drainesville say the Lincolnites carried off ten wagon loads of their dead. Their force must have been much less than was reported here last night. Some now assert that the enemy's Artillery did not exceed ten or twenty pieces.

Accumulated evidence makes it almost certain that our commanders were ensnared by a number of Union scoundrels, pretending to be "secesh," and co-operating with the Federal Generals. The large amount of forage in the vicinity of Drainesville was the tempting bait, and they very cunningly set the trap. They conducted our forces in between hills and woods to the very place, could easily, and without exposing themselves, make greatest havoc. Artillerists are quite confident that the rascals must have measured the distance from their cannons, to where our men were first exposed to them, which was just good range for field pieces, for their fuse was cut exactly the right length to even the very first shell they shot, and it exploded in the midst of our men.

This unfortunate affair turns out to be so much better than we feared last night, that the forces here are in comparatively good spirits about it. Although we deeply mourn our own loss, yet, we are glad that the Hessians have got nothing to brag about, for they come, at least, as near running as the Confederate troops did. They left the field "for good," while we now have the 9th Ga. Regiment and two others, encamped on the very battle ground. So we are *not second best* even this time.

John Black returned to camp to-day quite well. Marion Payne is expected in a few days. M. L. Sanders continues to be quite ill.

The weather still continues to be remarkably fine—not a drop of rain in the last three weeks. The little affair of yesterday, even if nothing *more* serious, should not, will probably deter our going into winter quarters for a short time.

Soldiers car, No. 3, arrived at Manassas last night, but it may be some days yet before we get anything from it, as we are still under marching orders. The enemy are rumored to be coming down upon us from the direction of Leesburg in large forces, so we may have a christmas frolic with them.

By the way, I wish a merry Christmas to all the readers of the *Courier*, had, for fear they should not see this until "the day after the feast," I will now wish them a happy New Year also. M. D.

Camp of the 8th Ga. Reg, near
Centreville, Va., Dec. 22, 1861.

**Dear Courier:** Another day is passing and nothing new of an exciting nature occurred. The rumor that the enemy were advancing by way of Leesburg, seems to be false. According to the most reliable information that I can get to-day, our loss on Friday at Drainesville, was fifty killed—belonging to Regiments as follows: Fifteen from 10th Ala.; nineteen from 6th S.C.; six from the 11th Va., four from 1st Ky., and six from Cutts' Battery. We have not been able to learn the number of wounded, except from the Alabama Regiment, nor the loss of the enemy, though it is now believed that their loss was much greater than ours.

Killed. Lt. Col. Martin, George S. Dunnelly, Geo. Litton, J. W. Graves, J. O. Bloxeton, S. L. Coleman, R. G. Dunlap, J. F. Martin, W. B. Lyon, A. H. Hanna, S. Bryant, J. S. Walden, T. Brownlee, C. A. Webb, and J. A. Calhoun—15.

Seriously Wounded. Col. J. H. Forney, J. W. Lendsay, B. Moss, H. Herzberg, N. Caldwell, H. Sprankles, W. M. Marague, McT. W. Chastain, J. W. Glover, J. S. Spence, P. D. Harris, Geo. T. Wilson, Henry Cates, H. H. Alexander, L. McClendon, Jas. L. Partain and G. W. Corley.

There are thirty others slightly wounded.

There are yet missing from this regiment S. W. Fuston, James Williams, Wm. Morris, Ira Chaney, T. Moss and A. F. McAdory.

It commenced to rain last night, and there is now every appearance of a long "season." We may have a very bad time to move and build cabins for the winter, but as we have no orders yet, probably it would better not to borrow trouble about the matter. M. D.

Camp of 8th Ga. Reg., near
Centreville, Dec. 27, '61.

**Dear Courier:** This is a stinging cold night, but as I am on guard duty, and am obliged to be up, I concluded to improve a few moments in writing you of matters and things in camp. This has seemed a very strange and gloomy Christmas to this Regiment, and especially to company A. At 2 o'clock on the morning of the 24th inst., M. L. Sanders of our company, died at our Regimental Hospital Tent. He had been too sick to set up since the 14th inst., and indisposed for some days before that. He had remittent fever, and for several days before his death, hemorrhoids of the bowels. He endured his intense sufferings with the utmost composure and patience, yet was all the while in a rather desponding mood, and several times, expressed the opinion that he would not recover. He was made as comfortable as possible under the circumstances, and he had no lack of attention. He was a general favorite with the company, and very much beloved for his uniform urbanity, kindness of disposition and generous nature. He never failed to do his whole duty, and that too, cheerfully. He was a faithful friend, an excellent soldier, and a consistent christian gentleman. His comrades in arms deeply deplore his loss, and cordially sympathize with his relatives in their great bereavement.

On the same morning of Mr. Sanders' death, and only an hour later, Lieut. Col. Thos. L. Cooper, of this Regiment, came to an untimely end. The circumstances attending his death were as follows: Himself with Capt. Wilcox, our Quartermaster, rode out on Monday morning to select a place for this Regiment for winters quarters, the Colonel's horse seemed to be a little scarry, and he spurred him for his foolishness. Upon this the animal struck into a lope, and directly commenced running, and Col. Cooper passed out of the sight of Capt. Wilcox. The Capt. thought nothing of it further than that he was probably letting his horse play a little, and kept on at his usual pace. But after riding some half mile, and not coming up to Col. C he became uneasy and commenced looking for him. By enquiring of some workmen on the roadside, he soon found his horse then had left the road, and had, evidently, been running through the woods. After tracking him back for a short distance, he found the Colonel, nearly senseless, lying upon the ground. It seemed that the horse had become uncontrollable, and in running through the forest, the Colonel had been dashed against a tree with great violence, and producing such injuries as to cause his death in less than ten hours. He was brought to this camp, and the best Surgeons called to his assistance, but he never spoke after the accident that so speedily proved fatal. A general gloom has been cast over the Regiment, on account of this great and unexpected bereavement. He had been constantly growing in favor of both officers and men ever since he came in command of the Regiment, was a good, efficient officer, and very much beloved. He was a man of no ordinary natural abilities, and, with experience, would have, without doubt, made one of the very best commanders in the army. But now he is suddenly cut down in the vigor of life and manhood, and that too in a manner especially deplored by soldiers.

Our Regiment commenced building their log cabins, for winter quarters, yesterday. The place is nearly in the direction of Manassas from here, and at a distance from Centreville of two and a half miles. It is on the East bank of Bull Run, where Rocky creek empties into it. This it will be seen that we will be in "striking" distance of this place in case of an attack. The camp will not be removed until the cabins are completed. Each company is to build their own huts, and nearly all the men go over and work through the day and return at night. The style adopted is that of double cabins, with a chimney at each end, and a petition in the middle, size 30 feet by 15, thus making room, intended for eight men, fifteen feet square. After we get fairly "set up" at housekeeping, it will afford us unfeigned pleasure to entertain our friends, and we would take, a kind of mortifying, it may be, yet particular delight, in showing our young lady friends how much better *they* would superintend household affairs.

Maj. Dunwoodie was elected Lieut. Col. of the 7th Georgia Regiment a few days since, and it is reported that nearly all of the five hundred and sixty men who had pledged to volunteer for the war have backed out. It is to be hoped that they will reconsider the matter, and come to a more patriotic conclusion.

All is quiet here now, except some slight "spiritual manifestations" growing out of the exuberant feelings produced by Christmas "Noggs," taken for the most part without eggs.

There are none seriously sick now in the company. M. D.

# 4

# "Good Gracious, It Is Cold"

## *January–April 1862*

As the new year began, the Light Guards kept busy building winter quarters for the first time. Melvin Dwinell explained how the cold weather slowed the work. Picket duty, never an enjoyable assignment for the troops, was even more trying in the bitter temperatures. Dwinell traveled home in January to attend to business. The *Courier*, like most businesses in Rome, was struggling as the county's economy remained in the doldrums. On his way back to Virginia, the editor got the chance to visit nearby Manassas and humorously told of his experiences in what he called perhaps "the muddiest place" in the Confederacy. In another letter, Dwinell explained the problems that were caused by putting Georgia's state hospital in Richmond. The Confederate capital was too far away from the army, and the city had become too crowded for soldiers to get proper attention in private homes. As proof, he provided figures that showed there was less mortality among sick soldiers who remained in camp than among those sent to the hospital.

In February, the Light Guards and other companies held elections for new officers. Lt. Sidney Hall was elected captain and Dwinell first lieutenant. In another letter, the editor criticized the "idle lookers on" who had not yet enlisted in the army. "Now is the time to volunteer for all those who possibly can, and have not already done so," he wrote. In other correspondence, Dwinell referred to the devastating Confederate defeats at Forts Henry and Donelson on the Tennessee and Cumberland Rivers. He insisted that the losses had not hurt army morale.

Dwinell also told readers about life in camp since the regiment had finished building its winter quarters. The accommodations were arranged on "streets," a street containing the tents and crude log cabins that housed the men of one company. In the next letter, he described the humorous scene of a windstorm hitting the camp and the soldiers scrambling around to keep everything from blowing away. By the time the storm ended, all but two of the tents had blown down. Dwinell movingly described how a Floyd County woman made the long, demanding trip to camp to get a furlough for her ill brother. The young woman traveled by train to Manassas and then walked seven miles to the camp.

During the winter, Gen. Joseph E. Johnston had been making plans to withdraw his army from Centreville to a position behind the Rappahannock River, about thirty-five miles to the south. By the beginning of March, the preparations were in full swing, and in a letter written in mid-March, Dwinell reported that the regiment was on the advance. The marching was difficult, however, and many men fell out. He told how some enterprising troops found horses that had been set loose by the quartermaster because they were not considered to be of use any longer. The men made improvised bridles and saddles and rode the horses instead of marching. Dwinell also told how drinking alcohol was being discouraged by making it almost impossible to get. He wrote, "This is a good move and it would be still better if commanding officers found it as difficult to obtain it as private soldiers do."

In another letter, Dwinell described how the effects of war were "sadly apparent" in the area where the army was camped. All the fences and trees of grand plantations had been cut down to provide wood for campfires. Moreover, horses had trampled carefully tended shrubbery, and officers had taken over fine homes for their headquarters. "The gentleman on whose land we are now encamped, says he had not cut a live tree on his farm in the last twenty years, and now, in a week, his beautiful oak and hickory grove has been nearly all cut down," Dwinell wrote. On April 7, the regiment was on the march again, this time in a miserable mix of snow, sleet, and rain. The troops had not reached Fredericksburg when they were ordered to turn around and march back to Orange Court House. The bad weather was too much for Pvt. Robert P. Barker of the Miller Rifles. The young man, who had been suffering from lung congestion, was found dead in his bunk.

Camp of 8th Ga. Reg., near
Centreville, Jan. 7, 1862.

**Dear Courier:** The writer finds himself in a deplorable situation again—*nothing to write*—and this is as much worse than "nothing to wear" as that is worse than peace and plenty in all things. There is nothing of unusual interest here, except the "keen nipping air," as it cuts and bites and twists the countenances, of all exposed to it, to contortions painfully hard, and shrinks up the bodies of all animated nature. Some three days since we had a fall of about two inches of snow, and since then, "jewhillikin," how cold it has been. Some say cold as h-l, but those who talk most learnedly about that place, all concur in its being a very *hot* place. Others say cold as Greenland, but they have never been there, and, hence, their testimony may, very properly, be taken with some degree of allowance. It is very hard to tell exactly how cold it is. If I only had a *Thermometer*, that would indicate exactly how many degrees below zero the thermometer is, and yet that, to most minds, is a very vague and unsatisfying test, and conveys no very clear idea, except to the scientific. But, good gracious, it is cold, *freezing cold.* I may have experienced colder weather—probably have—but most heartily wish it were warmer now.

This Brigade is making rather slow progress in building winter quarters. Before the "cold spell" commenced, our Regiment had the *pens* up for our cabins, and most of the *ribs* for the roof are in place. But there is difficulty in getting shingles or boards to cover the roofs with, and the ground is frozen so hard as to render it quite useless, to attempt doing anything towards laying up the chimneys or *daubing* the walls. It will probably be as late as the 20th inst. before the habitations are completed.

The first five companies of this Regiment went out on picket this morning, and a bitter cold time of it they are likely to have. It is terribly severe on some, especially those in delicate health, to be thus out without tents, and on the ground frozen so hard and covered with snow too. But, bad as it is, the fancy of it is worse than the reality, for the boys build up their big log fires, and with jest and song, do much towards dispelling from the mind a realization of their unpleasant situation.

Our Generals still insist upon believing, that a great battle is near at hand, but the general observer sees no indications of an immediate fight more than were evident, at any time, in the last two months.

Dr. Miller, Capt. Magruder, and Capt. Norton, have all returned to camp safe and well. M. D.

Winter Quarters, 8th Ga. Reg.,
near Centreville, Feb. 9th, 1862.

**Dear Courier:** Without any incident on the rail, worthy of note, your correspondent arrived in this camp this morning. A very decided and praiseworthy improvement in the conduct of soldiers on the thoroughfares above what it was six or eight months since, is noticeable. There is less drinking among them, they are less boisterous, more courteous towards each other and also citizens, and, although not as tastily dressed, are decidedly more genteel in their general deportment. The great majority of all the passengers on the various roads are officers and soldiers of the army, and army movements, the merits of officers, and the phases of the present revolution, is the staple of conversation with all. While the general feeling desponds not in the slightest as to the final favorable result of the war, there is a strong belief that the "tug of war" is yet to come, and is now, probably, not far distant.

Manassas is, perhaps, the muddiest place at the present, in the Confederate States. Its general depth in the streets, seems to be about twelve inches, completely mixed up, and as is complete a loblolly as one could wish to see. The place of entertainment called a *hotel*, can only be reached by *wading*, nearly knee deep, through this most disagreeable admixture of dirt and water. This tavern was densely crowded with guests last night, and the floor in the office room was at least an inch thick in mud. After some of the visitors who could get beds had retired, a servant came with a spade and commenced shoveling out the mud upon the floor, and he could take up a respectable spade full with very little or no scraping around at all.

The wagon road, between Manassas and this camp, is about as bad as one could possibly conceive. The railroad track is now laid and the cars run about two and a half miles in this direction, which of course is very advantageous in obtaining supplies. The work is progressing rapidly, and it is hoped that the road will be completed to near this place in about two weeks.

It has not been as cold here during the past three or four days, as it had been previously and the snow that had been four inches deep, is now nearly all melted away, except in shady places. Although there are quite a number of cases of slight indisposition, occasioned by colds and perhaps by the very indifferent, or, probably more correctly speaking, the very bad water we here get. There are none of the Floyd co., boys decidedly sick, except Mr. Davis, of the Miller Rifles, who has Rheumatism.

On last Friday, the 7th inst., nine of Ransom's Reg. of N.C. Cavalry, while on picket duty near Fairfax Courthouse were taken prisoners. It is believed that they were betrayed by one of their number who deserted some two weeks before. This may or may not be the case, but at all events they were censurably negligent of their duty at the time, if the facts are correctly reported. It is said that entire number on the post referred to had put their horses in a stable, and were themselves in a house eating dinner at the time, a very considerable number of Federal cavalry charged up, surrounded the house and a sharp skirmish ensued. Not one of our men escaped. A large number of balls were shot into the house by the Lincolnites, but without killing or wounding any of the inmates. The Federals made a hasty retreat with their prisoners. They were pursued by a squad of our men, who accomplished nothing except to lose two more men, taken prisoners. It is said that in this same expedition the Yankees took one of our wagons and trains. The first half of our Regiment came in from picket this afternoon. They say the orders to pickets and out-posts are now much more strict than ever before.

Lucius M. Lamar was promoted to Colonel, John R. Towers to Lieut. Colonel, and E. J. Magruder to Major, of this Regiment.[1] They are all excellent officers, and so far as the writer has been able to learn, their appointment gives great satisfaction to both officers and men.

Two from each company, a commissioned officer and one non-commissioned officer or private, have been sent home for recruits. Lieut. Hall and Serg. R. F. Hutchings, have been sent from the Light Guards, Lieut. Scott and Serg. Estes, from the Miller Rifles, and Capt. Yarbrough and one of his men from the Floyd Infantry. It is high time that our army was being recruited, and, unless men volunteer promptly, to fill the ranks, there will probably be a draft ordered before many weeks.[2]

Winter Quarters, 8th Ga. Reg.,
near Centreville, Feb. 12, 1862.

**Dear Courier:** As the sanitary state of the troops in the service, and the arrangement for treating the sick are among the most interesting features of the campaign, to friends at home, your correspondent proposes to devote a portion of this letter to those subjects.

In the general arrangements for the sick and wounded, there are some things deserving of commendation, and others disapprobation. In the first place it was a great mistake, on the part of the State of Georgia, to establish her principal Hospital in Richmond, a city some 175 miles distant from the place where the great body of her troops are stationed. For, if a man is much sick or severely wounded, he will be sure to suffer exceedingly, on this long journey, even if he does not, as several have done, die on the way. In the second place, there are several objections to having a general hospital in any city: the noise and confusion incident to all large places, the vitiated atmosphere and general unhealthfulness, especially in summer, render all such places far less desirable, than a healthy place in the country, where pure air and good water may be had in abundance. Another very important objection to a city, is the temptations there held out to the convalescent young men, to engage in various dissipations, so prejudicial to health. For these considerations, and others that might be urged, it would seem better, if Georgia would bestow at least a part of her munificence, upon the various Regimental Hospitals in camp and provide means and men, to procure suitable articles of diet for the sick and by improving their beds and shelters, and make them in every way more comfortable. After this is done, then let suitable hospitals be established, as near as possible to the seat of war, and yet out of danger from the enemy, at some quiet, healthy place in the country, and near the railroad. In such a place there will be nothing to divert the attention of the Hospital Officers and their assistants, or to distract the sick and convalescent.

In the early part of the campaign, very many, who were sent to the General Hospital at Richmond and other places, were very kindly taken by families, living in the vicinity, to their own homes, and there received as tender care as could be possibly administered by stranger hands. But now Richmond is so crowded, that it is next to impossible, for a sick soldier to get a place in a private family, and in smaller places, where government hospitals are located, the first glow of generosity and patriotism has subsided, and the fair and lonely daugh-

Richmond, c. 1865. Drawing by Alfred R. Waud. Despite its later date, Waud's sketch conveys what a busy city Richmond was. Library of Congress.

ters of Virginia, now feel it more of a task to provide for and wait upon the "soldier boys;" and as the government has got their arrangement systematized, and there does not seem to be that necessity for individual effort, that there was at first, these labors of love and mercy have, to a large extent subsided. So now, if a sick soldier is sent from camp, he can count upon nothing better than what can be obtained in the General Hospitals themselves.

These being the circumstances, in nine cases out of ten, the invalid had better stay in camp, probably in his own cabin, with his messmates to wait upon him, than to leave for the General Hospital, with the present prospect of obtaining better quarters. When a man is taken sick, he is very sure to compare his situation here in camp, with the comforts and tender nursing from the hands of affection, he had been accustomed to receive, when diseased at home, and ardently desire to be carried *somewhere*, think he will surely bettered by the change. But the statistics of this Regiment show conclusively that there has been less mortality among the sick who have remained in camp, than those who have been sent elsewhere. It should be borne in mind, that these sent away are the medium class, neither the sickest nor those nearest well:

SEPTEMBER

| | | | |
|---|---|---|---|
| Whole number of sick treated | | | 359 |
| " | " | sent to Gen. Hospt'l | 40 |
| " | " | deaths in camp | 1 |
| " | " | out of camp | 13 |

OCTOBER

| | | | |
|---|---|---|---|
| Whole No. of sick treated | | | 381 |
| " | " | sent to Gen. Hospt'l including | 100 sent |
| | | in expectation of a move | 130 |
| " | " | deaths in camp | 9 |
| " | " | out of camp | 1 |

NOVEMBER

| | | | |
|---|---|---|---|
| " | " | of sick treated | 309 |
| " | " | to General Hospital | 58 |
| " | " | deaths in camp | 1 |
| " | " | out of camp | 7 |

| | | DECEMBER | |
|---|---|---|---|
| " | " | of sick treated | 322 |
| " | " | sent to General Hospital | 25 |
| " | " | deaths in camp (1 killed) | 2 |
| " | " | out of camp | 4 |

| | | JANUARY | |
|---|---|---|---|
| " | " | of sick treated | 337 |
| " | " | sent to General Hospital | 19 |
| " | " | deaths in camp | 1 |
| " | " | out of camp | 6 |

The above table gives an accurate idea of the amount of sickness in our Regiment, and mortality from disease. The whole number of the Regiment during these months, was between 700 and 800 men. Very many of the cases were only slight indisposition, and detained the men from duty only a few days. The writer has not been able to get full statistics, under this head, for the first three months the Regiment was in service. August, however, was the most sickly month, 624 cases having been treated, yet with but two deaths in camp; the number of those out of the 60 who were sent away, that died, is unknown.

Camp Sam Jones, near Centreville VA.
February 14, 1862.

**Dear Courier:** This is Valentines Day, but precious few tricks of love are likely to be played off either *by* or *on* the soldiers, in this division of the army. It is not improbable that some, perhaps many, deep felt protestations of affection, may this day be written by the soldier boys, to their fair enameratas, far away, but they will not be upon fancy tinselled paper with cupids, billing doves and garlands of flowers, pictured all around upon the margins but upon the plain, coarse paper "thoughts that breathe, and words that burn" will be inscribed—coming from the heart, and much more likely to go to heart, than the sparkling effervescence of poetic fancies, so common in this class of epistles.

The hardships, privations and dangers of a campaign, some how, have a tendency to make men earnest minded and practical, and they come to despise the frivolities of the "weak, piping times of peace." Some—and it is to be feared that this class will include a number of the youths—the buds of hope and promise of the land—will be, by indulgence in the peculiar vices of camp life, not improved, nor yet, probably, much worsted in their character and habits; for if they are disposed to dissipation, their opportunities would have been far greater for indulgence, at home, than in the army. But others—all those who maintain strict habits of mental and moral purity and physical abstemiousness will come out from this fiery ordeal purified and strengthened, and with greatly enhanced abilities for usefulness in the world. War is not an unmitigated evil; if it accomplishes no other good, it at least makes despicable the almost universal worship of Mammon, awakening higher aspirations and developing some of the noblest virtues of humanity.

As for news, there is nothing of startling interest at this point. Two days since an order was sent to our Brigade, to make requisitions for every thing, including tents, needed to put the various Regiments in readiness to march. The news from Roanoke Island of course threw a shade of sadness over this army. But now that we have tolerably full particulars of the battle, we have more reason to rejoice than to despond. It was a defeat, it is true, but a most glorious one, and if our gallant forces there, had not been compelled to fight against an odds of more than four to one, they would have conquered the rapacious invaders.

On yesterday there was an election in the Light Guards and Miller Rifles.

In the former company 1st Lt. S. H. Hall was elected Captain, and the former 2d Lieut. was elected 1st Lieut., both without opposition.[3] The office of 2d Lieut. was contested by Robt. T. Fouche and J. T. Moore, the former of whom being elected. In the Miller Rifles Dunlap Scott was elected Captain,—Montgomery 1st Lieut., and, there being no vacancy in the office of 2nd Lieut., Dr. Boyd was elected 2d Lieut. Jr.[4]

There is now no snow on the ground, and it has been moderately warm for the past two or three days, but it has turned cold again this evening. There are now less cases of indisposition than there was five or six days since, and those then complaining are nearly all recovering. The Miller Rifles and several other companies have dug wells, and get therefrom very good water. The Light Guards are now digging a well. M. D.

Camp Sam Jones, near Centreville, VA.
February 18th, 1862.

**Dear Courier:** In the intensely exciting events of the past ten days, the army of the Potomac has taken a *lively interest*, but as yet no active part. How soon we may be called upon to *act* no one can predict. Now, while these lines are being traced, heavy cannonading is heard in the direction of Leesburg. Saturday and Monday, during several hours of those days, similar sounds were heard towards Evansport. Those distant rumblings under the present aspect of affairs, keep us reminded of the storms raging elsewhere, and admonish of its near gathering towards the centre and culminating point, in some line of the "onward to Richmond" movement.

The great events that are to decide this war, and with it the fate of our glorious young Republic, now seem to be fast crowding upon each other, and before many months the valorous deeds of the chivalrous heroes, who devoted their all to the Confederate cause, will be ready for enrolment on fame's fair escutcheons, for the admiration of generations yet unborn. But where, then, O where will be the names of the thousands of lethargic and slothful, the timorous and the miserly, the unpatriotic and selfish, who, with a cold, blind, trembling, cowardly infatuation, have deceived themselves, into the belief that their ten thousand excuses, which they work-day and night to make, for not doing their plain and unmistakable duty to their country, that they are thereby deceiving others also.

At every important point where our enemies are threatening an invasion, or an advance, they *greatly* outnumber our valliant hosts, and in some with an excess of *five* to *one*. At Fishing Creek, Fort Henry and Roanoke Island, the only reverses our arms have met in the last three months, the Southern braves were actually overwhelmed and crushed, by the sheer force of brute numbers.

How will it be at Savannah, Charleston, Norfolk, Evansport, or wherever the next battle shall be fought? What say you, men of Georgia, will you hazard the sacrifice of thirty-five thousand men, now in the field, in order to give ease, and the privilege of money making, to as many more, who ought to be by their sides, to support and aid them in going forward. Don't think the early volunteers are cowards—that is not the class that first steps forward for the defence of their country. They don't mind fighting fifty or a hundred per cent more than their own numbers even with great odds in quality of arms—but to be crushed to death by brute force, while thousands of their neighbors, who have, perhaps, more at stake, are mere idle lookers on, is more than human nature can be expected to tolerate without complaint. And then beside being so useless, it is the worst possible policy for our common cause. Every defeat to the Confederate arms protracts the war, possibly, for months, and makes it more desperate. Now is the time to volunteer for all those who possibly can, and have not already done so. From nearly every company in this division of the army, Recruiting Officers have been sent home, for men to fill up the ranks. This shows how anxious our Generals are upon this subject, and from it one can judge somewhat of the deficiency. A recruiting officer may now be found in every city, town, village and hamlet in Georgia. How many will at once respond to their patriotic appeals.

In the way of news, there is not much here to write. D. R. Jones, formerly of Georgia, but more recently in command of South Carolina troops, is now our Brigadier General. On last Saturday the Snow fell to the depth of about four inches—the deepest of the season. Monday there was sleet and rain, and now the snow has mostly disappeared. There are no cases of dangerous sickness among the Floyd boys. Col. J. R. Towers is to leave for home on furlough to-morrow. M. D.

Camp Sam Jones, 8th Ga. Reg.,
Feb. 21, 1862.

**Dear Courier:** As there is nothing of peculiar interest to write about, I propose in this letter to give your readers a brief description of our camp, and, perhaps, a little peep inside the cabins.

Camp Jones lies on the East bank of Cub Run. When the camp was laid off it was in the midst of a forest of oak, hickory, poplar, gum, &c., &c., but now between obtaining lumber for the cabins and the consumption of fire wood, a belt of about three fourths of a mile in width, has been all cut away, leaving a rocky, hilly, rough and stumpy clearing, containing about four hundred cabins and some two hundred tents.[5]

The ground around here is so rocky in many places, that were it desirable to plant wheat, it would have to be shot from a gun into the crevices between the rocks; and, if grass should grow in these little interstices, sheep noses would have to be rasped down to a point, in order to enable them to nibble it off.

The non-commissioned officers and privates all have comfortable cabins, while most of the officers are still in tents. The reason why the officers have not cabins is, because they were left for the last, and before those for the men were completed, the supply of lumber, suitable and at hand, gave out—and it has not yet been possible to get more hauled—there being hardly horses enough to transport provisions and forage. The cabins made of rough logs, with stone and mud chimneys, present rather a rude and crude appearance but each Regiment is laid off in regular streets, a street containing on either side four or five double cabins, and accommodating the men of one company. Each room in these is fifteen feet square with a large fireplace, dirt floor, crude beds for eight or ten men, a tolerable looking table, covered with oil cloth, and a grotesque lot of rough chairs, or stools, and a mess chest. Around the spacious fireplace may be seen pots and kettles, ovens and bake pans, spiders and frying pans, tea kettles and coffee pots, and whatever else deemed indispensible in a cook room. The groups that assemble round these fires, particularly after supper, at night, are all dressed in the dull, dingy suits of soldier clothes, but, though there is none of the bandboxy appearance of town fops, there are cheerful, honest faces and a high-toned manliness of bearing that mere dressing would not give them anywhere. Some spend their long winter evenings in reading and writing, others in little interesting games, and still others, who are more socially disposed, in telling long yarns, singing songs, and occasionally by way of variety, we have fiddling and dancing, and "a good time generally."

For the past two weeks it has been horrid walking about this camp—so awful muddy that one can hardly get about at all. And the new road between here and Junction—about two feet below the old one—is literally strewn with wrecks of wagons and the unsightly remains of faithful steeds.

There is no news here worth mentioning, unless, perhaps, to those who love to "whirl in the dizzy masses of the dance," it may be interesting to learn that there is to be a grand military ball at or near Manassas; on the 25th inst. I know of no place there, or "thereabouts," but a mud puddle—vast and deep—that might suit *webbfooted* ducks—nor where any *ducks* are to come from for such a frolic at such a time.

This Regiment was paid off, up to 1st Jan., last Wednesday, so money is quite plenty here, just now, and the *sutlers* are doing a firstrate business.

Most of the boxes that came in Car No. 4 are still at the Junction, and are likely to be, until they get a better engine and more cars on the Centreville track, which is now completed to within a mile and a half of this camp. M. D.

Camp Sam Jones, near
Centreville, Va., Feb. 24, '62.

**Dear Courier:** The wind is actually howling through camp at his time—10 o'clock P.M.—and has been blowing, a perfect storm since eleven this morning. Not a continuous gale, but in gusts and squalls of tremendous power. The weather for the last week had been mild with occasional rains, but this morning old Eolus seemed just to have let loose the pent up winds, and Boreas soon overcame his milder competitors, and has since had triumphant sway. When the wind first struck this camp the scene was quite amusing. There were some thirty tents, in which nearly all the officers of the Regiment were quartered, and as they commenced fluttering and flapping their snowy wings in a most vehement manner, the inmates all ran out; some catching hold of the tent poles, some hold of the flys, while others seized the guy ropes, all endeavoring to keep their tents from blowing over. Coat tails streaming, hats were flying high and far through the air—followed by a wishful look of the owners, who had a comically puzzled expression of countenance—in doubt whether to relinquish the tent or persue the deserting hat, and, with general confusion in command, the scene was very interesting as well as ridiculous. The wind increased, and as the swells came stronger and thicker, one by one "down came a fellows shantee." Then would come such a scramble, to put out the fire and save the loose papers and other "tricks" about the tent as would amuse any uninterested observer. In less than two hours every tent but two in the Regiment was prostrate. The Hospital tent was one of the first to blow down. The sick were carried immediately to the cabins of their respective companies, and it is hoped suffered no serious detriment from the misfortune. The officers have obtained shelter with their various companies, and will probably be comfortable until the storm blows over or "caves in" from sheer exhaustion. It is now quite cold and getting colder.

The only item of war news here of any possible interest is a little disaster that occurred to the North Carolina Cavalry Regiment last Saturday. They were on picket duty and the enemy surprised them, taking five or six prisoners. It is very strange that our pickets are so careless; in ninety-nine cases out of a hundred, it is their own fault—generally laziness—if pickets are surprised. A force of nearly 3,000 of our troops were sent in persuit of the captors, but of course were just a little too late to overtake them.

The recent sad news of disasters at Roanoke, Forts Henry and Donelson does not at all dispirit the men, but seems rather to nerve them with stronger determination to stay the tide and expel the ruthless invaders from Southern soil. *Something* has got to be done *somewhere* to retrieve our sinking fortunes, and if the army of the Potomac does not do it, then where for the present is the hope of country. The reverses were, no doubt, needed to arouse the people from the lethargy into which they had sunk, and fire them up to the determination to put forth their full strength. It is now evident that nothing short of the very best and most strenuous efforts will save the country from a long and most disagreeable war.

The general health of the Regiment continues tolerably good. Of the Light Guards, Stephenson, McGuire and Phelps, are the only sick ones, and they are all gradually recovering.[6] M. D.

Camp Sam Jones, Near Centreville Va.
February 28, 1862.

**Dear Courier:** The intense excitements, the fierce contests and defeats, after deeds of noble daring in some instances, and most wretched management in others, that have taken place in other sections, recently, have as yet had no counterpart in the Army of the Potomac.

Busy preparations are being made here, for a movement of some kind; whether it be for an advance or a retreat it would not be prudent to communicate, even if one knew. This Regiment has been ordered to pack up and send off all baggage that is not absolutely necessary for present use, and the essential baggage, above what the men can carry on a march, is ordered to be held in constant readiness for a move.

The tide of recent reverses must be turned, and it hardly seems probable that will be done, without, at least, the assistance of this army, that has now been so long idle. Joseph E. Johnston is not the General to be outwitted or whipped either, unless, forsooth, by the treachery of pretended friends, and, when it is engaged, the country may look for a good account from his command.

There is nothing of particular interest here at this time. The men are intensely busy, trying to kill time and keep themselves warm. This keeping warm, by the way, is no very easy matter, in this latitude and at this time of the year. No teams are now allowed to haul wood, except for the officers, and the men have it to "tote" on their shoulders, over a distance of nearly a half mile. Between their love of comfort and hatred for this kind of exercise, some men seem to be, frequently, in a very ridiculous quandary, and they will get wretchedly cold before they overcome their disinclination to labor, sufficiently to start off for a "turn" of fuel.

It seems to be the intention of our new Brigadier General, to keep his men occupied, from this date forward. An order was read out yesterday, for two drills each day—one at 9 A.M., and the other at 2 P.M., beside dress parade. These drills to be continued one hour. In addition to this, all the commissioned officers are required to recite a lesson in tactics, every day at 11 o'clock.

The monotonous feeling of camp life was varied last Wednesday, in a most interesting manner, by the appearance of four ladies in our midst. It was a "sight good for sore eyes," good for home sickness, good for the headache, and especially good for the heartache, good for anybody, anywhere, but by none anywhere so fully appreciated, as by soldiers in camp. We were indebted for this visit to the sickness of one of the Light Guards and the heroism and affection of his sister, Miss E. S. McGuire, of Floyd county. She had heard of the illness of her brother George, and, fearing that it might be of a most dangerous character, determined, in company with her uncle and brother, to overcome all obstacles and go to his relief. After being delayed several days on the way, she succeeded in arriving at Manassas. She was then several miles from our camp, and there was no possible chance for conveyance, but she was not to be defeated by any small considerations. She arrived at Manassas at 5 o'clock,

P.M., remaining in the car all night, and by chance made the acquaintance of three young ladies, from Winchester, Va., who had been left by the Manassas Gap train, and who would be obliged to remain at Manassas during the next day. These being perhaps, a little romantically inclined, she persuaded to accompany her, and they all, in company with two gentlemen, started the next morning, and walked to this camp. Not, on ordinary roads, to walk seven miles, even for a lady, is not such a wonderful performance, but over such roads as we now have here, it is by no means a small undertaking. We gave up the best cabin in the company for their accommodation, and they seemed to appreciate our efforts, to make their stay in camp as long as possible. They left on Thursday morning, after Miss McGuire had succeeded in getting a sick furlough for her brother.

The sick of this Brigade were all sent off yesterday. Owing to some confusion in orders, or accidental delay in the cars, they were all compelled to remain in an old field, about a mile from camp, from 10 o'clock A.M. till 8 P.M., and a bitter cold day it was, too. Their sufferings were intense, in their weak state, both from exposure and want of food. But their relief did not come with getting on the cars, when they did arrive. For, between here and the Junction, the cars ran off the track, and it was nearly daylight before they arrived there. M. D.

Bivouac of 3d Brig., 1st Div., A.P.
Near Fauquier, White Sulphur Springs,
Tuesday, March 11, 1862.

**Dear Courier:** My last letter was closed at Gainesville, at 4 o'clock Sunday evening. We continued the march from that place seven miles farther that evening, to a little village named Baltimore. Halted at 7 ½ o'clock and bivouaced for the night. Most of the men soon had good fires—the fuel, as usual, being the rail fences in the vicinity—ate sea biscuit and meat from their haversacks, and were sweetly sleeping around the numerous fires. We had marched fifteen miles that day, and it was the first march our Regiment had ever made, with the men carrying their knapsacks and blankets. They had taken but little exercise during the past two months, and this was, consequently, very severe on them.

Monday morning. The line of march was taken up at 7 ½ o'clock. It commenced raining about sunrise and continued raining very slowly most of the time until 2 o'clock. This made the road very muddy, and hard walking. During the first days march, a great many blankets and various articles of clothing were thrown away—probably in the whole army a thousand blankets or more, mostly picked up by citizens and free negroes—and not a few were left at our bivouac of Sunday night. We arrived at Warrenton, five miles distant, at 11 o'clock, continued the march about a mile after crossing the Rappahanock—which is here only a moderate sized creek—and bivouaced in a grove.

Numbers of men fell out of ranks during the day, from exhaustion, and inability to keep up with their Regiments. Each Regiment has a wagon in the rear to help these along, by taking the whole or a part of their baggage. A majority of these stragglers came up during the night and early next morning.

Tuesday morning. The sun was up "bright and early" this morning, and it seemed particularly early to the half rested men. It is a delightful atmosphere, soft and balmy, and we have a prospect of a more comfort on the march than on yesterday. We came up with the wagon trains last night, and waiting for them to get started, did not take up the line of march until 10 o'clock.

One sees many ridiculous scenes and there is no small amount of fun, even with and in spite of all the fatigue and hardships of the march. Many of the boys who fell out, caught horses, that had been turned loose by the Quartermasters as worthless and there are lots of them—and improvising saddle and bridle, put up their loads and mounted on top of it. Their appearance is laughable in the extreme—"fantastics" are nowhere in comparison. It is quite interesting to notice how quick a body of troops, on the march, will be down at the command "Rest." There is hardly a movement in the Manuel forms, executed quicker or more together. Most of the men recline on their knapsacks. Another thing is quite noticeable, and that is the great quiet pervading the ranks, especially after the first few miles.

Wednesday morning, 12th. This Brigade marched only seven miles yesterday. The road being only a mud one since we left the Springs, the wagons of course moved very slowly. Left bivouac yesterday at 10 A.M., and did not arrive at our present one until 6 P.M. The march was an easy one, the men going through the fields, a large portion of the distance, and very few men fell out of ranks. Our present bivouac is eight miles from Culpepper C.H. It is a beautiful morning, and the army seems more cheerful than any time since we started.

At 7 ½ o'clock the Regiments were formed, but did not take up the line of march until 9 1/2. Arrived at Culpepper, a distance of eight miles, at 2 o'clock P.M., and without halting, proceeded to our present bivouac, one mile South of the town. We will remain here tonight and how much longer your correspondent has no knowledge.

All communications to members of the 8th Georgia Regiment, may as well be directed to Manassas, probably, for the present. M. D.

Bivouac of 3d Brigade, 1st Division,
Army of Potomac, Near Culpepper C.H.,
Friday, March 14, '62.

**Dear Courier:** The last letter of your correspondent was closed at this place, Wednesday evening. It seems that the army has been halted here to rest and bring up the stragglers, and lest the men should "founder," *three drills* were ordered for yesterday—Battalion drill at 8 A.M., by company at 11 A.M., and by Brigade at 4 P.M. it was misting and raining slowly nearly all day after 11 o'clock, and, on that account, the Brigade drill was dispensed with. The men complained bitterly at having to drill the very first day after halting, from a march of forty-five miles and one of the severest—taking their loads and the condition of the roads into consideration—that has been by this division of the army since the war commenced.

This morning our Regiment received a small number of bell tents, that our Quartermaster borrowed—enough to allow three or four to a company, according the size of each. The Light Guards reported 34 men present and obtained three tents. This indicates that we will remain here for some days longer, at least.

There are a thousand rumors afloat in regard to the movements of the enemy, since our army commenced falling back. I will mention a few that seem to be reliable: It is reported that the Federal cavalry scouts took possession of Centreville on Monday, and took quite a number of prisoners—some of them sick soldiers who had failed to get off—some citizens and a few troops who had been left there to destroy any Government property remaining. It is said that on Tuesday, scouting parties of Lincolnites advanced as far as the Stone Bridge—on Bull Run which was blown up as soon as our troops had all crossed—and, that our cavalry there had a skirmish with them, in which seven of the enemy were killed and our loss only two, slightly wounded. It is reported that Stuart's entire Brigade of cavalry is in the rear of our army covering its retreat. It is rumored that three or four of the Tiger Rifles who were straggling were taken prisoners Wednesday, at Bristow station, four miles this side of Manassas. It is said that nearly all of the extra baggage of our Brigade was burnt before being moved from the vicinity of Centreville. This included the trunks of most of the company officers, containing all their clothing in many instances, except what they had on when the move commenced. "They say" that the Federal flag was raised in Leesburg—a town, by the way, of some three thousand inhabitants—before our forces were out of sight. It is said that a considerable quantity of stores were destroyed at Manassas.

Most of the men of this Brigade, who fell out on the march, have come up to their respective regiments. The whole country is in a state of confused excitement—hundreds of families were packing up and moving—ahead of the army and following it. The citizens had no intimation of the move of the army until it was actually commenced. Most of the able bodied men were away from their homes, and the consternation, in families, can be better imagined than described. Many servants have run away—some from the Yankees and others from their lawful protectors. While the great majority are moved back with their owners into the country—some are left in charge of their Master's property. Some of the families remain at their homes—about the towns a considerable portion of them.

The orders against selling all intoxicating drinks to troops, are very strict. In Warrenton the Provost Guard were ordered to destroy all that was kept there for sale, and a considerable quantity was poured upon the ground by them.

Before leaving Centreville, hundreds of broken down horses were sent off to recuperate. There are still thousands in the army, that, unless they get better treatment, will soon be dead or useless—many of them naturally fine animals, and only needing more food and better treatment, to restore them to their former good condition.

It is just reported that no mail is now sent off from Culpepper, nor has been for the last two or three days. If this is true, two letters written to the 'Courier' since we left Centreville, have been lost. This will be sent by private conveyance.

I know of none of the Floyd county boys that are much sick—sore feet and lame shoulders are about the worst complaints heard. Several that were indisposed before the march have been improved by it. Lt. Moore, Serg. Scott Hutchings, and John Pinson, did not make the march, but took the cars at Manassas, and are now in Gordonsville. They were unwell. Some five or six recruits to the Miller Rifles arrived yesterday. Maj. Magruder is still unwell at Gordonsville. In this Regiment, Lewis, of the Atlanta Greys, is the only Captain present.

A tragedy was enacted in the town of Culpepper last night, that has occasioned considerable talk to day in this Brigade. The facts as given by a reliable informant, are substantially as follows: Four of the Tiger Rifles, of Maj. Wheat's Louisiana Battalion, some time in the night, being intoxicated at the time, went to a dwelling and demanded lodging for the night. This was denied them, and, as they insisted the door was locked against them, and Lieut. Hardwick, of Company B, 8th Georgia, who happened to be a guest in the house, ordered them away. They broke in the window and fired two or three shots into the house. Finally one of them showed himself at the window, and

Lieut. Hardwick shot him through, killing him instantly. The other three desperadoes were afterwards arrested. Lieut. H. early this morning reported to Col Lamar, what he had done, and also to Gen. Smith, the commander of the Division of the Army. Of course everybody regards it as a case of justifiable homicide.

9 o'clock P.M. No intimation has yet been given of further movements. We had a Brigade Drill this afternoon the first one since Gen. D. R. Jones has been in command. He pronounced the drill very creditable. M. D.

Bivouac of 3d Brig., 1st Div., A.P.,
Sunday, March 16, 1862.

**Dear Courier:** Yesterday it rained nearly all day, and a considerable part of the time very hard. For this reason, although ordered to be ready to march at 7 o'clock A.M., the Brigade remained at its bivouac until this morning. It was a most disagreeable day, cold as well as rainy, and with a moderately high wind. We had no drills, and nothing of particular interest occurred in our immediate vicinity. It is reported that a portion of our cavalry, under the command of Gen. Stewart, engaged the advanced scouts of the enemy near Warrenton Junction, and after killing several, took seventeen prisoners. On our side none were killed, and only one slightly wounded.

This morning we fell into line at 9 o'clock, and commenced the march at 10. The weather through the day has been quite pleasant—an agreeable mixture of sunshine and cloud shadow. Our route being nearly South, towards Orange Court House, and consequently nearly parallel with the Blue Ridge, from which mountain we are distant some 25 miles. The view was one of the most delightful ever beheld. The mountains themselves so beautiful, just high enough to be charming, and excite the liveliest emotion of admiration, are yet not so high as to create the almost painful sensations of awe and grandeur, their ever gently changing outline, must please the eye of any lover of the beautiful at any time. But this morning, their undulating sides, checked with woodland and mountain farms, was most delightfully variegated, by sunshine and shade, and as the fleecy clouds arose from their sloping sides under the influence of the sun's genial rays, the scene was beautiful beyond description.

The force of the expression, "by the powers of mud," was never fully realized by the writer until to-day. From this place to Culpepper, the mud in the road constitutes one continuous puddle and uniformly about a foot deep. Yet the troops were disconcerted very little by it, for they were marched through the fields and woods nearly all the way, and thus found very tolerable walking.

There has been but little straggling to day, and the men all seem to be in better health and spirits, than eight days since, when we commenced the retreat some say in *spite* of the hardships and exposure of the march; but it may be that their improved health is occasioned by the purer air, and the abundance of wholesome exercise they are now taking.

The Brigade halted at 4 o'clock P.M. for the night, having marched only eight miles to-day. The distance to Orange C.H., from here, is said to be eleven miles. It is now cloudy but a little too cold to rain; we are bivouacked in a pleasant grove, and have a prospect of a tolerably comfortable night. The hard biscuit gave out last Wednesday, and since then rations of beef and flour, sugar and coffee have been given out.

Monday Morning, 8 o'clock. This morning we were aroused from our slumbers by the reveille drum at 4 o'clock. The *order* was to take up the line of march at daylight, but it was not actually done until 7 o'clock. Like yesterday the sun is not unclouded, and the air is cool and brash, with a Northerly wind. The Brigade is now halted to rest. It is seldom the march is continued over two miles, and generally not over one. These rests are from fifteen minutes to a half hour long. The rest would never exceed fifteen minutes, probably, if the troops were not delayed by the wagon trains. Since 9 o'clock the wind has lulled and the day has been bright and warm. The country throughout which we are now marching, is somewhat broken, but the land in the valleys is productive, the farm house large and fine looking, and quite as good in appearance as the best class seen in towns. They generally stand three or four hundred yards from the road, and in the beautiful flower yards, there are hot houses. All things indicate great wealth and refinement.

It is now 1 o'clock, and we have marched only seven miles, now being a mile north of the bridge over Rapidan River, and four miles from Orange C.H. We have been at our present resting place about an hour, waiting for a bridge to be built or repaired.

The bridge over the Rapidan is quite a novel affair, improvised for the occasion. It is at a ford in the river, the water now being less than three feet deep at any place. The bridge is constructed by placing a number of wagons, with the bodies taken off, in a line across the stream, and so near each other, that plank will reach from one to the next, and these planked over constituted the bridge.

The fatigue of the march is occasionally relieved by music, from the excellent Brass Band belonging to the 8th Georgia Regiment, which, by the way, is the only Brass Band in the Brigade.

4 o'clock P.M. We have halted for the night a mile and a half North of Orange C.H., having marched 9 miles to-day. The men are now all as "busy

as bees," in cutting wood, building fires, bringing water, making preparations for getting something to eat, where unto the days labor strongly invites them and scraping together leaves for a bed.

The Regiments appear quite small on this march. The members regularly in ranks being only 250 or 300 to each. But besides this number, there is a detail of about 150 from each Regiment, for front, rear and wagon guards. The men are not compelled to keep in their regular places in ranks, and, to one at a distance, they look like a drove of men. M. D.

Bivouac of 8th Ga. Reg., near
Orange C. H., Friday, March 21, '62.

**Dear Courier:** This Regiment—and perhaps it is not prudent to speak of any larger forces, lest by some possibility, the enemy might thereby be advantaged—left its bivouac one and a half miles Northeast of town last Tuesday noon and marched to this place, which is two miles West of the Court House.

Nothing of peculiar interest has occurred since arriving here. The lame shoulders and sore feet of the few, who have been thus afflicted, are getting well, and the general health of the Regiment is decidedly better than it was before commencing the retreat Since leaving Centreville we have been almost entirely cut off from all communication with the outer world beyond our own immediate vicinity. Newspapers, the great, and by far, the most reliable source of news, have been about "as scarce as hen's teeth." Until yesterday, I had seen but one in two weeks, and the state of suspense in which we were kept, was painful in the extreme. Vague rumors had reached camp of the recent fight in Arkansas, and our defeat at Newbern, but these were so extravagant and conflicting as to render them painfully unsatisfactory.

Lieut. Col. J. R. Towers, with six or eight recruits for the Miller Rifles, arrived here this morning. Maj. Magruder visited us on Wednesday and expects to return to duty in a few days. The indications are that, we will not remain here very long—but how far or where we will move to, it would be imprudent, even if one knew, to communicate.

Since Wednesday evening it rained almost constantly until this morning. Only two tents are given out to a company, yet most of the men, by making booths and covering them with their oil cloths, kept themselves tolerably dry. Being in an oak and hickory grove, there is a plenty of wood at hand, and none but the very lazy suffer much.

We hear very little of the enemy's movements. It is said that McClellan is very much disconcerted at this move of our forces, and that he says that "he had rather meet the devil in *advance* than Gen. Johnston in *retreat*." He may meet them both yet—the first a little after the second.

Whisky drinking has been nearly stopped by making it almost impossible to get it. This is a good move, and it would be still better if commanding officers found it as difficult to obtain it as private soldiers do.

Since writing the foregoing, information has been received, that seems to be reliable, that some of Steuart's cavalry had taken seventy-four traitors, all mounted on fine horses, well armed and having with them twelve thousand dollars in gold. They were giving aid to the enemy, who have retired, as it is said, to the Potomac, and were, when taken prisoners, within five miles of McClellan's lines. This detectable set passed here, in box cars, under guard, for Richmond yesterday. It is hoped they may have a sweet time—see *stars* and *feel stripes*, since they are so fond of these emblems. M. D.

Camp of 8th GA., Reg., near Orange C.H.,
March 26th, 1862

**Dear Courier:** This writing is not so much to communicate important news, as to gratify what is thought may be a no small anxiety, on the part of many of your readers, to know what, no matter how little, has been done by this command since my last communication. The fact is nothing, beside the usual routine of duties and drills, incident to a regular military camp, has been performed by this Regiment. It is not deemed prudent to speak of other and larger forces, except, perhaps, some such movements as having been accomplished, are now of general knowledge, and may be reasonably supposed to be known to the enemy.

It is currently reported that the headquarters of Stewart's cavalry is now at Centreville, and that the Feds have retired near to or perhaps across the Potomac. It is also currently rumored, that Gen. Jackson, who had retired some 40 or 50 miles down the valley, has returned to near Winchester.

It seems that the quantity of Government stores burned at Thoroughfare this side of and at Manassas, was not as great as first reported; it is now stated at 376,000 lbs bacon, 700,000 lbs corned beef, besides a large quantity of flour, molasses, vinegar, &c.; say $250,000 worth in all. It is said that the Chief Quartermaster of the Army of the Potomac, Maj. Barbour, was asked by Gen. Johnson how long he desired in which to move all the stores in his possession; he said eight days. The General allowed him this time, and yet he fell short of his estimates, by still having, at the expiration of the time, the amount above stated, if the report is correct, and the writer deems it worthy of credence.

We have no idea as to how soon or to what place this Regiment may be ordered. The Commissary is requested to keep in constant readiness four days rations of hard bread, and the Colonel to hold his command in readiness to execute light marching orders at a moments notice.

It seems probable that a much more rigorous discipline will be enforced this season than has hitherto been exacted. Without doubt, the efficiency of the army may thus be greatly enhanced, and most likely the volunteers, owing to the great and imminent peril of the country, will cheerfully abide by it.

The blighting effects of war are sadly apparent, in this beautiful section where we now are. For instance, an army encamps on the plantation of some worthy planter, who, from his first settlement in life, has been in possession of the same homestead, where he expects to end his days, and it had been the care and pride of himself and family, to add, to the extent of their ability, to its beauty and comfort. The beautiful hedge surrounding the yard, the tasteful shrubbery and charming flowers, have all been nursed with tender care, and their growth anxiously watched, in the grove near by, every shade tree has interesting associations connected with it, and the place, as a whole, has value attached to it *real* as any, to those who appreciate it, and yet such as would not and could not be taken into account by Government apprisers. To a lover of the beautiful and tasteful, a place may have a value as important to him, as that of the dirt and fences to the mere utilitarian mind and yet this value be entirely unappreciated by the latter. Where we are now, some beautiful residences have been taken by officers for head quarters. The houses, deprived of the careful supervision of the industrious housewives, soon become tarnished, and to have a sort of dissipated looks, as if they had just been on a "spree," the pailings were more less broken down, the shrubbery and shade trees broken down and gnawed, by horses being hitched to them, the flower beds trampled down, and the whole place to have a haggard appearance.

The gentleman on whose land we are now encamped, says he had not cut a live tree on his farm in the last twenty years, and now, in a week, his beautiful oak and hickory grove has been nearly all cut down, and consumed for fire-wood by the troops. The things are much more grievous to Virginians, because they are less migratory in their habits, than they would be to Southerners.

Thirty-eight recruits came to the Floyd Infantry to-day. The balance of the new delegation from Floyd, are expected to-morrow. The general health continues good. There are no new cases of sickness.

9 o'clock P.M. Orders have just been issued to prepare four days cooked rations and be ready to march by seven to-morrow morning. No wagon at all is to accompany the Regiment, except, probably, the ordinance wagon. Hard

bread is issued. The officers and men will carry one blanket each. It is surmised that we are to go towards Winchester, to assist Jackson.

Thursday morning 27th. The Regiment was in readiness at 7 o'clock to march, but after standing about an hour in line we were dismissed, with the order to be in readiness to march at a moments warning, and it was further stated, that we would not probably march to-day.

Camp of 8th Ga., Reg.,
Near Orange C.H., Va.,
April 1, 1862.

**Dear Courier:** This is a delightful morning. The brilliant sunshine and the calm, balming air—the blithesome notes of woodland warbles and the joyous strivings of the infant spring, to break loose from the dingy, swaddling clothes, in which winter, the wrinkled old crone—has so kept her bound, and the hushed state of all animated nature, induces a moody state, "and o'er one throws a loving languor that is not repose." How different this morning is from that of two days since, Sunday. Then when we first looked out after the not undisturbed slumbers of a cold, rainy, sleety night, every bough and branch and twig has completely enveloped in ice. It was a drizzling, cold, dark morning, and as we stood around our steaming smouldering, smoking fires, that seemed feebly struggling for existence, vague apprehensions stole over us, lest our limbs too would soon be clad in the same cold coating. The fire would'nt [*sic*] burn, the bread wouldn't bake, the coffee would'nt boil, the meat would'nt fry, and the dolorous groupes, shivering around these smothering smokes, presented a dark picture of glowing sadness. But *this* morning is such a delightful one, and then the contrast is so great that every one is obliged to appreciate it very highly. It may be well that nature, with even unbounded resources and skill, does not make all pleasant day and pretty faces, for she enhances the good by contrast with the bad.

We are spending our time here in a very quiet way attending to the usual routine of soldiers' duties, and getting very little news from the wide world apart. There has been no sensation for us since last Friday morning. The loud roll beat then at 3 o'clock, and the order was issued for the command to be ready to march, and every thing ready to move camp by 6 o'clock—each man being provided with four days' cooked rations in his haversack. We were in line by 6 ½ o'clock, stacked arms and awaited until ten, and then received notice that the order had been suspended, and we have remained in suspense ever since.

It is reported that some 25,000 of the enemy are just the other side of the Rappahannock—some twenty-five miles from there—what their intentions may be—or what we shall do in case they advance, is of course only a matter of conjecture.

Captains Scott and Yarbrough, with their recruits, came this morning. Capt. Hall, with his, is at Gordonsville and expected up this evening.[7] No new cases of sickness among the Floyd boys. M. D.

Camp of 8th Georgia Regiment,
Near Orange Court House,
Saturday April 5th, 1862.

**Dear Courier:** Perhaps almost anything may be more interesting to your readers, than nothing at all, from this camp. The many anxious hearts at home will, at least, be gratified to learn that the general health of this command continues good—very good—even better than it was one week since that there has been no one of their much dreaded, yet hoped for, sanguinary conflicts, which they have seen with their "minds eye" in fancy's startling pictures, and that we are all still alive, and breathe with a full supply of sound limbs, healthy stomach and a plenty of wholesome food to fill them with, and spirits as buoyant as air.

The lax discipline of winter quarters, has given place to more strict regulations; the returning warm days of Spring, gives strength and vigor to the men, and the large number of recruits, recently received, swells the average number of men to a company, to some 75 or 80 men, thus making the efficiency of this portion of the army, nearly twice as great as this was two months since. The *numerical* strength of three Regiments, in this Brigade, has been increased about forty per cent, but the *vim* and *ambition* of the men—which are more important in a hard march or fight—more than one hundred per cent. It may be that "*conscience* makes cowards of us all" in the ordinary relations of life, but it is really strange to what extent a little indisposition takes the "pluck" out of men, for general fighting purposes, and falters the step to meet "grim visaged war, with his wrinkled front."

Yesterday and the day before, we had a Brigade drill at Montpelier, a mile and a half South of camp, the place improved by President Madison and where he resided in his lifetime.[8] This is a place of rare attractions, and when its surroundings and the scenery are considered, one of almost unparalleled picturesque beauty and loveliness. The residence is about a mile South of the plank road, and, though somewhat undulating, the ground gradually rises, as you approach the House through a large open field, well turfed over and very smooth, and destitute of shade, except three circular pine groves, about fifty yards in diameter. The carriage road, not enclosed, through this field, does not run direct, but meanders by long and gentle curves, so as to give one approaching the residence, several charming views of the place. About twenty acres are enclosed with a white pailing, in front of the house. This enclosure has but little shrubbery and no trees, until you get within some hundred yards of the dwelling. To the left and rear is a grove of considerable size, of oaks, hickorys, poplars, chestnuts, &c. To the left of the residence, and leading to the ice house, is a very pretty avenue of white pines. In the immediate vicinity of the house, and surrounding it, there is an abundance of shade trees, nearly all very large, and many of them having a very venerable yet vigorous appearance. The ground slopes on three sides from the house. It is two stories high, with a basement, is built of brick, stuccoed and painted a light cream color, the main body being higher and wider than the two wings, that extend out from either end. There is a moderate sized portico in the center of the main building, supported by five pillars. The house has a mansion like appearance, with an air of substantial durability and comfort.

From the portico the view of the landscape in front, is of uparalleled magnificence and beauty. The place is sufficiently elevated for one to see the gently winding valley of the Rapidan, some six miles distant, and the Blue Ridge, with its long sloping sides, in full view, and, at the nearest point only about ten or twelve miles distant, with its beautifully undulating outline, bounds the horizon in a long stretch, and embracing about the sixth of the circle. The only element of complete and perfect beauty that seems to be wanting is a large stream or body of water. As it is, it has never been the writers fortune to see scenery, that so completely charms, and with such pleasant emotions fills the mind of the beholder.

The spot of greatest interest on the place, is a small burial ground, about a quarter of a mile to the Southwest of the house, where rest the remains of the great, the pure, and the good Madison, whose public career, without being particularly brilliant, was yet characterized by the highest writers, and whose life, with earnest zeal, was devoted to the permanent welfare of the Republic. The cemetery is about forty yards by twenty-five in size, and enclosed by a brick wall four feet high. The monument over the remains of the illustrious President, is a plain granite shaft, beautiful is its symmetry and simplicity, and the only inscription that can be seen from a little distance is Madison, and this is the most pathetic, touching and eloquent epitaph your correspondent ever saw. Is it not strange, that many men, whose greatness and many virtues were very little known in life, should have such extraordinary characters ascribed to them upon their tomb stones. Not unfrequently the epitaph tells you what the deceased *ought* to have been, and not what he really *was*. As you approach near the monument, you observe the dates of the birth and death of Madison, and this is all there is inscribed upon it. Some twenty other graves are in the same yard—most of them of the relatives of the President.

Col. Goulding of the 9th Georgia Regiment, died suddenly at Orange, C.H., on Thursday, 3d inst. He had been absent on sick leave two or three months, but had returned, hoping to be able to do duty, yet he did not get to his Regiment before the "grim destroyer" claimed him for his own.

The Spring seems backward; the white maples are just in bloom, and the buds of other trees are now swelling. "It is the month before the month of May, And Spring comes slowly up this way." M. D.

On the road between Orange C.H. and Fredericksburg, 8 o'clock A.M.,
Monday April 7th, 1862.

**Dear Courier:** Our Brigade received orders yesterday at 5 ½ o'clock P.M., to be ready as soon as possible to march with four days rations, and the men to carry their blankets. At six the drum beat to fall into line, and at half past six the 8th Georgia Regiment was ready to march, leaving the few tents we had standing, and all the heavy baggage, except a small allowance of cooking utensils. At eight we left camp, but as there were various causes of delay, did not leave Orange until 12 ½ o'clock. The march was continued without stopping at all until 3 o'clock A.M., and yet did not make over seven miles from the Court House, or a little less than 10 miles from camp. At 4 o'clock the Regiment was roused up—most of the men having lain down by comfortable fires—and moved only about a mile further, where they halted until 7 o'clock, took their scanty breakfasts of fat bacon, hard biscuit and coffee made in tin cups.

It is reported that the entire Federal force between Orange C.H. and the Potomac, has been removed, in the last few days, and that very few are left at Alexandria or even at Washington City itself—they all having gone down the Potomac as the report goes.

Wednesday morning 9th. On Monday morning we continued the march about six miles from Orange C.H. We bivouaced in a grove beside the road, and there remained until 10 o'clock yesterday morning, when the march back to this old camp was commenced. Since Monday noon it had been falling weather nearly all the time, snow, sleet and rain alternately, and sometimes all together. We spent a miserable night Monday, having no tents and very poor booths, very many men got wet, and nearly all very cold. The road, between here and the little Post Office called Deersville, where we turned back, is an old dilapidated plank road, bad enough, yet vastly better to march upon than a mud one would have been yesterday. Everything considered, the march yesterday, of fifteen miles, was the most disagreeable one the 8th Georgia Regiment has yet made.

The cause of this movement, so far as subordinate officers and privates are concerned, is a mere matter of conjecture. Without doubt the move was commenced with the expectation of going to Fredericksburg, but probably some new move of our enemies, caused a change in our programme. The Regiment arrived at this camp at 4 o'clock P.M. Everything, tents, cooking vessels, &c., had been sent off, and the few vessels we took on the march have not yet got back, the wagon having stalled somewhere on the way. The blankets were nearly all wet, and last night was by no means comfortably spent by a majority of the men. We have had three miserable nights in succession, and our food has been less in quantity and as wholesome as usual. The hills all around are white with snow, and have been since yesterday morning.

Thursday morning. It continued to rain and sleet all day yesterday, and the men suffered much from the cold and wet. Last night was one of the most disagreeable we have seen in the service.

Gen. David R. Jones, who has been acting Maj. General for some three weeks, but whose nomination to that office had not been confirmed at last accounts, has been ordered to Richmond, and Gen. Toombs is now in command of this Division.

The wagons are now loading up all the extra baggage—the quantity being very small, in comparison to what it was when we evacuated Centreville—and they are about to start to Richmond. Our Brigade is expected to start on the cars for *somewhere* to-morrow. The sun is now shining with cheerful brightness, and the earths surface is rapidly loosing its brilliant silver grey, and assuming its wonted hue of sober brown.

This morning the Miller Rifles were greatly horrified at finding one of their men, Mr. Barker, dead in his bunk. He complained of being unwell last night, and had a chill, but he was not considered very ill—he staid in the same booth with Sanford Williamson, was awake and conversed about an hour before day, and was not even then considered by any means dangerously ill. When a little breakfast had been prepared at about 8 o'clock he was asked if he would have some, and making no reply, one of his messmates went to him and found him dead. It is supposed that he had congestion of the lungs.

The glorious news from Corinth has produced quite an exultation among the troops.[9] M. D.

# 5

# "This Duty is Telling Fearfully upon the Men"

## *April–June 1862*

The Eighth Georgia was not back at Orange Court House long when orders came to move again. Gen. George McClellan had decided on a new strategy in an effort to capture Richmond. He was moving his army by ship down the Chesapeake Bay to land at the tip of the peninsula between the James and York Rivers. McClellan planned to march up the peninsula to the Confederate capital, possibly without having to fight a battle at all. Confederate leaders recognized what McClellan was doing and ordered Gen. Joseph Johnston to move his army east along to the peninsula and confront the Federals at Yorktown. On April 11, the Georgians packed into train cars bound for Richmond. The men were so exhausted, Melvin Dwinell wrote, that they fell asleep immediately. From Richmond, they boarded a flotilla of canal boats and schooners, drawn by steam tugs, which carried them down the James. The editor described passing the historic settlement of Jamestown.

Just two days after arriving in Richmond, the Eighth Georgia saw combat. The men were rushed to support a North Carolina regiment that had been working on fortifications and was surprised by Union troops. The Georgians charged toward the works the Federals had just taken and soon had them on the run, Dwinell told readers. The Union army tried to retake the fortifications but was repulsed. The Light Guards soon settled into trench duty, and Dwinell described the demanding task of being constantly on guard. After living in the trenches for many days, the men had become a "hard looking set," he wrote. "Many have not had clean clothes in two weeks, have been sleeping on the mud and in the muddy trenches, and eating fat meat, when they could get it, with their fingers, after broiling it on a stick."

On May 3, the Confederate army began to secretly withdraw from its position and march back toward Richmond. About the same time, Dwinell became sick and was sent to the city to recover. The illness did not keep the editor from keeping up his correspondence to the *Courier*, and he sent six letters from the capital. He even did his best to report the fighting at what Southerners would call the Battle of Seven Pines. The Eighth Georgia was not involved, but other Georgia units suffered heavy casualties. Dwinell provided a partial list of the men from the state who were killed or wounded.

Johnston was wounded at the Battle of Seven Pines, and President Jefferson Davis tapped Gen. Robert E. Lee to replace him. The aggressive Lee began making plans for a spring campaign to destroy the Union army. When Dwinell returned to his regiment in mid-June, it had moved outside Richmond. The men resumed picket duty and occasionally exchanged fire. Dwinell told readers how an artillery shell hit the camp and wounded several members of the regiment.

Gen. Robert E. Lee. Photograph by Julian Vannerson. Library of Congress.

The series of battles known as the Seven Days Campaign began on June 27, and the Eighth Georgia spent the day in a position of support. The next day there was miscommunication between Confederate commanders, and the Eighth Georgia was one of two regiments ordered to attack across a broad field. Dwinell described how the Light Guards charged across the field and fought through woods before capturing a Union rifle pit. But the force was too small to hold the position, and they had to retreat when they faced "murderous" fire from the enemy. Dwinell wrote that it had been "a disastrous day"—and indeed it was. Some twenty men from Floyd County's companies were killed or wounded at what became known as the Battle of Garnett's Farm. Among the casualties were Maj. E. J. Magruder, who lost part of his nose, and Lt. James M. Montgomery, who later died at the brigade field hospital. Many other men went missing.

The hard fighting was not over, however. After a long day of marching on July 1, the Eighth Georgia was part of an assault at the Battle of Malvern Hill that proved to be one of the most tragic of the war for the South. The Confederates marched out of the woods into an open field and were easy targets for the Union artillery. Men fell everywhere. In one letter, Dwinell graphically described the death of two members of the Light Guards. All in all, however, the Eighth Georgia suffered relatively few casualties as compared to other regiments. Within a week, the regiment was back on picket duty, and Dwinell reported that the men were holding up "wonderfully well" considering all they had been through.

Camp Winder, near Richmond, Va.,
Sunday, April 13th, 1862.

**Dear Courier:** Our brigade did not get off from Orange C.H. until 6 o'clock Friday evening. We then got into box cars, without seats, forty-seven men to the car, and our situation, thus crowded together, with guns, knapsacks, blankets, haversacks and canteens, can probably be better imagined than described. At first chances to sit on their blankets, lean against the sides of the car, were eagerly caught, but there not being room for all to be thus accommodated, they soon began to sit through the middle and lean against one another. The fatigues and exposures of the preceding five days, had so exhausted their strength, that most of them were soon asleep, even in their cold and uncomfortable positions. A brief review of what had been done since Sunday the 6th, will give the reader an idea of their exhausted state.

A brief account of our movements, up to Thursday morning, was given in my last. At 5 o'clock P.M. of that day, we were ordered into line of march, and left camp again just at sun set, and marched down to a field, a little beyond the town, expecting every moment to get upon the train, until 3 o'clock A.M., when an order was published that we would remain where we were until Friday evening. The Blue Ridge in full view was white with snow, and the stiff breeze from that direction seemed naught but rarified ice itself. Consequently—although about a mile of rail fence was exhausted in building fires—there was but little sleep that night. Speaking of fences, by the way, reminds one of the fact that the notorious "rail-splitter" of Yankeedoodledom, is expected to have possession of the country evacuated by our men, and if would exercise his powers, only as his pet name would indicate, and in such manner as he really has capacity, he might prove a blessing, and supply a desideratum to the agricultural interests.

Arrived at this camp at 10 o'clock yesterday morning, and the high and dry ground and clean white sand was a pleasing contrast to the red clay mud we had been marching through for several days before leaving the vicinity of Orange C.H. We are in very comfortable barracks, of which the number here is sufficient, probably to shelter 20,000 troops. The camp is near the Reservoir, and also the city cemetery. The latter is a place of rare beauty and picturesqueness.

It is on the side or a bluff, some 200 feet above and five hundred yards from the river, the rapids of which are in full view and greatly enhance the charming loveliness of this delightful place. The primitive growth of trees is to a large extent preserved, the grounds are quite broken—a fact that both facilitates and enhances the artictic beauties that have been lavished upon them. There are a large number of beautiful monuments, and among them that of President James Monroe. This is of granite, not large, simple, and would not be conspicuous were it not for the little cast iron, Tower in Gothic style architecture, and open work that covers it. Perhaps the most interesting portion of the burial ground is that part where the soldiers, who have died in Richmond, are buried. These number some six or seven hundred. These graves are in regular order, and as close together as they could well be dug.

There is very little sickness in our regiment at this time. It would seem that the more hardship and exposure the men endure, the healthier they are. They look rough and dirty, but strong and healthy. The remarks made by citizens, was heard more than once yesterday, as we came through the city, speaking of this Brigade, "these are no paper soldiers, but they look like they had seen real service."

Sunday, Noon. It is now just reported that orders have been received for our regiment, *and others*, to proceed to Yorktown, as soon as transportation can be provided—probably this evening. We expect to go by boats. M. D.

Bivouac of 8th GA. Reg't.
Lebanon Church, four miles from
Yorktown, April 15, 1862.

**Dear Courier:** We arrived at this place yesterday at 5 o'clock, P.M. Left Richmond at 9 P.M. Sunday on canal boats and schooners, propelled by steam tugs, in company with the 9th and 11th Georgia Regiments Toombs' Brigade left about two hours before we did. Had a tolerably comfortable passage on the boats, but were considerably crowded, and everybody hungry. "The honey, heavy dew of slumber" fell upon the eyelids of the writer at about ten o'clock, and hence he was oblivious to passing scenes and scenery until sun rise Monday morning. We were moving in a due east direction, and, as the sun arose clear, the scene calm and lovely, was not devoid of beauty. The James river, or at least part of it, we passed after daylight, varies in width from one and a half to two and a half miles. The banks are low, in fact almost no bank at all on the left hand side; the current is slow and the stream now very muddy. The boundary of the low, flat lands that stretch out on either side of the river cannot be seen from boats, in many places, and the soil is said to be very fertile—these lands even now readily commanding one hundred dollars per acre. Passed Jamestown, the place famous for having been the first permanently settled by the whites in America, at 9 o'clock, A.M. There are now some fortifications here, barracks and a small garrison. Within fifty yards of the river stands a portion of the brick walls of the first churches built in Virginia. There is one modern farm house with out buildings near by, and this is all that marks the place of the original town. About a half mile back from the river are some half dozen houses, all but one or two very ancient in their appearance, and much dilapidated. From respect to the garrison, probably, our flag was raised and the band played as we passed this place.

Nothing further of interest occurred on the trip. We landed at King's Point, fifteen miles from Yorktown, at 11 o'clock, A.M. By the river we were ninety-two miles from Richmond. At noon we took the brief march to this place, eleven miles distant, the men bringing their knapsacks and blankets. The Light Guards have just got sabre bayonets for their rifles, and most of them were busy, on the boats, putting them to their guns. Rations of hard biscuit and bacon were issued last night, and after eating a hearty supper, the men slept soundly.

The enemy have been shelling Yorktown since Sunday morning, but have produced no serious damage at last accounts. They fire slowly—not averaging more than once in ten or fifteen minutes—and we had not returned a single shot up to last night. Gen. Magruder is in command at Yorktown. It was expected yesterday that the great battle would commence—we making the attack—this morning; but as Smith's and Longstreet's divisions, also all the artillery and cavalry of the army of the Potomac are still behind, it is probably delayed on that account. It is reported that McClellan is in command of the Lincolnites, and that their entire force here, is one hundred and sixty thousand strong. Our force is said to number about sixty-five thousand. It is thought the line of battle will be about twelve miles long. The battle will doubtless be a most desperate and bloody one, but we are full of hope that victory will finally prch upon the righthous standards of our glorious cause. We shall go into the conflict, not with boasting, but an earnest effort to

> "In the God of battles trust;
> Die we may—die we must;
> But where, O where, can dust to dust
> Be consigned so well,"

as in defense of all that is sacred or near and dear to a spirited and free people.

Our Regiment has here, six hundred and thirty-two men, and they were never, apparently, in better fighting condition

Ten and a half o'clock A.M. It is a bright, warm morning. The heavy booming of cannon is still heard in the direction of Yorktown at slow and irregular intervals. We have as yet received no orders to-day, further than to get a full supply of 40 rounds of cartridges, and be ready to fall into line of battle on the shortest possible notice. The enemy, in force, are said to be within three miles of us.

Lieut. Col. Turnepseed, of the 9th Ga. Reg., was this morning elected Col. of that Regiment. It is now half past twelve and nothing of special interest has yet occurred. M. D.

In the Intrenchments, near Dam No. 1,
April 18, 1862.

**Dear Courier:** On Wednesday, the 10th, the 3d Brigade was moved to the front. At 11 o'clock, we passed in range of the enemy's guns and a shell burst in about 200 yards from us. This was sent with the compliments of Yankeedoodledom as a salutation. From this time, until 3 P.M., these shells were bursting in our very midst and near by, almost continuously. A musket ball from one of these, hit Wm. Aycock, of company A, on the shoulder, but did not penetrate his clothes even, only producing a slight stinging sensation. One of the Atlanta Grays was similarly hit. At 3 ½ o'clock, we heard heavy musketry in the direction of Dam No. 1, distance one mile, and soon received orders to go there to support the 5th North Carolina Regiment. We went as fast as possible, through the thick bushes of the woods. When loading, the cannon balls, bursting shells, and grape shot were flying thick as hail about us. The enemy had surprised our pickets and taken possession of our trenches. When we came in sight, the 5th N. C. Regiment were peppering them at a lively rate. The 7th and 8th Ga., the former ahead, rushed with a whoop into the conflict. The Federals commenced running before we came up, and soon we had quiet possession of the trenches again. These two regiments then took possession. At 6 ½ we were attacked by a single regiment of Lincolnites. They were trying to make their way to one of our batteries, to charge it. They came through the water very gallantly, opposite the 8th Regiment, but our fire was too hard for them, and after a very severe loss, they were repulsed. Nobody hurt on our side.

These trenches are very small and slight, 2 ½ feet deep, same width at bottom, and evidently thrown up in a hurry. About fifty yards from these was a small creek, which has been damed up and now flows a width of some 100 yards. The trenches change direction to correspond with the course of the stream.

There was no further fighting that day, except the artillery, on both sides kept up a constant and heavy firing. The enemy had six pieces and we only four at this place. The casualties on our side, on our entire line, is reported at 40 killed and 100 wounded. That of the enemy must have been very heavy. At this particular point the loss was mostly sustained by the N.C. Regiment. They lost 12 killed, besides Col. McKinney, and had 23 wounded. The 7th Ga. lost two killed and seven wounded. No one was sufficiently hurt in the 8th to keep him from duty. Lamar and Wilson behaved with great bravery, well as mortals possibly could do.[1]

The trenches are kept full all the time, regiments relieving each other every 24 hours. The enemy have long range guns, and their sharpshooters keep up a constant firing at any one they can see. Last night the Federals made two efforts to breach Dam No. 1, once at 12 o'clock and again at 3 ½, but were both times repulsed, without loss on our side. Four or five of our men were killed yesterday by the sharpshooters, and some ten wounded, but none of these of the 8th Ga.

The big fight seems to hang fire, and we half mistrust it will not come off here at all. Last night we were in line of battle after 12 o'clock and came in the trenches at 4 ½, this morning. There is but little skirmishing of any kind today. M. D.

Bivouac of 8th GA. Reg.,
April 22, 1862

**Dear Courier:** I have begged a few scraps of paper, and have time to give a brief summary of transactions here since 11 o'clock A.M., last Friday when my last letter was closed. The 8th was then in the trenches between Dam No. 1 and No. 2 where we continued until 8 o'clock Saturday evening, having gone in at 4 o'clock Friday morning. This duty was extremely severe, the men being required to keep awake all the time—which, by the way, is impossible—an attack being momentarily expected, and the order being to hold the position against any force. Nothing worthy of note occurred further than that cannonading was kept up nearly all the time by the enemy—mostly directed against our batteries—and their sharpshooters constantly shooting at our men in the trenches if one happened to expose himself, until o'clock Saturday afternoon, when a flag of truce was sent over from our side, requesting the enemy to send over and remove their dead, killed on Wednesday, and many being near our trenches, had become a most disagreeable nuisance. The enemy *preferred* that we send them over; this was agreed to, and thirty-seven were carried over Dam No. 1 by our men; there are probably twice as many more in the pond, which was not searched. This short armistice was intensely enjoyed. It was a sweet re-relaxation from the awful anxiety experienced since Wednesday morning. The men left their places in the trenches, and for *two hours* experienced the sweet delights of peace. Never did time seem to fly on swifter wings. On one side of the pond the men sauntered about in listless leisure—on the enemy's side they were in line, and as neat and prim as an old maid. Their army is evidently much better disciplined than ours.

Saturday night at 8 o'clock, and just as our Brigade was being relieved from the trenches, a false alarm was created, and all along our line between Dams No. 1 and No. 2, nearly all the men fired, and some two or three times. None of the 8th were harmed. In the 9th two were killed by the enemy's pickets, five or six wounded by our own men; in the 7th Ga. one was killed and six or seven wounded by their own regiment. This most mortifying affair created great confusion, it being as dark as it ever gets to be, at the time and raining beside. The panic lasted but a short time, however, and when quiet and order was restored, we were marched to our position—some 400 yards—on the rear, the place of the reserve. The men were all thoroughly wet, without blankets or oilcloths or shelter of any kind, yet most of them as soon as their guns were stacked, lay down on the wet ground and were soon asleep. At about midnight there was another general firing by our men in the trenches, &c., and like the first, without cause, our regiment was in line in less than five minutes, ready to support those in the trenches if need be. One by one, however, they again lay down and were soon asleep. At day light the same unfortunate affair was played over for the third time. The great fault lies in the fact that our men will fire without orders when they *think* they see an enemy. I believe the Lincolnites throw forward a few of their pickets occasionally, at night, into the pond, which, in many places, is only a foot or two deep, just for the purpose of drawing our fire.

On Sunday the firing along our line for three or four miles, was more general than it had been at any time before. There was no considerable fight though that I have heard of. The men spent the time in cleaning up their guns. Sunday night at 8 o'clock our regiment again went into the trenches for twenty-four hours more, at 9 o'clock there was a tremendous discharge of musketry from our line about a mile below us; the feint did not extend to our regiment this time. I am happy to state. At 2 o'clock P.M., Monday, the enemy sent over a flag of truce to ask for an exchange of prisoners. They particularly desired a missing Capt. As we did not have him—he probably being in the pond with many of his men—no exchange was effected. It is rumored that they have fourteen of our men, Alabamians, taken some two miles above, near Winns' Mill, last Wednesday—Lee's Mill, another important point, is two or three miles Southwest, or below here, as the creek runs. The trenches are very muddy, and Sunday night we suffered much from cold. Many of the men have now got their oilcloths and one blanket each. Yesterday the enemy's cannon were nearly silent and ours entirely so. To-day the Fed's fire occasionally, say every half hour or so, and there is not much firing between the pickets. The enemy's sharpshooters annoy us very much. They are firstrate shots, and their guns hold up well six or seven hundred yards. A few men have been wounded by them, but none killed that I have heard of. It is woods all about here, all the way up to the enemy's line, except an opening cut down in front of our battery, opposite Dam No. 1, but as the growth is not very thick in many places, they manage to get a good many bullets through to us. Just back of the enemy's pickets, there is a large field in which they have their batteries, all thrown up last Wednesday night.

It seems doubtful now when the general battle will be fought, and many think it will not be here at all. It is rumored that enemy are now preparing to move probably to Fredericksburg. Nearly one half of the men who left Richmond with us are now unfit for duty, mostly from fatigue and loss of sleep. If our entire force here is in the same situation, McClellan can soon whip the fight without firing a gun. The men complain very much, and there is no little murmuring. It is thought that some of the brigades, kept two or three miles back, might be brought forward and relieve ours. I believe Gen. Magruder is still in command on the peninsula, although Gen. Joseph E. Johnston is here.

This morning the sun shone out bright and warm, but now—1 ½ p. m.—it is raining again.

Wm. Jones, Capt. of a Chattooga co. company, was elected Major of the 9th Georgia Regiment a few days since, Major Manger having been promoted to Lieut. Col.[2] No man in the 8th Ga. Regiment has yet been hurt, either by the enemy, or the foolishness of our own men. Our time we expect will come soon for a full share of the casualties of war. M. D.

Bivouac of 8th Ga. Regiment
Near Yorktown, VA., Saturday, April 22, '62.

**Dear Courier:** Not so much because I have anything of importance to communicate as to relieve the painful anxiety of friends at home, do I write you a few lines at this time. My last was closed at 10 o'clock A.M. last Thursday. Since then there has been no particularly exciting events in this immediate vicinity. We took the usual tour of 24 hours in the trenches, commencing at 7 o'clock Thursday evening. Our sharpshooters, armed with the Enfield Rifle, yesterday, went forward of the trenches down to the water's edge, and even crossed over on Dam No. 2, and skirmished with the enemy's pickets. One of our sharpshooters was shot in the side, but not fatally injured, it is thought. Capt. Bell, of the 9th Georgia, was accidentally shot in the mouth by one of our men.

The most cheerful expression of countenance since we have been on the peninsula, by the men generally in the 8th Ga., was seen yesterday, when it was announced that the commissary had drawn eleven hundred pounds of bacon, a hogshead of sugar and plenty of flour for the Regiment, and that a portion would be ready for supper. There has been considerable suffering for want of wholesome food, but what really produced most pain was the fearful apprehension that matters would become worse, and some men, to use a soldier's expression, *"hogged"* more than their share, and as is usual in such cases, when there is a probability of a scarcity, every one wants more than his usual allowance. It is hoped that the Quartermaster and Commissaries have now got their wits and means sufficiently at command, so as to prevent further complaint. The main cause of this trouble is believed to be beyond our brigade.

One of the 15th Ga. Regiment was wounded this morning while in the trenches, I did not learn how seriously, further than that they brought him up on a litter. The enemy fired several shots into Dam No. 1 yesterday evening but did not break it.

Both the health and spirits of the men are better now than two days since. Longstreet's Division is on our left. This morning about sun-rise, there was heavy skirmishing heard along his line, and supposed he made a *sortie* inside the enemy's line. It was announced that he would do this yesterday evening, but we heard nothing of it then. It was thought probable whenever he did do it that it would bring on a general fight. It rained all night and has continued up to this time, noon, to-day. This is the worst rainy country I ever saw, and we are very scantily provided with blankets and oilcloths, and have no shelter at all. We have no idea *when* the general fight will come off, it at all, here. Our Regiment goes into the trenches again at 7 o'clock to-night. M. D.

Bivouac of 8th Ga. Reg't.
Near Dam No. 1, April 24, 1862.

**Dear Courier:** Our usual rounds of duty continues at this place, with, perhaps, less extraordinary interest than might be supposed. Since my last letter was closed at 1 ½ o'clock P.M. on the 22d, there has been less firing between the pickets than there had been before, and less cannonading by the enemy. Every hour or two however, they throw a shell, either at our batteries or into the midst of the quarters of our reserve for the purpose, it may be, of keeping our men on the strain of anxious expectancy.

Our forces, beside doing picket duty, are continually throwing up additional breastworks and redoubts, and in every possible way strengthening the position. Yesterday some of our sharp shooters, the Texas Rangers, crossed ever on Dam No. 2, and took a Yankee prisoner. He said it was McClellan's intention to make the grand attack last night, but it is not likely that he knew anything about it.

There has been more firing between the pickets this morning than there was yesterday, but no general charge. An order was issued this morning, by Gen. Magruder, just before daylight, to be in readiness, as all indications pointed to an attack this morning. It is now half past eight, and no demonstration is yet evident to us here.

Night before last the first four companies of our Regiment lay in the trenches. These have now become intolerably muddy, and, as it was very cold, we suffered exceedingly. One third of the men were kept standing in the trenches at a time, for the purpose of keeping a sharp lookout. It was very dark, and of course they could see but a short distance, but the utmost silence was observed, and no large body of men could approach without being heard, especially through the water, which extends up to within forty yards of the trenches. There was no alarm that night or the last. This duty is telling fearfully upon the men. Beside the great fatigue to which they are subjected, the want of sleep and exposure, the most trying of all is the continual expectation of an attack, which seems imminent all the time. If it were possible, by reason of all other considerations, to keep this out of mind, the occasional bullets that whistle by, and the cannon balls or shells that whiz over our heads, demonstrate the nearness of bitter enemies. This feeling of apprehension is not cowardice, and men are very seldom in a situation, where it is experienced more than a few moments or hours at most, at a time. But we have now been under this excitement nine days. All this time rations have been both poor and scanty, having very little meat and not enough bread, no coffee but little sugar, and, besides a few peas twice, nothing else whatever. After all, our men hold out wonderfully well. The Light Guards reported twenty-three for duty this morning.

A man of the 15th Georgia was shot this morning, while standing in the trench near our battery. Fronting Dam No. 1. He was shot in the breast, producing a bad, but, it is hoped, not fatal wound.

There are a thousand rumors afloat, in regard to French interferences, an armistice, peace negotiations, &c., all of which are much talked about by the soldiers, and, in some sort, supply the place in the mind's hankerings, of the morning papers, very few of which get to us here.

The soldiers here are a hard looking set. Many have not had clean clothes in two weeks, have been sleeping on the mud and in the muddy trenches, and eating fat meat, when they could get it, with their fingers, after broiling it on a stick.

It is now 9 o'clock—all quiet yet and it is a bright and pleasant morning. M. D.

Bivouac of 8th Ga. Reg.,
April 28, 1862.

**Dear Courier:** Just to illustrate the condition we are now in, it may be justifiable to mention the circumstances under which I now write. My shirt and all my under clothing is off, and the boy Van is washing them near by, while I am wrapped in overcoat and blankets, and rather impatiently waiting for the aforesaid nether garments to dry. I have not had a change of under clothing in fifteen days, and this is the best and first opportunity I have had, to have those I had on to be washed. The men generally are not quite as bad off. Their baggage belonging to the brigade, is now only a half mile off, and most of them have a change of underclothing along; but the officers baggage has been sent to Williamsburg, some nine of ten miles distant from here.

Yesterday our Regiment had another turn in the trenches. We were stationed immediately behind Dam No. 1, and in the vicinity of one of our batteries. This is one of the most dangerous and important posts on our line. While we were there, the enemy threw six or eight shells, which burst very near the Regiment, but no one was injured. Tom McCay, of the Light Guards, yesterday, while going to the trench, had the first joint on his first finger on the left hand shot off, and the second finger slightly bruised.[3] So far as I know, this is the severest injury as yet suffered by our Regiment, and even this, it is probably, was done by our own men, shooting off their guns for the purpose of cleaning them. It is perfectly outrageous that this is allowed.

Yesterday was a cloudy day but no rain. We went into the trenches at 8 o'clock Saturday night, and as it was very cold suffered much.

I have hardly left the Regiment since being on the Peninsula, and can give no information in regard to the distribution of our forces, further than that our Division is from Dam No. 1 to Dam No. 2; Cobb's Legion is on our right, towards Dam No. 2, and Longstreet's Division on our left. Winn's Mill, I am told is about 2 ½ miles to our left, and Lee's Mill nearly the same distance on our right. D. R. Jones has returned and assumed the command of our Division; that throws General Toombs back to his old Brigade. There are plenty of traces of the old fortifications thrown up here by Washington, to repel the British in the old Revolution. Instead of being in a straight line, they are zigzag like a rail fence and only about twenty feet between angles. This was probably to prevent successful flank firing by the enemy. It is most devoutly to be hoped, that our defences and men may do as well as did those, and that a victory here may be crowned with such glorious results.

Ten thousand rumors are afloat among the troops, and many of them of the most extravagant nature. A specimen one, rife in our Regiment is to the effect that Rome is now in the possession of the enemy. Cut off as we are, from the newspapers, which with all their faults, are yet the correctors of misrepresentations and perverted facts, we know not what to believe, and our only source of information, is the very irresponsible "they say" of the multitude.

This is a bright warm day, and its genial atmosphere is of immense value improving the feelings and health of the men. It is now half past one. The most momentous event of the day, that has come to my knowledge, is the fact thae a party of Texan Rangers, who crossed over Dam No. 2, this morning, were driven back by some five or six hundred of the enemy, having five of their number wounded, none seriously however. A single bomb shell from our battery put the enemy to fight and they have not come back since.

3 ½ o'clock P.M. It is now reported that one of the Atlanta Grays, named Gill, was shot through the thigh while working on the breast works near Dam No. 1 to-day. It is only a flesh wound. There is no apparent prospect of a general fight soon. Our Regiment goes into the trenches again to-night. M. D.

Richmond, Va., May 3, 1862

**Dear Courier:** Since Wednesday morning, the date of my last, nothing of very great interest occurred at Dam No. 1 or its vicinity, except that Lieut. Armstrong, of the Ga. Regiment, was killed by the enemy's sharpshooters, until Thursday evening, when an order was issued to our Brigade to cook what rations they had on hand. This of course seemed to *mean something*, but exactly *what* it meant no one could tell. The day, "May Day"—and O how different were the surrounding circumstances under which it was spent, from all the other May days of the writer's life—had been rather more quiet than usual. In the night much noise, occasioned by moving wagons, on the enemy's side of the line, was heard. About midnight, three day's rations were issued to our Brigade (and how many others it may not be prudent at this time to state) and the men were required to cook them immediately, and other orders were issued indicating a march. Before day quite a number of our artillery wagons were in motion. Our baggage train was ordered to Williamsburg—an old town, once the Captal of the colony of Va., I believe, a place of some two or three thousand inhabitants and about fourteen miles from Yorktown and five North of James river. For over three weeks our army had faced the *invading* enemy, our line of pickets distant only 300 or 400 yards from theirs; they have been repulsed in three efforts to advance; and, as they are so well protected by the breast works, and so near their gunboats and Fortress Monroe, it would hardly be *policy* for us to attack them; and we could only *"bag"* of them, in case of a successful attack, the number actually killed, for we could not possibly cut them off. Whether our line is to be moved back, I do not know, but it would seem for the above suggested reasons, that if we could get a position anything like as strong, that it would be vastly better for our cause.

A vast number of our troops, who have been on the peninsula, are sick. Yesterday evening there were at King's Landing, twenty-two hundred and sixty, waiting for the boats to take them to this place.

The hospitals here are very much crowded. Rev. Mr. Crumly is untiring in his efforts to relieve these poor sufferers, and accomplishes a great deal, but one man cannot do everything. In one hospital, I am informed, they had one hundred more patients last night than they had beds. Though unable to do duty, I feel "like a fish out of water," away from the Regiment. Hope to rejoin the boys in a few days. M. D.

Richmond, May 10, 1862

**Dear Courier:** I have been in this city now a full week, and though able to be up most of the time, have been able to learn very little of what is transpiring in the place, and still less of the movements of our army. There is perceptible here quite a stir, amounting in many cases to panic. Government stores, machinery and archives are being, as I think, either actually removed, or, at least, put in readiness to be sent off at the shortest notice; many private families are moving off, while others are sending to some place of supposed safety, all except the articles of absolute necessity for housekeeping.

The reports of the advance of the enemy are vague and confused, and their present position, is at present a matter of doubt to most persons here. There is, however, no doubt but that they are in possession of West Point and Fredericksburg *in force*. They have possession of, at least, the North bank of the James River, as high up as King's Point opposite Williamsburg, and probably somewhat higher. Our army is, at last accounts, still falling back, probably seeking for an eligible position for a general fight. It is not improbable that our stand will be the Chickahominy Creek. Our rear guard is almost continually skirmishing with the enemy's advance, and so far with uniform success.

Of the movements of the 8th Georgia Regiment, I have been able to learn but little. The following however, may be relied on: the Regiment went into the trenches near Dam No. 2 at 8 o'clock Friday night, the 2nd instant, and remained there until 8 o'clock Saturday night, when they were relieved by two companies, and as soon as possible took up the line of march for Williamsburg, where, after a most fatiguing march, they arrived at about 10 o'clock Sunday morning. Here they halted some two hours, got breakfast and a little rest, and proceeded some eleven miles further this way, to a Creek, where they were ordered to halt and await further orders. Here they remained until 11 o'clock on Monday, when our informant left the Regiment.

He states that the men were so much fatigued and exhausted, that they were obliged to fall out of ranks on Saturday night and Sunday morning. Before they were two miles this side of Williamsburg, they heard the fight on the other side of the town.

Of the Floyd county boys who are now here sick, there are none who are unable to be up, so far as I can learn. No passes are now being granted to leave the city. Many will join the Regiment as soon as they are allowed to do so; this will, probably, be as soon as it makes a permanent halt.

It is said that there are now some twenty-five thousand sick soldiers in Richmond, and thousands have been sent to Lynchburg, Farmersville and other places in the last week. Considering the number, the mortality among them is small.

I cannot learn that the 8th Georgia Regiment has been in any skirmish since the retreat commenced. Frank Cane, Jr., of Greensboro, was killed by the enemy's sharp shooters on the 2nd inst.[4] He belonged to the Stephens Light Guards, and was a son of Judge Cane. He was the only man of our Regiment killed on the Peninsula. M. D

Richmond, May 19, 1862.

**Dear Courier:** Several days have elapsed since my last communication, for several reasons. In the first place, *indisposition* not *sick*, but "ratherish unwell," as Charles Lamb would have said; in the second place, not being with the Regiment—the especial object of my interest—I had nothing of peculiar interest to communicate, and in the third place, nothing of general interest has yet occurred of which your readers have not been advised. On Wednesday there was a great and general *panic* here on account of the advance of the enemy's gunboats to our obstructions and defences, at Drury's Bluff—some eight miles by land and fifteen by water below here—but as they were repulsed, and confidence thereby given in our defences on the river, there has since been much less anxiety in this city. Many families are, however, moving away to North Carolina and the interior of this State, and, as I believe, nought but the skeleton of the Capital of the Confederate States yet remains here. People living to the East of this place are nearly all moving back here, and to points beyond, and a general expectation exists of a great battle very soon near this city. Johnson and McClellan both are almost continually changing their positions, *slightly* advancing and retreating—and evidently watching each other with a jealous eye.

Our defences and the obstructions in the James river, below here, have been greatly increased, since last Wednesday, and even Federal gunboats will now find that a "hard road to travel." The confidence in our ability to defend Richmond is daily increasing, and the determination to do so *at all hazards* has already become quite general. The expectation is that the great fight will be a most bloody one whenever it comes off, and it seems impossible for it to be long postponed. So far as I can learn, the general feeling of our army is that of entire confidence in their ability to whip the dastard invaders.

Last Friday was observed as a day of fasting and prayer, with great perfectness is form and apparent spirit; even the Sabbath is not generally so well observed as was that day. The fact that some 150,000 of the enemy are threatening this city and are only twelve to twenty miles from the place, has a wonderful influence in making the people in *earnest.*

Our Brigade—the 3d and 1st Division Army of the Potomac—which constitute a part of the reserve, under present arrangements, and it is now bivouaced in less than two miles East from this city. They have been in none of the skirmishes since we left the Peninsula. From there we came up to the city. I learn that the general health of the Regiment is improving and those who are here in the various hospitals are rapidly recovering. Three of Pulaski Guards have died of disease in the last fifteen days, but no others, from our Regiment, that I have heard of.

This is a cold, gloomy, rainy day, and, as yet, no *sensations* have enlivened the dismal aspect of affairs. It really seems strange that two such large armies should stand menacing each other so long and yet full confidence is felt that Gen. Johnson will manuevre our forces as to whip the fight when it does come—God grant that he may, and that this horrid war may be ended by a glorious victory at early day near this city. M. D.

Richmond, June 2d.

**Dear Courier:** The almost utter impossibility of obtaining anything like reliable information, is the only excuse offered for not writing sooner after the commencement of the recent battle near this city. On Friday from 4 o'clock P.M. until Saturday morning it rained almost incessantly, and much of the time, poured down in torrents. It seems that on Friday afternoon, a portion of McClellan's army, variously estimated at from 20,000 to 50,000—but generally rated at 35,000—men, crossed the Chickahominy. This stream in ordinary times is only a small creek but has low banks and a swampy bottom on either side, and rises rapidly with heavy rain, and spreads out over the swamp from 100 to 300 yards wide. This swamp is covered with a very thick growth of timber and undergrowth.

Our Generals knowing these facts, supposed McClellan's force to be by these circumstances cut off from reinforcements, attacked them near Bottom's Bridge, about eight miles from the city, Saturday morning. The Federals were already entrenched, and had a large amount of artillery. The fight soon extended along a line of four miles, and became one of the most desperate of the war. We had no artillery in the early part of the action. Our men charged their batteries in instances over an open field five hundred yards wide, in face of their cannon throwing grape and canister with the utmost rapidity, and took them at the point of the bayonet. The fight became general about noon, and continued until dark. The enemy had three lines of trenches, and from the two in front they had been driven back with a loss of all their artillery on these lines—some thirty pieces—several thousand stand of arms, a large amount of camp equipage, tents, baggage, commissary and ordinance stores, &c., &c.

The Hessians fought bravely, disputing every inch of ground; yet before the desperate charges of the chivalrous sons of the South, fighting for all that freemen hold dear, they fell back full three miles on this memorable day. Night then closing in, ended the fight for the day. Whenever the enemy opened a new battery our men charged it immediately with a shout, and it is said that late in the day when the feds heard this shout, they would not wait even to *see* the conquering heroes, but would anticipate the result of the charge and run at once, abandoning their guns and everything impeding hasty flight.

The loss has been heavy on both sides; that of the Lincolnites is of course unknown. According to the most reliable information, our loss in killed is in the vicinity of three hundred, and fifteen hundred wounded. It is to be hoped that this is an over estimate, as first reports are nearly always exaggerated; but a gentleman told me that he counted one hundred and sixty three of our dead on the right of the field. The wounded have been brought to the city as rapidly as possible, and are being very carefully provided for, the citizens, many of them at least, doing all they possibly can to relieve these unfortunate sufferers. 'Tis said there are an unusually large number who are only slightly wounded.

The victory, though not, perhaps, quite *complete* is nevertheless a most decided one, and will tend to greatly retract the "onward to Richmond" movement, even if it does not cause McClellan to abandon it until he is reinforced.[5]

On yesterday, Sunday, morning at 8 o'clock, the Yankees renewed the fight, which was continued for two and a half hours, with great activity on both sides. The enemy then gave back, and as a "trap" was expected our forces did not pursue them, hence no very decided advantage was gained by either side. Since then, it has been quiet on the whole line, except about the usual amount of skirmishing between the pickets. Yesterday our men were moving off the wounded and burying the dead. The fight was commenced Saturday on our side by Hill's and Longstreet's Divisions. Stewart's and Magruder's came up later. The 8th Georgia Regiment, neither any part of the 3d Brigade was in the fight. The 12th Miss., 6th Ala., 3d Ala., and the 12th Va., suffered great losses.

We lost a large number of officers Gen. Pettigrew, Col. Lomax, 3d Ala., and Gen. Hatton, of Tenn., were killed. Gen. Joseph E. Johnston was *slightly* wounded some say–others that his injuries are even *dangerous*.[6] Gen. Garland also was wounded severely. It is reported that we took 500 prisoners. The battle could be distinctly heard from Church Hill, in this city, even the rattle of musketry, which here sounded like the rushing of a mighty storm. The people were of course much excited, yet there was no panic nor indications of insanity. Most of the congregations at the churches yesterday morning were dismissed by the pastors, and the ladies requested to go home and cook for the wounded and men still on the battle field, and most generously did many of them do this.

6 o'clock Monday Evening. So far as I can learn, it has been quiet along our entire line to-day—in fact it seem almost ominous. Our troops are all in the very best of spirits, and though for the most part they refrain from boasting. There is a feeling of entire confidence in regard to the result of the great fight whenever it comes off. Such news as I may be able to obtain, will be sent to the *Courier* as soon as possible. The weather has hitherto been cool, but yesterday it was warmer, and to-day it is almost hot. M. D.

Richmond, June 13, 1862.

**Dear Courier:** Quiet yet pervades our lines, so far as fighting is concerned, and the "bloody conflict" *seems* no nearer than a week since. There is a possibility that Stonewall Jackson's successes in the Valley may put a very different phase on affairs here than what otherwise they would have assumed. What the notion of *this* army in reference to his movements, it would not be prudent to state; but Gen. Johnston—who, by the way, is reported to be convalescing—is a great strategist, and, if he does not out general McClellan, then present appearances are no criterion to judge by.

The 8th Ga. Regiment has not moved during the past week, but remain on the Nine Mile road, five miles from the city, near the residence of Mrs. Price, called Woodstock. The health of the men is now very much improved, and a larger number are now reported for duty than at any time since the battle of Manassas. Their duties are comparatively light—each company being on picket post but one day out of five—and, that they have no tents or but few blankets, yet they have nearly dry ground to sleep on. They get a plenty of flour and half pound of bacon per day, beside rice or peas for rations.

The enemy pay their respects nearly every evening, by sending some dozen or more of shells into the camp, but nobody has been hurt yet.

We may possibly be on the "pad" in a few days for some distant field—there is no telling in these war times what a day may bring forth.

The Car came through safely, under the careful management of Mr. Samuel Johnson, and no favors from home have ever been so joyfully received. The hardships and suffering of the past two months prepared the boys with a keen relish for the good things. The clothing was very much needed. God bless the ladies; they surely do not know how much their affectionate efforts in behalf of the men in the field cheer their hearts and nerve their arms. M. D.

Bivouac of 8th Ga. Regt.,
Woodstock, Va., June 18, 1862.

**Dear Courier:** This is the first time I have had the pleasure of addressing you from the quarters of the "bloody Eighth" since early in May. Woodstock is no village, but merely the beautiful former residence of Mrs. Price on a high bluff on the South side, and about a mile distant from the Chickahominy River. It is all open ground between this house and that stream and for some distance beyond, in some places, while in others, the woods on the other side skirt its banks. This river, that is already famous, and is likely soon to be swollen with the "crimson tide" from two immense armies, here makes a large curve—nearly a half circle—and we are in the "horseshoe."

This is the twelfth day our Regiment has done picket duty at this post, but as only two companies are out on the advance posts at a time, while the balance are held as a reserve, the duties are considered quite light. It is a healthy place, we get plenty of rations, and the consequence is a greatly improved state of health among the men. Companies that a month since reported only twenty-five or thirty men for duty, now report from fifty to sixty, and nearly all have a robust and hearty look.

Nearly every day, the Yanks shell us for an hour or two, but as yet only one man has been hurt on our side, a member of the Stephens Light Guards, wounded last Sunday. Mrs. Price's residence has been completely riddled, three cannon balls having passed through the roof, one through the walls and a shell bursted in the parlor. She had fortunately moved away in time to save most of her furniture. We have a battery just to the west of the house, and are now throwing up a redoubt on the north and east side, utterly ruining the very elegant and tastily ornamented yard. The house is about the centre of our regimental line, and probably the enemy throw more shot at it and the battery than at other places, yet they give us a sort of miscellaneous shelling once a day. To-day six or eight of their shells burst within twenty or thirty yards of companies A and B, whose position is in a narrow ravine, the banks of which are about twenty feet high. This makes a very complete protection, and as long as we remain in this "hall" there is but little danger.

There has been considerable firing between the pickets on our right today, and much moving noticed among the enemy, and it is thought by many that the great fight may commence tomorrow. If the enemy advance on our forces, we will have, in this immediate vicinity, at least, greatly the advantage. Our great danger lies in the possibility that the enemy may, with large force, drive back our forces above or below, and then, by a flank movement, cut us off.

On our Brigade line, there is no firing now, between the pickets on the outposts, and the feds show great anxiety to hold friendly intercourse with our men. They occasionally exchange papers, coffee for tobacco, &c., but all this is contrary to strict orders. The weather is now fine and has been for the past three days. The Chickahominy, here at least, is within its banks, and the time seems propitious for the great fight.

P.S. 7 o'clock, P.M. A heavy skirmish is now taking place on our right, opposite General Toombs' Brigade. M. D.

Bivouac of 8th Ga. Regt.,
Woodstock, Va., Friday, June 20.

**Dear Courier:** This has been rather a sad day in our Regiment owing to the fact that five men were seriously wounded at about noon. Four were members of the Pulaski Volunteers, viz: Robt. Lawson, Color Corporal, L. C. P. Jones, W. J. Mullis and J. J. Armstrong. The first two are reported to have since died; Armstrong's left knee is most horribly mutilated, and Jones is thought to be mortally wounded. Besides these one of the Atlanta Greys, whose name I did not learn, was slightly wounded in the heel. A piece of the same shell that produced these sad effects, struck within a few feet of Col. Towers, and another piece struck Capt. Scott's bunk, he being inside. This is the first serious disaster to our Regiment since being stationed at this post. One of the usual artillery duels was going on, and to which the men have become so much accustomed, as to hardly use sufficient caution, because previously, though hundreds of shells have struck very near, yet no one had been seriously hurt by the enemy. In the excitement of battle one can see men killed or horribly wounded, with comparative indifference; but when men are at leisure, to see and think of nothing else but the awful sufferings of their companions in arms, with whom they have stood "shoulder to shoulder" in many well contested battle fields, the soldier then as deeply spmpathises with the distressed, as if his vocation was less bloody.

The spring campaign has been very severe, and has told disastrously on our army, especially on the recruits. In the Miller Rifles, since the army fell back to Richmond, the following men have died, viz: Elisha Hawkins, B. F.

Reynolds, John Estis, and Jas. Perry; these all died in the Georgia Hospitals in Richmond.[7] It is reported that of the Floyd Infantry ten recruits have died, but I have not heard their names. The Light Guards have lost no men since our lamented young friend Scott Harden. There are none of the Light Guards or Miller Rifles that are known to be seriously ill at this time, though several are at Hospitals at Lynchburg, Liberty and other places, who have not been recently heard from.

Col. Towers' fine horse, "Bill Ramey" died of disease to-day. This loss is the more severe as such animals are now very scarce.

The difficulties, when on the Peninsula, and since, in preserving a suitable degree of cleanliness of clothes and person, has in numerous cases, resulted in such annoyances as would naturally be expected, where large bodies of men are crowded together. The weather continues fine.

So far as your correspondent can discover, there is no indications of an immediate general fight.

The Light Guards and Miller Rifles join in acknowledging the receipt of and returning thanks for a box brought by the last car, of most excellent dried fruit from some unknown donor. It was divided between these two companies and the Floyd Infantry. M. D.

Bivouac of 8th Ga., Regt.,
June 25, 1862

**Dear Courier:** This writing is merely to inform you that nothing of peculiar of general interest has occurred since my last letter. The shelling, in our immediate vicinity, has been much greater on both sides today than for several days previous, but no one hurt on our side, except a very slight wound in the hand of one of the Artillerists, and two horses wounded. Companies A and B are in a small ravine to the right of our batteries, while the balance are to the left, and separated from us some two hundred yards. Our situation is very secure one. If the Yanks could burst a shell at precisely the right place, they might hurt us severely; but as they cannot see our position—a hill intervening—it would be a chance shot that would burst in our midst. Occasionally they burst unpleasantly near. This morning the fragments of one fell in less than ten feet of us. Now as I write—2 ½ o'clock p.m.—the enemy's shells are passing over and a little to our right, at the rate of three in five minutes. Of course some apprehension is felt, but the loud whizzing of these missiles produces by no means the *fright* upon the men that it did while they were novices; in fact, many are entirely too careless, and unnecessarily expose themselves. It is so exciting to go out on the brow of the hill at a point where both the enemy's and our own batteries can be seen, and there watch the fight, that many are disposed to gratify their curiosity in this way, and a guard is now put out to keep such from unnecessary danger.

At 6 o'clock P.M., yesterday, orders were issued to cook three days' rations, and other indications pointed to a general fight to-day. So far as musketry is concerned, the picket lines in our vicinity have been more quiet yesterday and to-day than previously.

An Irishman, named Riley, deserted last week from the Oglethorpe Light Infantry (co. B), and it is stated in a recent copy of the *N. York Herald*, that he went over to the Feds.

The general health of the Regiment continues good, the men are in good spirits and fine fighting order. Our greatest annoyance, so far as personal comfort is concerned, is the myriads of flees and mosquitoes, that are most persistant in their petty torments.

Ample supplies of good bacon and flour are now issued for rations, with peas about half the time and rice and molasses occasionally—-coffee is "played out" except for those who can send to Richmond for it and pay $2,50 a pound. Sugar sells in the city at 75 cents per pound; Molasses at $5,00 per gallon; chickens a 1,00 a piece; butter a $1,50 per pound, and eggs a $1,00 per dozen. Those who try right hard can get very common corn whisky in the city at $4,00 per bottle. The very cheapest kind of calico shirts sell for $3,00 each, tolerable colored shirts at $6,00 to $8,00, and fine ones at $10,00 or $12,00. Good sewed shoes $16,00 a pair and heavy boots $25,00 to $40,00. The above may serve as specimens of war prices in Richmond.

Major C. H. Smith returned to duty last Monday. Col. Cothran and Cicero Smith made us a visit yesterday. We are always glad to see friends from home.

Gen. Joseph E. Johnston is reported to be gradually recovering.

4 o'clock P.M. The cannonading has considerably increased in the last hour—the enemy now firing about three shots a minutes. Their nearest battery is sixteen hundred yards from ours, and the most distant one they are aiming against this regiment, about two miles. They are now blazing away at us from four batteries. There is no telling what hour a general fight may be brought on, but neither army will be likely to cross the open field before our brigade. M. D.

Bivouac of 8th Ga. Regt.,
Woodstock Va., June 27.

**Dear Courier:** The great and long expected conflict, commenced in good earnest yesterday, the attack being made by Gen. Hill's Division, near the extreme left of our line. The conflict began by taking the bridge near Mechanicsville, strongly guarded by the enemy, and covered by batteries of their best guns. The charge here is reported to have been most gallant, our men having, for some half mile before reaching the bridge, to march right in the face of the Yankee cannon, pouring grape shot and canister upon them with almost incredible rapidity. Our brave men charge at double quick, and took first the bridge and then the batteries, at the point of the bayonet. This was the beginning of a series of grand successes made yesterday evening.

The enemy were without doubt surprised, yet they are said to have fought far better than their cause would seem to prompt them to, even gallantly. But they could not stand the impetuosity of freemen, fighting for all that is dear to noble minds, and excited almost to frenzy, by the brutal outrages of the insolent and haughty, yet dastardly and contemptible foe. Our forces drove the would be subjugators back, full five miles, before 8 o'clock, taking batteries, camps, cannon, small arms, camp equipage, commissary and medical stores, &c., in large amounts. The fighting continued till it was fully dark—the infantry not ceasing until after eight o'clock and the artillery until nearly nine.

The fight commenced about seven miles to our left, and, though we could see nothing but the smoke of battle we could hear sufficiently distinct, even the musketry, to shake the occasion exceedingly exciting. The Yankees immediately in front of our brigade, were shelling us with great rapidity all the time after 2 o'clock P.M., thus depriving us, to a large extent, of the enjoyment of the battle scene. We expected attacks all night, and companies A and B were deployed as skirmishers on the picket line, which post they occupied until daylight, when they were ordered to return—all except six or eight men—to the bivouac. When it was fully daylight it was discovered that the enemy's pickets in front of us had been withdrawn, and also all the cannon from the batteries that has been playing upon us daily, during the past month. Gen. Anderson asked permission to carry our brigade across the river and pursue the retiring enemy. This request was denied and it is now understood that we are to hold our present position during the great battle, unless driven from it, or needed to support the forces on our right.

The fight on our left was resumed at daylight this morning. Longstreet's command had been moved round to the left yesterday, and he was in command. It is said that Gen. Lee was there this morning and in command. The fighting was very brisk until 6 ½ o'clock, the roar of artillery and rattle of musketry being almost incessant. After that time it was more spasmodic until 10 ½ o'clock when it ceased until noon.

This morning, as yesterday, our forces swept everything before them, and the enemy has now fallen back about seven miles on the river, and fully twice that distance on the outside of their line. This morning the dastards commenced burning their camp equipage, and probably but little valuable property has fallen into our hands to-day. Since 10 ½ it seems that our forces had come to some difficult places in the highroad of success, they had previously so rapidly traveled.

The enemy are now all driven back to opposite our post. From 12 till 2 o'clock there was heavy fighting going on, some two miles back of the enemy's front line, and opposite to us, but with what results, we, from this point, cannot determine. They have been skirmishing and firing upon each other with artillery, nearly all the afternoon, but neither side has advanced.

It is now 5 o'clock P.M. For the past hour but little firing has been heard.

So far our loss is reported to be almost incredibly small, but no estimate of numbers have yet been made public. Our Regiment has not been shelled today at all. Our troops in sight are now advancing again. It is reported, and probably true, that Stonewall Jackson arrived at Hanover Court House, with a part of his command, on Wednesday. It seems that Jackson and Longstreet with their line of battle are at right angles with the enemys primitive line, and it is believed, are driving all before them.

Although, so far, everything has gone on swimmingly, yet the fate of the great battle is by no means decided—we may yet meet great reverses.

President Davis, dressed in a blue homespun suit, and straw hat, is here watching with eager eyes the tide of battle. His looks, physically, indicate exhaustion from severe and continued labors; calm confidence and hope predominate in his expressive countenance. Mr. Mallory, Secretary of the Navy is with him.[8]

The day has been bright, and would have been excessively hot, but for a delightful breeze. The fight may last for two or three days yet. M. D.

Bivouac of 8th Ga. Regt.,
Woodstock, Va., June 28, 1862

**Dear Courier:** This has been a disastrous day to the "bloody eighth." Yesterday at dark, we were moved out about a mile right oblique to the front from Mrs. Price's house, to be in supporting distance of Toombs' Brigade, who had been engaging the enemy in the vicinity of James Garnett's residence. We got in position at 9 o'clock and lay on our arms all night, expecting, if the enemy did not advance on us, to attack them at daybreak this morning, but for some reason we were not ordered to advance until about noon. We were then ordered to advance on, and charge a very strongly fortified and large battery of the enemy mounting fifteen guns, distant from us about 900 yards.

It is said that one Regiment of Tommbs' Brigade were ordered to make the charge with the 8th, but for some reason they did not do so, and we, with only about 450 men, dashed ahead. As soon as we had got in sight of the enemy's pickets, the Light Guards and Oglethorpe Light Infantry were thrown forward and deployed as skirmishers. The Regiment was moving forward in line of battle, and three companies were so deployed as to cover the entire front.

The skirmishers had not advanced 50 yards, before Sergt. W. S. Hutchings was severely wounded in the upper part of his left thigh. Lt. Moore stopped to take care of him, and the balance pushed forward. The enemy had a very heavy picket force, and with their excellent long range guns, they made it very hot for us, as we advanced on them. They could not stand the impetuous charge, and fell back in good order, but disputing every inch of ground. We had to charge through a field some 300 yards wide, while the enemy were under cover of woods. Our boys pressed forward, in spite of the murderous fire of the vandals, and soon gained the woods, where we were on an equal footing with them. Soon after striking the woods we came to a thick jungle, in a swamp and almost impassable. Our line was, however, kept much more perfect, than, considering the nature of the ground, could have been reasonably expected. After passing the swamp, we had to ascend the hill, on which the redoubt is built. The hill side is covered with pine timber, and all the undergrowth has been cleared away. On, on, charged the Regiment. Coming up to their rifle pits, we took them at the point of the bayonet. Up to this time the charge had been most successful on our part; but it was now painfully apparent that our force was too small, and that we were only occupying the front and right of this stronghold of the enemy.

They immediately moved a heavy force, with two cannon, down on our right flank, and were about cutting us off, when the order to fall back was given. The retreat was somewhat precipitate at first, but order was soon restored. While in the pits the men were completely protected from the Yankees, but as soon as they started back, a most murderous fire was poured upon them. If there had been another Regiment on our right, thus preventing our being flanked there, all agree that we could have taken the battery easy.

The list of casualties on our side, though a sad and painful one, is yet not so long as might be expected. According to the best information up to this time, 5 o'clock P.M., our entire loss in killed, wounded and missing, is between seventy-five, and a hundred.

Battle of Malvern Hill. Drawing by Alfred R. Waud. Library of Congress.

Col. Lamar was severely wounded and taken prisoner. Col., was taken prisoner; Maj. Magruder was slightly wounded in three places, a small piece shot off from the top of his nose, a flesh wound on the point of his right shoulder, and a bruise on the side from a piece of a shell. He is in good spirits and says he will fight the Yankees again in a few days.

The following is a list of all the killed, wounded and missing in the Floyd companies:

Light Guards. Killed—Stafford. Severely wounded—J. T. S. Johnson and W. S. Hutchings.[9] Marion Payne slightly wounded in the face; W. S. Booton, slight flesh wound in the right thigh.[10] Missing—Robert DeJournette and Wm. McKay.[11] It is believed that Dejournette remained on the field to take care of Johnson.

Miller Rifles. Killed—J. M. Martin, S. D. Asbury, W. A. Hardin and S. B. Wimpee.[12] Severely wounded—Lieut. Montgomery, Emmet Lee, F. M. Reynolds and J. A. Frix.[13] Slightly—J. W. Robinson, T. C. Estis and C. P. White, head.[14] Missing—H. L. Ware, and W. H. May, Lieut. Chas. Harper was taken prisoner.[15] He went inside the enemy's lines, after the fight, with a flag of truce, to look after the wounded, and, probably, unthoughtedly carried his pistol in his belt; this the Yankees discovered, and, charging him with acting in bad faith, took him prisoner. Of course he did wrong to go armed, while claiming the protection of a flag of truce, and I am afraid, they will hold him, though no one who knows him believes he intended to take a dishonorable advantage, even of the most despicable foes.[16]

Floyd Infantry. None Killed—Wounded—J. Hicks, J. R. Manning, and W. J. Dennon.[17] (I have not learned the extent of their wounds.) Missing—G. W. Pinson, and J. M. Green.[18]

It is altogether probable that a considerable portion of the missing are unharmed, and will soon come up to the Regiment.

The extent of the injuries inflicted upon the enemy is of course unknown, but believed to be very considerable. Five prisoners, all belonging to the 33d New York, were taken. Your correspondent had the pleasure of taking Capt. Hamilton, and is rewarded by being allowed to keep his fine pistol and sword. The pistol is of English manufacture, and of the very finest kind. Of course such trophies are very highly prized. Capt. Hamilton says he is a native of Brooklyn, New York; the other prisoners are all foreigners. M. D.

Bivouac of 8th Ga. Reg.,
July 2nd, 1862.

**Dear Courier:** The fight progresses and the excitement thickens, but the decisive blow has not yet been struck. Being in the midst of these stirring scenes, I can give but little information, except such as pertains to the action of our own brigade.

After the unsuccessful charge on the battery by the 8th Ga. Regt., (in which it was supported on the left by the 7th Ga.—a fact unknown to me at the time of writing on Saturday last) it was moved back about half a mile, where it remained until about 10 A.M. Sunday morning. It had been previously ascertained that the enemy had evacuated this stronghold, and the Brigade was ordered forward. They moved about six miles into the enemy's line and there supported Gens. Kershaw and Cobb in a brisk fight, but were not actively engaged. The enemy were driven back. After nine o'clock the Brigade was ordered to move back. It was raining hard, intensely dark and very muddy, and the men had a most disagreeable time until past midnight—in moving back some four miles. Monday morning—it being known that the enemy had retreated to near the James River—we commenced pursuit, marched by a circuitous course, starting towards Richmond, and then curving round and moving down the river. Halted at 11 o'clock and bivouced for the night. This march was a little more than the men could stand, and a large number fell out of ranks after dark. Most of these joined the Regiment in the morning. We were now, I suppose, about twelve miles from Richmond and two or three from the river.

Monday evening Gen. Longstreet's Division engaged the enemy near here, in a most desperate struggle. He twice charged their battery, taking it the second time—just before dark—but with great loss. The enemy *always* "skedaddle" as soon as their cannon are lost, and so the capture, in this case gave us the victory. Tuesday morning our army moved in pursuit, in columns of brigades. We had gone only about a mile, when it was ascertained that the Yankees had moved to the right, towards their gunboats. Our columns filed and moved by the right flank back some three miles, and then struck out towards the river. The enemy was found in a most advantageous position, but, for a wonder, without artificial fortifications. Then commenced the fiercest fight, and one with the largest numbers engaged, on both sides, that has yet occurred before Richmond. Brigade after brigade charged the Federal battery, of at least thirty guns, gave way and moved to the read. It was impossible to get our cannon into positions anything like equally advantageous.

Our Brigade made the charge at about 6 o'clock P.M., but before getting within rifle shot of the enemy, the storm of grape and canister was so great that Gen. Anderson gave the order to fall back—intending to move but a short distance to the rear, for the purpose of getting a more advantageous route to the much coveted battery. The order was not understood, or at least the intention was not known, and the Brigade fell back so far, and got so much scattered that it did not advance again. We had been under shells and all sort of cannon shot over three hours. The cannonading, in amount, far exceeded anything ever heard in this vicinity. Other Brigades, however continued to make the trial, but all without securing the prize. The fight lasted until after 10 o'clock. Each army held its position, yet it is certain the enemy believed themselves whipped, for before daylight this morning, they had "skedaddled" again. The loss was heavy on both sides, but I have no means at present, of learning how great.

Of the Light Guards, Hugh McCullough and Monroe Phelps were killed, advancing towards the foe.[19] Only sixteen of the company went into the charge.

Of the Miller Rifles only eight beside Capt. Scott went into the charge. None were killed, and but one, (Chambers) [*sic*] was wounded.[20] His wound is severe, but not thought to be dangerous.

The Floyd Infantry were in the fight.

It had rained hard all day, and no movement has been made of importance, that have heard of. Our cavalry are in pursuit of the enemy. Our men are nearly all broken down through fatigue, but are in good spirits. I write under great disadvantages, both from my own feelings and external circumstances. M. D.

Bivouac of 8th Ga. Regt.
Saturday, July 5th, 1862.

**Dear Courier:** Since writing to you on Wednesday, there has been no considerable fighting as far as I have been able to learn. The main body of the enemy has retreated to a large bend in the James river, where they are protected on three sides by that stream and on all sides their gunboats. Their retreat ought to have been cut off, and it reported that Gen. Huger is now under arrest for not occupying a certain portion to which he had been ordered for this purpose. The battle on Tuesday, July 1st, was fought on Crews' Farm, that of the 30th ult., on Frazer's Farm.

Thursday we remained in bivouac near Crews' Farm all day. The Brigade started on Friday, at 4 o'clock A.M. for this place. Nothing of peculiar interest occurred on the march. Stonewall Jackson's army is here, and many other troops. We are now twenty-five miles from Richmond, eight from Charles City C.H., and nine from Long Bridge. Appearances last night indicated that our forces would attack the enemy—who are in line of battle about three miles from here—early this morning. But it is now 8 ½ o'clock, and no demonstration has yet been made. Although the enemy has been retreating for now over a week, yielding one stronghold after another, yet it does not seem that they have been thoroughly and irrecoverably whipped. The Confederate army are now provided with sixty rounds of cartridges and preparation are being made as if a grand general engagement with the enemy, now concentrated, was expected.

The truth seems to be that the Federal army is so large, and their retreat has been conducted in such good order that is almost impossible to whip them all. No one field is large enough to meet them all at once, and while we are "walloping" one or two divisions, the others retreat, and seek an advantageous position.

The health of the men in our Regiment has improved with the last few days of diminished fatigue. The Light Guards yesterday had twenty-four men in ranks. There are none of the Floyd boys very sick that we know of—the absent ones having fallen to the rear, mostly from fatigue, and are coming on with the wagons. Scott Hutchings is doing well in Richmond, and expects to start home in a week or so. Marion Payne will probably join the company in a few days. Wm. McKay is probably a prisoner, as he has not been heard from. Col. Lamar is said to be doing well in Richmond. In their haste to get away, the Federals could not carry him, so he and some two hundred of their own wounded fell into our hands on last Monday.

5 o'clock P.M. All remains quiet so far as I can hear. We only have moved about half a mile to day. Captain Dawson is now in command of our Reg-

iment, and Lieut. R. T. Fouche is commanding his company, the Stephens Light Guards.[21] Most of the boys have spent the day in sleeping. M. D.

Sunday, July 6th, 1862.

**Dear Courier:** We still remain in the same place I wrote from yesterday and all has remained quiet along our line. Jackson's army is now in this immediate vicinity, and we are not certain but that our Brigade is under his command. It is thought that the position of the enemy in front is naturally better than our own, and that they are fortifying. Of general movements we can see nor hear nothing, but just have to keep our position and await orders.

A few particulars of the fight on the 1st inst., may be interesting to our readers. Monroe Phelps was killed a full half mile from the enemy's battery while making the charge. He was shot through the bowels by a cannon ball, cutting him nearly in two and mutilating his body in a most horrid manner. He was a modest young man, clever in all his ways, brave as the bravest, and always did his duty without murmuring. Hugh McCullough was killed at the furthest point to which the Regiment went in the charge. He was shot with a rifle ball just under the right eye, and fell instantly dead. A better or more useful soldier cannot be found. He was always busy doing good, and not only cheerfully performing his duty, but constantly sought out ways for serving his country and companions in arms. The remains of these two were brought out to near the road on Wednesday, by members of their company, and decently buried, their names and Regiment being marked on the head stone.

Tuesday morning we marched over the battle field of Monday evening, and our boys got a supply of Yankee rubber cloths, blankets, paper, envelopes, haversacks, &c. Hundreds of the dead and dying were still on the field, and the scene was heart rending and sickening in the extreme.[22]

10 ½ o'clock.—orders are issued to fall in, and I must close for the present. M. D.

Bivouac of the 8th Ga. Regt.,
Monday, June [*sic*] 7, 1862.

**Dear Courier:** Our Brigade moved yesterday only about a mile and a half to the front and we are now on picket duty on the left of our line. We have a picket guard in front, in sight of the enemy's pickets. The river is about a mile and half off—McClellan's main force being this side and little up the river from us. We heard their bands playing very distinctly last night. I suppose their gunboats can shell us whenever they please.

The men hold up wonderfully well considering the hardships they endure and the scanty fare. We get nothing to eat but fat meat and hard bread, and little enough of these. Cooped up here with the regiment in the woods I can learn nothing of general movements. Firing has been heard both up and down the river this morning—only a few cannon shots, however. 'Tis rumored that we have some field batteries on the river bank below, for the purpose of cutting off the enemy's transports. Two prisoners who voluntarily came into our line yesterday and surrendered, say that on Saturday the 28th ult., that Gen. McClellan had an order read to all his forces on his left, stating that his right wing had whipped out the Rebels on his right, taking a whole division prisoners, and that his right wing was then in Richmond. These men may have lied, but I would sooner believe that their General did. The general report from prisoners is that the Federal army is very much discouraged and entirely sick of the war. They are now aware that they have been deceived in many ways, but yet good discipline is maintained, and McClellan is reported to have 70,000 in one body, and daily expecting reinforcements. But God has blessed our arms with great success, and, with a continuation of His divine favor, we hope to make the victory complete. The gunboats is all that saves the invaders now.

The enemy were all day yesterday cutting down trees in front of us by thousands, but for what purpose we cannot discern. They are probably fortifying, making roads, bridging the swamp, &c., &c., but it may all be done for the purpose of making an early and safe departure on their transports and gunboats. The Lord grant that this may be their object, for it seems extremely rash for our Generals to attack them in their present position and strength, and under cover of their gunboats. But it may be possible to *starve* them out of their present position, and if so, they may bet their fill yet; so one hardly knows what to wish. If the reports are true, General Huger is responsible for the present favorable position of the enemy. Can it be possible that a *South Carolinian* GENERAL has finally betrayed our cause, just on the eve of the greatest victory the world ever saw! But he should not be condemned before an investigation. M. D.

# 6

# "The Sight of the 'Old Eighth' Is Now Saddening"

## *July–September 1862*

After all the fighting of the spring and early summer, the Eighth Georgia finally got some much-needed rest. In a letter on July 11, Melvin Dwinell said the men were enjoying the "sweet relaxation," even though everyone knew "this 'good time' can not be expected to last very long." In other correspondence, he provided more details of the fighting during the Seven Days Campaign and corrected a mistake when he wrote that the Light Guards were part of the charge during the fighting on July 1. Dwinell wrote, "Our ranks are now rapidly filling up," but he also expressed his suspicion that not all the men who were absent had been genuinely ill. "It is lamentably true that there are vastly too many men, even in our army, who 'shirk' their duty in times of great danger," he stated.

In early August, the men welcomed back their old lieutenant colonel, John Towers, who had been in Union captivity and exchanged. The Eighth Georgia was part of a force that was sent to counter a Federal probe near the old Malvern Hill battlefield. The intense heat made marching difficult, and what it all meant, the men did not understand. Because Gen. Robert Toombs commanded the other Georgia brigade in their division, Dwinell was sure that any real fighting was unlikely. Dwinell candidly noted that the troops increasingly questioned the general's "qualities as a fighting commander." Although Toombs often talked boldly, Dwinell wrote, the "men cannot comprehend the reasons for some of his actions if he is really so very anxious to fight."

In July, Dwinell traveled to Lynchburg, Petersburg, and other places "for the purpose of looking up men and baggage belonging to the Brigade." He took the opportunity to visit hospitals in the towns and found them to be in generally good condition, certainly far better than they were several months earlier. In another letter, Dwinell described what he said was "a very decided change in the religious tone of the army" in recent months. "There has been no great public demonstration in the way of revival meetings, or anything of that sort," he wrote, "Yet a quiet but deep work has evidently been going on in the hearts of large numbers of the patriot heroes now in the field." Many regiments held regular prayer meetings, and numerous men could be seen reading their Bibles daily.

In mid-August, the Eighth Georgia was on the move again. Gen. Robert E. Lee hoped to catch and trap the Union army commanded by Gen. John Pope. A week later, the regiment was moved up to support several batteries of Confederate artillery that were exchanging fire with Union artillery. For five hours, the men were under constant shelling without being able to return fire. Dwinell called it "one of the severest ordeals to which it is possible to subject even the best of troops." Fortunately, the Floyd County companies suffered only a few casualties.

Lee had decided to divide his army in an attempt to get around Pope's army. The Eighth Georgia was one of the regiments commanded by Gen. Stonewall Jackson that marched around the Union force in one of the most daring moves of the war. On August 28, the two armies met again on the Manassas battlefield. Dwinell had become ill and was one of several members of the Light Guards in the rear, so he provided only a general description of what was a tremendous victory for the South. Although the Light Guards were in the vanguard of the fighting at Second Manassas, the company had only minor casualties. Dwinell closed his letter by telling readers, "When or where you will next hear from us the Lord only knows. If no great reverse overtakes our army, we may be in Maryland before you read this letter."

Indeed, the Army of Northern Virginia followed up its victory at Second Manassas by invading Maryland early in September. They left behind thousands of men from various regiments, including many members of the Eighth Georgia. Dwinell was among these soldiers. In fact, few members of the Rome Light Guards—and none of the officers—took part in the Battle of Sharpsburg, or Antietam, as it was known in the North. Aside from describing the battle as "one of the bloodiest of the war," Dwinell had little information about the shattering loss for the Confederacy. By the time he rejoined the regiment, only about 150 members were present for duty. After four months of heavy fighting, the sight of the Eighth Georgia had become "saddening," the editor frankly told readers. Many of the men did not have shoes or a change of clothing, and virtually all of them were exhausted from the constant fighting of the past several months. Every officer in the regiment had signed a petition requesting that the Georgians be assigned to post duty to give the men time to recuperate. "There is such a thing as killing the life and fire of a regiment long before the last man is killed," Dwinell wrote. "It would seem that our officers have been trying the experiment on the Eighth, to see just how much a body of troops could endure."

Bivouac of 8th Ga. Regt.,
July 9th, 1862.

**Dear Courier:** Since my letter of Tuesday last, nothing of exciting interest has occurred in our Brigade, or, so far as I can learn, within our lines. The Brigade remained on picket post until yesterday eve, when we ordered to move to this place, some 14 miles in a direct line, towards Richmond, but the way we came, zigzagging by small cross roads, we marched fully 20 miles. The march was continued without halting, except to pass mudholes and other impediments, until after daylight, when we rested about two hours, and arrived here at 11 A.M.

We are now some 10 or 12 miles from the city, and probably 6 or 8 miles from Drewry's Bluff—I cannot learn the distance to the latter place. Our rations gave out last night, and the way the commissaries were abused, for supposed indifference to the wants of the men, who endure the hardships of this terrible war, was without stint or measure. It has been intolerably hot during the past three days, and when the Brigade arrived here, the men wore out with fatigue and want of sleep, were almost famished with hunger, and ready to melt with heat. Rations were issued at 1 o'clock P.M. and now—3 P.M.—better humor prevails, as the demands of hunger have been satisfied.

The other brigades that had been in the vicinity of the position we left yesterday, withdrew before us, and we covered the retreat. After offering battle four days to the Yankees at that point, it was probably deemed useless to keep troops longer in that position. How long we are to remain here, or where next moved to, is of course unknown to me.

Many little incidents of the late battle would doubtless be interesting to your readers. I will give one. C. L. Johnson of the Light Guards took one of the enemy's sharp shooters on the 2nd inst. under the following circumstances: Johnson went over to the hospital on the other side of the battle field, where the wounded Hessians were being cared for by their own surgeons.[1] He saw a Yankee coming up with a rifle on his shoulder. He approached him and said, "unless we get our wounded off soon the rebels will get them." The Yankee said "that is so." Johnson asked him permission to take his rifle and examine it. This was readily granted and Lorraine then told him that he was a prisoner. The gun, which J. retains, is a splendid one, with globe sights, and the Yankee boasted that he had picked off several rebel officers with it. The scoundrel stated that every regiment in the Federal army, had a corps of sharp shooters whose special business in battle is to kill officers, and that they get fifteen dollars a month extra pay. Such scamps, thus bribed to duty even hazardous, ought to receive more severe punishment that of mere imprisonment.

The men in our brigade have not had an opportunity to change their clothes in now nearly two weeks, and their looks and feelings can probably be better imagined than described.

There are no new cases of serious sickness in the Floyd county companies, and the boys are in good spirits' but greatly desire rest and the chance to clean up.

Yesterday evening the Federals fired several salutes of twenty-one guns each. What was the occasion or why this number, we cannot divine. It may be in reference to something pertaining to the twenty-one *loyal* States. 'Tis to be hoped that they will soon be compelled to use this manner of guns, or a less one, for their national salute.

5 o'clock Thursday morning. Orders are issued to march—probably to a position on the river, two or three miles below Richmond. M. D.

Camp of 8th GA., Regiment.
Friday, July 11, 1862

**Dear Courier:** Thank God we are more and more in *camp*, with a good supply of "flies" to shelter us from the sun and rain. This location is three miles from Richmond, on the Charles City road, and the prospect is good for a few days, at least, of quiet and rest. What a "change has come over the spirit of our dreams" already! How changed is the general expression of countenance from what it was four days since. Now sweet relaxation and calm, pleasing placidity has taken the place of the stern rigidity of grim visaged war, "and instead of forming battle lines "to fright the souls of fearful adversaries," we eat our "grub" and smoke our pipes with none to molest or make us afraid. Of course, this "good time" cannot expected to last very long. The enemy are not all dead, nor are they a thousand miles distant. When they get a little rested from the fatigues of last week and the week before—for they were very much out of breath after their skeedaddling—yet new leaders and a portion, at least, of their new levy of three hundred thousand more troops—when all this is done, then probably—if our cousins across the big waters do not think this foolishness had continued long enough and interfere to stop it—they will again commence the "on to Richmond" movement. But, for the present, the "weak, piping times of peace" are enjoyed with great gusto, and the troops are disposed to verify the old adage "when the old cat is away then the rats and mice will run and play." No one who has not been placed in similar circumstances, can possibly appreciate the present feelings of this army. During fourteen successive days they were all either actually under the fire of the enemy, or momentarily expecting to be; were making rapid and forced marches, with short allowances of rations, no changes of clothing, and none of the ordinary comforts of even camp life. But what of all this! A most glorious victory over the proud and haughty foe has been achieved, and those who have done and suffered most are proudest of their part in the struggle.

Our ranks are now rapidly filling up. It is lamentably true that there are vastly too many men, even in our army, who "shirk" their duty in times of great danger. It may be a curious fact that always just before battles there are an unusually large number of *sick*; some become fatigued very quick and absent men, on their way returning to their respective commands, find it unaccountably difficult to find them. Well, I suppose this is "accordin to nater," as Pathfinder would say. None wish to be killed, and comparatively few are ambitious to establish a fighting reputation. Yet, it is true, that every man ought to do his duty and he should not be excused from it under any mere *pretense.*

There is no news in our camp worth writing. There was a fine rain last night and this morning, and now the air is pure and pleasant. So far as I can learn, the wounded are all doing well, and are receiving the best possible care. A. C. A. Huntingdon was elected 3rd lieut. in the Miller Rifles last Wednesday. He has been a faithful good soldier, and has doubtless merited the promotion he has received. Capt. G. Oscar Dawson is now in command of this Regiment, and has been since June 28th. The 7th Georgia is in command of

Capt. Carmichael.[2] The loss in officers, in the recent fights, was unusually large. M. D.

Bivouac of 8th Ga. Reg.
July 17th, 1862.

**Dear Courier:** Human hopes are everywhere and at all times fallacious, but at no place or under any circumstances more so than to an army in the field. When I last wrote to you, we were in camp, surrounded with the means of comparative comfort; but yesterday morning at 5 o'clock, orders were received by our Brigade, to be ready to march out on picket in one hour. So there was a hasty packing up of "duds," falling in, and moving off. Our picket post reserve is on the Darbytown Road three miles East from camp, and the videt post, about a mile in advance of the reserve. Our regular camp, is between the Charles City and Darbytown roads, and to the South of the former.

There is nothing of peculiar interest to communicate from the past. It is understood that we are to remain here but two days. Last night there was a heavy shower, and all hands got a thorough soaking. The reports for rations are made out two days before they are actually issued, and, as the convalescent sick and stragglers are coming into the Regiment at the rate of from twenty-five to fifty a day, there is a continued shortness of supply, and, consequently, much complaint among the men. It don't do well to try to starve soldiers for if this is done they become mutinous directly.

The Floyd Infantry were *not* in the charge with the Regiment on the 1st inst., and it was so stated in my letter of the 2d, but the printer, by leaving out the word *not*, reversed the meaning.

Robt. Wade was elected 2d Lieutenant Junior in the Miller Rifles yesterday, to fill the vacancy occasioned by the resignation of Dr. Boyd.[3] Under the present law, and the construction of it given by our Generals, companies in our Regiment can only elect the 2d Lieutenant Junior, all other vacancies are filled by regular promotion.

Joe Dunnahoo, of the Floyd Infantry, is reported to have died at the hospital in Richmond, a few days since. This patriotic soldier, like many another, suffered and died for his country, without having an opportunity of meeting the enemy in the field, but they will all be remembered by a grateful country, as martyrs to our glorious cause.

The remains of J. T. S. Johnson, were enclosed in a good plain coffin, and buried near the Brigade Hospital on the Nine Mile Road, about four miles from Richmond. The deceased was one of the best of soldiers, constant at his post, and cheerfully doing his duty. Of his bravery there can be no doubt, when it is known that he volunteered to be one of the color guards—a place of known danger.[4]

"After life's fitful fever he sleeps well."

All is quiet both along our lines and those of the enemy, so far as I can learn. There are some rumors of movements, but any disclosure would be imprudent.

If the friends of the Regiment should send another car, a suggestion or two may not be out of place. Bread, cakes, (except ginger cakes) pies, and cabbage in warm weather, nearly always spoil on the way. Boxes containing vegetables of any kind should be well perforated, so as to give a free ventilation. Dried fruit would be particularly acceptable—and there is nothing better than Irish potatoes and onions. Potatoes sell here for 50 cts a quart, and onions at a dollar a dozen. It is hardly possible for a soldier to get vegetables of any kind.

Richmond Va July 28 '62

**Dear Mother:**

My health is now good, and has been, generally, since I wrote you last. I still belong to Co. A. 8th Reg—am now 1st Lieut.

A letter directed to my Co. and Reg. Richmond Va. might reach me. Remember me kindly to all relatives and friends and accept my hearts warmest affections for yourself and my dear Father—Your Afth. Son Melvin

Camp of 8th Ga. Regt.,
August 1st, 1862.

**Dear Courier:** The reason of my not writing, during the past two weeks, is owing to absence, visiting Farmville, Lynchburg, Liberty and Petersburg, for the purpose of looking up men and baggage belonging to the Brigade. The hospitals in those places were visited, and found to be in good condition; and with the exception of those in Lynchburg, and a portion of those in Petersburg, not half filled to the extent of their accommodations. System, order and cleanliness generally prevail, and in every way the hospitals, in Richmond and all the other places that have come under the writers observation, are now much better than six since. The wounded in the recent fights, in the main, are doing remarkably well—in fact much better than could have been reasonably expected—and so far as your correspondent could learn, no very malignant disease anywhere prevails. A few weeks since the typhoid fever was raging rather fearfully at Camp Winder in Richmond, but it has now considerably abated. An effort is being made to reduce the number of sick in the hospitals in Richmond, but some fatal epidemic might rage there during the sickly months of August and September. To effect this, sick camps, for each brigade, are now established near these several commands, and to these camps all new cases are carried. Especially at this season of the year, this is, without doubt, far better than being sent to large hospitals.

Our present camp is ten miles Southeast from Richmond, and probably about two miles from the James River. Our distance from Drury's Bluff is said to be nine miles. We are on picket duty, and our camp, is said by the citizens living near, was occupied by the American forces in 1812, and was then named Camp Holley.[5] The Brigade has been here since the 24th ult.

Absentees are gradually returning, and our Regiment now reports about four hundred for duty. The country around is rather level without being flat, and mostly piney woods. The waste is abundant and good, and the situation has every indication of being a healthy one.

What is being done by the army in the vicinity of Richmond, of course, would not be prudent to state, but the country may be assured that it is not idle, or losing any of its efficiency. Most of the regiments, except a comparative few belonging to those brigades that did not go the peninsula, and that also suffered most severely in the recent fights—are now in better condition, and numerically stronger than when the grand series of conflicts commenced. During the first two weeks of last month, the 8th Georgia Regiment was a "skeleton," in numbers, sure enough. As an example to illustrate the lean supply of officers at one dress parade, the following facts are given in regard to the positions of the officers of the Rome Light Guards: Capt. Hall was in command of the regiment; the 1st lieutenant was in charge of his own company. Lieut. Fouche had command of Co. I, and Lieutenant Moore acting adjutant. Owing to their own good fortune, probably, and not to any direlection of duty on the part of the officers of other companies, it is yet a fact that the Rome Light Guards have come nearer having a full attendance of officers all the time during the past three and four months, than any other company in the regiment.

There recently has been no lack of rain here. Yesterday it rained nearly all the time. When not raining it is exceedingly hot—the great humidity of the atmosphere preventing copious perspiration, and producing a kind of stifling sensation.

Whortleberries and blackberries are abundant in this vicinity, and their free use, doubtless, contributes largely to the good health of the troops. If sugar could be had, delicious pies from these berries could be made in abundance.

Last night about 12 or 1 o'clock, we heard rapid and continuous cannonading, probably some eight or ten miles down the river. Its cause or result has not been made known here yet. M. D.

Camp of 8th Georgia Regiment,
August 4th, 1862.

**Dear Courier:** It is hot, hot, hot—too hot to move, and too hot to sit still—too hot to stand, sit or lie down—so hot, in fine, that "one feels like laying off his flesh," as has been quaintly observed, "and sitting in his naked bones to cool himself."

Our camp is in a field, but we are provided with good fly tents, and nearly every mess has a bush arbor, erected in front and yet the scorching rays of this dog-day's sun penetrates everything everywhere. Languor and debility is the prevailing characteristic of present appearances throughout this camp. What a horrid time this would be for a great battle! Yet it might be comparatively to our advantage; for if those "to the manor born" suffer from the great heat, how much more must our foes from the cold regions of the North. But so far as fighting is concerned, there seems to be no indication of a general conflict in this immediate vicinity soon; yet McClellan's position is such that he might make a sudden advance upon our forces on either side, or even both sides, of James River, any day.

Camp duties are now sufficiently arduous to furnish an ample provision for that amount of physical exercise necessary for good health. Our Regiment furnishes seventy men each day for fatigue duty—throwing up entrenchments—one company a day for a picket post about a mile and a half from here, and the whole Regiment goes on picket for one day, to Malvern Hill (the battle ground of July 1st) once in nine days. Malvern Hill is about four miles from this camp.

There is no excitement here whatever, and our principal enjoyment is obtained from the "good news" in the morning papers. No one more fully realize the cost or more full experience the pleasure of victory than the veteran soldier of several hard fought battles. Our long catalogue of recent successes, has had a greatly inspiring effect in the Confederate army.

There are very few cases of sickness in this Regiment; none of serious character. The absentees continue to return, and the ranks are speedily filling up. The "old Eighth" yet has over seven hundred names on its muster rolls, but only about four hundred in camp.

Car No. 6 will be looked for with much pleasure. M. D.

Camp of 8th Ga., Reg. Aug. 5.

**Dear Courier:** In no sublunary affairs do "coming events cast their shadows before" with less clearness than the soon-to-be movements of skillful Generals to the men in line. When my letter of yesterday was closed there was no apparent prospect of excitement today, yet it has turned out to be a day of no small interest and of exceedingly great fatigue to the 8th Georgia Regiment. This morning at 5 o'clock the Regiment left camp for Malvern Hill—distant four or five miles—for the purpose of doing picket duty. Before half the distance had been marched, brisk cannonading was heard in that direction. Nothing was learned in regard to this firing until the Regiment was in less than a mile of the Hill, when a courier came up and communicated to the following as a statement of existing facts. The Ga. Troopers, Stribling's Battery and the 17th Ga. Regiment composed our force picketed there. At about 11 o'clock last night a courier came to them with the information that our pickets on the post to their left had been driven in by the Federal cavalry. The commander at the Hill is said to have sent word back to the commander of the post on his left that if he would hold his reserve post, then the former would hold the Hill, at least, till reinforcements could come to his assistance. Our forces at the Hill received no further news of the enemy's movements during the night nor of the intentions of our forces on their left, but at daylight discovered that the Yankees were on two sides of them, while the river full of gunboats was on the third. The forces of the enemy was judged to be a brigade of infantry, two or three regiments of cavalry, and a battery of artillery, in position ready to open upon our, apparently, devoted little band. The best disposition of our forces, at that place, that time and circumstances would admit, was hastily made before the enemy's battery opened. Stribling's Battery returned their fire with spirit until their ammunition gave out, which occurred just as the 8th Ga. Regiment had got up in supporting distance. The 8th had been shelled from the gunboats as we moved down the road, but without effect, and it was halted under cover of some woods about five hundred yards from out Battery—company A was deployed out in front as skirmishers, the cannonading still going on briskly from the field batteries on both sides. Soon some dozen of our cavalry pickets came dashing up the road and said they were obliged to run to save themselves, as they were being surrounded. Within less than a half hour from the time we had got into position, our artillery, having exhausted their ammunition, came up the road, followed by the cavalry, while our infantry force came round under cover of woods, and thus left the famous Malvern Hill in complete possession of the foe. *What should be done* was now a painful question, and this was only intensified by an order from Gen. Toombs—who commands the picket post in this vicinity—to hold the position that had just been surrendered. Major Picket, of the 17th Ga. Regiment, was the ranking officer present, and he very soon, and without doubt, wisely, declared that we should fall back until the expected reinforcements should be met.[6] This was no sooner decided upon than the enemy's cavalry were seen advancing up the road towards us. Our small company (the Ga. Troopers) soon formed and charged down upon them but were at once repulsed. But the vandals did not choose to charge up to our infantry. They very soon, however, and before we could get into good order from the confusion occasioned by the Troopers, in their retreat, dashing through our men in a narrow lane, brought forward two pieces of cannon and opened on us at a distance of less than 500 yards. Captain Dawson moved his Regiment at once into a wheat field on the left and continued the retreat as rapidly as good order and the very difficult walking through the heavy growth of uncut and tangled grain would admit of. We thus marched for over a half mile under as rapid fire as the Yankees are capable of, but thanks to their bad aiming and the meager protection of the slightly rolling ground no one was hurt. Major Picket, without being discovered, probably took this Regiment up the road in complete safety.

The retreat was continued to within a mile and half of camp before information was received that the reinforcements had been sent round by another road—probably because the river road is in dangerous proximity to the river. Geo. Morton was indisposed and is missing. The 8th was ordered to a position on a cross road where it remained about half an hour, when it was ordered back to camp. Arrived there at 10 ½ o'clock, A.M., but were not dismissed before another order came to form line of battle about a mile distant. So off we moved again. The day has been intensely hot, and the men already having marched nearly ten miles, were greatly exhausted. Arrived at the place designated and rested in a delightful shade until 1 o'clock P.M., when orders came for another move. We were now marched down the river road to within sight of the Federal pickets and set to watch them. Company A was put on the out post, the balance of the Regiment acting as a reserve. The instructions were if the enemy should be seen to advance in force, then the pickets would shoot at them and fall back. We had to wait but a short time before our pickets on the road—P. Cohen, S. Beal and R. D. Boggs—saw the Federal cavalry advancing. They fired and ran in. The Regiment was some 75 yards from the road in thick pine woods—the Federals dashed down the road in large numbers, firing volley after volley, in the direction of our forces.

As soon as the pickets came in the Regiment commenced the retreat, but even then the cavalry got ahead of us, and nothing but the thickness of the woods prevented their charging in on us. The cavalry alone was not feared, but we had strong reasons for apprehending that a heavy infantry force was at the same time moving down upon our left. We moved back in a hurry, for about a mile. No body hurt however. Two or three men who had gone to a spring for water have not yet come in—they may have been taken prisoners. Arrived at camp again at 10 o'clock, P.M., completely tired out.

Nine o'clock Wednesday morning. We were ordered up at one o'clock this morning, struck tents and packed up, and we were ready for another jaunt today. A fight is expected. The baggage has been sent to the rear.

11 o'clock—Our brigade is in reserve. A rumor has come in that our cavalry scouts have been to Malvern Hill and even beyond, and that no enemy has been found. I supposed we have only held it for thus long for the purpose of securing the forage in that vicinity. I exceedingly regret to hear that Marion Stovall is missing, and it is feared that he was taken prisoner.

6 o'clock, P.M. The rumor that the Federals had again evacuated Malvern Hill was not true. Our Brigade is now said to be in the same position that it was just before making the charge on the 1st of July. Your correspondent being indisposed, has not been with the Regiment to-day. It is reported that we have very large forces in the vicinity of the Hill, and heavy skirmishing between the pickets has been going on. A great battle is expected soon. Large numbers from the 8th Regiment were exhausted and broken down, and returned to the rear today. M. D.

Thursday Morning, Aug. 7, 1862.

**Dear Courier:** Since closing my letter last night, I have learned that our cavalry engaged in the skirmish of Tuesday morning was compose of parts of three companies, viz: Georgia Troopers, Fulton Dragoons and Co. R. of Richmond Ga. Hussars.[7] Gabriel Jones of the Miller Rifles has been missing since that time, and it is feared that he was taken prisoner in the retreat. Last night about nine o'clock a discharge of musketry was heard in the direction of Malvern Hill battle field. It sounded like a volley from a regiment shooting, and was followed by a scattering fire for a few minutes. Nothing has been heard from it up to this time—eight o'clock.

It was exceeding hot during the middle of the day yesterday, and there is every prospect of its being so again today. I have heard no firing yet this morning. It is thought by some that the enemy's demonstration down here, in the vicinity of Malvern Hill, some 12 or 14 miles from Richmond, is for the purpose of trying to draw the attention of the majority of our forces to this place, and then rush up with their gunboats and heavy infantry forces on transports, as near as they can with safety to Drury's Bluff; land behind us and rush on to Richmond.

Gen. Robert Toombs. Library of Congress.

Two o'clock, P.M.

Toombs' Brigade and our own are now on Malvern Hill again—at the very place where the great battle of July 1st was fought. The enemy evacuated last night. The field is considerably changed in appearance since the writer last saw it. The ground then charged over seemed entirely naked, but now it is covered with a very tolerable growth of corn. The enemy's advance here was probably only a feint to cover some other movement, but what it is has not yet transpired. Your correspondent joined the Regiment again this morning.

The firing last night was by some of Cobb's Legion, firing upon some Yankee cavalry scouts, who had dismounted and were skulking through the woods. Two of the vandals, wounded, were found on the ground this morning. Some ten or twelve Yankees were taken prisoner "hereabouts" last night.

Friday Morning, 8th.

Before our Brigade left, we made a thorough reconnoisance of Malvern Hill. The high table land extends South, towards the river, about a mile beyond the battle ground. Our troops were carried to an extreme bluff. As the Brigade in advance approached this verge of the highland, they saw the Yanks drawn up in line of battle to the left, and less than a half mile distant, but they skedaddled immediately.

We were told by negroes on the hill that the vile Hessians left their camp in the middle of the night. These same unfortunates say there was 20,000 of them—some say it was Gen. Sumner's Division. We are now satisfied that our retreat on Tuesday morning, was not only prudent but timely, and skillfully managed.

The Brigade left Malvern Hill at 4 o'clock P.M. yesterday, and arrived in camp at about sundown. We have done three days of very hard duty, but nobody has fired a gun, except some half dozen who were on picket post Tuesday afternoon.

A grand demonstration by the enemy is expected soon. It now seems probable that it will be on the other side of the river. Everything is quiet this morning.

Col. Towers and Billy McKay, having been exchanged, returned to this vicinity last Tuesday.[8] They are now in Richmond, and are expected in camp to-day. It is a very clear and hot morning.

In Camp, 5 o'clock P.M.

The Regiment has been quiet to-day, except fifty men have been throwing up breastworks. It is rumored this evening that the enemy are again advancing towards Malvern Hill. What all these movements and counter movements will amount to we cannot divine. Gen. Morton and Gabriel Jones have neither been heard from yet. It had been exceedingly hot to-day and is becoming quite dusty. M. D.

Camp of 8th Ga. Regt.,
August 11th, 1862.

**Dear Courier:** It may be a violation of a strict construction of the third commandment to address a few lines to you, yet I feel it to be a sort of religious duty to improve this earliest opportunity—Sabbath—though it be to inform the numerous friends of this Regiment in Rome and vicinity, that the expectation of an immediate fight, on this side of the river, has passed away, and all has been quiet on our lines since last Thursday. It is now very evident that the enemy re-surrendered Malvern Hill on that day without a fight, because they feared to contend with the force they saw approaching. An old negro at their headquarters said he heard one of their officers say that it would be useless for them to contend against three such columns coming from as many different directions. So we re-took the Hill without firing a gun—the foe receding as our forces approached.

The popular idea, in the army, of Gen. Toombs' qualities as a fighting commander, may be inferred from the general talk throughout our Brigade on Thursday morning. The almost universal expression was, that "there is no danger of a fight to-day, for Toombs' Brigade is ahead." Of course a man who talks as strong and loud as he does, has made strenuous efforts, for himself and command, "to have a place in the picture near the flashing of the guns." But the misfortune to *him* is, *common* men cannot comprehend the reasons for some of his actions if he is *really* so very anxious to fight.

Last night two wagon loads of the contents of Car No. 6 arrived in camp. These arrivals of good things from home produced the happiest emotions the soldiers ever experienced in camp. If the loved ones at home could know but half the pleasure they thus produce is so sweetening the hard fare of army rations they would, I am sure, feel more than compensated for the trouble and expense incurred. Ten thousand thanks to all those who have so kindly and generously cheered the hearts of the hardy soldier boys. Some of us who have neither "kith nor kin" from whom such affectionate remembrances might be expected, feel particularly grateful for the generous supplies received. Two wagon loads of the boxes arrived in camp last night, and were soon opened with eager hands. So far as examined, nearly everything came through in perfect order, and the contents of the boxes was precisely such things as are most acceptable.

Messrs. Davis, Rogers and Barber deserve credit for having, with untiring energy and carefulness, secured the early and safe arrival of the Car.

This morning at 2 o'clock the Brigade was ordered to strike tents pack up and be ready to march by daylight. This was unexpected, and particularly unpleasant to the Floyd county boys, as, with the move, would probably come the loss of all the good things from home. As usual no intimation was given as to where we were going. The column was put in motion towards Richmond at 6 ½ o'clock, and at 10 we arrived here at our old camp, three miles from the city. The boxes left behind have all been brought up, and we now have another prospect of enjoying their contents. Unless there is another move ordered, the balance still in the city will probably be brought out to-morrow. These are very precarious times, and we are liable to move almost any hour.

Mr. Kaufman had a severe attack of sun stroke last Friday—hoped to be better. There are no other cases of severe illness among the Floyd boys that I have heard of. M. D.

Camp of 8th Ga. Regiment,
August 12, 1862.

**Dear Courier:** This morning three days' rations were issued with orders to cook them, and be in readiness to march at the shortest possible notice. This was very unwelcome tidings to the Floyd county boys. They had just got a full view and a slight taste of the good things from home, by Car No. 6, and the idea of having to leave them all was provoking indeed. It is now late in the afternoon, and no farther orders have come yet. It is thought, probable, that we may go to reinforce Stonewall Jackson, but some think we are bound for East Tennessee. The good news from Jackson is cheering. A gentleman has just told me that he saw 29 Yankee officers in *"hand cuffs"* who had been taken last Saturday by Jackson's men. One of them complained and commanded that he would be carried to the commander of the post to be relieved of his arms. He was carried to old Gen. Winder, whom he asked if he was not to be treated as a prisoner of war. The brief reply was that he was no prisoner of war, but a vile plunderer and murderer—and the guard was ordered to take the aforesaid Yankee away immediately, the General refusing to hold any continued conversation with him.

These officers are said to have told their guard that they had never heard of President Davis' Proclamation providing measure of retaliation for their thieving and plundering in the Valley under the orders of Gen. Pope. The general impression in our army is, that these retaliatory measures will work admirably. The rumor is that Yankee officers have already attempted to disguise themselves as privates. If they hang one of our citizens or commit any of their inhuman threats, it is to be hoped that their officers may swing at least two for one. To-day has been perhaps the hottest day of the season.

Tuesday morning 6 o'clock. No orders to march received yet. M. D.

Bivouac of 8th Ga. Regiment, near
Gordonsville, August 14, 1862.

**Dear Courier:** Yesterday morning at 1 o'clock the long roll beat in our brigade. Tents were struck, baggage packed, and the Regiments were in line ready to march at 2 o'clock. The order soon came to move towards Richmond, where we arrived just at break of day. The marching of the Brigade to the vivinity of the Capital Depot, made it evident that this force was going to join Jackson's army in the neighborhood of this place. Toombs' Brigade took the cars before us, and we were delayed till 10 ½ o'clock in getting off from Richmond. Nothing of interest occurred on the route. Stopping a short time at Beaver Dam Station, we had a chance to see the result of Yankee depredations at that place some two weeks since. They burnt the depot and a store-house, containing 175 barrels of flour and a considerable quantity of arms and ordinance stores. Arrived at Gordonsville at 4 o'clock P.M.; remained in line about two hours and were then marched in a southerly direction, about three miles to this place, where we bivouaced for the night. It is understood that the Brigade will move a short distance to-day to some place where it will remain until the wagons got through from Richmond.

Southwest Mountain, where the battle was last Saturday, is some twenty-five miles from Gordonsville and about four miles from Culpepper C.H. A gentlemen who says he walked over that battlefield four times on Sunday asserts that he there counted 600 of the Federal dead, and could only find about 50 of ours.[9]

We are now in a high mountainous country, with good water, and the prospect for good weather is much better than in the flat, dide-water country we have left. It may not be generally known that the tide ebbs and flows regularly twice every twenty-four hours, on the James River, as high up as the Falls opposite Richmond. In a full tide, the water there rises about two feet.

Kaufman still continues very sick—is now at a private house in Richmond; Captain Hall has a swelling on his ankle, that incapacitates him for marching, and he remained at Richmond.[10] This is the first time he has failed from sickness to move with the Regiment since we have been in service. Billy Omberg has been detailed as forarge Master in the Ordnance Department.[11] W. A. Choice to write at division headquarters, and Barna is attached to the band.[12] The butcher of our Regiment, named Glenn, formerly of Philadelphia, was drowned while bathing in James River last Monday. He was a pleasant young man and very capable and efficient in his sphere.

The air here is pure and bracing, and much cooler than in the vicinity of Richmond. M. D.

Bivouac of 8th GA. Regiment,
Near Gordonsville, Va.,
August 15, 1862

**Dear Courier:** We still remain at the place where we bivouacked on Wednesday night. All is quiet around here, and, so far as heard from, throughout Jackson's army. The enemy are reported to have very heavy forces at Madison Court House—about 25 miles from here—and also at Culpepper C.H., about the same distance East. Whatever indications there may be of the particular place of the grand assault nothing like satisfactory information has come to the knowledge of the writer. Preparations, on both sides on a grand scale, are being pushed rapidly forward, and a grand battle is likely to commence at almost any time. No intimation has yet been given, as to whether our Division will be moved to the front to "open the ball," or remain somewhere in this vicinity as a reserve.

The pleasant oak woods in which we are, make a fine place for troops to rest, and it is being fully enjoyed by the vast throng around us. The men are, for the most part, either sitting in groups engaged in conversation, or reclining upon their oil cloths and blankets, reading or sleeping. Most of those reading are using their Bibles it may here be remarked, that there has been a very decided change in the religious tone of the army, going on during the past six months. There has been no great public demonstration in the way of revival meetings, or anything of that sort. Yet a quiet but deep work has evidently been going on in the hearts of large numbers of the patriot heroes now in the field. Prayer meetings are now held, in many of the Regiments, every night, and they are much better attended than formerly. Except at these meetings, the voice of prayer is not often heard in camp, yet hundreds may be daily seen, who, judging from the expression of countenance frequently raise their hearts in thanksgiving, supplication and praise, to the Great Disposer of Events, for his gracious mercy shown in preserving their lives from the ravages of disease, and the awful conflicts of the bloody field. May it not be that the prayers of pious mothers, wives and sisters at home, for the conversion of their relatives in the army are being answered? With nearly all who have Bibles, their careful perusal is now a daily practice, and profanity has greatly diminished, throughout this Division, at least, of the army. May the good work go on, until not only profanity, but all other immoralities shall cease in the Confederate army, and having enlisted under the banner of Christ, every man feel a calm and holy reliance in the protection of Providence, and be willing to live or die as an all wise and just God shall determine.

3 o'clock P.M. Orders have been issued to cook three days' rations and be ready to move, but where to, no one in the Brigade knows. We have neither rations nor cooking vessels, so what is to come of the order time must determine. M. D.

Bivouac of 8th Ga. Reg't,
Near Gordonsville, Va.,
August 16, 1862.

**Dear Courier:** A short time before closing my letter yesterday, orders had been received to cook three days' rations, when we had neither rations nor cooking vessels. At 9 o'clock last night one day's rations of fresh beef was issued, and most of the men spent a considerable part of the night in "jerking" the meat. This was a novel process to many of us, and consists in cutting the beef into thin strips, and drying it over a fire that is not quite hot enough to cook it. Thus prepared it is quite palatable, and is said to keep much better than when regularly cooked by any usual process. At 6 o'clock this morning hard bread for one day and bacon sufficient for two days, were issued, and we were informed that flour enough for two days would be issued in an hour or two. Now, all this may seem very unimportant, yet these facts were unpleasantly interesting to the troops, from the fact, that we were under orders to prepare for three days fatigue duty, marching or fighting, and the strong presumption was, if we started with a short allowance of provisions, there would be no means of getting a supply until the expiration of the three days, and even then it might be doubtful—circumstances, like that, make up the little anxieties of camp life.

There was a current rumor last night, and it was generally believed, that on this morning our whole army would advance—Jackson's corps taking the lead and Longstreet's following up to act as a reserve. At 11 o'clock we were ordered to "fall in," but before morning the order to march was countermanded, and we were informed that the Brigade would remain where it is until to-morrow morning. Our wagon train from Richmond is now coming on and within three miles of here, and it is most likely that there will soon be cooking vessels and flour too, enough to provide cooked rations for two days yet before we leave here.

When the order was published this morning to remain here another day, there might have been seen a very interesting change in the expression of countenances along the line. Geographically speaking, the *longitude* was greatly diminished, while the *latitude* was equally increased, and the whole *face* of the country became vastly more pleasant. Some men when *far away from the seat of war*, and who have never been in a hard fought battle, may boast of their bravery and speak of their eagerness to meet the foe, but three or four bloody conflicts wears off this "raw edge" and produces a dread of fields of carnage and strife. But acting from deep and stern convictions of duty, they, being *manly men*, hesitate not to promptly respond to their country's call. It is not because some men are more reckless of danger than others, that makes the difference between the brave and the cowardly, but it is because some men *dare to do right*, and *will do their duty*, while others are too *lazy* and *selfish* and *mean* to do either.

Are not many of our conscripts too craven hearted to be *really good* members of society anywhere? How many of them are there who are not quite as able to do military duty—through they may have been exempt after a strict surgical examination—as one tenth of the volunteers now in the field? If all but strictly able-bodied men were taken from the ranks of volunteers, the lines would be more than decimated. Now, is it right to compel these patriotic men to still incur the hardships and dangers of the field, fighting for the cormorants and parasites, while these latter gloat in their increasing [unable to read] extorted from the widows, orphans and families of those who have given up all for their country's sake? It is probably impossible to make the burdens of war fall equally upon all, but no reasonable effort should be spared to approximate as near as possible to this.

3 o'clock, P.M. Col. Towers has returned and taken command of the Regiment. The last rumor is, that we will move towards Fredericksburg in the morning. M. D.

Beside the Road near Brandy Station,
August 22nd, 1861

**Dear Courier:** After closing my letter of Tuesday and Wednesday, we advanced some two miles and bivouaced for the night about four miles from the Rapahannock, where the brigade remained until 2 o'clock, P.M., yesterday when the order was to move. At first we moved back a mile or two, then formed all to the right and took the road to Brandy Station. Last night bivouached a half mile below here. Culpepper C.H. is seven miles to our rear. Jackson's forced entered that place Wednesday at 3 o'clock P.M, without opposition.

Yesterday was notible on account of two executions in Longstreet's corps. The first was of a spy taken yesterday morning, and hung at 1 o'clock. He was dressed in a Confederate Uniform and claimed at first to be a Col. in our army, but when asked what regiment he commanded he named one of Hood's Brigade. This Gen. was present and of course knew the statement to be false. He was then examined and found to have a yankee uniform under the Confederate, and to have forged papers purporting to be dispatches for Gen. Jackson, and also a pass through the picket lines from Gen. Longstreet. He did not deny being a spy, but claimed to be an independent Pennsylvania scout. The evidence against him being conclusive, he was executed at once.

The second execution was of a deserter by the name of Johnson, who deserted from the Wise Artillery, when we were at Harper's Ferry last year. He has since been serving in the Federal army. He was hung to an apple tree near Stephensburg, a little old village that we passed through about 4 o'clock, P.M.

It is rumored that a portion of Jackson's command has crossed the Rapahannock, but this needs confirmation. We are now headed towards that stream in the direction of Rapahannock Station, distant some five miles, I believe.

It is reported that the enemy are fortified on the other side of the Rapahannock and a desperate fight, on the banks of that River, is not improbable. The fact that the federals have fallen back so far without any great resistance, has had the effect to greatly encourage our troops, but whether this is any real cause of gratulation, is yet to be seen.

Our rations gave out last night, and none have yet arrived to replenish with. It is now 11 o'clock and the men need breakfast, but they may have to endure a hard fight or long march with nothing to eat. Cannonading is now heard ahead of us, and it seems almost certain that a battle is at hand.

5 o'clock, P.M. We have not moved since 11 o'clock. Rations were issued at one and the cooking vessels came up.

No fight yet. The enemy are now said to be fortifying on this side of the river, stirring times may be expected to tomorrow. Quite a rapid cannonade is now going in front of us, and to the left.

Bivouac of 8th Ga. Reg.,
Sunday, August 24, 1862.

**Dear Courier:** Yesterday our Brigade passed through one of severest ordeals to which it is possible to subject even the best of troops—that of being under a heavy cannonade, when they could do nothing but grin and bear it.

At eight o'clock A M., it was ordered that one regiment of Gen. Evans' with one of Col. Anderson's should charge a Federal battery on the South bank of the river, at Rappahannock Station, and be supported by the balance of Col. Anderson's Brigade. We had already been marched to within about a mile of this battery, and drawn up in line of battle.

At the command the Brigade moved forward as silently as possible. When within about 800 yards of the battery to be charged, we came to a beautiful open field, with no obstruction whatever except a cedar wicker work fence, running across the field at right angles with course, and about midway between us and the battery. The ground, slightly inclined towards the battery, seemed fearfully smooth, and the yawning cannon stared our men full in the face. On moved the Brigade in almost perfect line and in good order. Besides the battery to be charged, three others could play upon this same open field and we had not been long in sight before they opened on us. At first their shots went overhead, but they soon came fearfully near, and directly charge after charge of shrapnel and canister swept through our slowly moving but firm and steady line; yet strange to say, occasioning very few casualties, when within 250 yards of the battery the Brigade was ordered to lie down flat upon the ground. Just at this juncture Holcombe's South Carolina Legion, of Evans'

Brigade, passed on to our left, to charge the battery. The order of the Brigade commencing on the right, was the 9th, 11th, 7th, 1st and 8th Ga. Regiments. The first three were on ground entirely flat, and in full view of one of the batteries, while the two last were on rising ground and partially behind a hill. It was over this hill and just in front of the 8th, that Holcombe's Legion charged *towards* the battery. The only advanced about 100 yards beyond the 8th, when the enemies fire became so intolerable they turned back. About fifty, however, remained behind some breast works the enemy had thrown up there the night before. Seven of their men were killed and twenty wounded.

The constant expectation was that the enemy would advance their infantry and try to drive us back; but this they did not do, and we lay five hours under the severest kind of cannonade. When we had been there two hours one of our regiments came up to the hill in front of us, but could not stand the fire and left immediately. Not one of our Brigade fired a gun. The 8th and 1st Regiments were not as much exposed, but the hill behind which they were, seemed to be an object of special apprehension by the enemy, and it received largely more than its share of attention.

The Brigade finally being in a position where it could do nothing, was ordered to move off by regiments, seeking as safe a passage out of range of the enemy's cannon as possible. The 8th was not fired into as we moved off, but the 7th 9th and 11th were. So far as ascertained the casualties in the 8th were twenty-seven wounded—there are four mortally it is feared. There were only three wounded in all the Rome companies: Lieut. Fouche, a slight bruise on the forehead; Bean, of the Floyd Infantry, very slightly, and Quarles, of the Miller Rifles severely in the arm, which was so badly shattered that it is feared he may die.[13] The 1st Georgia had three killed and twenty-one wounded; the 7th had eight wounded, one mortally; in the 11th there were two killed and twenty-seven wounded.[14]

The Brigade moved back about three o'clock P.M,. and after halting a while marched to the same bivouac where they stayed the night before. Soon after we left, the Federals moved back their battery that was on this side of the river, and for some time previous, long lines of their troops were seen moving up the river on the other side. Our artillery moved up and opened on them from the hill they had just left, but our forces could not cross the river to give them pursuit. They burned the railroad bridge, and several buildings, among them several fine residences in the vicinity.

Monday Morning, August 25.

Yesterday morning soon after daylight, we were again on the move. Marched slowly all day and bivouacked last night at a little village here called Jefferson, a mile and a half from the river, and two miles from Warrenton Springs. A bridge had been built here for us to cross on, but the enemy got possession of and burned it yesterday evening. Our Generals seem to have been anticipated in this movement and failed. 'Tis said that one Brigade of General Jackson's forces crossed over on this bridge Saturday, but were compelled to return. Heavy cannonading was going on all day yesterday, between our artillery and the enemy's stationed on opposite sides of the river near this bridge.

It is now 8 o'clock, and orders have been issued to be ready to march.

Tuesday Morning.

Nothing of particular interest has occurred since yesterday morning. We marched up the river some three miles and bivouaced last night near the turnpike running from Warrenton to Washington, Rappahannock county. None of our forces have yet crossed the River that I have heard of. There is said to be a good crossing some six miles above here, and Jackson is supposed to be there. The Yankees were trying all day yesterday to burn the bridge on the pike. Their batteries and ours on opposite sides of the river kept up a heavy firing.

Yesterday we subsisted on fresh beef and green corn without salt. This morning rations have been issued. If Jackson comes down on the other side, our forces will probably attempt to force a crossing here. The want of rations will force us forward or back soon. The country is exhausted, and the cars only run to Orange C.H. M. D.

The Plains, 20 miles from Manassas Junction,
Thursday, Aug. 28.

**Dear Courier:** We left our bivouac near Waterloo Bridge Tuesday noon, and marched back from the river round under cover of hills and woods, so as to conceal the movement from the enemy in front, and after describing, in our course, three sides of an irregular square, came up to the Rappahannock and forded it at 5 o'clock P.M. The march was continued on the road leading to Salem, passing through Orleans, a small village, at 8 o'clock, and halting at 11 o'clock P.M., seven miles from Salem. Resumed the march next morning at 8 o'clock, and continued till noon without any notable occurrence. Then halted for rest in a grove one mile from Salem. We had been here but a few moments when a courier came dashing in, with the intelligence that the enemy were advancing on us in the direction but beyond the town, and that their cavalry already had possession of the place. Gen. Lee was in the advance of our forces, and was only half a mile from Salem when he discovered the enemy's cavalry, and turned back. Our forces were soon thrown into an advantageous position, the natural defences being good. From the 8th Regiment, it being in front, companies A, B, and K were thrown forward as skirmishers, and ambushed in the margin of the woods. All things being ready to give the enemy a warm reception, his advance was awaited with anxious solicitude. Scouts were sent out in all directions from which it was possible for the enemy to advance, to ascertain if possible, their number and intentions.

After about two hours it was learned that only a regiment of cavalry had made a raid into Salem, coming probably, from Warrenton, which is only some twelve or fourteen miles to the right, for the purpose of picking up stragglers from Gen. A. P. Hill's Division, that had gone through the place the day before. The citizens report that they took twenty-one of our men prisoners, some of whom, who had gone ahead, belonged to our brigade. To what regiment or company they belonged I have not learned. The Yankees were probably frightened at seeing so many of our pickets, and they paroled all their prisoners and left in hot haste.

Our forces marched into Salem about 4 o'clock, made a short halt, and one company being thrown forward as skirmishers, followed by the 8th Ga. Reg., in a body as a support, and about 300 or 400 yards behind it the balance of the forces. The march was continued without interruption to this place, distant five miles from Salem. M. D.

From the Plains near Manassas
Monday, Sept. 1, 1862

**Dear Courier:** We have been in the midst of stirring and important movement events since I closed my letter last Thursday morning. The march was resumed at 10 A.M. of that day. Four miles below the Plains is a passage through the mountains called Thoroughfare Gap—the same that the Manassas Gap Railroad passes through. Some intimation had been received that the enemy were going to dispute the passage through this defile, and it was approached with caution. The 9th Ga. Regiment was deployed forward to feel the way, followed by the 8th. The passage through is about a mile long. As our troops approached the enemy opened with artillery, planted on hills on the east side. Our Infantry moved on nearly through before encountering anything except cannon shot. The Regiments ahead were deployed up to the left of the road, and were ascending the last high hill before getting to the open fields on the east side of the Gap, when the Yankees opened a tremendous volley of musketry upon them. The advance fell back a little, but when our reserve came up the enemy gave way. Anderson's and Toombs' Brigades were both engaged. They fought a Division of Federals under Gen. Rickets. Our loss was small, eight or nine killed, and some twenty-five seriously wounded. Of the Rome Light Guards, J. M. Jack was killed; Geo. K. Sanford severely wounded in the head; Daniel Miller wounded in the check, and Mr. Bordett slightly in the shoulder.[15] David Harper, of the Miller Rifles, was killed, and Mr. Estis had his right ankle so badly shattered that it was amputated.[16]

Our division went through the gap before sunset. This was quite a triumph. The enemy had three batteries just keeping the woods hot with grape and shell while our artillery could not get into position to bear on them at all. Forty one of the villainous invaders were found dead on the battle field.

Friday morning the march was renewed on towards Gainesville, distant some seven miles, where we struck the Alexandria and Warrenton Turnpike, and taking the left hand, proceeded towards Centreville some three miles then took position for the night, near the railroad.

A. P. Hill's Div. had been desperately fighting all the evening, and was said to be out of ammunition.

The next morning, Saturday the troops were being rapidly marshalled on both sides. As near as I could ascertain the Warrenton pike was our battle line. At about 2 A.M. the cannonading commenced and was kept incessantly for the balance of the day. The musketry opened about noon and continued with occasional interruptions until night. Our regiment after being a long time under shells, was lead into the conflict by Capt. Dawson, Col. Towers being reported slightly wounded has gone to the rear. Just as he had given the order to fire, Capt. Dawson was wounded, and the enemy coming up in overwhelming force just in front, the regiment fell back a short distance. The fight between Infantry was now general along the whole line and continues until dark. This was an awful bloody, yet glorious day to the Confederate army.

Our loss was tremendous, but the enemy had been driven back along the whole line, except a short distance on their center. In our Brigade it is said that every Field Officer was either killed or wounded, except Col. Anderson commanding. Col. Wilson of the 7th was killed, Col. Beck of the 9th wounded, Lt. Hardwick, A. A. G., wounded. In the 8th Capt. Phinizee was killed; Capt. Hulsey severely and probably fatally wounded; Lt. Huntington, of the Miller Rifles slightly wounded, Lt. Fouche lamed himself in getting over a fence, and was not up with the Regiment at the time the charge was made, yet he was slightly wounded by a piece of shell.[17] Webb Leigh was the only one of the Light Guards any way seriously wounded. He was hit by a piece of shell near the shoulder.[18] There may have been others of the Floyd county boys who suffered, but if so your correspondent has not heard of it—he has been sick and in the rear since Thursday morning. Lt. Fouche had command of Co. A in the fight at the Gap, and Lt. Moore at the time of the charge on Saturday. Capt. Hall has not yet came on from Richmond. Capt. Scott, since we left Gordonsville, has been in command of the Division rear guard.

Gen. Ewell was very severely wounded last Friday.[19] A portion of the fights Friday and Saturday, was on the old ground of July 21, last year.

It is now reported that all our forces have crossed Bull Run, and that the enemy are in full retreat towards Washington. Their wagon train left Warrenton last Saturday week, so it seems they feared trouble, even that long ago, and went beyond Centreville.

*When* or *where* you will next hear from us the Lord only knows. If no great reverse overtakes our army, we may be in Maryland before you read this letter. If an army was ever completely mobilized, then the Confederate army is so now. The crisis of this war now seems at hand, and with Heaven's blessing we hope soon to see a favorable issue. M. D.

Winchester, Va., Sep. 11th

**Dear Courier:** Since closing my letter of the 2nd inst., I have not been with the army. I was sent to the rear after the battle of Aug. 30th, on account of indisposition, and went to Salem and remained there until the 8th inst., when I came here. There were large numbers of men, who, from sickness and exhaustion, had broken down on the march, before arriving at the battle field of Bull Run, making quite an army of stragglers. As early as Tuesday the 2d inst., we would hear that Jackson, A. P. Hill and Longstreet were all on the move, but which way they were tending was not so easy to learn.

On Saturday it seemed to be a well authenticated fact, that all three of the above named Generals, with their forces, had crossed the Potomac in the vicinity of Leesburg. This is now known to be true. We cannot learn here the exact position of our forces in Maryland—probably they are in the vicinity of Frederick City. All stragglers and men in the rear of our army when it left Bull Run, were ordered to this place, where they were to await orders. There are now nearly two thousand men here, who have come in squads of from two to fifty; some few with arms, but most of them without them. There are also here hundreds of wagons and teams, ordered to report and await orders. Things seem to be somewhat confused. The cause is probably owing to the fact that a Federal force still lingers between this place and the Potomac, that was expected to have run before now. They are said to be in possession of Charlestown, Harper's Ferry and Martinsburg as well as some intermediate points. We can get very little satisfactory news either from our own or the Federal army. The scattered and disorganized troops here, are very anxious to get to their regiments, but are not allowed to leave.

Winchester is completely cleaned out, so far as goods are concerned. The Yanks evacuated on the night of Tuesday the 2d inst., after destroying all their stores, except a small quantity of provisions in one store house—probably overlooked in the hurry—and some cannon balls and a small quantity of powder. They spiked and left in their places in the fortifications, nine large cannon.

The citizens who had been run off by the vandals are returning, glad enough to find their homes once more surrounded with sympathetic hearts and cooperative arms. The stores are nearly all closed, and those open have only a few remnants of goods that are nearly valueless. The Federals did not steal very much grain in this vicinity, but they took every fine, serviceable horse they could lay their vile hands on. In some cases they gave a receipt for property.

It has been exceedingly dry here for some weeks, and the corn crop has suffered materially.

It is expected that a force will soon be sent, to clean out the Federals this side of the River. It seems that by good management on the part of our Generals, the last one might be bagged. Why they have not run before this time, seems very strange, inasmuch as the main body of our army is now nearly between them and the main Federal army, and in a situation to cut off their supplies. But whatever they may do or attempt, Gen. Lee will be sure to whip them out in some way or another.

We are completely shut out here from newspapers—having seen none of later date than the 3d inst.—and of course are exceedingly anxious to hear the news.

Sept. 12, 9 o'clock, A.M. No news has yet been received. The stragglers continue to come in; there are now probably, between 2,000 and 3,000 here. They are being thrown into temporary organizations and put into camp. Perhaps one fourth of them have guns and equipment. There is a rumor afloat here this morning, to the effect that Jackson is moving back across the Potomac, for the purpose of capturing the Federals on this side. M. D.

Winchester, Va., Sept. 16, 1862

**Dear Courier:** A considerable portion of the stragglers who were well enough to do duty left here yesterday to join their respective regiments on the other side of the Potomac. A large number of these men had just came on from the Richmond hospitals, many had broken down from fatigue and improper diet, others had become sick on the long series of forced marches, not a few had been slightly wounded in some of the numerous bloody battles fought this side of the Rapidan while the balance—no inconsiderable portion—were ordered to the rear because they were barefooted. Before leaving they were thrown into temporary organizations—men of the same brigade or division making companies. Those still unable to do duty, including the barefooted, were ordered to remain here in the hospitals, so far as these afford accommodations, and the remainder to find for themselves the best quarters they could in private families. It is but just, here to remark, that the citizens of this place and vicinity have been and still are generous and kind to our soldiers to the utmost extent of their ability. The Yankees treated them most shamefully, not even allowing marketing or fire wood to be carried into the town, except by persons who would take the oath of allegiance to the hated Lincoln dynasty, and helped themselves to horses, hay, grain, and everything else they desired and could lay their hands on, some times giving receipts, but frequently taking these things without promise of remuneration.

Most glorious news was this morning received from Harper's Ferry. Sunday evening our forces took the Maryland Heights at the point of the bayonet, the enemy spiking their guns and saving their own miserable lives by hasty flight. This gave us three important positions, Loudon Heights and one important position on Boliver Heights, beside the first named. It is reported that at day break yesterday morning Jackson demanded of Gen. White, the Federal commander, the unconditional and instant surrender of the place, including the entire Yankee force, about 10,000 men, and an immense amount of army stores and ammunition. White *asked time* and Jackson *opened on him* before sunrise, with his batteries. One brigade attempted to cut their way out and are said to have been literally cut to pieces, and the slaughter generally is said to have been great in the enemy's ranks. After enduring our deadly fire for two and a half hours, the Yankees run up the white flags at all points and unconditionally surrendered. Beside the forces and property, about 3,000 contrabands were taken, and some 30,000 stand of extra small arms, 2,000 horses and forty pieces of artillery. These figures are currently rumored, but it may be more or less erroneous. The Federal loss in killed and wounded is reported to be between three and four thousand; our loss only *seventeen*. The reason of White's standing fire at all is, it is supposed, that he expected McClellan to come to his relief on the other side of the river. It seems that McClellan did start to aid the Federal forces at the Ferry, but could not get through our forces below or opposite the place, so he went on above Frederick City and came into the rear of A. P. Hill near Boonsboro'—cut off and burned his wagon train—attacked him at 11 o'clock A.M., and for the first two or three hours got the better of the fight. At about 2 P.M., as the rumor goes, Longstreet's corps came to the assistance of Hill and then the tide of battle turned. The fight is reported to be a most desperate one, but the Yankees could not stand the invincible Southrons, and reluctantly fell back, still contesting every inch of ground. It is said they were driven back six miles. The fight continued till nearly or quite night, and *both* armies are said to have fallen back from the positions they held at sunset. The losses, on either side at Boonsboro' are not reported, neither does it appear from the *final* movement that our victory was as complete as would have been desirable.

The above is sifted out of a large number of rumors more or less conflicting, yet these statements are at least the nearest approximation to the truth we can get here up to this time. M. D.

Bivouac of 8th Ga. Reg., near
Martinsburg, Va., Sept. 21.

**Dear Courier:** Our Brigade left the vicinity of Shepardstown, 12 miles below here, at sunset last night and arrived at this place at 8 o'clock this morning. We are now attached to Gen. Hood's Division, which is composed of his original Brigade—1st, 4th and 5th Texas and 18th Ga. and Hampton's Legion—Whiting's Brigade—2d, 11th and 6th N.C, and 4th Ala., and now our own Brigade. This evening the men are cooking three day's rations, and a march is expected to-night, but which way, is only known to a very select few. Many think into Maryland again, while others surmise various places, back into the Valley.

The Yankees made an unsuccessful attempt to cross the river, yesterday, near Shepardstown. They were repulsed with heavy loss by Jackson's forces.

Last Wednesday's fight is said to be one of the bloodiest of the war. The battle was at Sharpsburg. All our forces in Maryland, except A. P. Hill's command, making some sixty thousand men in all, were engaged on our side, against, at the lowest estimate, 120,000 of the enemy. All present agree in the statement that most vigorous and desperate fighting was kept up for nearly eleven hours. Only about 250 men of our Brigade was in the fight with the Brigade. The 11th Ga. Regiment was guarding baggage, and 25 men from each of the other Regiments were on picket; these latter had desperate fighting. Toombs' Brigade and Anderson's are both spoken of in terms of the highest commendation on account of their valiant conduct that day.

There were 13 killed and wounded from the 8th Ga. Among them Larkin Greer, of the Light Guards, killed by being hit by a piece of shell in the head, mutilating it in a most horrid manner. R. D. Watters, of said company, was severely wounded in the left knee by a musket ball, and Stinson slightly in the hand. None are known to be killed or wounded from the Miller Rifles but Lieut. R. Wade, J. R. Davis and Jack Eason are missing. Of the Floyd Infantry none suffered except Wm. Smith who is missing.

The Brigade never before had so good a position for doing good execution. And they are said to have improved it to the uttermost, killing large numbers of the enemy, but I have heard no satisfactory estimate of numbers. Gens. Branch and Garland were killed on our side. Gen. Starks was killed the Sunday before.[20] The victory was complete, our forces driving the enemy back on both the right and left, while they drove back our pickets and the centre yet did not advance even there. The next morning they sent in a flag of truce and asked leave to come on to the field to bury their dead. It was not consistant with the plans of our Generals to pursue them far, and on Thursday our forces fell back.

Instead of 41, we captured 81 pieces of artillery at Harper's Ferry. This ordnance is all of the very best kind.

Gen. Toombs was wounded in the hand Thursday night, while visiting the posts with two of his aids, when some five or six mounted men were seen approaching. Capt. Troup cried out "who comes" and the response was "friends—don't shoot." As they approached nearer it was discovered that they had on Federal uniforms. They were again challenged as before, and received the same answer. Capt. Troup then asked them what State they were from, and being answered Massachusetts be said "for that reason I will shoot you," and he fired. The Yankees then fired and run, hitting General Toombs in the left hand and Lieut. Grant in the arm.

None of the commissioned officers of the Light Guards went into Maryland, and company, (fifteen men) was commanded by Sergt. R. F. Hutchings while in that State. Capt. D. Scott has been in command of the rear guard since the army left Gordonsville.

Sept. 22, 5, o'clock P.M. No move yet; the day has been spent by the men in washing their clothes and cleaning their guns. We have just had Inspection of arms. The Regiment, including officers, is about one hundred strong. Tis said that about 2,500 men joined our army in Maryland, but the three counties our division went through (Montgomery, Frederick and Washington) are strong Union.

TUESDAY MORNING 2d P.S. The Miller Rifle boys, Lt. Wade, Davis and Eason came into camp this morning.[21] They were taken prisoners last

Wednesday and have been paroled. No news this morning. I have just been into Martinsburg, and found this to be the dryest town yet. Not a store open or any chance to buy anything at all. The citizens say there are no goods in the place, but there are probably considerable quantities hid out. There are many union men here and they will not sell goods for Confederate money. M. D.

Bivouac of 8th Ga. Reg. near
Martinsburg, Va., Sept. 27, 1862.

**Dear Courier:** One week ago tomorrow morning our Brigade arrived at this place and nothing "here or hereabouts," has since occurred, that would be likely to interest your readers. The stragglers have been gradually coming in, and the weary and broken down have been taking the much needed rest. Our Regiment now reports 150 men for duty, and the Brigade 1,057.

The sight of the "old Eighth" is now saddening, yet encouraging to every well-wisher to our cause. Many of the men are without shoes (these are allowed to go to the rear,) or change of clothing, and even the clothes many of them have are much the worse for wear, and if troops have ever seen severe service, than our Brigade has since the 8th of March last, and it has had its effect upon even the hardiest in ranks. Hard marching, exposure, indifferent and insufficient rations and severe fighting will "tell," as the rowdies say, on the best of men. Yesterday every officer now on duty in the Regiment signed a petition to the Secretary of War to the effect that the 8th Ga. Regiment should be assigned to post duty at some location in Ga., and its place here be supplied by some full Regiment now doing that duty in the State, that has never yet been in the field, so as to give the Eighth a chance to recuperate its men and fill up its broken ranks. This seems to be a very just and reasonable request, and it would doubtless be of great advantage to the service if Mr. Randolph would grant it.[22] Our Regiment does not wish to shirk duty—its history proves the contrary—or get out of active service, except for such a short period, say three or four months, as will enable them to do it efficiently. There is such a thing as killing the life and fire of a regiment long before the last man is killed. It would seem that our officers have been trying the experiment on the Eighth, to see just how much a body of troops could endure and "stand up to it." Since being in the service the Regiment has lost, in battle, in killed, wounded and missing four hundred and forty eight men; from disease, and discharged for other reasons than wounds three hundred, making a total loss of seven hundred and forty-eight men. It should be remembered, however, that many of the wounded after, in many cases, months of pain and anguish, have recovered and returned to their commands.

The petition referred to will be sent to our Senators, in Congress to present, and if our friends in Ga. can do anything to assist in the attainment of the object desired, such efforts will gratify the Regiment.

Some amusing sights and incidents were witnessed by our troops in Maryland. As they marched into Hagarstown—a place of some 5,000 or 6,000 inhabitants—an old man was seen standing out on his piazza looking pale with excitement and his lips trembling as he saw Brigade after Brigade file past, with Confederate flags flying and the bands playing "secesh" tunes, many paroled Yankees were standing around and lots of citizens who evidently hated the sight of our forces. The old gent looked at our troops then at the despised Yankees and his tory neighbors, as if he was fully conscious that would inform against him should they ever have an opportunity. But his excitement increased as our troops came pouring in, and at last with a trembling, yet strong voice, he exclaimed, "I can't stand it any longer—huzzah for Jeff Davis and the whole Southern Confederacy." Such instances were however rare. The Southern rightsmen generally, it is said, seemed afraid to make any demonstration of joy or approval. A large portion of the people being Unionists, and our movement into that State, being regarded rather as an experiment, they feared lest they should again fall into Federal hands and then be made to suffer for any sesesh sympathies they might exhibit to our troops. All private rights were scrupulously regarded by our troops, and the Union men received as full protection as those who favored our cause. As our army approached many Union men fled, but when they learned they would not be harmed, they returned, and some of them became even noisy in their condemnation of the "rebellion." Our band serenaded some ladies, and after playing several of *our* tunes, one of the asked the band if they would play the "Star Spangled Banner." This was asked in rather a faltering voice and the leader pretended not to hear it. But was'nt that a stunner?

Goods could be purchased with Va. State bank notes, U.S. money or specie, at old time prices—bacon from 8 to 12 cents, sugar from 10 to 12, and coffee 20 cents, and other things, except tobacco, in proportion. Some few Marylanders took Confederate money at par. These sold whatever they had that soldiers could use readily.

At 2 o'clock yesterday orders were issued to Longstreet's corps to provide two day's rations on the haversacks and be ready to march at daylight that morning. It is now 9 o'clock and our Regiment has only moved about ½ of a mile unto the road and stacked arms. No intimation has been given as to which way we are to go, but the general impression is that we are bound for Winchester—distant 22 miles—or some point beyond there.

Sunday P.M. Sept 28th. It is currently reported that enemy are in possession of Harper's Ferry, Charlestown, Leesburg and Shepherdstown.

Yesterday we marched to Bunkershill, zizzagging on small roads to the left of the Pike and marching at least two or three miles farther than it would have been by the Pike, on which latter road the distance is only 10 miles. To day we have marched towards Winchester, on the Pike, 5 miles, and leaving us yet 7 miles from that place, where we are bivouaced, probably for the night. Some troops coming from the direction of Winchester are passing our bivouac and it may be that preparations are being made for warm work in this vicinity soon. The latest rumor from the enemy is that they are advancing in heavy columns through Harper's Ferry.

Monday morning, 8 o'clock. All quiet and no News. George Morton, Gale Jones and Marion Stovall who was taken prisoners at Malvern Hill about the first of August, are paroled.

# 7

# "The Health and Spirits of the Men Are Improving"

## *October–December 1862*

The Eighth Georgia did not get the post assignment the men desperately wanted. However, Melvin Dwinell reported that the troops were getting some badly needed time to recover. Within a few weeks, most of the men had been properly supplied with shoes and clothing, thanks in part to "friends at home" who made generous donations to the army. During the reprieve from fighting, Gen. Robert E. Lee took the opportunity to reorganize his army. Col. George T. Anderson's brigade had been temporarily under the command of Maj. Gen. John B. Hood for a large part of the summer. In early October, Anderson's brigade was permanently reassigned to Hood. Dwinell traveled to Richmond in early November to get the regiment's blankets and overcoats that had been stored in the city. He traveled by stagecoach and told readers about enjoying the beautiful sights of the Shenandoah Valley. The winter supplies arrived just in time because the weather soon turned cold and the camp was hit by an early snowstorm.

Dwinell continued to give readers of the *Courier* insightful pictures of camp life. In one letter, he noted how, in the first few days in camp after a long march, the men often were in good spirits. However, if the troops remained in camp too long "laziness would steal over them like clouds in the night," and they would begin quarreling. During the extended periods in camp, some men got into serious trouble that resulted in court-martials. The most common offense was being "absent without leave," Dwinell wrote.

Transgressors often were given sixty days of hard labor, forced to wear a ball and chain, and ordered to forfeit two months' pay. Those found guilty of the more serious crime of desertion were branded with the letter "D" on their left hips, had half their heads shaved, and were drummed out of camp. For minor infractions, soldiers would have to stand on top of a flour barrel for several hours a day. One of the games the men liked to play to relieve their boredom was called "wrap jackets." The schoolyard game involved two contestants who locked their left arms and then flailed at each other's backs with switches held in their right hands. After listening to the sounds from one game, Dwinell predicted that the two men would "carry marks for several days to come."

On November 19, the army broke camp and the next day began marching in a cold rain toward Fredericksburg, Virginia. Part of their trip was made on the Orange Plank Road, once a generally good wood and macadam road, but one that over time had become "so dilapidated as to make it exceedingly hard to walk upon." The poor condition of the road made the march "the hardest our Regiment has ever made," Dwinell wrote. The rest of the march was easier, and by November 22, the Eighth Georgia was in line for battle about three miles from Fredericksburg. Except for "numerous sore feet," he reported that the men were in good condition.

With the vast Union army nearby, Dwinell said the troops expected another battle soon. But after several days, the men settled into the routines of camp life once again. The Eighth Georgia was assigned to picket duty in late November and got to see the stately mansions that dotted the countryside. Many of the men had never seen such grand homes, he wrote. While in camp, the troops stayed busy with other tasks. Dwinell described how they learned to make their own candles and soap, the latter item being increasingly hard to get.

In a letter on December 6, Dwinell wrote that the expected battle had been delayed for so long that some wondered if it would not be fought until the spring. Of the chance that Union general Ambrose E. Burnside would attempt to cross the river with his army, Dwinell boasted, "we could 'riddle him into doll rags.'" Moreover, he observed, a Confederate victory might convince "old Abe" to give up. The Battle of Fredericksburg eventually was fought on December 13. The Eighth Georgia came under fire and was repeatedly in line for battle. In the end, the regiment did not take part in one of the major Confederate victories of the war. However, skirmishers saw action, including some members of the Floyd companies. Dwinell dutifully noted the deaths of James Boggs and Henry Garrett and the mortal wounding of George Aycock. A few days after the battle, he got the chance to visit Fredericksburg. The sight of how the occupying Union troops treated the once-beautiful town made the editor's blood boil. "The demons of the infernal regions turned loose for the special purpose of plundering and destroying, could not have done worse," he wrote.

Looking back over a remarkable year—and perhaps feeling sentimental—Dwinell used his last letter of 1862 to describe the camaraderie that had developed among the troops. He told how the "common toils and sufferings, privations and dangers" had bound together the army "man to man, heart to heart, and arm to arm." It was "one of the consoling effects of this calamitous and wicked war." That commonality, however, could not disguise the differences among the troops, Dwinell noted in a more lighthearted passage. From their dialects, mannerisms, and appearances, he could often tell what Southern state the soldiers were from.

Bivouac of 8th Ga. Regiment,
Near Winchester, Va.,
October 6, 1862.

**Dear Courier:** During the past week nothing of peculiar interest has occurred in our camp. It has been fine pleasant weather; rather hot in the middle of the day and cool at night, yet on the whole rather agreeable weather. No rain yet and perhaps the dust—immense clouds of which are constantly rising—is the most unpleasant element in the atmosphere.

Our former acting Maj. General David R. Jones has been furloughed for two months, and our Brigade and that of Gen. Toombs, transferred to Hood's Division, formerly Whiting's, and Drayton's Brigade to McLaws' Division. There is much speculation in camp as to what our next movement will be, but of course this is all idle. Absentees are constantly coming in, and our Brigade is now much stronger than when it crossed into Maryland. A petition has been signed by nearly all the officers, and forwarded to the Secretary of War, to the effect that Col. Geo. T. Anderson, who has been acting as our Brigadier General since the first of April, be commissioned a Brigadier General, and assigned to the command of our Brigade. His conduct, both in camp and field, prove that he is eminently deserving of this promotion, and it is the ardent desire of the entire command that he should receive it.

On Saturday last I had the pleasure of meeting, in Winchester, with Mr. J. M. Selkirk, Gen. Agent, Rev. W. H. Potter, Cor. Sec'ty, Dr. James Camak, Agent for Va., and Wm. Jones, Agent for the Augusta Branch, of the Georgia Relief and Hospital Association. It would do one's soul good to see these efficient and active gentlemen, so busily engaged in their missions of relief and mercy. There are a vast number of sick and wounded soldiers in Winchester, and with the very limited hospital room and scarcity of Physicians many are almost necessarily neglected. These good Samaritans never "pass by on the other side" a sick or wounded soldier, but go to and administer to the necessities of all Georgians that come in their way, and then seek out, not only through the hospitals and general places of resort of the sick, but seek out, through the byways and hedges, for suitable objects for their charitable labors. Their arrival was most opportune. They brought a large supply of underclothing, which was most acceptable, as not a single article can be purchased in Winchester. Also the supply of medicine distributed by Dr. Camak has been of untold value. He has administered with his own hands to over three hundred patients.

Rev. Wm. M. Crumley is also here, and still unflagging in his efforts, is doing all that can be done, for the relief of the suffering soldiers. Those who loved him in prosperity, may possibly form some idea of how they would regard him if they were sick and destitute, among strangers, and without the commonest comforts of life, when he should show his benign countenance, and, after administering in all ways in his power to one's physical relief, then pouring into his soul the oil and wine of Divine cansolation. God will surely bless the supporters of the Georgia Relief and Hospital Association, and their agents who so efficiently carry out its objects. Thousands of soldiers will rise up in the day of judgment and call them blessed.

Capt. Scott has just heard of the death of John A. Hardin, of his company, at Danville, on the 27th of July.[1] He died of typhoid fever in the hospital. W. F. Leigh, of the Light Guards, died a few days since, from a wound received August 31, at Manassas Plains. He was on the litter corps, and, when wounded, actively engaged in taking from the field our wounded men. He was an excellent soldier, as brave as the bravest, always did his duty promptly, and was a young man of fine promise.[2] I have learned since noticing the death of Larkin Greer, that when killed he was standing over a wounded Yankee that he had just carried out of musket range, when a cannon ball cut him down. It is not hard that a good man should thus, while mercifully taking care of a wounded enemy, be slain by our merciless invaders and would be subjugators?

Col. L. L. Floyd and W. W. Ware, of the Miller Rifles, the former slightly wounded, and the latter there as a nurse for Serg. John Bailey, were taken prisoners by the Federal cavalry last Monday, and immediately paroled.[3] Wm. P. Martin, of the Light Guards, was taken prisoner on the 18th ult., near Sharpsburg, Md., and paroled a day or two afterwards.

Our army is very destitute of clothing and shoes, and there seems to be no immediate prospect, at least, of getting a supply. This reminds me of a retort made by one of our soldiers to a Unionist in Maryland, who was making some "oderous" comparisons between the appearance of the Federal and Confederate troops. The Unionist said his army were all well uniformed, in a neat and genteel style, while the rebels were shabbily dressed in all sorts of styles, and dirty and ragged at that. The very appropriate and spirited answer was, "when we go to kill hogs we always put on our old clothes."

The week's rest we have enjoyed here has greatly improved the health of the men, and indications of their returning wonted spirit and vigor are everywhere seen. There has been but slight frost one or two mornings yet, but serious apprehensions are felt lest cold weather should catch us here without winter clothing or tents. The equinoctial storm seems to have been postponed this year, probably for good reasons, but when a long, cold rain does come—as it surely must soon—the troops will necessarily greatly suffer. But surely our army will not remain here much longer. The country is completely exhausted of provisions and forage, and it is ninety miles to Staunton, the nearest railroad station where supplies can be had, we will be obliged to either advance into Maryland, or fall back soon.

Capt. Hall has not yet returned. Capt. Yarbrough of the Floyd Infantry, is sick and gone to Richmond. John P. Duke was elected 2nd Lt., Jr., of that Company a few days since.[4] There is less complaint in regard to rations now, than there was a week since. M. D.

Winchester, October 8.

**Dear Courier:** A simple statement that we are all quiet here may not be uninteresting to your readers. There has been no sensation to disturb the usual quiet of our camp in the last few days, except a very current rumor that there were four cases of small pox in the 7th Georgia Regiment. Two or three surgeons said that there was no doubt but that these cases were genuine small pox and such a run for vaccine matter and such an anxiety to be inoculated you never saw. But yesterday, when the oldest cases were five days old, a careful examination was had, and the disease pronounced to be chicken pox; so that now the boys breathe freely again.

On Monday our Division was reviewed by Gen. Hood and yesterday by Gen. Longstreet. The ranks continue to fill up, and the health and spirits of the men are improving. We are getting a little clothing and a few pair of shoes. These things come in very small lots. One pair of shoes to a company at a time, and perhaps one suit of clothes. By such driblets it will take a long time to put the army in a comfortable condition. One difficulty in the way of getting a full supply at once, is, as I understand, want of transportation from Staunton here. It is reported that one officer from each Georgia Regiment will soon be sent to that State for the purpose of getting clothing, shoes, hats, &c., for the soldiers.

To-day we received the sad news of the death of R. P. Watters of the Light Guards. He was wounded in the knee in the battle of Sharpsburg, and left at Sheperdstown when the army fell back. His leg, though badly wounded, was not amputated, and it is reported that he died a few days since. One of the Macon Guards of our Regiment, named John Watson, was with Watters at the time of his death. Watson went through Winchester on his way to Staunton yesterday, and as he had been wounded, he will probably go on to Richmond and perhaps to Georgia. Mr. Watters was one of the very best of soldiers, a kind and sympathetic companion, and his loss is deeply deplored by his numerous friends. This is another evidence that "death loves a shining mark."[5]

The weather still continues warm and dry. No intimations are given as to our probable movement, except perhaps the fact that the convalescent sick and wounded are being sent to Staunton as fast as possible. M. D.

Bivouac 8th Ga., Reg.,
Winchester, Va., Oct. 13th, 1862.

**Dear Courier:** Nothing can be more monotonous than an encampment of troops when no immediate battle or movement is expected. The roar of the enemy's cannon or the rattle of his musketry, has not been heard by this Division of our army for over two weeks, and we have been all this while quiet in Bivouac. Thank Heaven for this respite, short though it be, from the fatigue of forced marches, and the terrible excitements of battle. What a *rest* this is and how it is appreciated, none can know but those who have experienced the agonies of "the bloody strife" on hard contested fields. The severe drafts on body, mind, and spirits made by a spirited campaign, reduce the participants to a half lethargic state of stolid indifference from which it takes time and rest to awaken them. These opportunities being afforded, however, they soon revive, and, ere long, every "Richard is himself again."

The Small Pox excitement has nearly abated, though according to the *last* decision of our Surgeons—and after several others, first one way and then the other—the disease, in a mild form, called Varioloid, now actually exists in our Brigade. No cases have yet been reported outside of the 7th Ga. Reg't. There are only 6 or 8 patients in all, and none of these are considered in an anywise dangerous condition. The general health of the army is, perhaps better than at any previous time, and the ranks continue to be filled by stragglers, and those who have been sick and wounded, returning from the Hospitals.

The weather has changed at last. It rained nearly all Friday night, and ever since then it has been cold and cloudy with drizzling rain, a considerable part of the time. The troops are poorly provided for this weather, having no tents and only a meager supply of blankets.

Of the movements of the enemy in our front we hear little that is reliable. The most probable reports concur in the statement that few or none are camped north of Harper's Ferry, on this side of the river. Their cavalry occasionally cross over at Shepherds town, cruise round for an hour or two, then return. It is reported that Gen. Stewart of our army crossed over into Maryland last Friday, with two thousand cavalry, and eighteen pieces of artillery, for the purpose of making a reconnoisance. This may or may not be true. There are some indications that we will leave here soon. M. D.

P.S. 2 o'clock P.M. There were six new cases of Varioloid reported in the 7th, this morning, and since noon the Regiment has gone off somewhere into Quarantine quarters.

*Rumor* says the 1st Reg't Georgia Regulars, are to start for Georgia to-morrow, probably to do Post duty. We all wish the 8th could meet the same good fortune.

Bivouac of 8th Ga. Regiment
Near Winchester, Va.,
October 16th, 1862.

**Dear Courier:** Time wags on at ordinary speed and no important movement has yet been made by this Division of the Army. The varioloid still continues to spread slowly in our Brigade. Last Tuesday the 7th Ga. Reg't. was sent some four miles towards Strasburg from Winchester into Quarentine quarters. Several cases have since appeared in the 9th and 11th Regiments, but none in the 8th. We all have orders to be ready to move by one o'clock today, to the vicinity of the 7th Ga. Reg. We of the 8th, are told that strict quarentine rules will not be established over us until the small pox appears in the Regiment neither will be put very near the 7th. The main object seems to be to get our Brigade, that has been so much exposed to this infectious disease, away from the balance of the Army, so as not to jeopardize others. In no case has this disease proved fatal here, but, on the contrary, all the patients are said to be doing well and are not very seriously sick. As she is, perhaps generally, Madam Rumor was mistaken in asserting that the Ga. Regulars were to start for Georgia a few days since. They are still here, and, for ought I know, are likely to be as long as the rest of the Brigade.

Gen. Stewart returned from the raid into Maryland mentioned in my last on Sunday or Monday, having made a most glorious success of the trip. He is said to have divided his force into two or three Divisions and crossed the river at Shepardstown, Williamsport and some other place. He scoured through the country as far as Chambersburg, Pa., which place he took with all the cannon the Yanks took from us at Sharpsburg—some dozen pieces, and a considerable amount of Ordnance stores. Somewhere in his perigrinations he is said to have taken two thousand horses, a considerable portion of them being in droves, and just coming in from Pennsylvania for the use of the Federal army. He is also said to have brought safely within our lines not only all these horses and cannon, but 400 prisoners. He went entirely round McClellan's grand army and recrossed the river at Leesburg. At some place he is said to have encountered the enemy and cut his way through a full division of the vandals. His loss was very small, and the expedition is said to eclipse even his celebrated raid round the army before Richmond. He destroyed a large amount of Federal property, including two or three Railroad bridges, telegraph wires, &c., &c., the whole estimated at two millions dollars in value or more.

Friday Morning, Oct. 17. At one o'clock yesterday the Brigade left Bivouac and marching through Winchester, came to this place, Kearnstown, three and a half miles this side, and bivouacked, in an open field, on the battle ground of March 23d, for the night. It rained hard from 6 to 8 o'clock, wetting the men and rendering the ground, which is covered by a thick mat of grass and weeds, a most uncomfortable bed for the night. The 7th Ga. Reg't. is in Quarentine quarters less than a half mile from our bivouac. I hear that there has been fifteen cases of small pox, in all, in that Regiment, and no new ones since they came out here, but that two have since died. This is *hearsay*, and may or may not be so.

There has been no cases reported yet in either the 8th or the 9th Regiments, and only two or three in the 11th.

It was understood yesterday evening that we were to proceed to Cedar creek, near Strasburg, and our present place of bivouac is of such a character as would indicate that the commander did not expect to remain here for any considerable time.

At 2 o'clock this morning the men were aroused from their broken slumbers on the "cold, cold, ground," ordered to cook what rations they had, and be ready to march at daylight.

It is said that the enemy are reported to have crossed the Potomac in large numbers at Harper's Ferry, and that there was a cavalry fight at Charlestown yesterday, and for those reasons we were to be in readiness to march back. But it is now eleven o'clock, and we are still waiting orders to move. M. D.

Bivouac 8th Ga., Reg.,
near Old Forge, Va., Oct. 20, 1862.

**Dear Courier:** The rumored fight, near Charlestown, last Thursday, turned out to be only a cavalry skirmish, and our Brigade, including the 7th Ga. Regiment, together with Toombs' Brigade, left Kearnstown at 10 o'clock last Saturday morning, and marched about ten miles to this place. We are now in what is called the Little Valley, (taking the right from the Pike at Kearnstown in our march here) two miles from Old Forge, four miles from Middletown and seven from Strausburg, near Cedar Creek, and in the midst of mountains. Fremont came through on this same route last summer, making an unsuccessful effort to head off Gen. Jackson when he fell back from Winchester.[6] The citizens here say that the Yankee army had been on forced marches with only half rations for a week before reaching this neighborhood, and that during the two days they halted here, they committed all sorts of depredations, to procure eatables. We had expected to find here a good country to "forage" in; but the speculators had secured it before our arrival, and the little butter, eggs, chickens, lard, bacon, honey, &c., left, are fully up to the extortionary prices of other places. But in spite of this, the men, many of them, will buy honey at a dollar a pound, bacon and lard at 75 cents, and other luxuries in proportion. They have lived so long on fresh beef and flour, with less than half the salt they desire, that they have become desperate for something good to eat. Fresh pork has been *promised* several times lately, but it has not yet come to hand. Beef and flour with nothing else but a very little salt, do not make a desirable diet for any considerable time, say three or four weeks together, and men become almost frantic when confined to it, and they will pay almost any price for something else to eat. Some speculator brought a little salt into camp a few days since, and sold it "like a flash," for a dollar a pint. Ordinary sized apples have frequently been sold at a dollar a dozen.

The general health of this portion of the army is excellent. No cases of small pox have yet appeared in our Regiment, and it is said to be abating in those Regiments where it has broken out.

The weather has been fine since the rain last Thursday night, having bright, pleasant days, and clear, frosty nights. M. D.

Bivouac of 8th Ga. Regiment.
Near Old Forge, Oct. 23.

**Dear Courier:** The most interesting thing to communicate from this place, at this time is, that there is nothing of particular or even ordinary interest to make known. The small pox, concerning which, perhaps, our friends feel more anxiety just now, than anything else, has not spread, except, perhaps, two or three new cases in the 9th Georgia Regiment, and even in regard to these, there is doubt yet whether it is that disease or not. All the old cases are reported to be doing well.

This is certainly a very much out of the way place. On our way here the roads, after leaving Kearnstown, became small and poorer as we advanced, until it might be reasonably apprehended, that "the road would," as Willis Gayland Clark said, "dwindle down to a squirrel's track and go up a tree." The latest Richmond paper received here, was one of October 17th, and we can hear nothing from our army on the Potomac.

Capt. Scott of the Miller Rifles, Lt. Shelman, of the Oglethorpe Light Infantry, from Savannah, and Lt. Young, of the Pulaski Volunteers, all started for home last Monday, for the purpose of obtaining clothing for our Regiment. The men are greatly in need, and it is sincerely to be hoped that our friends at home will be able to furnish them with a tolerable outfit for the cold winter campaign. It should be remembered that, although the government furnishes some, occasionally, a little clothing, but this is rather incidental and altogether uncertain, and that the soldiers main, and almost entire dependence, is upon supplies sent him from home.

The members of the Floyd county companies belonging to the Regiment, have been instructed to write to their friends, and notify them of what articles they stand in need of; this was necessary because men cannot carry more clothes than they actually need for present use, and if more is sent them it is liable to be lost upon the first long march that is made. A change of under clothes, a comfortable uniform, an overcoat, two blankets, and a pair of shoes, is all the clothing a soldier can take care of, even in the winter, and if more is sent him, the chances are at least, that he will loose the surplus. The above named officers will probably remain in Georgia some sixteen or twenty days, and persons wishing to send clothing, boots, shoes, hats, caps, &c., to members of this Regiment, should send them to some point that will be probably designated by these officers, and there boxed by them and sent on immediately.

The weather continues fine, and the general health of the Regiment is very good.

Since leaving the other side of Winchester, Col. Geo. T. Anderson has been in command of that portion of the Division in Quarentine, viz Toombs' Brigade and ours; Col. Towers acting as our Brigadier General, and until he left for Georgia, Capt. D. Scott in command of our Regiment, now Captain Malone commands this Regiment. M. D.

Camp of 8th Ga Regiment,
Near Orange, Court House,
November 8th, 1862.

**Dear Courier:** The silence of your correspondent during the past sixteen days, is accounted for by the fact that he has been on detailed duty to Richmond, to procure overcoats, blankets, &c., stored there last spring for the Regiment. The trip from Winchester to Staunton by stage coach, was a delightful one. We were fortunate in obtaining a seat in a fine coach, has tolerable good teams, and, it being a beautiful autumn day, the romantic scenery of the rich and far famed 'Valley of Virginia," fully sustained its high reputation for beauty and apparent productiveness. There is no other mode of traveling so advantageous as a seat on top of a stage coach, for "seeing the country." Utilitarianism may clamor for rail road cars, and young go-a-headativeness, with miserly greed, anxiously count on time and space annihilated; but he who has a soul realization of the fact, that "a thing of beauty is a joy forever," enjoys a richer feast, and really lives faster, in a reasonable way, by traveling slower through a romantic country, and thereby getting full views instead of tantalizing glances of the "sights" on the way.

Richmond has again assumed much of its wonted liveliness and general business appearance. The busy hum of cheerful voices is everywhere heard, and the lively steps of thrifty trade are on every walk of the city. The hotels are not crowded, but this is, in part, accounted for by the fact, that in the office of each claiming to be "first class," is a large playcard inscribed "Price of Board, Five Dollars and Fifty Cents per Day." Entertainment in private houses is from fifteen to thirty dollars a week.

Many members of the army are seen about the city, but perhaps not more than would be reasonably expected, considering that nearly all go through this city in passing to and from home, hospitals, and the grand divisions of the army, and including those having government business.

The two Brigades that had been in quarantine near Old Forge received orders to march on the 29th ult. They proceeded to Strasburg, thence down the line of the railroad towards Front Royal, to the Suray pike, thence up that road to the town, thence on to Madison Court House and Gordonsville making the march of ninety-seven miles in six days. The weather was, delightful, the roads good, and the march is said to have been enjoyed to as full an extent as such severe fatigue well could be.

Arriving at Gordonsville on Monday night, the 3d inst., and remained there until Wednesday morning, when they proceeded to 1 ½ miles beyond Orange C.H.; remained there one night and then removed to our present camp, five miles northeast of the Court House, and about midway between the Rapidan and Robinson rivers.

It turned cold Thursday evening, snowed nearly all day yesterday, and the ground was white with its fleecy blanket this morning. We now have the same tents we used before leaving Richmond last August, and with the partial supply of old overcoats and blankets, recently obtained from that city, most of the men are comparatively comfortable.

Saturday Noon. Orders have just been issued to pack up and be ready to march at a moments notice. Various conjectures are made as to where we are going. Heavy cannonading was heard yesterday evening in the direction of Warrenton Junction, and it is not improbable that we will go that way.

Geo. Thos. Anderson, formerly Colonel of the 11th Georgia Regiment, but who has commanded our Brigade since last February yesterday received his commission as Brigadier General. Probably no officer in the army has been more faithful to his duties in camp, or more deliberate and brave on the field of action. It is expected that he will continue to command our Brigade.[7]

There is no mistake now, but that the 1st Ga. Regulars have been ordered to report at Macon, Ga., and they are to leave here as soon as a certain Batallion arrives to take their place. The Small Pox has nearly all disappeared and the general health of the brigade continues good.

Maj. Little of the 11th Ga. Reg. from Walker co., was to-day elected Colonel of that Reg't, in place of Col. Anderson, promoted.[8]

7 o'clock Sunday Morning. Tents are now being struck and we will soon be on the march, unless the order is countermanded. M. D.

Camp of 8th Ga. Regiment, near
Rapid Ann, Nov. 11, 1862.

**Dear Courier:** The order for the 3d Brigade to move last Sunday morning was countermanded at about 10 o'clock, and we are still here, although yesterday the order was again issued to pack up and be ready to march at a moment's warning. The expectation of a fight has been realized, but how general the engagement was not yet been reported in this camp. Cannonading commenced on the Rappahannock last Saturday, and was continued with skirmishing between pickets and cavalry forces up to Sunday night. On Monday mornings Gen. A. P. and D. H. Hill engaged the enemy about eight miles from Culpepper C.H., and the fight continued until late in the afternoon. No particulars have been received here further than that the enemy were driven back about three miles, sustaining a heavy loss in killed and wounded, and three pieces of artillery. This fight was about twenty-three miles from our camp, yet the cannonading was distinctly heard, nearly all day yesterday, and, being under orders as we were, the expectation every moment, was that we would go to the support of our friends then engaged. We have heard no cannonading to-day, and as no orders have been issued to be ready to march, the fight at the Rappahannock probably ended yesterday.

Stirring times are expected, and an order to march will not be surprising at any time. The movements of the enemy will probably control our own, so it is altogether which way we will march, even if we leave here at all, at any very early day. 'Tis reported that the Abolition invaders are arriving in large bodies at Fredericksburg. If this is so, our army will probably soon move back, at least across the Rapid Ann, and perhaps to Gordonsville. It does not seem probable that we will remain here very long.

Since last Friday the weather has been fine for the season; clear days, with a bracing atmosphere, and keen cool nights. There is no talk of winter quarters, and our army will, probably, have none this year. The general health of this command continues first rate, and the small pox has disappeared from the Brigade. M. D.

Camp of 8th Ga. Regiment, near
Rapid Ann River, Nov. 17, 1862.

**Dear Courier:** There is nothing of particular interest just now, transpiring in our Brigade. The small pox has entirely disappeared from this command, and it is now evident that the whole excitement upon this subject, was—as the "Old Boy" said when he shaved his hogs—"a great cry and little wool." With the exception of the snow last Friday week and rain last night, the weather has been uniformly fine since we came to this encampment, and, after receiving some of their old clothes left at Richmond last spring, mending those they previously had, and drawing a few more from the Quartermaster, the men have been most sort of half comfortably clad, and good health and good humor have prevailed. It is a noticeable fact that just a few days after long fatiguing marches—as soon as the men have rested and had, for a few successive meals, enough to eat—they are in the best possible good spirits. But if they remain more than a week or ten days quiet in the same camp, they eat too much for the exercise they take, physical exertion becomes irksome, and laziness steals over them like clouds in the night. Then there is any amount of grumbling towards everybody, and in regard to everything; the men even quarrelling among themselves about their own cooking, bringing wood and water, &c., &c.

The enemy are reported to have fallen back to the other side of the Rappahannock, and last Saturday Capt. John Lane—a son of "old Joe Lane" of Oregon—was ordered forward to the river with his battery, in order to feel of the enemy's line. He kept up a brisk cannonade for about three hours at the enemy across the river, but with what result has not yet been reported here.[9]

Yesterday orders were received by this Brigade that the command should be put in readiness to fight, at a moment's warning, with two day's cooked rations constantly on hand. We here can *see* no indications of an immediate fight, but, of course, we have no opportunity to know or judge of general movements, or even special ones a few miles from camp.

In the last few days several orders have been published, giving the results of general court-martial. From these it seems that by far the most common crime in our army is "absence without leave"—on account of extenuating circumstances, the punishment inflicted by the court in many cases, was not so severe as it otherwise would have been. Very many were charged with desertion, but on trial only found guilty of absence without leave. In a majority of these cases the penalty ordered to be inflicted was for the culprit to be confined for sixty days at hard labor, wearing during this time a twelve pound ball attached to a chain to his ankle, and to forfeit two months' pay. One or two guilty of desertion, were ordered to be branded with the letter D on the left hip, have one half of the head shaved and be drummed out of camp. A few for minor crimes were condemned to stand some four or six hours per day for thirty days upon the head of a flour barrel, set in some conspicuous place in the Regiment. Two of the Floyd infantry, Buckanan and Mathews, were tried last week in a Regimental court-martial for being absent without leave.[10] They were sentenced to confinement under guard for 30 days working six hours a day, and to forfeit one month's pay. These men would possibly have been more severely punished, if they had been tried by a general, instead of a regimental court marshal.

TUESDAY MORNING, Nov. 18. All quiet and no news this morning. The weather continues warm and cloudy, but there has not much rain fallen yet. M. D.

Camp 8th Ga. Regiment,
Rapid Ann River,
November 19th, 1862.

**Dear Courier:** At six o'clock yesterday evening, orders were issued to the brigade, to cook three days rations of bread and of meat, and be ready to move at day light this morning. Consequently last night through our camp the busy hum of earnest voice was everywhere heard, while calm but careful preparations were being made to provide against hunger, on the expected march. Experience is said to be the best school master, and eighteen months' service has taught this regiment something in regard to the least practical method of carrying out orders to prepare rations and be ready to move. When we were "green," noise, bustle and hurried confusion followed the issuance of such orders, and the thing was over done, and badly too. After the lapse of a few months, the men learning that orders to "get ready" were not half the time followed by those to "move," they became slack, and, instead of making an excess of preparations, made none at all. But being caught a few times in this "fix," and nearly starving on long and fatiguing marches, they have finally settled down on the conviction that it is best to get "ready" whenever ordered to do so. It may be a curious fact to the "inexperienced," that men, while on severe and continuous fatigue duty, do not desire more than about half the food they crave, when lying about camp and taking but little exercise. If, however, the march is only ten or twelve miles a day, the men will eat in a single day what would do them very well for three successive days, if they marched twenty miles or more, each day.

Reville was beaten this morning at 4 o'clock, and at daylight tents were struck, wagons loaded, and everything ready to start. Up to 10 o'clock last night Gen. Anderson, even, did not know which way we were expected to move, but now, (9 o'clock) it is generally believed that we are to go—if we move at all—towards Orange C.H.

"Wrap jackets" is just now the game that attracts the attention of the listless crowd, and the way the switches of two combatants near here, wrap and slash carries conviction, that they will carry marks for several days to come.

At 9 o'clock the order to move was countermanded, the baggage was brought back, tents pitched and the men commenced to eat their rations. At 9 ½ P.M., another order was received to move immediately, and in accordance with this, in a half hour tents were again struck, wagons loaded, and the Regiment in line ready to march. At 3 ½ o'clock we moved off in the direction of Orange C.H. Which way after passing there, I cannot tell, but probably towards Fredericksburg. It rains slowly.

Capt. Yarbrough and Geo. Hutchings arrived yesterday.

THURSDAY MORNING, Nov. 20. We did not get so far as Orange C.H. last night, but bivouaced 1 ½ miles from town, at the same place we had stopped at twice before—last March and two weeks since. We were ordered to be ready to march at daylight, but it is now 7 ½ o'clock and we are not yet ordered into line. It is rumored that this movement is a general one and that the whole army is falling back while the enemy are advancing by way of Fredericksburg. It is still lowering.

9 ½ o'clock. We are now passing through Orange C.H., and the head of the columns has turned down the Fredericksburg road. M. D.

At "Rest" on the Road Side,
1 o'clock, P.M., Nov. 21, 1862.

**Dear Courier:** After leaving Orange C.H., yesterday, we took the Fredericksburg Plank Road, and followed it about sixteen miles, then turned square to the left, marching about one mile, when we came to the old Fredericksburg road which we took, turning again to the left, and continued on about two miles further, and camped for the night.

The march yesterday was the hardest our Regiment has ever made. It rained a considerable part of the day, and the old plank road is so dilapidated as to make it exceedingly hard to walk upon, having frequently to jump, and take long straining steps to reach from one plank to another. In good weather and over a good road, we could have made the distance—twenty-one miles—very easily. But as it was we marched almost continuously from 8 A.M. until 4 ½ P.M., and as rapidly as the men could be urged forward, and only proceeded as far as was marched easily in seven hours, in our trip from the Valley. It rained nearly all night, but as the tent flies were given out to the men, they got along very comfortably.

Last night one day's rations was issued and cooked. This is a cold misting day, but it has not rained much since 7 ½ o'clock—the time we resumed the march.

Saturday. 9 ½ A.M. Yesterday the march was continued some twelve or fifteen miles, when we camped about a mile from Spotssylvania C.H. The march was resumed this morning at 7 ½ o'clock, and at the Court House we took to the left, and are now proceeding in the direction of Fredericksburg, which is 14 miles from the C.H.

Spottsylvania C.H. is remarkable on account of the absence of the usual concomitants of country villages. The Court House, jail, one hotel, one dwelling, and two churches—all neat brick buildings, with a few outhouses, constitute the town.[11]

If Fredericksburg is our destination we have made a considerable circuit round to the right of a direct course from Orange C.H. No rain since yesterday morning, and as there is less clay in the soil along here, the walking is much improved. It is, for the most part, a very poor country between here and Orange C.H.

It is rumored that the enemy are in large force on the other side of the Rappahannock river opposite Fredericksburg, and that they yesterday gave the citizens till 9 o'clock to evacuate the place, threatening that they would commence shelling the town at that hour. We have heard no artillery this morning as yet.

3 o'clock, P.M. At noon our Brigade was within 2 ½ miles of Fredericksburg, but at the time we turned to the right and have since been countermarching and turning about till I can hardly tell our present distance from town but probably not more than three miles.

We have not seen the place yet. The Brigade is now in line of battle in column of regiments. This is probably rather for convenience in camping than any expectation of an immediate fight. Back a mile or so from here we could distinctly see the enemy's camp fires on the other side of the river. Probably to-morrow we may have stirring times. Humbly trusting in the God of battles, we will try to do our duty.

Orders have been issued to cook two day's rations, and we will, probably unless some movement of the enemy shall necessitate one on our part also.

9 o'clock Sunday Morning. Tents were pitched last night, but orders were issued to be ready to march at a moment's warning. All quiet this morning. M. D.

Camp of 8th Ga. Reg't. near
Fredericksburg, Monday Morn'ng
November 24th, 1862.

**Dear Courier:** This is a beautifully bright, calm, cold morning and the pure sunbeams dance in innocent glee on the sparkling hoar frost, while all nature rejoices in the blessedness of peace and with its still, small, yet earnest voice, condemns the bitter strife and bloody carnage, now preparing in this vicinity. How strange that enemies should force us to fight them, while the voice of Providence is everywhere and at all times heard denouncing their unholy cause. They seem to be blind by their folly, and maddened by their own wickedness. Surely they are.

Blind as never bat was blind, with a dead, bloodshot blindness of the heart. They are deaf as a dead adder's oar, with a swimming swollen senselessness of soul.

It is not remarkable that they should recognize in their numerous defeats—wherein, to all mere human appearances, they had greatly, the advantage at the beginning of the battle—no higher agency than that of their Generals. Can they not see that by removing Scott, McDowell, and McClellan, Halleck, and then McClellan again, respectively from supreme command, that they only create consternation and confusion in their general plans of warfare and thereby diminish their own strength.[12]

It may be Heaven's decree that they shall perish by their own blind folly. At all events, God grant that they soon cease this war that they are unnecessarily waging with so much bitterness.

The two great armies again face each other, with only the Rappahannock river to keep them apart. Busy preparations are going on behind the curtains, and there is no knowing how soon the tinkling rattle by the pickets may call attention to the opening scene in the bloody tragedy to come. The grand *debut* of Burnsides, as principal character, will be waited with great solicitude, and if he fails to make a good thing of the play to the present lessee of the Yankee stage, why then he will be hissed off and have to follow in the footsteps of his disgraced predecessors. If Burnsides should fail, will "Uncle Sam" then see that the fault is in the *play itself,* and not by reason of any incompetence on the part of the principal actors.[13]

Yesterday we moved about three miles, and our present camp is ½ mile east of the railroad and some five miles from Fredericksburg, on dry ground in oak and hickory woods.

Except numerous sore feet, our brigade is in good condition. Our regiment left camp near Rapid Ann River, 409 strong in the aggregate, and this morning reports 373. Two or three new cases of Small Pox have recently appeared in the 7th Reg't, and probably, for that reason, we are now some two miles away from the balance of the army.

Yesterday the dastardly enemy fired a few cannon shot at a train leaving the town, mostly loaded with women and children, to whom they had given notice to leave in three hours. Thus giving an implied threat to shell the place. Fortunately no lives were lost, but no thanks to the vile wretches who perpetrated this outrage.

They have, doubtless, discovered a larger force on this side of the river than they expected to encounter, and now they will probably stop and ditch a while, or, as it is already rumored, they may, by an other "masterly movement," change the base to some other distant approach to Richmond.

Wednesday Morning, Nov. 26th. Matters remained quiet all day yesterday and continued so this morning. It is said that their gunboats cannot come nearer than ten miles from Fredericksburg, in the present state of the river. M. D.

Camp near Fredericksburg, Va.,
Nov. 29, 1862.

**Dear Courier:** The monotony of passing events has not been disturbed by anything of particular interest during the last three days. On yesterday (Friday) morning our Regiment went on picket. Our post was at an evacuated mud fort, on the banks of the Rappahannock, about four miles below the city. The large rich farms in view, with the stately mansions of the aristocratic owners, press the conviction that this portion of the State is in possession of the Virginia gentlemen we "read of" in romances or in historical sketches by enthusiastic writers. There are many beautiful residences in this neighborhood, and some that are, indeed, quite grand. The river opposite our picket post is about 150 yards wide, is a clear, pacid stream, and, with a kind of dignified composure, rolls leisurely along its meandering channel towards the Chesapeake Bay. The tide on the river here rises nearly four feet, and it seemed queer to some of our boys that the water at high tide should not be salt; they supposing that *modus operandi* of the tide was a huge move, starting from some place far out in the ocean, and rolling on the top of all intermediate waters, finally expended itself against the shore, or, per chance far up some inlet or sluggish stream.

There was nothing of note that occurred on our picket that will do to publish just now, except the arrest of two men, at different times, who had crossed the river. One claimed to be a member of the 47th Va. Regiment and said he lived on the other side of the river, and had been, for some, at home sick. We sent him up to headquarters for examination. The particulars in regard to the other I did not learn. We were allowed no fire on post, but, as last night was comparatively pleasant, the suffering was less than what was apprehended. We got back to camp at 8 o'clock tonight, all in good health and spirits.

About general movements, of course, all the "small fry" *know* very little, yet each has a right to think and whatever seems to him probable. The rumor comes quite direct to us over the under ground railroad from the Abolition army; that Burnside has now gone to Washington for the purpose of asking, from his serene highness, Abe the 1st, permission to delay his "onward to Richmond" for thirty days. If that is so *he* will not attack us here; for, if he is not superceded before that time elapses, it will then be too late in the season to think of moving an army over the country so abounding in water courses. But who knows but that the plan of the Richmond fight may be played over again. Jackson is near as then, far to the right of the Federal army, and if he should again dash down upon his right, he would find some way—and I think the means are already at hand—to get to him in front, and, with God's blessing on our side, the wicked invaders might again be driven back.

Capt. Scott, with clothes from home, has not yet arrived, but it rather anxiously looked for. We are now subsisting upon hard bread and beef, and not getting quite enough of these.

The companies are preparing their pay rolls for six months up to Nov. 1st, and the men will probably be paid off for that time, Monday.

Monday morning, Dec. 1. All quiet this morning, and no news. M. D.

Camp near Fredericksburg, VA.,
December 3d, 1862.

**Dear Courier:** There is no exciting news to communicate from this place at present. It is reported that the Abolitionists are making preparations to cross the river in two places. If they make the attempt, the general feeling in our army, so far as I can learn it is, that will be most signally defeated, but it may not be until after a very sanguinary conflict.

So far as one "cooped up," as we are, can see, the preparations of Gen. Lee are to meet any force from Burnside is likely to bring again him. But of general plans or movements, one can know but little. He is like the rustic, who, in the midst of it, said he could not see the city because of the houses. The fact is, the very nearness of a few objects excludes the more distant and perhaps more important ones and thus prevent the possibility of generalization. By a general order, not only the enlisted men, but all the officers are also prevented from leaving the quarters of their respective brigades, except by special permit from the Major General. In addition to this fact, you will take into consideration this other one, that "camp rumors" are so numerous and conflicting, that none of them can be believed, you will realize that we are lamentably ignorant of the very scene in which we are acting. The earliest news which we get in regards to matters about Richmond is through the Fredericksburg papers.

At 3 o'clock P.M. yesterday an order was issued for the men to fall in and form a line of battle, immediately, upon hearing a signal gun, but the gun has not been heard yet—and there is now no expectation of being startled by it soon.

Our regiment is supplied with fly tents and by keeping up good large log fires at the night, the men keep quite comfortable. The other regiments of the brigade sent their tents to Hanover Junction when we moved from the Rapid Ann River, and consequently they now have some reason to complain of the cold, though the weather continues mild for the season.

Our men are making some advancements in their culinary attainments. I have watched Messes making Soap in the last few days. While others are manufacturing candles. The former of these articles, so essential to health, it had become almost impossible to buy but the boys now make a very good article for "home consumption," and thus make a great saving to the government.

Lieut. Huntington, of the Miller Rifles, met with quite an accident today. While cutting some wood his ax glanced and gave him a severe wound in the foot, completely severing one of his toes.[14] Jas. L. Phillips, of the Light Guards, has received a certificate of disability from the brigade surgeon and sent to Richmond. He has been sent to Richmond. He will probably be discharged. He is subject to fits, and had a severe spasm a few days since. If he only had the physical ability, he would make one of the very best of soldiers. He is willing to attempt more than he has strength to perform. He has been discharged once before.[15]

The clothing from home arrived at the depot this evening, but has not yet been brought to camp. Capt. Scott is expected to-morrow.

Thursday Morning. Late yesterday evening orders were issued to the commissaries to provide three days rations and for the men to keep this amount on hand. At ten o'clock last night orders were received to be in readiness to fall in at a moments warning, but all remains quiet up to this time. There is no doubt but that some movement is anticipated by our generals, very soon. It was rumored last night that the enemy were crossing the river at Fort Royal, some 22 miles below here, in force. The ground is now white with frost, but the sun is shining beautifully, and if we have to fight or march, this will be a splendid day for it.

Thieving is becoming quite a common crime in the army. Last night when our boxes come, a guard was sent over to the railroad to protect them. A scamp came up and took up one of them and walked off with it. He was ordered halt but neglected to obey and continued his course with the box. The guard shot at, but missed him. He droped the box and made his escape. M. D.

Camp 8th Ga. Reg. near
Fredericksburg, Dec. 6, 1862.

Dear Courier: The long expected fight has been so long delayed that there now seems to be some doubt whether it comes off at all this season. There has been no important move in our immediate vicinity since my last. The most exciting affairs on the Rappahannock, that I have heard of was the crossing over of 48 men at some point below here, who took 51 prisoners and cleared out one post of the enemy. Another nice little affair occurred some 10 miles below here last Thursday. Two regiments of cavalry and two batteries of artillery went down to attack *five gunboats*. Before the artillery got into position a broadside from one boat killed one man in Capt. Norman's battery. This was the only loss on our side. The batteries took position on a high bluff and within 150 or 200 yards of the boats. At this place the boats could not shoot over the banks, because of their highness. Capt. Norman is sure that he sent three or four balls through one of the boats. At all events they headed about and steamed off down the river as rapidly as possible.

Friday morning it commenced raining, and continued to rain and sleet until about 4 o'clock, P.M., when it commenced snowing in good earnest and this morning the snow was full three inches deep. To-day has been clear, but cold—the snow only melting on the south side of the hills, &c. This is by far the coldest time we have had this season.

The new clothes from home come in the best time possible, and they are now making many a one comfortable who else would have suffered. This Regiment is now very well supplied—thanks to the exertions of friends at home—and we will need but little more clothing this winter.

Sunday morning. All is quiet yet. It is horrid cold this morning, and our Regiment has to go on picket to-day. This will be pretty hard on the five companies who go on post, for there no fire is allowed. M. D.

Camp 8th Georgia Regiment
Near Fredericksburg, Va.,
December 10th, 1862.

Dear Courier: The situation of our army and that of the enemy, also remains as it was when I wrote you last, and "camp life" is as dull and monotonous as it well can be, considering the proximity of the two grand hostile armies. There seems to be no apprehension of an immediate fight. Whatever *opinions* may be entertained, or, however, men may *think* in regard to an early conflict here, they all have a sort of *instinctive feeling in their hearts* of safety, that gives entire quietude on this subject. If however, Burnsides should have the hardihood to attempt to cross the river, it seems that, by a judicious arrangement of our batteries and infantry force, we could "riddle him into doll rags" before he could establish a line of battle on this side. Of course he has a vast army, but from the best information I can get, if he fights us here, we will come nearer meeting the enemy with equal numbers, than we ever have in any great battle, before. And besides our troops are in excellent health and spirits, and they will, if called upon, "put up, at least, as good a fight" as they ever have done. Many think they see the "beginning of the end of the war," and are persuaded in their own minds, that a general victory here, would probably induce old Abe to give up his "big job" of subjugation.

Although it has been clear with bright sunshine every day since, the snow that fell last Friday has not all melted, even in the fields, yet. So you can judge how cold it is.

On last Sunday our brigade moved camp about a mile, for the purpose of getting fire wood convenient. If, by the way, the army remains here much longer, fuel will become scarce. Already the farmers in this vicinity think they are ruined. They did not have much woodland when the army came, and on many farms more than half of what they had is already cut down and consumed. Provisions and forage are also becoming hard to get at. One Quartermaster now hauls corn 22 miles, and the whole country is cleaned of beef, pork, wheat and anything else soldiers can eat. It is no small amount that satisfies 100,000 men and 15,000 or 20,000 horses. Those states and sections that have never had a large army camped in their midst, know nothing of the devastations of war.

Under the present arrangement for picket duty in our brigade, each company will have to go out only once in twenty-five days, and remain only one day on post. This makes picket duty very light, and we have not drilled at all for ten days past.

THURSDAY MORNING. At 6 o'clock this morning we were aroused by signal guns, fired near Fredericksburg. Since then there has been heavy cannonading constantly kept up. It is now 7 ½ A.M. and we are in line of battle. M. D.

In Line of Battle, near
Fredericksburg, Dec. 14.

**Dear Courier:** This is the fourth day of the battle here, and our Brigade has not yet been, generally, in the active engagement. Our position (Hood's division) is in the centre, Gens Thos. Cobb and Richard D. Anderson are on our left and A. H. Hill and Jackson on the right.[16] Gens. Gregg and Cobb were killed yesterday. James R. Boggs was killed yesterday while skirmishing in front of the Regment. Serg't Geo. L. Aycock, of the Light Guards, was mortally wounded while lying in line with the company. He was shot in the head and died last night. Henry Garrett was very severely wounded this morning by grape shot. There have been *no other casualties* in the Rome companies as yet. We have been under heavy fire since 9 o'clock yesterday morning, and have slept three nights in line of battle. There was a general fight of infantry forces both to our right and left yesterday. The enemy were everywhere repulsed. The pickets keep a constant firing this morning, but there is no general engagement of infantry as yet, to-day. It is now noon, and the cannonading has quieted down somewhat. I cannot write more now. M. D.

In Line of Battle, near
Fredericksburg, Monday, Dec. 15.

**Dear Courier:** Yesterday heavy skirmishing was kept up opposite to our line, and heavy cannonading at several points. From 4 o'clock till sun set a flag of truce was up, probably for the purpose of removing some of the dead, but its cause was not certainly known in our Regiment. No general engagement of infantry was heard of by us.

Friday morning our Brigade went on picket, and remained till 9 o'clock last night. We are now back on the bluff, about three miles from the river. The left of the Regiment extends nearly opposite to Dr. Reynolds' residence, and about six or eight hundred yards to the rear of it. We are in the woods, and have a very good rifle pit for protection against infantry. In this vicinity there are said to be three lines of battle, one in front and the other in our rear, but we can see neither of the others. After descending the bluff, which is some hundred feet high, there is spread out before us a plain three miles wide to the river, the surrounding hills making it nearly semi-circular in shape. A. P. Hill's forces are below this amphitheatre, and Cobb's and R. H. Anderson's above. Our artillery is planted thick all around on these hilltops. When our Brigade left picket post last night, that post was vacated except by 150 men left as skirmishers with instructions to fall back if the enemy advanced, thereby to draw them in under our artillery. This morning our skirmishers left on picket post under the command of Major Magruder were relieved. They report all quiet during the night.

The "old Eighth" was under a heavy fire all day Saturday, but the only men actually engaged were our skirmishers thrown out some 200 yards in front of the line. These skirmishers took sixty-one prisoners, perhaps more correctly speaking, that many Yankees were driven into our line by an advance of the 16th N.C. Regiment, on our right, together with the advance of our skirmishers. Our boys got a large number of oil cloths, blankets, guns, accoutrements, &c., &c.

The report that Serg't Geo. K. Aycock was dead, was erroneous. I have just seen a man right from him, who says he is doing well, and the Surgeon thinks him in a fair way to recover. His skull was fractured, and the Doctor has removed some small pieces that pressed upon the brain. Henry Garrett died yesterday evening, and he and James Boggs are buried near Dr. Reynolds' residence. They were both excellent soldiers, brave and faithful, and much beloved by their companions in arms. The three above named and one of the Atlanta Grays, C. W. Fraser, and three of the Oglethorpe Rifles, taken prisoners, *is all the loss* as yet (Monday noon) suffered by our Regiment.

Gen. Pender's Brigade of North Carolina Troops, now joins us on the right. The men have been furnished with spades and axes, and are now very busy improving their breastworks. It has been very quiet all the morning, yet a general engagement is expected to commence every moment. The officers and men are all in good spirits and confident of success whenever the tug of war comes. It seems that the Abolitionists will soon be compelled to advance or retreat, one or the other. They are now confined to the river bottom land, while we hold all the surrounding heights on this side of the river. Several of their best batteries fire upon us from the other side of the river.

There is very little wood this side of the river, within thre lines, and although the past three days have been remarkably warm and pleasant, this weather cannot be expected to continue long at this season of the year.

It is now 12 ½ o'clock and all quiet as yet.

Billy Barron arrived yesterday. M. D.

In Line of Battle near
Fredericksburg, Dec. 16, '62.

**Dear Courier:** This morning we were surprised to learn that the Abolition army had all recrossed the river. 'Tis said that they commenced the move at daylight this morning. Our scouting parties took about 1,000 of the vile wretches this morning, who had straggled behind. A plenty of them can still be seen on the other side of the river, and their heaving guns are sending an occasional shot over this way. Some of their wagons are moving down the river, and the general impression with us is, that the whole Yankee army are preparing to move down to Port Royal, at least in that direction. There was no general fight yesterday, and but little skirmishing this morning. Our Brigade moved down to the right, to the railroad near Hamilton's Crossing.

Burnsides has certainly done a losing business here. The Abolition loss can hardly be less than 8,000, in killed, wounded, and prisoners, and may be 3,000 or 4,000 more than that, while our entire loss does not exceed 3,000. The banks of river being higher on the north sides than on the south, our forces are prevented from pursuit by the Yankee artillery, which is covering their retreat, and so our victory is not so decisive as would have been desirable; and yet it is a great victory to have repulsed "the Grand Army of the Potomac" that moved up to Fredericksburg a few weeks since so boastingly and with such imposing numbers. Burnsides has certainly acted very discreetly in retreating when he could. The judicious selection of positions and arrangements of troops, by General Lee, was such as to have enabled our army to have whipped out the Yanks, even if they had advanced in a force of 200,000 strong.

What our next movements are to be of course time will develop; it is not improbable that a long march is in store for us at an early day. A little rest now would be highly appreciated by the "Rebels." For five days and nights our Brigade has been in line of battle, although in that time it has marched six times, short distances (a mile or two) each time. It rained an hour or two this morning, about daylight, and since then it has been turning colder. Sergeant George Aycock is reported to be better, but the Surgeon says his wound is very severe.[17] There have been no casualties in our brigade since Saturday.

Wednesday Morning. Last night we moved back to the camp ground occupied previous to Thursday. We expect our tents to-day. Some of the Yankee officers acknowledge a loss of five to one in the recent battle. This is a fine morning, bright and pleasant. M. D.

Camp Near Fredericksburg,
December 17, 1862.

**Dear Courier:** The following list of wounded, from the 21st Ga. Regiment, is probably correct, as far as it goes, and includes all that were carried to their Brigade Hospital:

Thos. J. Verderey, Adjt. of the Regt., killed on the field.

M. E. Mayo, Co. K, slightly; W. Gibons, Co. I, slightly; J. C. Bennett, Co. F, slightly; W. A. Duke, Co. D, slightly; W. Wood, Co. G., severely; R. W.

Stuart, Co. B, slightly; W. E. Blevins, Co. H, slightly; W. T. Faib, Co. A, severely; Lieut. J. Rucker, Co. C, slightly; A. Heusly, Co. A, severely; Serg't J. Camp, Co. A, severely; H. H. Henderson, Co. H, slightly; Sergeant B. H. Dodd, Co. D, slightly; J. B. Crabb, Co. D, severely; J. C. Benedict, Co. C, severely; F. M. Wiley, Co. H, slightly; J. Gatlin, Co. H, slightly; J. T. Phillips, Co. D, slightly; J. L. Reynolds, Co. F, severely; W. Bennington, Co. H, severely; J. Norton, Co. K, severely.

The following named of the 19th and 38th Ga. Regiments were carried to Anderson's Brigade Hospital:

Of the 19th Lieut. M. T. Hamilton, Co. F, slightly; C. B. Gladney, Co. F, severely; H. M. Reed, Co. F, seriously.

Of the 38th Regiment J. C. Harris, Co. D, slightly; R. M. Simpson, Co. D. severely.

The following is believed to be a full list of killed and wounded in General George Anderson's Brigade:

James R. Boggs, Co. H, 8th Georgia, killed; Henry J. Garrett, Co. E, 8th Ga., killed; Serg't L. Aycock, Co. A, 8th Ga., severely wounded, Isaac Collins, Co. H. 7th Ga., severely; Ransom Deigs, Co. I, 7th Ga., severely; N. H. Fowler, Co. F, 7th Ga., severely.

The 38th Georgia Regiment suffered very severely in the fight, Col. Atkinson, Acting Brigadier Gen. of Lawton's Brigade, was killed; Captain Lawton, brother of General L., and Acting Assistant Adjutant Gen., was also killed; Lieut. Col. Scott, of 12th Ga., killed; Captain John W. Hooper, of 19th Ga., was slightly wounded in the foot.

When the Abolitionists recrossed the river they left most of their dead on this side; most of them, however, had been collected in heaps of from twenty to two or three hundred, yesterday they sent over details and were burying them. It is said that in one field of four acres, upon the left, a thousand dead Yanks could be seen. Our pickets took possession of Fredericksburg early yesterday morning.

D. C. Bussey, of the Light Guards, died at Lynchburg on the 2d instant.

Thursday Morning. We got our tents yesterday and last night had comfortable lodging. It is fine weather. I cannot leave the Regiment to get news, and so send you such items as come to hand. M. D.

Camp 8th Ga. Regt., Near
Fredericksburg, Dec. 20, 1862.

**Dear Courier:** On Thursday last I got permission to visit town and the left of the battle field; but, as we were ordered out yesterday morning into line of battle and kept there all day, on account of some supposed movement of the enemy, this is the first opportunity of writing of what was there seen. I walked from our present camp, about three miles below the city, over the right of the battle ground, discovering nothing of particular interest except two or three dead men who had been overlooked, several dead horses, and the places where two Yankee caissons had been blown up. It is easy to tell where there had been hard fighting, from the litter of haversacks, cartridge boxes, old clothes, etc., etc. Following up the railroad track the "Old Burg" was entered near the southern side. I passed on up Main street, which runs parallel with the river, then went through two or three cross streets, and beheld such sights as, perhaps, were never before seen in this country. Through the entire place, which probably contained, in times of peace, some six or eight thousand inhabitants, but *three* buildings not hit by cannon balls or shells are remembered to have been seen. Some houses were literally torn to pieces, others had six or eight ball holes through them, and still others a less number. Here you would see where a ball had passed through a window, there through a door, in another place through the brick walls. The insides of many buildings were torn to the fragments by the bursting of shells. The proportion of houses burnt is comparatively small, not more than six or eight were seen in the city. Bad as all this is, it is nothing in comparison with the evidence of vandalism of the Abolition troops. The demons of the infernal regions turned loose for the special purpose of plundering and destroying, could not have done worse. Every house was entered in some way, to some the doors were battered down, to some only panels

Aftermath of Battle of Fredericksburg. Photograph by Alexander Gardner. Library of Congress.

were knocked out and into others they crawled through the windows. To enter these houses and see the wanton destruction committed by these vile wretches is enough to boil the blood in the most stolid breasts. Beds were cut up and torn to pieces, fine carpets defiled by the most filthy means, splendid mirrors dashed to atoms, and all sorts of fine furniture ruined. In some instances it looked like fine parlors had been entered by some half dozen savages with axes in hand, with which they had cut and knocked until every article in the room was utterly ruined. Even "hobby horses" and children's toys did not escape the general destruction.

It must not be inferred that they did not *steal*, oh, no! Every thing of value that they *could* carry off was sent across the river, and will probably be carried home as trophies of abolition valor—fit illustrations of their character. They got most egregiously whipped in a fair fight and then vent their spite by most wantonly sacking a defenceless town.

A few citizens and some ladies had come back to see the loathsome sight of their homes thus wickedly desecrated, some troops came round sight seeing, yet the place has every appearance of being deserted and was painfully quiet.

Leaving the city we went over the battle ground on the left of our lines. This is on the outskirts of town, not more than a mile from Main street, and is where McLaws' Division committed such awful destruction on the advancing columns of the abolition hordes. Our front line along here was in a road and behind a rock fence. The position was a most admirable one for defensive operations. There is a bluff about fifty feet high and two hundred yards in the rear of this line, where was our second line and artillery. The Yanks, as soon as they left the cover of the buildings in the town, were exposed to our cannon, and they were unable to get a single one of their batteries into position so as to play on our infantry. Their line advanced, however, in good order, being under cover of a hill from our infantry until within about 150 yards of our front line. Here our men poured it into them as they came up over the little hill. They were repulsed. Again and again, and yet still they persisted in the attack. These were Sumner's best men and he was determined to carry that point, if possible, at any cost. But they were finally forced to give back. They could not quite stand the fire of the "ragged rebels." Some idea of the enemy's loss may be formed from the number of dead left on the field here. The Yankee officer commanding the detail to bury their dead said that they buried six hundred on Wednesday, and he supposed there were about three hundred left to bury on Thursday. All these had been left on the field, and on not more than four or five acres of ground. Many who fell dead, and nearly all the wounded during the fight were carried back to the camp and thence across the river immediately so that their number of killed at this place can hardly be less than a thousand. The usual proportions of wounded to the killed being five to one, would make their entire loss here, besides prisoners, six thousand. On our right the enemy's loss in killed and wounded was not less than three thousand, and it is reported that we took, along the whole line, two thousand prisoners, thus making the entire Yankee loss eleven thousand. This estimate is lower by far than the usual one made here in camp. Our loss is now estimated at twenty-two hundred.[18] M. D.

Camp 8th Ga. Regiment,
Near Fredericksburg, Va.,
December 31.

**Dear Courier:** Did it ever occur to your mind what a mighty "band of brothers" the army of the Confederate States is becoming? How that common toils and sufferings, privations and dangers, together with mutual rejoicings over, hard won victories, and a living, active, universal hatred of the detested Yankee nation, has bound together our entire army—man to man, heart to heart and arm to arm—in golden bands of indissoluble strength and unlimited endurance? But this is really the case, whether you have thought about it or not, and it is one of the consoling effects of this calamitous and wicked war. The absence of all selfishness, and the general prevalence of generous sentiments, keeps down all rivalries and bickerings between regiments and States, and the whole army "dwells together in unity."

This by no means prevents wit and repartee and the rallying of men, from any state or section, upon their imputed characteristics and provincialisms.

It is really interesting to notice the little differences of dialect, and the peculiar cant phrases of different States, and, in very many, if not a majority of cases, a short conversation with a soldier, particularly, if he be a man of only ordinary education, will furnish satisfactory evidence as to what State he is from.

The Virginians are sure to use the word *indeed* unnecessarily, and confirmatory expression. They seldom say "yes sir" or "no sir," but almost invariably respond, "yes *indeed*" or "no *indeed*," as the case may be.

The North Carolinians say "weins" and "youins" instead of *we* or *our*, and *you* or *yours*.

The Georgians do a "mighty" deal of "toting."

The South Carolinians are not so readily distinguished by any word or phrase that they use, as by an apparent expectation on their part, to be regarded as a little braver, or more chivalric than any body else.

Floridians are proverbially small, with sallow complexion, and are generally disposed to be rather taciturn. In bravery and powers of endurance, they beat their appearance all to pieces.

The Alabamians have no State peculiarities, by which they are readily distinguished, and the same may be said of Mississippians, unless it be that the latter have a disposition to indulge in the slang peculiar to the Mississippi boatman.

The Louisianians are rather cosmopolitish in their manners, have a tinge of French friskiness and politeness, and are merry under all circumstances.

The Texans have a "rough and ready" air of recklessness, and seem to really enjoy the excitement of fighting.

Arkansians may generally be known by the huge bowie-knife, looking for the world as if it was made by a country blacksmith, hung by their side.

Tennesseeans are large, generally have red hair or at least are of light complexion, and have a very decided bias towards hog driving and stock raising, in their illustration and comparisons.

The amount of intelligence and genteel breeding is very equally distributed among the different States. Each State has in the ranks a very large number of as well raised, affluent genteel men as can be found in the best society anywhere.

It is wonderful what a rage cant phrases and peculiar sayings and doings, there are in the army. It is probable no exaggeration to state that "here is your mule," has been said a hundred million times by soldiers in this army, during the past year. But that is nearly "played out" now. Another thing that has been nearly, as popular, is, when a citizen or private soldier, or an officer of low rank, is seen riding a horse in any way at all eccentric, he is sure to be called on to "fall off and grab a root." Another sensation that has recently had a great run is, to call upon the person, showing some, ecentricity in dress or personal appearance "to come out of that—I know you are in there, for I see," so and so. To illustrate a man wearing an uncommonly high pair of top boots, is ordered to "come out of those boots—I know you are in there, for I see your head." One of the most ridiculous examples of this, that has came under the writers observation was, in case of a man having a very long gootee, who was thus addressed: "spit out that horse—I know he is in there, for I see his tail." If a man perpetrates a witicism he is said to be "shelling" the crowd, and so if one jokes another, he is said to be "shelling" him, and if the repartee is not ready and adequate, the whole crowd cry out, "lie down, lie down, he is shelling you." But thus speaking of shells reminds one of the literal ones, and the "pet names" by which they are called. The very large bomb shells, thrown by the Yanks at us, are called "flour barrels" and the long ones fired from rifle cannon, "lamp posts." When a cannon ball goes far over us, when in line of battle, and hence on to the rear, the boys all say "there goes a commissary hunter."

Thursday Night. New Years Day has been pleasant, and very quietly spent by the troops here. Nothing of public interest has transpired here during the past week. On last Saturday our brigade moved across the railroad and nearly to the telegraphic road. We are now about four miles from the city.

Toomb's Brigade has been transferred to Gen. Pickets Division, Rylander's Battalion has got here at last, and has joined our brigade, and the Ga. Regulars are probably now on their way to Macon, Ga.

Capt. Dunlap Scott has recently been appointed Provost Marshal of Hood's Division. M. D.

# 8

# "Once More I Take My Pencil in Hand"

*January–May 1863*

As the new year began, the Eighth Georgia remained camped outside Fredericksburg. Anxious to get back to Rome and attend to the financial affairs of the *Courier*, Melvin Dwinell complained that Confederate commanders were not granting furloughs except in "very extreme cases." Another letter told the story of a young black man with smallpox who allegedly was ordered by Union troops to swim across a nearby river to the Confederate lines. When Rebel troops learned what the man was suffering from, they told him he had to go back, and he drowned trying to return to the Yankee side. "Cunning devils might have thought of such a plan, but no enlightened human being besides a Yankee would ever had the presumption to attempt to execute it," Dwinell wrote.

Dwinell also raged at President Abraham Lincoln's issuance of the Emancipation Proclamation on January 1. He claimed the proclamation was an act of desperation by a president—"Abraham the First"—who ruled tyrannically. Later, he described how the troops enjoyed a late January winter storm by organizing a big snowball fight: "The contest was very amusing—more exciting than a horse race and more laughable than any comedy on the stage." Dwinell finally received the furlough he wanted, and the editor returned to Rome in mid-February for two weeks. The town had been turned into a vast Confederate hospital, and many of the largest homes were being used to care for injured soldiers. The uprooting of homes and businesses for military hospitals only aggravated the struggling economy. While some merchants remained

Abraham Lincoln, c. 1865. Photograph by Alexander Gardner. Library of Congress

determined to keep their stores open, many others were selling out. A notice in the *Courier* said the editor would be glad if everyone with outstanding debts "would call and settle" while he was home. During his return trip to Virginia, Dwinell was delayed at several stations. With plenty of time to observe the passengers, he noticed how women traveling alone received more help than ever from men. He suspected that this was the case because men helping women could travel in train cars reserved for ladies.

While Dwinell was home on furlough, two of Lt. Gen. James Longstreet's divisions were dispatched for Richmond. The Confederate command believed the capital was threatened by the large number of Federal troops to the south. The Eighth Georgia marched through Richmond and set up camp near Petersburg. In a mid-March letter, a rested Dwinell said the men were enjoying the best rations they had eaten in a year. On March 27, which President Jefferson Davis proclaimed a national day of fasting, humiliation, and prayer, the entire brigade attended a religious service. Rev. William Monroe Crumley preached a sermon that Dwinell predicted would "be long remembered" by the troops. In another letter, the editor referred to the recent food riots. Hundreds of women in Petersburg and Richmond were angry about the rising cost of goods, and Dwinell denounced the "extortioners and speculators" who charged outrageous prices.

On April 8, the Eighth Georgia broke camp and marched down the road toward Suffolk, Virginia, about one hundred miles away. The weather was good and the marching generally easy, Dwinell wrote. Along the route, the soldiers saw a farm where cotton had been grown, "a sight that cheered the hearts of Southern boys." By April 11, the troops had taken up their positions in the Confederate lines near Suffolk. They spent the next several days building breastworks and going out on picket duty. Although the Eighth Georgia came under fire repeatedly, only a few men were wounded, and most injuries were minor. As was often the case during long sieges, the men looked for various ways to amuse themselves. Dwinell told how Confederate troops had a good time putting an effigy of a soldier in an observation post on a tall tree. The "sell took finely," he wrote, as the Union artillery spent the better part of a day trying to knock out the observation post.

Camp 8th GA. Regiment,
Near Fredericksburg, Jan. 9, 1863.

**Dear Courier:** It is remarkable how ardent the attachments of soldiers to their *successful* Generals becomes, and the more terrible the conflicts they lead them through, and the greater their own sufferings the warmer are their affections and the greater is their admiration for the man whose orders they have obeyed. In consideration of this fact as it really exists in a great army, it is not strange that governments have, in times of revolutions, been jealous of the power of successful Military chieftains. But to return to the first idea of the comparative little *fighting* a soldier has to do. Our regiment has been in ten regular pitched battles in about twenty months, or on an average one battle every two months. Though this is considerable more fighting than has been done by the average of regiments in the Confederate army, yet even this affords us long intervals of dull, monotonous camp life, that drags heavily upon the spirits and health of the men, and puts to a severe test their military discipline.

The health and discipline of this army are both good at the present time—much better than they were six months since. Being right in face of the enemy here, and from twelve to fifteen men from each regiment going out on picket every two days and standing on one bank of the Rappahannock while the enemy's pickets are on the other bank, thus seeing them and being sufficiently near to hear them talk, although conversation with them is prohibited, keeps up a lively sense of prudence and an appreciation of the necessity of strict discipline. But still after all, we are having a decidedly dull time. It hardly seems as though there will be any more fighting here this season, and yet Gen. Lee will not grant furloughs except in *very extreme cases*. And now, just at this season of the year, nearly every man in the army is extremely anxious to visit home in order to make some arrangements for his business during the next twelve months, or, if he has no urgent business, why then it is just the time and is most desirous of seeing the "loved ones at home." Any amount of applications for leave of absence have been sent up, nearly all of which have been *very politely disapproved*. The General regrets that the demands of the service will not admit of the granting of furloughs *just now*. This "throws a damper" over the high hopes of the ardent applicant and makes him feel very much as a young man is *supposed* to feel (for the writer would not have his young lady readers think he knows anything about it) when he gets a negative response from a young lady whose hand he has solicited, but which refusal is accompanied with the hope that they may always be *friends*. Aside from the anxiety to go home we are getting along very pleasantly, although it has been "cold as krout" during the past two or three days. Except a little rain on last Tuesday we have had bright days, or at least neither rain or snow since December 15th. The army is now comfortably clothed and shod.

Last Wednesday our Brigade was reviewed by Gen. Hood, and to-day the Division by the same officer. Our Division as now arranged is composed of the following Brigades, in their order from the right: Jenkin's, Anderson's, Law's, and Robinson's; the latter being Hood's old Brigade. Toombs' Brigade has been transferred to Picket's Division, and they are now said to be building Winter quarters.

If it was warmer I might write a little more, but I declare my feet and hands are almost frozen, and I must go to the fire and warm—so good bye for the present. M. D.

Camp 8th GA. Regiment, near
Fredericksburg, Va., Jan. 15, '63.

**Dear Courier:** The public mind is now so completely absorbed in the history of passing events in Tennessee, Mississippi, and North Carolina, that the less said about our army here, further than that "all is quiet along" the lines of the Rappahannock, the better. All the necessary preparations seem to be making to give the abolition hordes—should they attempt another "onward to Richmond" from this point—quite as warm a reception as they got before, and they will surely not be allowed to escape in the same way again. But it is not so very *quiet* in some sections of our picket line as it was a week since. Some little incidents have occurred that make the posts in the city and its immediate vicinity quite interesting. I will narrate two that seem to be well authenticated. A few days since, at a post a little above town, some North Carolinians, then stationed there, noticed a negro being driven towards the river by three or four Yanks, they pressing him forward with the points of their bayonets. This, of course, excited curiosity of our men, and they watched closely to ascertain what this strange preceding might mean. The negro seemed to move forward reluctantly, but was forced on by the bayonets of these vile abolitionists, the *pretended* friends of his race. When they got him to the very waters' edge he seemed by his movements and gestures, to expostulate them, but all to no purpose. He was forced to plunge into the river and swim towards our shore. When he got about half way cross, our men hailed him and asked him what he was coming over to our side of the river for. He answered that he had the *small pox*, and that for this reason the Yanks had compelled him to come. Our men threatened to kill him if he came to our shore, and so the poor fellow turned back to try once more the *tender mercies* of his *friends*, but had swam but a short distance before he sank to rise no more. This is but a little incident, yet it speaks whole volumes of abolition history and illustrates their style of warfare. Such low-lifed, sneaking, devilish tricks characterize their efforts to subjugate a high-toned, chivalric and brave people. This negro they had, probably, coaxed, with flattering promises, from his master, but as soon as a loathsome, contagious disease had developed itself upon his person, they thought it a good trick and an easy way to kill off the rebels, to send him back, and thus spread the fatal malaria in their ranks. Cunning devils might have thought of such a plan, but no enlightened human being besides a Yankee would ever had the presumption to attempt to execute it.

Another interesting occurrence took place not long since between one of our pickets, a member of 10th Ga. Reg., stationed in or near the city, and a Yank stationed on the opposite bank of the river. The Yank insisted on talking to our men, who took no notice of him until the vile scamp said, "Do you want to know what we all come down South for? I will tell you anyhow. We came to ruin secesh women." This fired the blood of the chivalric Georgia boy, and the words had barely escaped the lips of the disgusting incarnate, when, forgetting orders, crack went his rifle, and down dead fell the abolitionist. Since that event it is reported that there has been considerable firing by the pickets on both sides in that part of the line. Several ladies and children are reported to have left the city in the past day or two, and it is said this has been done because Gen.

Burnside had given notice that he intended to shell the place again. This may be all so, yet is barely possible; or at all events, if Burnside intends to fire upon the town again, it is probably merely for the purpose of dislodging our troops there, and not with the intention of again crossing the river.

Last Monday was a rainy day, since the weather has been pleasant. Good health and the very best of spirits prevail. Last Sunday Gen. Lee sent round an order to the effect that two men and one officer from each company might get a short furlough. The applications have gone up and answers are expected tomorrow. M. D.

Camp 8th Ga. Reg. near
Fredericksburg, Va., Jan. 20, '63.

**Dear Courier:** Once more I take my *pencil*—about an inch and a half long—in hand—resting on an old memorandum book, (that I have carried in my pocket ever since the war commenced,) upon my knee for a writing table—to inform you that we all who have not been killed in battle, nor wounded, nor been lately sick—are well, and hope these few lines will find you and all of your readers—except those few who have stopped the *Courier* because a little more than half its cost is now charged for it—enjoying the same blessing. But these discontinuants may have *good* reasons for their course that are unknown to me, so I hope they are all "enjoying the same blessing." And even if I had not hoped so, they would have done me great injustice, by supposing that I wished them *ill.* For at worst, I could only have desired that they should have felt a little kind of sheep-stealing guiltiness when, every night, they review their matters of conscience. But I didn't go to say anything about this matter, and now more than half wish I had not. But "what is writ is writ—would it worthier."

This letter was commenced with the idea (in the writer's mind) of accounting for the many errors that appear in these letters after they are printed, and this shall now be done in short metre. They have nearly all been written with only facilities as are mentioned above; frequently under very exciting circumstances; often when the writer was greatly fatigued, and nearly always in a hurry, so as to be sent off by some opportune chance. These being the circumstances, and the chirography, always bad, made worse by using a pencil, instead of a pen and ink, the real wonder is, not that the printers have made so *many*, but so *few* mistakes.

If the reader has persisted in going through this long rigamaroll of a prelude, he—or she, as the case may be—will now surely conclude that the writer has made "too big a go for a pony;" for there is little matter of real interest to communicate, and this little can be expressed in a few lines.

Last Friday morning we were somewhat startled by learning that an order had been promulgated to company commanders "to allow no men to leave camp, as you may be ordered to move at a moment's warning." This order was followed, about two hours afterwards, by another "to cook two day's rations." "Well, well, what is out now?" was the common enquiry. The Surgeon came along directly and relieved the doubt by saying that he had orders to get a supply of *splints* and *bandages* and have all things in readiness for "field duties." This was rather a damper on the spirits of the men; for, as it is said, that the most dauntless dislike to have their own coffins paraded before them, while conscious, so the common run of soldiers hate to see the Surgeons scraping the blood rust off their probes and "carving knives" and getting in readiness their tourniquets and bandages. Yesterday it was rumored through camp that the cause of these orders was the ascertained fact, that the enemy were building a military road so as to enable them to approach the river at two points, hitherto inaccessible, one about the city and the other below, and the consequent apprehension, or rather expectation that they intended an early advance.

To-day an order was sent around "to keep constantly on hand two days cooked rations." Yesterday an order was read to the Regiment that the Commissary General had found it necessary, on account of recent interruptions in Railroad communication, to reduce the rations of salt meat to one fourth pound every day, and that in lieu of the other fourth pound one fifth of a pound of sugar would be issued to each man daily *in addition to the regular allowance of sugar*. What a good joke the last clause contains will be understood when the fact is known that up to a week ago the men had not received, in all, a half pound of sugar each in the last three months.

A few furloughs have been granted in the last two days, and more are *hoped* for.

It has been exceedingly cold for the past three days.

Wednesday morning. Last night was one of the worst we have seen this winter. About dark the weather moderated a little and it commenced to rain. The wind continued high all night, and the rain was incessant. Several of the tents have been blown down and everything so wet, it looked like a hard chance to get any breakfast. Wonder if this storm won't give the Abolition fleet scissors? M. D.

Camp 8th Georgia Regiment, near
Fredericksburg, Jan. 30, 1863.

**Dear Courier:** Current events in Abolitiondom all point to the fact that the great crisis of the war is fast approaching. Lincoln, in desperation, has made his last mad leap in his Abolition proclamation; the iron grasp with which he crushed freedom of speech and an untrammeled press has been broken, and now, not only disaffection, but outright opposition to his tyrrannous rule, spreads like wild fire throughout the length and breadth of his betrayed, befooled, and almost enslaved dominions. The present cringing, fawning, dough-faced Congress, that has hitherto been his pliant tool, and that of his rabid Abolition advisers, expires on the 4th of March, and will then be succeeded by one containing a clear Democratic majority, who have been elected for the very purpose of opposing his tyrannical rule.[1] The term of service of over two hundred thousand of his best troops will expire in May and he, in vain, seeks for any reasonable prospect to supply their places. And then, what is, perhaps, the worst of all to him, is the rapidly sinking condition of Federal finances, and this, not because, of any sudden panic, but for the reason that the money lenders of the world have no sort of confidence in him or the success of his war of subjugation.

All these things combine to make Abraham the First desperate, and it may be expected that no plan of wanton barbarism or bloody cruelty will be too savage for his undertaking, or any scheme, trick, or device be too low-lived and mean to receive his approbation, provided it promises success. As a drowning man will catch at a straw, so he will jump at any chance to save his sinking fortunes. But he sees that he "has been weighed in the balance" and even Northern public opinion "and found wanting," and that he may be impeached and deposed is now by no means beyond the range of possibilities. His only way of salvation lies through *success*—immediate and completely overwhelming, over the Rebels—in fact an entire subjugation of the South.

The New York *Tribune,* in a recent issue, points out a plan by which, if the rebellion is not crushed in three months, he, Horace Greeley, will then be willing to accept of *peace on any terms.*[2] His plan is as follows: The bankers are to be assured that this is positively the *last time* they will be called upon to furnish money during the war, and on the strength of this assurance the aforesaid will furnish five hundred millions of dollars, the amount now needed to crush the rebellion; the entire militia of all the loyal States is to be called out for three months, and with them Maryland is to be kept down, Washington City to be protected, and Fortress Monroe and all other posts of comparative safety, to be garrisoned; all the forces now in service are to engage the rebels in their various strongholds, and two hundred thousand *colored* Unionists, in small, organized bands, are to scour those portions of rebeldom most densly populated by those of their own race, arming and setting them free as they go, and exterminating the white race. Now, as Greely is old Abe's "right bower," who knows but that this or some other equally crazy plan may be adopted. At all events the entire militia of the State of New York has recently been ordered to report to Gen. Wool.

In consideration of these facts, the duty of the Confederate States is plain. All possible preparation ought to be made to overcome our merciless enemies, in what, as it now seems probable, will be their last desperate effort at subjugation. The Government is doing all in its power, and the officers and men in the field will cheerfully do their duty when the hour of trial comes. The only fears to be apprehended arise from the weakening, and what is even worse, the demoralizing effect upon our army, of the number of absentees from their several posts.

There are at least one hundred thousand officers and men now out of camp who ought to be there. Most of these have had Furloughs or sick leaves, which have expired, and they are now putting up, at best only some frivolous excuse for their absence from duty. A man can hardly be absent without leave and the members of his own company not know it, and it tends to disaffect every one who is faithful. Another thing that has hitherto kept thousands of men out of the army that now ought to be there, is the obsticles that have been thrown in the way of enrolling conscripts.

This is no time to be "meally mouthed," or for any one, from motives of mere delicacy, to shrink from a faithful discharge of duty; and, while the soldiers in the field shall do the fighting, there is a contest hardly less important, that ought to be successfully engaged in by the ladies, old men, exempts and other non-combatants at home; and that is to drive off the lazy shirks, the would-be drones in the great national hive, from their retreats of blissful ease and security at home. Mothers must give up their sons, sisters their brothers, and lovers their sweethearts, until the last grand struggle for our independence is over. Physicians, when called upon to give a certificate of disability, should be careful that they do not do it just as a personal favor, and thus forget their duty to the country. Let them put on a hard face and refuse to commend a furlough to all but those who are actually unable to do duty in the field. All such certificates, however, have to be signed by Army Surgeons, where there is one within reasonable distance of the applicant.

But to conclude, the indications are that the severest fighting yet to be done in this war will be done very soon. Let our ranks be filled up and then success will be easy and *sure.*

As for news, there is none here of much interest. There is no doubt but that the enemy did make an effort to cross the river last week, but their artillery and baggage wagons stuck in the mud so that they had to turn back. Last Wednesday it snowed all day and on Thursday morning the snow was 10 to 12 inches deep. Yesterday there was the greatest frolic at snowballing I ever saw. Brigade met brigade, they threw out skirmishers and advanced on each other in regular lines of battle. The contest was very amusing—more exciting than a horse race and more laughable than any comedy on the stage. A full description of this fight might prove entertaining if this letter was not already too long.

A. F. Pemberton and H. A. Smith start for home to-morrow, on furlough for 29 days.

Camp 8th Georgia Regiment, Near
Richmond, Va., March 10.

**Dear Courier:** After various haps and mishaps, diverse delays and petty annoyances—none of which, however, are particularly interesting, except vexatiously so to the sufferer—your correspondent arrived safely in camp on the evening of Saturday, the 8th inst. The cars on all the roads are intensely crowded, and of course there is any amount of pulling, hauling, "scrouging" and tearing about at every place where the passengers change cars, every man having determined that *he* will have a seat at any rate. Some who are particularly "sharp" seldom fail, but it is good average luck to get seats over two roads out of three.

Probably gentlemen never appeared so gallant to the ladies as they now do in travelling. If a lady, about a station, is seen looking after her baggage or trying to press her way to the ticket office, or doing anything else that seems to indicate that she has no gentleman accompanying her to attend to such things, at least half dozen gentlemen are sure to tender their services. But it must be confessed, that is done not so much from motives of pure politeness as from the selfish desire of thereby securing a seat in the ladies' car. There is generally but one car in a train reserved for ladies, and into this no man is allowed to enter unless he be the escort of a lady, and hence the great anxiety to secure a lady friend who will do the favor of passing him by the guard, into this much coveted coach of pleasant comfort.

The general rule now seems to be to miss connections at the termini of the various roads and the exceptions to make them. The writer was delayed at Augusta, Charlotte, Raleigh and Petersburg. Of all those places Augusta seems most to be in the enjoyment of peaceful ease and comfort; perhaps no city in the Confederate States has suffered less from the devastating effects of the present horrid war. There are more fancy dry goods and dandyfied looking men in Petersburg than in any other place on the route, and yet there are so many hospitals and broken down soldiers there that the general appearance is greatly saddened, and every right thinking man is vexed at the contrasts he sees, between foppishly dressed citizens and the diseased, careworn, poorly clad, but brave defenders of the "swell heads" around them. It may be wrong to desire to thrash them, yet it is very provoking for a soldier to see fat, slick-headed citizens strutting about and bearing no evidence in their personal appearance that they are bearing their part in the present struggle, but are, on the contrary, taking advantage of the absence of those in the field to amass fortunes for themselves. Petersburg is not the only place where the soldier sees these hateful sights, but there are more of them there than in some other places.

Our present camp is on the Petersburg Track, five miles from Richmond and two and a half from Drury's Bluff, on only tolerably good ground and with a very short supply of good wood. The men all have tents with chimneys to them, and on the whole, in a very comfortable condition. They are nearly all in excellent health and spirits, and more men are now reported for duty than at any other time since the battles before Richmond. The Miller Rifles now have in camp forty five men, the Floyd Infantry thirty two and the Light Guards forty one.

There is no knowing how soon or where we may move, yet there are no indications of any immediate departure from this place.

The boys are having a good time generally. Two from a company are allowed to visit town every day, and most of them have too little money to be anxious for a second trip in the same month.

Yesterday was beautiful; shining bright and pleasant as May, but to-day we have cold rain and sleet, and a gloomy prospect for our small woodpiles. M. D.

Camp 8th Ga. Regt., near
Richmond, Va.,
March 16th, 1863.

**Dear Courier:** It would do your readers good if they could just look in upon our brigade, and walk the streets of our tented city. The nomadic life led by our army corps, has induced all to reduce their movables to the least possible amount, and yet the actual *necessaries* for sustaining life, have so far, been nearly always at command.

All have got a protection of some kind from the weather; some have nice wall tents—those are confined pretty much to their staff officers—some have the sibley tent, some the bell tent and some the fly tent, others have simply a straight fly with blankets hung at the end, still others have a log pen with a fly stretched over for a roof. Nearly all the tents, however are old, dingy and rotten, but they are vastly better than nothing for keeping off the frequent cold rains, sleets, snows and raw, cold winds of March. Long habituated to the privations of camp, the men have the complacent air of contentment, and really enjoy any little addition to their customary comforts. Now for instance, we are getting a better variety of rations than at any previous time in the past twelve months. Beside flour and alternately bacon and dried beef, we now get full rations of sugar and rice. It is surprising how good natured and happy soldiers, who have been on short allowances for a long time, suddenly become when they get enough wholesome food to eat, and a sufficiency of rest to enjoy it. They become more spirited and ambitious, wear cleaner clothes, and these are put on in better taste; and, instead of appearing depressed, wear an exultant expression of countenance.

Rev. W. W. Bennett, General Tract Agent of the Methodist Church, preached a most excellent sermon yesterday, to the largest religious congregation the writer has ever seen in this brigade. There is now a greater interest manifested upon the subject of religion in this command than at any previous time. Some forty-five or fifty have professed conversion in the last two months, and twenty-three have joined different branches of the christain church—the others prefer to wait and join the church at home. Two received the ordinance of baptism by pouring at the close of services, yesterday morning, nine received by immersion in the evening, administered by Rev. Mr. Walker, former editor of the *Christian Index*, of Macon, Ga.

In order to secure some of the advantages of a regular church membership at home, there is now organized the "Georgia Soldier's Christian Association of Anderson's Brigade." It already numbers one hundred and fifty members; meets every Saturday at one o'clock, and is believed to be a very efficient aid in promoting the cause of religion.

Last week two men, belonging to the 11th Ga. Regiment punished for desertion, in a very strange way, and the trial was not, if correctly reported, in accordance with the Confederate Army regulations. The facts are given by what seems to be good authority, as follows: The men were tried by Regimental Court-martial, found guilty and sentenced to forfeit one month's pay and suffer such other punishment as the Regimental commander should deem proper to inflict.

This officer then told the prisoners that although their case might be properly carried up to a General Court martial, yet if they would inflict each upon the naked back of the other, twenty lashes, he would not prosecute the case further. This they consented to do, and the Regiment was drawn up in a hollow square, with the culprits in the centre.

They were stripped to the waist and a long keen hickory placed in the hands of each, with the instructions that one should give the other ten licks, and then alternate. The first ten blows are said to have been tolerably light, but after that nearly every lick brought the claret. The general impression is that these men will not desert again, or, at all events if they do, they will be particularly careful not to be caught.

Petty larceny is becoming outrageously common; confined, however, almost entirely to articles of food and cooking vessels. A few nights since some one "lifted" Major Magruder's dough that was set by the fire to "rise," together with the skillet and some fifty pounds of flour.

It is not yet known whether more furloughs will be granted at present. If they are, R. J. Franks and W. S. Lansdell will be recommended from the Light Guards. The old members drew lots for the chances.

The Regiment is still increasing in strength.

The only instance that has come to my knowledge of any large theft, was the stealing of two hundred and forty dollars from Lewis E. Graves, by a man named Glow. The money was all recovered and the thief is now under guard. M. D.

Camp 8th Ga. Regt. near
Richmond, Va.,
March 21st, 1863.

**Dear Courier:** Last Wednesday morning, just at daybreak, an order was issued to the troops in this vicinity—and it may not be proper to state what commands were here or how many—to pack up *immediately*, and be ready to move off on a long and tedious march. No time was given for cooking or to make any except the most hasty preparations. A little after sunrise the Brigade was formed and moved off towards the city. Of course all were very anxious to know the *cause* of this very sudden and unexpected movement. The news boys soon came along with the morning papers, containing the news of a cavalry fight some six or eight miles beyond Culpepper C.H., and it was soon noised along the column, that we were bound for Fredericksburg. It was a beautiful morning, and the troops were as gay and blithesome as the joyous birds, caroling the sweet songs of spring for the first time this season. There were some little delays of starting, yet we passed through the city, between 11 and 12 o'clock, and the boys had a regular feast of fun, taunting paper officers and the shirks that always loiter about town. Cheer after cheer went up for the ladies, who in large numbers freely bestowed their approving smiles and cheered on the troops to deeds of noble daring. The march was continued almost without respite until to within about two miles of Ashland, making full twenty miles, and halted at sunset for the night. Directly the order to go to Fredericksburg was countermanded, and the forces were ordered to return to their former camp. Thursday was given for rest and to cook rations. At about 4 o'clock P.M., of that day, it commenced to snow. At daylight it was about six inches deep and still snowing. The march back was commenced at 6 o'clock A.M., and a sweet time indeed was had wading through the still deepening snow. When we arrived at our old camp at 3 o'clock P.M., the snow was about ten inches deep. The troops though very weary, were yet in good spirits, and had straggled less than on many previous marches. The tents that had been left in Richmond, were brought back here yesterday, and after two nights exposure, last night there was good sleeping.

To-day the weather is mild, it is misting a little, and the snow is getting moist. Furloughs are still being granted.

The prices of goods in Richmond are high, but there is a very good supply in the light and fancy line. At an auction sale a few days since, fools cap paper, not ruled, sold from seventy to eighty-three dollars per ream. Some hundred reams were sold at such prices—letter do., at from forty to sixty dollars. It was English paper that had run the blockade. Wooden pen handles sold as high as fifty-one dollars per gross. M. D.

Camp 8th Ga. Regt., Near
Richmond, Va.,
March 27th, 1863.

**Dear Courier:** This day has seemed more Sabbath like, than almost any Sunday in camp since the war commenced. At sunrise the Band played two or three pieces of sacred music for a reveille, and that seemed to aid in giving a subdued and religious tone to the general feeling. It was a beautiful morning, and, though perhaps not general, yet large numbers of the officers and men were trying to keep this day, set apart for our Chief Executive for humiliation, fasting and prayer, in its true interest and spirit. All drills and other military duties that could be consistently dispensed with, were ordered to be omitted for the day, and a strict observance of the day was enjoined.

At 11 o'clock Rev. W. H. Crumley preached in our brigade, to probably the largest religious assemblage that has ever convened within its lines. This most excellent man is considerably reduced in flesh, and looks care worn. Few men have been more active or untiring in this war, than this devout christain, and none have done more for the temporal and spiritual wants of Georgia Soldiers than he. Yet the same glow of eloquence still warms his lips, the same light beams from his loving countenance, and his great warm heart still gushes forth with the same pathetic strains, of love to God and good will to man, that have so often in times past, thrilled the hearts of his audience. The congregation was deeply interested and this Fast-day sermon will be long remembered by many.

Maj. Gen. Hood and Brig. Gen. Anderson, were among the attentive listeners.

It is now 8 o'clock at night and "a change has come over the spirit of our dream." The Sunday quiet has given way to the rapid click-clack of numerous axes, the hurrying to and fro with buckets and camp kettles, of water and other preparations, for cooking rations. An order has been issued to cook three day's rations and be ready for a long march. It is rumored that we will take the direction of Petersburg. It seems that active operations, for us, at least, are about to commence. M. D.

Camp 8th Georgia Regiment, near
Petersburg Va., April 4, '63.

**Dear Courier:** In my letter of the 27th ult., it was stated that our Brigade was under orders to march on the 29th. This order was countermanded on the 28th, and we remained in our camp near Richmond, until last Thursday the 2d inst. Left camp at 7 o'clock A.M., und marched on the Petersburg Turnpike, an excellent road and in good repair, twelve miles and bivouaced for the night, four miles from Petersburg. Resumed the march at eight o'clock Friday morning, passed through the city, and pursued an easterly direction for three miles, to our present encampment.

It is reported that the enemy are at Suffolk, thirty-five thousand strong, and that they are making demonstrations indicating an early advance in this direction. Now if they come the arrangement and strength of our forces are such as to give them a very suitable reception, but for obvious reasons, it is not prudent to make any statements, either of the strength or disposition of our forces in this vicinity. Present indications point to lively times at some location between here and Suffolk, and probably it will be at Blackwater river, before many days. Our troops are in excellent health and spirits, and they are very confident of victory whenever they may first meet the vandal foe in this campaign.

This is a cold raw day, the wind blows, and the temperature of the atmosphere is that of December, rather than of April. The Spring has been so cold and wet that the wheat crop is looking badly in this section, and for the same reasons the corn lands have not been put in readiness for planting. Many farmers are quite indifferent about planting at all for fear that their crops will be destroyed by the enemy. Let me observe right here, that the great apprehension in the army is, not that they will be unable to whip our enemies in the field, but lest they themselves will be overcome by gaunt want and the raving madness of actual starvation. What is being done in Upper Georgia to prevent this horrid state of affairs? Will every man plant all the corn he can? It is to be feared that some, actuated by their miserable, miserly feelings, will try to deceive themselves and their neighbors, and stealthily plant tobacco or cotton, so as to satisfy their own greedy love of gain, while they hope somebody else will raise food for the soldiers. If such there be, we would warn them beforehand, that if the soldiers are starved into submission or forced to leave the field, no laws will be strong enough to protect the ill-got gains of such cold blooded enemies. There are a plenty of vile cowards even now, at home, who would tremble in their boots if they knew one half the soldiers say of them. Men who have periled their lives upon a hundred battle fields are not going to submit to a set of sneaking, crawling, slimy reptiles at home, who are sucking up the life blood of the nation, and who are now gloating over the price for which they have sold their souls. O, ye extortioners and speculators! laugh now, in your sleeves, like demons, and feed your snakish love of gain, but remember that for all these things you will be brought into judgment by the soldiers on their return from the war.

Women's raids on the provision and other stores are the rage here now. One was made in Petersburg last Wednesday. The fair creatures were prevailed upon to quietly retire to their homes however, without committing any depredations and await one week. The City Council has appropriated $30,000 for their relief, but it is not yet known whether they are satisfied. On last Thursday, a demonstration of a more serious character was made in Richmond. The Female mob broke into several stores, and took there from gents boots, brooms, leather, and variour other articles that were not food. 'Tis said there was not an American in the crowd. They knocked down one of the city police with a ham of bacon, and bruised him up pretty severely. The city battalion was called out to suppress the riot.

These affairs are greatly depricated by the citizens. Many of the women engaged in these scandalous affairs have no near relatives in the army.

Bivouac of 8th Ga. Regt.
South Hampton County,
April 9, 1863.

**Dear Courier:** We are again on the pad. Left Petersburg yesterday at 7 o'clock A.M., taking the Jerusalem plank road, running out in a Southerly direction, and continued it eighteen miles, and bivouaced last night near a church called Hawkinsville. 'Tis supposed that the church has that name, from the fact that it and a small dwelling were the only buildings seen in the vicinity. It was a fine day, the road tolerably good, though the planking is very much dilapidated, and the march was made with comparative ease. Our route lay through a rolling country, with sandy soil, mostly second growth pine timber, and, and as would be inferred, for the most part a very poor country. There were, however, a few tolerably good farms on the way, and on one of these was a sight that cheered the hearts of Southern boys. It was a field containing some fifty acres, on which last year cotton was raised, and the stalks were still standing. The week was about medium size for our section of country, and seemed to have been very well fruited.

To-day, Thursday, has been equally as pleasant as yesterday, and we have continued our march eighteen miles on the same road, and are now within eight miles of the county site of this Blackwater county. From near Petersburg to our present locality, we have passed no clear, colorless streams, but, on the contrary, they all have, in an eminent degree, that peculiar color, on account of which the whole section of country has received its name.

The men all started with three days rations in their haversacks, which, with their guns, accoutrements and blankets made them a heavy load. Most of them, however, have stood up to it manfully. No tents are along except a few for staff officers. Last night it was calm, clear, and frosty, and to-night promises to be its fellow.

The same troops that left Fredericksburg on the 17th of February, are in this expedition. To be more specific would perhaps be imprudent.

Friday Noon. We are now at Jerusalem, and moving on towards Franklin, on he Weldon and Suffolk railroad. M. D.

Bivouac 8th Ga Reg., Eight Miles
from Suffolk, Va., April 12.

**Dear Courier:** My last letter was closed at Jerusalem, Friday noon. The march was continued that day to Franklin, where we bivouacked for the night. This is a mere railroad station, containing some dozen buildings in all, and is twenty one miles, by the carriage road, from Suffolk. Here four days rations were issued, and it took the men nearly half the night to cook them. Reveille was beaten at daylight next morning, and, at a little after sunrise, we were again on the "pad." Franklin is on the West side of the Blackwater river, which is here less in size than the Etowah above Rome. This stream has no more right to be called the *Blackwater*, than the Nettaway, or any of the numerous creeks crossed in passing from Petersburg to Franklin. Yet for the mere purpose of designation it may be well enough.

The advance yesterday was slow and cautious, having numerous scouting parties of cavalry and infantry skirmishers in advance of the main column. The Blackwater river, that rises about six miles East of Petersburg, and runs in a Southerly direction, has hitherto been the dividing line between the opposing forces, and as late as Friday, the abolition cavalry scouts came to within two or three miles of Franklin, and some 30 of the rascals that day took dinner at Carrsville, a very neat little village on the Rail Road. These scamps have a very cool way of helping themselves to anything they may desire, which happens to be within their reach. In this case a party of them rode up to a house just as dinner was ready, and seeing the table ready set, without invitation, immediately filled all the seats around it, and commenced helping themselves. They consumed all the food on the table, besides various other things that they called for and the family were afraid to deny them; and then, instead of showing any appreciation of favor, merely stated that they would be back for dinner again the next day, departed.

Our main force is within three or four miles of Suffolk, and our regiment is now on picket to prevent a surprise attack from the rear. The impression prevailed generally yesterday evening, that we would attack the enemy within their entrenchments, early this morning, but it is now 2 ½ o'clock, P.M., and all quiet yet. Yesterday evening a balloon was seen up inside the abolition lines, and last night several rockets were seen in the same direction. Heavy, but slow cannonading has been heard for the last half hour, but it is believed to be much farther off than Suffolk.

The weather has been fine, and the men have stood the march very well, considering the hardship of marching 70 miles in four days, carrying their rations, besides guns, accoutrements, and blankets.

Monday Morning 7 ½ o'clock. No fighting yet. Yesterday we moved some six miles to the left, and forward. It rained a little about 6 o'clock, P.M., yesterday, and is misting this morning. It seems probably that we will have stirring times to-day.

It may not be prudent to state what forces there are here, or their disposition, for fear this letter might fall into the enemy's hands before it gets to Franklin. The enemy are said to be strongly fortified. Some firing has been heard on our picket line this morning. I have not heard where the cannonading was yesterday afternoon. I must close. God bless us in the impending conflict. M. D.

Bivouac of 8th Ga. Reg.
Suffolk, April 14th, 1863.

**Dear Courier:** Throwing up breastworks, planting batteries, changing positions, scouting and doing picket duty, is still the order of exercises. Last Wednesday our Brigade moved round from north of the city to the west side. It rained nearly all that day. At 3 o'clock p.m., the Light Guards were sent out on picket post. Our position was about 1000 yards from the enemy's breastworks. Their pickets are inside their fortifications, and yet their sharpshooters would throw balls 200 yards to our rear. They kept up a constant fire upon us all the time. In going to and from our outposts, we were in full view of the enemy, and although we went in and out, a single man at a time they would shoot from six to ten rifles at him, and if two men happened to get tolerably near each other they were sure to throw a shell at them. Yet strange to say, we stood out our 24 hours and had no one hurt.

We have now been for eight days on the hardest kind of fatigue duty, and begins to tell on the men. They are much in need of rest.

Our forces occupy the west and north sides of the city, the Dismal Swamp is on the south side, and on the east they have two railroads protected, for an outlet to them to Norfolk. Their fortifications are very strong, with a large number of heavy guns mounted. They keep an almost constant firing from these, shelling the goods promiscuously in all directions. It is estimated that they have fired at least 5000 cannon shots since we have been here, but they have done comparatively little harm. So far as I have been able to learn only four men have been killed, in our entire force here and some fifteen wounded.

There is no use surmising as to what will probably be done here. As usual, there are a thousand rumors afloat. Last year at this time we were at Yorktown, and in many particulars our present situation is identical. In two important particulars however we are better off—as we now get a tolerable supply of rations, and so far, there has been less rain.

This is a bright and pleasant morning, and we are just not resting after the false alarm, that the enemy were crossing the river below the city. M. D.

In Line of Battle, near Suffolk
April 14th, 1863.

**Dear Courier:** It is now mid-day, and there has been no general engagement yet. Our Brigade remained at its place of bivouac of the night previous until noon yesterday, when it moved forward to within about a mile of the city, for the purpose of throwing up a redoubt and line of rifle pits. We had been halted but a few moments, when the enemy commenced shelling us very heavily, from a gunboat and also a battery on the other side of the river. One of the 9th Regiment was slightly wounded in the foot, and one of Co. I, of our Regiment in the hand; these were the only sufferers. Afterwards we took three positions, farther back from town, and finally, about 10 o'clock P.M., returned to the first of these, when, in two hours, a very good line of rifle pits were dug in front of the whole Brigade.

Last night a redoubt was thrown up on the river bank, below Suffolk, and at daybreak this morning, we had a battery of four rifle guns mounted there. 'Tis reported that no boats have since passed, and it is believed that communication with Portsmouth and Norfolk, by water, is cut off. There is one gunboat below our battery and one above. These have kept up a very heavy and constant fire upon it all day, but with what effect I have not heard, though the presumption is that little or no damage has been done. Our pickets now extend to the river, and yesterday they fired upon one or two gunboats and several transports. They say they certainly killed one horse and wounded another, and think they wounded or killed several men. One boat having two guns mounted on it, was fired into, and our men distinctly heard the captain give the order, "grape them, grape the damned rebels." But as the gunners came on deck, our sharpshooters sent a few minnie balls whistling about their ears, and they scampered down below.

Several houses were burned yesterday by the Federals. When we were driving in their pickets, they set fire to a fine dwelling, about a half mile this side the Nansemond, and because the owner attempted to quench the flames, one of the vile wretches shot him through the neck. The wound, though very painful, is hoped to be not mortal. This is only an example of what good and true citizens are liable to suffer, who in the vicissitudes of the war, happen to fall within the Abolition lines. Thankful, indeed, should the residents of our own section be, that they are not thus circumstanced.

When the grand conflict will take place, or, even whether there will be one here at all, now seems uncertain. General Longstreet is here, and whatever orders he may issue, will be executed with cheerful confidence. I see no reason why a great battle should not be fought here, in a few days at farthest, except that it has already been so long delayed.

The Federals are said to be very strongly fortified in the town, and they have all been driven inside their strongholds. If they will come out and attack us, we have the utmost confidence of success. But as we have very little artillery here, and it comparatively light, it may be imprudent to attack them behind heavy breastworks, with any amount of siege pieces and heavy artillery.

4 o'clock P.M. No new developments so far to-day. The cannonading by the enemy still continues, but not as rapid as in the morning. They are shelling the woods for two miles this side the river.

Bivouac of 8th GA. Regiment,
Near Suffolk, VA.,
April 18th, 1863.

**Dear Courier:** A few lines are addressed to you now, not so much because there is anything of great importance to relieve the anxiety of friends at home in regard to the forces here. There has been no material change in the general programme of events since my last. Yesterday, however, the monotony was slightly interrupted by a Regiment of Yanks making a lash upon the picket line occupied by our Brigade. They were enabled to come down on our right flank for the reason that Jenkin's Regiment which is on our right, does not picket so far in advance by about 400 yards as ours. Three companies were occupying our advances post—one from the 9th, and one from the 11th Regiments. These were driven back some two or three hundred yards. They however, soon rallied, and without help from the reserve, drove the enemy back, and retook their former position. In this skirmish two of the 11th Regiment were killed—names not reported—and one of the 8th; Sergeant Flemming, Pulaski volunteers, seriously though not dangerously wounded. Our pickets occupy holes dug in the ground, and now go in and out after dark. Our Regiment is to go out for reserve tomorrow morning, and at night take the outposts.

No Gunboats or Transports have yet been able to go down the river since our battery was mounted on the bank last Wednesday, they are allowed to come up if they choose. One boat passed our battery on that day, and was disabled, and is reported to have been burned by the enemy a few miles below. We hold a continuous line from the Dismal Swamp of the South of the city all the way round to the river, striking it about a mile below the town. On Thursday, the vandals burned three houses between the lines. It is believed they were set on fire by missiles fired from muskets. Large amounts of corn and bacon are said to have been already removed from this vicinity, that had been hid out from the Yankees. There are many loyal citizens here, who had nevertheless to be very polite to the mercenary invaders. Not a few were *forced* as they say, to take the oath of allegiance to the Federal Government. Some of the latter class refused to sell to our commissaries, but hint a wish that they would impress whatever articles of food they have to spare. M. D.

Bivouac of 8th Ga. Regt.,
Near Suffolk, Va.
April 21, 1863.

**Dear Courier:** Late last Sunday evening, 300 or 400 of the Yankees crossed the Nansemond river, some six miles below the city, and after dark, advanced upon a battery we had there upon the bluff, and captured it together with two companies of infantry, from the 44th Alabama Regiment; making in all about 175 men, and 5 cannon. It was Stribbling's battery, from the vicinity of Warrenton, Va. General French has command of all the artillery here, and sufficient infantry to support it.[4] So to him, if any one, should be ascribed the blame of this surprise. Yesterday morning the whole of our Division, except Lane's Brigade, which was already near there, was carried round from the West side of the town, to the North, and down the river to the vicinity of the venturesome surprising *party*.[5] They had taken possession of an old fort, near where they took the battery, and immediately commenced entrenching themselves, and were reinforced until their numbers were variously estimated at from 1000 to 3000 men, with three gunboats in the river and several batteries just on the other bank to support. Our regiment was on picket at the time the balance of the brigade started to this interesting place, and did not get on the ground until nearly sunset. Just as we arrived, 100 volunteers from each brigade of the division, were called for to make a night attack upon this abolition force. Our brigade sent forward its quota immediately. Some of the other did not do it until evening. Hood decided that it was too late, and the attack was postponed. If the volunteer party had made the attack, and failed to capture the Fort, our brigade was expected to go to their support. It was a dark, cold, rainy night, and the idea of a night attack, always horrible, was rendered doubly so, by nature's doleful aspect. The news that the order for a night attack was countermanded, gave great relief and dissipated all our melancholy foreboding.

At daybreak our skirmishers advanced, came upon and captured the Yankee pickets, twelve in number, moved on to the Fort and found it empty. The birds had flown out it in the night as they came in, and so we again have undisputed possession of the North side of the river.

To day our brigade moved back to its former place on the West of the town. The firing still continued very heavy on the picket line. Last Sunday, Thomas Clark, of Atlanta, belonging to the 7th Georgia regiment, was killed, being shot through the head by a minnie ball while in front line of the pickets. Up to last Saturday night the entire loss in killed and wounded, from all our forces near Suffolk, was eighty eight (88); of these, Hood's division lost twenty two, and Anderson's brigade, eight. We have no means of knowing the enemy's loss.

The work of removing meat and grain from the adjoining counties of North Carolina is being carried on rapidly, and this, I believe, is the grand object of our expedition, though if, as it were incidentally, we could capture Suffolk, it would be gratifying.

Bivouac of 8th GA. Regiment,
Near Suffolk.
April 23, 1863.

**Dear Courier:** Some daring exploits have been performed here, worthy of commemoration. Among the most conspicuous are those of Lt. Gambrel and his brother, a sergeant, both of the 2d Mississippi Regiment. On the 13th inst., they armed themselves with Minnie rifles and pistols, and started on scout within the enemy's lines. They prowled around in the woods and bye-paths, going some eight or ten miles towards Norfolk, tore up a few rails on the railroad, took two prisoners, one of whom they brought back, and returned to their regiment on the night of the 17th. They had quite an interesting time with the prisoner they captured, but afterwards released. They took him on the night of their return, and while they were looking for a boat, with which to cross the river. It was very dark, and a soldier came up to them, whom they challenged; he replied that he was a Confederate soldier belonging to the 11th Mississippi regiment, Col. Lomax, and Robinson's Brigade.[6] The officers named not being the ones in command of those forces proved that he was trying to practice deception. Lieut. G. told him that himself and friend were Union soldiers, and that he was their prisoner. He readily surrendered, and they told him that as they were going on a scout within rebel lines, they would take him with them. They had learned that a small boat was in the cellar of a deserted house, and were forcing the doors to get it. The Yank said he knew of a good boat just a little up the river, and urged them to go with him for it, but this they of course declined to do. They succeeded in getting the boat out, and to the river all the while hearing clattering hoofs and sabres of their pursuers. But the boat was so small and leaky, that it would carry but two. Lieut. G. says he made up his mind to kill the pretended rebel, with a small crow bar he had, but his heart failed him, and, as it was so dark he could not parole, he turned him loose.

Yesterday the same brothers, with one other man, made a scout, down on our side of the river, for the purpose of detecting some parties, who were mistrusted of holding communication with the enemy. Lieut. Gambrel dressed in citizen's clothes, went to the house of a suspicious free negro. and represented himself to be a Union man, and desirous of getting over to the other side of the river, and asked the negro if he could not assist him. The negro replied that he could, that any steamboat would stop at his signal. Gambrel excused himself, and went and ambushed his two men near where the expected steamer, would stop, then returned to the negro. Soon a steamboat was heard approaching; the negro went out and made his signal and the boat hauled to. Gambrel approached it and the captain, scrutinizing him through the glass, said, "that is Thompson is it." Gambrel said "Yes," and that he desired to come aboard. "Very well," said the captain, "I will send for you.["] Directly a small boat, manned by five armed marines, came ashore. Just as the boat struck the bank, the men in ambush, rose and fired upon them, killing one and wounding another. The others immediately surrendered. The captain of the boat, seeing what was done, ordered a charge of grape to be fired at them; but this hurt no one. Four marines were brought off as prisoners, and they took some dozen free negroes.

These prisoners and others represent the enemy's force at Suffolk, at about 50,000. They have been receiving reinforcements nearly every day since we have been here.

The 10th Ga Battallion, Maj. Ryelander, has been pronounced unfit for duty on account of sickness, and recommended for Post duty.[7] They will probably leave our Brigade in a few days. The 59th Ga. Col. Jack Jones, is here to take their place.

Our men are taking up the Seaborn and Roanoke R.R., track and moving it back to Franklin. The other track, running from Suffolk to Petersburg, the Yanks had torn up and relaid it about 6 inches narrower, and it is rumored that our men are widening this to suit our rolling stock.

This is a very rainy day. There is but little sickness, and the men are in good spirits.

List of killed and wounded in Hood's division up to the event of the 21st inst,

Killed. D. J. Culpepper, Jones' Battery; Corporal J. R. Short, Jones' Battery; Captain J. M. Turner, 5th Texas Regiment. James Tucker, Company E. 11th Ga. Reg. Sergeant J. J. Clark, Company B. 7th Regiment; August Wilson, Company I, 7th Ga Regiment; and one of Lane's Regiment, name not learned.

Wounded. Sergeant W. Young. Co. K. 8th Ga Regiment; severe flesh wound in leg and arm; Private D. B. Morgan, Company D. 7th Ga—slightly in leg by shell; Corporal D. G. Flemming. Co. G, 8th Ga; severely in shoulder; R. A. Tounne, Company F. 7th Ga; slightly in leg by shell; Thomas M. Jones, Co. E, 11th Ga; severely in arm; Dan'l J. Jackson, Co. C, 9th Ga; severely in thigh by shell; J. R. Rhodes, Co. I, 8th Ga; slightly in hand; R. L. Gray, Co. C, 8th Ga; severe in foot; M. S. Reagan, Co. C, 9th Ga; severe in hand.

Since the above and up to the night of the 22d, the following have been reported:

Private Simmons, 5th Texas, Killed; Private DeLang, 1st Texas, leg amputated; Private Rowe, 5th Texas, slight wound in hand: John Peddy. of the 11th Ga, mortally wounded; J. F. Bohannon, Co. G 8th Ga, slightly wounded in the leg.

P.S. 6 o'clock, P.M. There has been less firing along the picket line today, than usual; probably owing to the little rain. There has also been comparatively little cannonading.

Our men occasionally play off a good trick on the Yanks. A few days since a Colonel of Davis' Brigade, made an effigy and placed it upon an Observatory the Feds had made and used, but which is now inside our lines. It is nothing more than a very high Pine Tree with the top cut off, and a small platform put on the top of the high stump. The effigy was placed on this platform, knelt down, and a stick, representing a telescope, resting on the railing, as if a person was making observations. The sell took finely, for the next morning the Yanks commenced firing cannons at it, and kept it up nearly all day. A similar trick was practiced by our pickets in the river. They placing an image behind a tree. M. D.

Bivouac of 8th GA. Regiment,
Near Suffolk.
April 25th, 1863.

**Dear Courier:** The principal news here is, that there is no news of particular interest. Yesterday and the day before were rainy days. To day it is bright and pleasant. Yesterday our Regiment moved from its regular place of bivouac (in the forks of the Rail Roads) round to the North East side of the town. We are now three miles from the City and one from the River, and keep out a picket near Reed's Ferry. We are some five miles from the balance of our brigade.

It is rumored that, for the past three or four days, there has been very heavy skirmishing along the extreme right of our lines, occupied by Pickett's Division. That on one day our loss in killed and wounded was seventy men. This may be true, or it may not. The cannonnading continued to be much less than it was three or four days since.

Captain W. Satterfield, of the 7th Ga, and formerly from Cartersville, I think, was complimented in an order from General Hood, a few days since, for gallant conduct on the 14th, when he with his Company charged a Gunboat and drove the gunners from the cannon.

A citizen who was driven out of Suffolk some months since, but who by taking the oath was allowed to visit the place three times a week, has given me some interesting facts in regard to affairs there. He says when our forces arrived, there were between 15,000 and 17,000 Federal troops in the place; he has not been in the town since, but believes they have been reinforced. He says nearly all the servants in and about the place, left their owners soon after the Yanks took possession. The few that remain at home, are hired by the month. He thinks there are some 300 contrabands in and about Suffolk—he has lost twenty-one. The Abolitionists have built up a little village, called Uniontown, for their pets; where some 1500 are domicilled. He says it has been rumored that an effort was being made to organize a Negro Regiment, and that they had daily drills a little outside of the city, but he had never seen any demonstration of the kind. He reports that Suffolk jail is nearly full of the very best citizens of the county. Gen. Peck has been in command over there, but we heard a salutation of thirteen guns three days ago, and it may be that he has been superceded.

We are now just in pretty shelling distance from the Gunboats but they have not yet disturbed us. Our batteries have been forced to leave the river-bank, and so the boats have nothing but our sharpshooters to obstruct their free passage up and down the river.

Benning's (formerly Toomb's) brigade is over in the border of North Carolina, guarding our forage trains. At last accounts they were doing a first rate business in the way of Bacon and Grain.

How much longer the present style of warfare will continue here, the Lord only knows. The officers, most of whom left all their clothing at Petersburg, would very much like a change. M. D.

Near Suffolk, Va., May 1, 1863

**Dear Courier:** Yesterday was rather a lively day on the left of our lines, though it resulted in no fighting except for artillery. At about 9 o'clock, A.M., notice was sent to Col. Towers that three steamboats had stoped in the river, about a mile and a half from our bivouac, and were landing troops. Directly another courier came, bringing confirmation of the news. Not long after another report was brought up from the point of interest, to the effect that the enemy had got possession of the old fort they occupied in their raid on this side of the river some two weeks since, and that they had in it, at least, *one* piece of artillery and 600 or 800 men. Law's Brigade was a little above this fort; Robinson's was some few miles towards the righthand, it was ordered to the left of Law's, opposite to the supposed landing. Our Regiment was moved a half mile down the river to support a battery and to prevent a landing being effected in that vicinity. A strong picket was put up on the bank above and below the old fort. The enemy seem to have discovered the movements of our forces, and gave us an unusually severe shelling; but beyond this there was no excitement growing out of the "advance movement." Late in the evening it was ascertained that the Yankees had landed a few men in a yawl boat, with the supposed intention of capturing our men on an exposed picket post—had run in these men, and that the gunboats had probably stopped at that place to protect their scouting party. Thus ended this mortifying cause of excitement. But before all this was found out, we had something of a little more substantial interest. The battery we were supporting was mounted out on the south bank of West Branch and about quarter of a mile from the Nansemond River, and consisting of only two guns, "Long Tom" and "Laughing Charlie." They had opened fire for the first time, in this vicinity, about noon. It seems the Yankees thought they would silence these "boys" with their gunboats. So about an half hour by sun, three came down the river and two came up, all stopping nearly opposite, and at once opened fire on the spunky little battery. They at first sent a few single shots, but very soon seemed to fire with as much rapidity as was possible from some ten or fifteen guns. The roar of artillery was deafening. Our two guns kept throwing well directed shots as fast as they could. The Yankees fired ten inch spherical shells for the most part. Just as dark was setting in, a peculiar commotion was discovered on one of the boats, and she is believed to have been disabled. They soon all withdraw down the river, and passed out of sight round a point. The "old Eighth," except two companies on picket, was stationed all this time about 600 yards to the right and rear of our battery, in a ravine, so that our opportunity for *hearing* the fight *was* good, but we could occasionally *see a* piece of shell that fell near. No harm was done to our battery or the men in it. Neither was any one hurt in the Regiment, except the following four, who were on a reserve post of pickets: Serg't Gabriel Jones of the Miller Rifles, hit on the hand by a piece of shell—skin not broken, but fore arm badly swollen this morning; Glenn, of the same company, and Stallings, of Floyd Infantry, stunned by a shell bursting very near them, and Serg't Barrow, of Floyd Infantry, slight wounds in the face—all these were injured by the bursting of the same shell.[8]

The two duels, mentioned in my last, are reported to have resulted only in a slight wound to one of the parties. It is a matter of gratulation that their honors are satisfied with so little loss of blood. Whether they will be reported and Court martialed, I have not heard.

This is a beautiful May morning, but, instead of starting out to a Sunday School Celebration, a steamboat excursion, or a pic-nic, we are very likely throwing up rifle pits. There has been but little firing in our hearing up to this time to day. M. D.

# 9

# "Stirring Events May Soon Be Expected"

## *May–October 1863*

In early May, the Eighth Georgia was on the march again. Brig. Gen. Joseph Hooker had crossed the Rappahannock River and was threatening Richmond. Gen. Robert E. Lee ordered Lt. Gen. James Longstreet to end the siege and rejoin the main part of the Army of Northern Virginia. Longstreet's corps marched briskly but did not arrive in time to be part of the Battle of Chancellorsville. The difficult march took its toll on the troops, and Melvin Dwinell was among the many men who became ill. The editor was sent to a hospital in Petersburg to recuperate, and in a letter home, a portion of which was published in the *Courier*, he wrote, "This is a dirty place, and hard to be sick at. . . . There are bed bugs enough to run a man crazy, and a general want of cleanliness about the premises that would be sickening to a well man." His correspondence stopped for four weeks, the longest pause during his time in the army.

When Dwinell rejoined the regiment on June 4, it was camped near Culpeper Court House. The next day the men were treated to a review by Maj. Gen. J. E. B. Stuart's cavalry brigades. He described the columns of galloping horsemen as "splendid." However, showing the lack of respect that foot soldiers often had for their mounted counterparts, he could not resist writing, "If they will only charge on the enemy with as much impetuosity." In the same letter, Dwinell wrote that "important movements are going on," and he told readers, "I will try to keep you posted on events as they transpire." The next day, the Eighth Georgia broke camp in the opening moves of the Gettysburg Campaign. During the march, the Light Guards recovered the company flag that had been presented to them when they first left Rome. The banner had been lost near Manassas two years earlier and was found by a local man who had taken good care of it. Dwinell said the men rejoiced to get back the flag, which bore the motto "Our liberties we prize—Our right we will maintain." By late June, the Eighth Georgia had crossed into Pennsylvania, and Dwinell wrote that the men marched through "one of the richest sections of country" he had ever seen. The editor was particularly impressed with the barns built by farmers. "They look as fine as churches and are twice as large," he wrote.

On July 1, the Eighth Georgia, along with the rest of Brig. Gen. George T. Anderson's brigade, left their camp near Chambersburg, Pennsylvania. They marched through much of the night and by the next afternoon were in line for battle at the little town of Gettysburg. Dwinell and the men had gotten news about the initial clash that had taken place while they were marching. The editor could report few details but said the fighting had been "severe." He described how the troops marched a half mile "through wheat field and woods, over rocks and fences," under "the most dreadful cannonading the Abolitionists have ever been able to bring to bear against [Confederate] forces." The regiment charged a strong enemy position repeatedly but was thrown back each time, suffering heavy losses. Dwinell was wounded in the left arm, and by the time the battle ended, he was part of a large group of "walking" wounded heading back to Virginia. In his letter about Gettysburg, written four days later, Dwinell did not conceal the heavy price the Confederacy paid for invading Pennsylvania. Casualties were "very heavy," he wrote. In fact, the Eighth Georgia lost half the men who fought at Gettysburg.

Dwinell entered General Hospital No. 9 in Richmond on July 13, and three days later he received a thirty-day furlough. In its July 21 issue, the *Courier* explained that its editor had returned home to recuperate. "He is looking well, though somewhat thinner and paler than usual," the newspaper noted, adding, "His wound is doing very well." It is not known what Dwinell did during the time he spent recovering in Rome, but he likely spent some time attending to the financial condition of his newspaper. In late July, the *Courier* announced another rate increase, saying it was necessary to cover the higher costs of paper and materials. Paper that once cost $2.25 per ream now was $16.50 per ream.

While at home, Dwinell's life took another turn. A group of citizens nominated him to run for the Georgia House of Representatives, and they made their idea public by publishing a letter in the *Rome Southerner*. In his reply, Dwinell said that he appreciated the "flattering attention" but hoped to return to the army as soon as possible. Still, he agreed to consider allowing his name to be put on the ballot. Ten days later, he announced that he would indeed be a candidate for one of the seats in the assembly.

Before the election was held, a fully recovered Dwinell rejoined his regiment, which had been sent to Charleston, South Carolina, to defend the city against renewed attacks by the Federals. He was not in Charleston long. On October 7 the Eighth Georgia boarded a train to Atlanta and then one to Chattanooga, Tennessee, where the two armies faced off against one another. While the election votes were being counted, Dwinell sent back several letters from Chattanooga. In one, he described how soldiers voted during the trip to Tennessee. Dwinell also noted that a number of soldiers in the regiment took the opportunity to make a quick visit home to see their loved ones. Although this was wrong, he said, it was understandable because many of the men had not been home since enlisting.

Because the ballots of Floyd County soldiers took time to be returned and counted, the election results were announced over several weeks. When the final results were tallied, Dwinell had far outpolled the other candidates, and he became one of two new representatives from Floyd County. Dwinell's superior officers, Anderson and Longstreet, refused to accept his resignation from the army, arguing that he should be able to take a furlough instead. Anderson wrote that he could not afford to lose so valuable an officer. However, the secretary of war apparently overruled the officers and accepted Dwinell's resignation. In his last letter to the newspaper, written on October 28, Dwinell described fighting that had taken place south of Chattanooga. It is not clear exactly when he left the army, but after two and a half years, the editor's time in the regular army had ended. So, too, had his "Dear Courier" letters from the war.

Franklin, VA.,
May 4, 1863.

**Dear Courier:** No detriment to our cause is likely to ensue from publishing the fact that Anderson's Brigade fell back last night, leaving Suffolk at midnight late last night, and arrived here this morning at 8 o'clock. Important movements are on land, but it may not be prudent to make them public at this time.

On the 1st inst., there was very heavy skirmishing along the centre of our lines. Anderson's Brigade, except the 8th Georgia, which was some five miles to the left, were more or less engaged; the 9th however bearing the heaviest part; and Davis' Brigade also took part. The Yanks advanced some two regiments from their breastworks, deployed as skirmishers, and had them supported by two brigades. They seemed determined to drive in our pickets. Our outposts along that part of the line, are stationed in the out edge of an abattis, some 600 yards wide, that the enemy had formed by felling trees and brush. Between this abattis and the enemy's breastworks, was an open field 1000 yards wide. Through this they advanced on both sides the Roanoke and Seaboard Railroad truck. The right of our brigade rested on the railroad and Davis' left. The Yanks moved out very gallantly, and succeeded in driving Davis' pickets back some sixty yards, but ours did not "budge a peg." The 9th Ga. is said to have behaved very gallantly on that occasion and the 11th also, though in a less conspicuous position. While their infantry was advancing, the enemy shelled our reserves most unmercifully. After about twenty minutes, they found the galling fire of our brave boys too much for their pluck, and so they withdrew again. The result was on our side one mortally wounded in the 9th, and six slightly, and five or six wounded in the 11th Regiment. It is said that eighteen Yanks were left dead on the field and that at least sixty of them were wounded.

There was another skirmish on our left yesterday, the 3d inst., in which Law's Brigade was principally engaged. Two regiments of the enemy crossed the river about 8 o'clock A.M., under cover of gunboats, and commenced an attack upon our pickets. Heavy skirmishing was kept up until 4 P.M. when the Yanks retired. Eight or ten of our men were killed, and some thirty-eight wounded. The enemy's loss is not known accurately, but is believed to be pretty heavy—say three or four times ours. As usual, they seemed to depend largely upon their artillery and gunboats.

Our men are of course very weary and much exhausted, from their march last night. We will probably rest here to day. This excursion to Suffolk has been a very severe tax on the physical energies and powers of endurance of the men. They never endured more unless it was at Yorktown, twelve months since. It is rumored that we are now our way to Petersburg, and some think even to Fredericksburg.

There are some three hundred sick at the hospitals here, "one of whom I am which," and expect to leave on the train for Petersburg to day. Most of the patients are suffering from diseases of the bowels, occasioned by bad water and unwholesome diet. M. D.

Petersburg, Va., May 6th, 1863.

**Dear Courier:** A portion of Hood's Division arrived here yesterday, and the balance came in to-day. From Franklin they marched to Ivoy, a station on the Petersburg and Norfolk Railroad, and from thence came here on the cars, a distance of 36 miles. What will be our next move is as yet unknown. If it was the original intention to go immediately to Fredericksburg, that may now be changed, for the reason that Gen. Lee has already run Hooker's murderous hosts all across the Rappahannock. If, however a pursuit is determined upon, it is not unlikely that Hood's famous command of tried veterans, may be called into requisition. But it is useless to speculate; of all the possible movements, it is hard to tell which are the most probable. As matters have now turned out, it may have been better if more troops had been left in the vicinity of Suffolk, to hold in check the vandal foe, who will now be almost sure to vent their spite upon defenseless families in that section, and to extend their large marauding practice to disagreeable distances into the country. They had better not, however, be so very venturesome.

There has been considerable excitement here to-day, on account of the seizure of horses by the military authorities. They are taking all in the city except those belonging to physicians. Hacks, omnibusses, carriages and vehicles of all descriptions, rapidly disappeared from the streets after the order was issued, and the horses that had been attached to them, were being led off to the Government stables. It was even laughable to see the distress of some citizens, when they were stopped in the streets, and their horses taken from them. The first notice they would receive, would be that an officer would hail them "hello friend, a word with you, if you please." They would stop and the officer would step and politely *request* them to deliver their horses. Some were dumb with astonishment, while others would fly into a passion, and rage like "a tempest in a tea pot." 'Tis rumored that some of these pressed horses are to take the place of broken down ones, in some of our artillery companies, while the greater portions are for cavalry service. 'Tis said that the Arkansas Post prisoners, most of whom are here, are all to be mounted for cavalry service, and to use these horses. There are various rumors afloat, in regard to detachment of Stoneman's Yankee raiders. It is said that parties are now in pursuit of them. But it is probably too late. They have, it is feared, escaped in the direction of Yorktown. They certainly made a bold dash, but it will be very mortifying to our army, if any considerable number of them escape.

This is a cold, rainy day, and our troops are doubtless suffering considerably. Few of our Brigade slept last night and none of them two nights before. The Brigade is bivouaced some two miles from town, on the Richmond road. I expect to join them in a day or two. M. D.

Bivouac of 8th GA. Regiment, near
Culpepper C.H.,Va., June 6, '63.

**Dear Courier:** The writer rejoined the Regiment at this place on the evening of the 4th inst. The command, after leaving Petersburg on the 6th of May, marched on through Richmond and to Frederick Hall, sixty-six miles, in four days. At the latter place they halted two days, and then proceeded to Raccoon Ford on the Rapidan River, where they remained until last Thursday morning, when they came to this place.

The health and spirits of the Brigade are good, and the men are in good condition for the hardships that are in prospect.

Yesterday was a gala day for the cavalry. Gen. J. E. B. Stewart has a force here, now numbering, say ten thousand. There can hardly be imprudence in stating the approximate number, for before this can be published in Georgia and get to the Yankee lines, this cavalry *can* all move, at least, three hundred miles, but what they *will probably do*, is not to be intimated. The general impression here is, that there were probably a plenty of spies on the ground yesterday, and as the enemy have a large picket force all along the east bank of the Rappahannock, six or eight miles hence, these spies have doubtless, ere this, reported the full particulars of the demonstration. The infantry in this vicinity went out to see the "show," and were well pleased. The horses are all in excellent condition, and the men and horses are both well drilled. Their charges, in columns of squadrons, were splendid. If they will only charge on the enemy with as much impetuosity they could hardly be blamed for running. Long rest of the most jaded, for man and beast, and rich clover fields for the latter, have very much improved this branch of the service.

The enemy are reported to have obstructed the fords, on the Rappahannock, by throwing in trees and timbers, stationed batteries and thrown up breast works, at all the noted passages of this famous stream. They seem to apprehend an advance of our forces; whether their conjectures are to be realized events will soon show.

An order for a Brigade drill at 8'o clock this morning was countermanded, and we were ordered to cook three days' rations and be ready for a march by noon. The current belief is that we are to advance. Important movements are going on, that it would, perhaps, be imprudent to communicate, but I will try to keep you posted on events as they transpire.

P.S. 8 o'clock P.M. The head of the Division is moving through town towards the Rappahannock and of course we will follow. We are told that no fires will be allowed to night. So of course it is expected that we will be near the enemy. M. D.

Bivouac 8th Ga. Reg't. near
Culpepper C.H., Va., June 8th, 1863.

**Dear Courier:** My letter of last Saturday, closed with the statement that our division was on the march towards the Rappahannock. We went about three miles toward Rappahannock Station, on the Orange and Alexandria Railroad, then turned to the right, and passing to the left of Stephensburg, proceeded down the river to a point some sixteen or eighteen miles from here, where at 11 o'clock P.M., we bivouaced for the remainder of the night. It rained nearly all the afternoon, thus greatly increasing the fatigue and otherwise rendering the march more disagreeable. No fires were allowed, but as the men were very wary, the "honey heavy due of slumber, soon rest up the pent up lids" of the grim visage host, and visions of home, all radiant with the love-lit eyes of affection, soon gladdened the hearts and softened the expression on the deep wrinkled features of the manly heroes in freedom's holy cause.

The march during the afternoon had been moderately slow, with frequent rest; but as soon as night set in, a lively quickstep was kept up without a single half, for the last eight or nine miles.

The bivouac was said to be four miles from Kelly's Ford, on the Rappahannock, where the enemy had a considerable force of artillery and infantry, and the general expectation in our division, when we lay down, was, that at daylight next morning, we would attempt to force a passage, and, if successful, would then move down and attack Hooker's right flank. This opinion seemed the more probable, from the fact that it was reported that the enemy had crossed just below Fredericksburg, some ten thousand strong. If he should make a strong advance, it would be such a good joke in interrupt his successful backward movement. But A. P. Hill spoilt all the sport by thrashing out the vandals, and destroying their bridges, but not until the most of the scattering scamps had made their escape.[1] So at sun rise yesterday, we were ordered in to line, and immediately took up the march back to his place, where we arrived at

1 o'clock P.M., having marched some thirty-two or thirty-six miles, in less than twenty four hours. Of course, the men were greatly fatigued, but now they are so far rested than the usual amount of mirthfulness and god humor prevails.

We now get for rations an abundance of first rate bacon and flour, and, occasionally, a little sprinkling of sugar and rice.

The army was never in better spirits, and they will do, with a hearty good will, what ever is demanded of them.

Tuesday Morning: Heavy cannonading is now going on in front, probably at some point on the river. It is likely that our cavalry is feeling the enemy's line a little. M. D.

Camp 8th Ga. Reg.,
Near Culpeper C.H., Va.
June 10th, 1863.

**Dear Courier:** Yesterday was a day of considerable excitement in this vicinity, occasioned by a fight participated almost exclusively by cavalry and artillery.

Accounts are still very unsatisfactory and contradictory in regard to details. Infantry are bad enough in all conscience, but cavalry are the worst sensationists beyond all doubt in the service, and the first reports brought back by freightened deserters from the battle field, yesterday, were of a most astounding character. It is not necessary to repeat the tales of these men who desired to justify their own running, by fabulous statements of its necessity, and the subject is only alluded to from an apprehension that some of these statements may be widely circulated.

From the most reliable information received, the facts seems to be about as follows: A large body of Federal cavalry, variously estimated from 10,000 to 15,000, crossed the Rappahannock at some three or four fords, from Kelley's to one just above Rappahannock Station, at about daybreak. They brought with them several batteries, and either a brigade or two of infantry, or they had cavalry dismounted. They crossed unobserved by our cavalry pickets, and completely surprised the cavalry camps in the vicinity of the various crossings. 'Tis said that they even went into one camp and waked up the men and told them it was time to get up for reveille. This is probably an exaggeration. The heaviest of the fighting was near Brandy Station, on the O. & A. R.R. Here our forces were at first driven back, but they afterwards regained their ground. The Yankees are said to have rushed through our artillery camp without even spiking the guns; the captain of the battery immediately had his horses hitched up, moved off a short distance, and opened fire on the very regiment that had so unceremoniously disturbed his morning slumbers.

The fighting is said to have been very desperate for several hours, and there were more killed and wounded than often happened in this branch of the service. Gen. Lawton's Brigade of infantry, some time in the afternoon, went to the assistance of the cavalry, and that was the only infantry, so far as I have been able to learn, that was engaged on our side. Of the artillery engaged I can learn but little. 'Tis reported that we lost one piece—which some say was recaptured—and took three.

The enemy advanced in three or four columns, and some got to the rear of our men before they had any intimation of danger being near. It is admitted by all that our men were most disgracefully and completely surprised, but after the loss necessarily consequent upon this fact, they made, with the exception of, say one brigade, (Jones) a very gallant and praiseworthy fight.

At the same time that three columns advanced to near Brandy Station a large force of about, 2000 Yanks moved on to Stephensburg, a little village some four miles down the river, where we had two regiments of cavalry. One of these, the 4th Va., is said to have been not only surprised, but completely panic stricken, and took to their heels with the utmost speed; the other the 2d S.C., after being surprised, did the best they could, but had to fall back before greatly superior numbers. They were pursued some two miles this side of the village.

Accounts of losses are very conflicting. According to what seems to be the most reliable, our loss in killed, wounded and missing, will not exceed 450, and nearly all of them were taken prisoners. Lt. Col. Frank Hampton is reported mortally wounded. A considerable portion of our wounded are slight sabre cuts. The enemy's loss is much greater. Our men took over 400 prisoners and the enemy left over fifty dead on the field. As they occupied the field through the early part of the day, a large portion of their wounded were carried off, still a large number were left in our hands. Their entire loss can hardly be less than 1000, including many officers.

They gave up the fight about 4 o'clock P.M., and before night the discomforted hordes had all recrossed the river. This movement was probably another of Stoneman's raids, but it happened to be nipped in the bud.

The infantry in the vicinity of C.H. moved out towards the battle field, about 1 o'clock P.M. Our Brigade went towards Stephensburg about two miles, and there halted until sunset, when we returned to our former camp. I regret I cannot give you more satisfactory news, but as I have been unable to leave camp to-day, have concluded to send what seems to be the most reliable of camp rumors, and trust to better opportunities for getting precise information in the future. M. D.

Bivouac of 8th GA. Reg.,
Near Culpepper Court House, Va.,
June 13, 1863.

**Dear Courier:** The cavalry fight on last Tuesday, is still the engrossing topic of conversation in camp. There is a disposition on the part of the infantry, generally, to be unreasonably severe in their criticisms, of cavalry service, particularly their efficiency in a fight. 'Tis firmly alleged that the bravery of one man is rarely sufficient to overcome the running propensities of six legs, and beside this, the very discipline of cavalry does not tend to make men *stand* to a fight like infantry. There is always much jeering and jesting between the members of the different branches of the service, and also some little rivalry.

It is said that it takes cavalry for a *show*, artillery for a *noise*, but infantry for hard, decisive *fighting*. The cavalry are notoriously unreliable reporters of their own fights and skirmishes. This is not because of any moral defect, but is owing to the velocity of their movements, being so great as not to admit of making close and accurate observations. Hence, in regard to the recent fight, *it* seems almost impossible to get a correct statement of the details. It is pretty well ascertained that Generals Hampton and Jones' Brigades were the principal, and perhaps the only forces engaged on our side; that they made several charges upon the enemy, who stood their ground, and fought them with sabres when they, came up; that the enemy made no charges after their first surprise charges in the morning, but invariably gave way after a short contest with cold steel; that our loss was some thirty-five killed, mostly by dismounted sharpshooters; that we had about one hundred and seventy-five wounded, about one third of whom are suffering from slight sabre cuts; that about two hundred of our men were taken prisoners, and that we lost something like four hundred horses. Of the enemy's loss very little is known, beyond the fact that we got over three hundred prisoners, beside some fifty or sixty wounded, and the possession of some thirty of their dead. They had ample opportunities to re-move those of their killed and wounded who were *hors du combat* before two or three o'clock P.M., so it is reasonable to suppose that their loss in killed and wounded must at least double ours. They also lost three pieces of their artillery.

This was probably the largest and severest cavalry fight there has been, not only since the commencement of this war, but ever on this continent. Now when it is noted that our two brigades lost only thirty or forty killed, and less than two hundred wounded—-which numbers have several times been exceeded by single regiments of infantry in an engagement—one grand difference between the two branches of service will then be readily appreciated.

It is generally considered disgraceful that our cavalry should suffer itself to be completely surprised, as it was on this occasion, but they are said, in the main, to have acted remarkably well after recovering from the panic incident to this.

There is no camp news of particular interest. Our bivouac is about 2 miles South of the Court House in a pleasant grove, with a tolerable supply of good water, and the men are in excellent health and spirits. One fact shows the uncertainty of substitutes. Phillip Cohen, of Co. A, mustered in one on the 2d day of May, when we were near Suffolk, and he ran away in less than five hours and has not been heard from since. But the one George McGuire, of the same company—who by the way has been a most excellent soldier—put in last week; it is to be hoped will "stick."

It is now noon. At 11 o'clock we received orders to fall in and be ready to march, how far or which way, no one knows, except—well, some of the big ones.

It may be interesting to the old "stagers," to know that Gov. Brown's electioneering documents are circulated very freely among the Georgia troops. This has evidently been done systematically, for every company, so far as I have been able to learn, gets its exact quota. There was an effort at a meeting of the Brigade, to pass resolutions endorsing his administration, and recommending his re-election, but they failed to pass.

Most of the soldiers are ardent supporters of our national administration, and will consequently oppose its opposers. The extent of Gov. Brown's opposition to President Davis' Administration, does not seem to be well understood by the soldiers generally.[2] M. D.

On the Road Side near
Upperville, Va., June 18th, 1863.

**Dear Courier:** Advantage is taken of a short rest, to inform you of the movements of our brigade. On last Monday morning, at sun rise, our brigade—and whether other troops or not, may not be prudent now to state—was in line ready to move. Eleven days rations were in the haversacks, and before reaching the city, an other days rations of hard bread was issued. For unknown cause the command was delayed so that we marched through town at 2 o'clock. The day was intensely hot, and the march was continued very rapidly until 2 o'clock, P.M., when we rested for three hours. But before this time some twenty men, overcame by heat, had fainted by the way side. They did not with two or three exceptions, faint entirely away, but would turn pale, get dizzy and fall. In most of these cases, wetting the face and wrists with cold water, with a little to drink, soon revived them. Wonderful rumors were current among the men, some gravely asserting that forty had died from sun stroke. Reliable information has been received that one man died, but even he did not belong to our brigade. There is no doubt but the suffering was intense.

We started out from Culpepper C.H. in the direction of Warrenton, but after going some five miles, took to the left, and late in the evening crossed the Hazel river, marched until eight o'clock, making a distance of about twenty miles during the day.

Tuesday was cooler and, as we marched about twelve miles, the men stood it finely. That night we bivouaced at Molcome, a station on the Manassas Gap Railroad, having forded during the day, Robertson's and the Rappahannock rivers, both were deep where we crossed.

The march was resumed at sun rise again on Wednesday morning, and making a detour around to the right, crossed the railroad at Piedmont, and took the pike for Upperville, a little town nearly at the summit of the Blue Ridge, and six miles distant from Piedmont. This morning was excessively hot, and as there was very little shade, many men, overcome with heat, broke down. Halted at one o'clock, for the balance of the day, having marched ten miles. This morning at sun rise the march was resumed, taking back down the pike about half a mile, then filed to the right and made a circuitous route round to Paris, marching, at least six miles over a miserable mountain road, to Paris, while the direct pike road is only three. Passed through Ashby's Gap at six o'clock A.M., and arrived at the Shennandoah river at ten. Here we crossed at the same ford where we crossed on the 18th of July, 1861.

Halted a mile on the North side of the ford, rested two hours and put in our haversacks one day's rations that a detail had been sent forward and cooked, then moved off for the ford opposite Snicker's Gap, distant ten miles, but as we made a detour to the left, our march was at least twelve miles. It was excessively hot until three o'clock when it commenced and continued raining until night. Some eight or ten men from the brigade, fell during the day, overcame by heat and fatigue. Arrived at Snicker's Ford at sunset, having marched twenty miles during the day. By the meandering course pursued we have marched, since leaving Culpeper C.H., about sixty miles in four days. Owing to the excessive heat it has been the severest march this command has ever made. The men all look like they had suffered from a spell of sickness and had fallen in weight on an average of ten pounds each. None of the Floyd county companies have took very sick.

Friday Morning. Under the present state of affairs it can hardly be imprudent to state that we have been in company with the balance of the division. Benning's and Robertson's brigades, now hold the ford opposite Ashby's Gap, and Anderson's and Law's that opposite Snicker's Gap. Our position is a very advantagous one and can be easily held against ten times the opposing force. We have a brigade of cavalry and a battalion of riflemen at Snicker's Gap, and it is said that the enemy are not nearer than ten miles. They may have gotten intimation of our movements, and concluded it would not be prudent to attempt to cut off Ewell by this course.[3] Gen. E. is beyond doubt, in Maryland, and it is rumored that our cavalry are now in Pennsylvania.

Of Ewell's victory at Winchester, you will probably get full accounts before this reaches you. The five million's worth of army stores, he is said to have captured, will be particularly serviceably more valuable than the five or six thousand prisoners.

5 o'clock, P.M. At one o' clock we got orders to recross the river and take position in the gap, at the summit of mountain. It was reported that the abolitionists were advancing towards that point, in strong force of both cavalry and infantry.

The two Brigades moved off very promptly, and forded the river without hesitation. The stream, in the deepest part of the ford, is not over two and a half feet deep, and our Brigade, as usual, pulled of their pants socks and drawers. The summit is only two and a half miles from the river, and in about two hours the two brigades had taken position, Gen. Anderson upon the left and Gen. Law upon the right of the road. Maj. Henry, with his artillery battalion, composed of sixteen guns, occupied a position near the road. Our position is certainly a very strong one. The enemy's cavalry pickets are reported to have occupied the Gap up to yesterday morning.

A Yankee courier is said to have been captured today, carrying an order to the Federal commander here, to hold Snicker's Gap at all hazards. The order was dated yesterday. The enemy will hardly attack us here unless they are greatly deceived about our strength. Of course a thousand rumors are afloat.

The latest from the front is that the enemy is about six miles distant and slowly advancing.

Saturday Morning—All quiet as yet. We had a rainy night, commencing with a heavy shower at 8 o'clock. It is very foggy and raining a little this morning. No exciting rumors are now afloat.

Sunday Morning—We recrossed the river to the North side last evening. No news this morning. M. D.

Bivouac of 8th GA. Reg't, Near
Berryville, Clark Co., Va.,
June 23d, 1863.

**Dear Courier:** Since closing my letter, on Sunday morning, nothing of particular interest has occurred, so far as the infantry is concerned, except that they have been most of the time in motion.

At four o'clock Sunday evening a report was brought into camp that the Abolitionists were driving back Stewart's cavalry, in the vicinity of Upperville. Our brigade was ordered to cross immediately to the south side of the river, and go to the support of the cavalry. Consequently we forded at double quick, few stopping to remove any part of their clothing. Marched to within a half mile of the summit and halted for the night. It was now ascertained that the Yankees had pursued our cavalry, one part to Upperville and the balance through Shephards' Gap, which is about five miles from Ashby's and Snicker's Gaps, being midway between them. The Federal cavalry are said to have acted with desperation, and they greatly outnumbered our cavalry, at least the latter say so, they gave way at first slowly but soon in great rout, and as fast as their horses could be made to carry them.

Of our losses in the fight, I have no certain information. It is rumored that we lost one piece of artillery and quite a number—some say a regiment—of prisoners.

Yesterday morning our brigade only passed up to the top of the ridge, in Snicker's Gap, then filed to the right and proceeded on rough mountain road, right along the very summit about five miles, then took a stand. Had been here some three or four hours, when it having been ascertained that the Yankees had fallen back the night previous, we were ordered back across the river, and crossing at Shephard's Ford, which is five miles from the top of the Gap, and came on to this place, five miles further, arriving here at nine o'clock, P.M.

It seems to have been Hooker's intention to cross the ridge at some of the Gaps, and thus cut Ewell off from the balance of our forces, and his base of supplies, but he has completely failed, and it is reported that all his infantry is at Leesburg, or beyond there. If Lee can divide his force he will probably whip him by detail.

We are now 22 miles from Harper's Ferry and ten from Winchester—Since the rain last Friday and Saturday, the weather has been fine. Most of the men who broke down on the march from Culpepper, have come up and are now well. As near as I can ascertain, four or five men of our division, died of sun stroke on that march.

The beautiful flag presented to the Light Guards, in 1860, is again in possession of one of the former members of the company, Commissary G. C. Norton has it. It was lost when we left Winchester, in July, 1861. Was found by a servant and has been cared for by a Mr. McGuire, of this county. The company is greatly rejoiced at the recovery of this memento of the Ladies' esteem. Whether they have shrunk from the duties implied in the motto, "Our liberties we prize—Our right we will maintain," let others judge.

Gen. Lee has completely non plussed Hooker this time, and what are to be our future movements, 'tis useless to conjecture. M. D.

Bivouac 8th Ga. Reg.
Franklin co., Va., June 27th, '63.[4]

**Dear Courier:** Since closing my letter on the eve of the 25th inst. our division has not been idle. That night, though we had marched 20 miles during the day, the men had to cook two days' rations—had Reveille at 2 o'clock, Friday morning and got underway at 5. It was four miles to ford at Williamsport—Forded the Potomac there between 7 and 9 o'clock, the water being no more than 2 ½ feet deep in the deepest places. It commenced to rain at 2 o'clock and we had a rather a gloomy time, but we were halted two miles this side of W. where whisky rations were issued, the men built good fires from Union rails and cheerfulness and even hilarity soon became universal. At Noon again resumed the march, taking a Northerly direction, towards Greencastle, PA. The first two or three miles was once a dirt road, which the heavy rain of the morning had made very muddy and the marching was horrid. But the men kept up finely; in fact here has been less straggling during the past three days than I have ever known in our Division. At four o'clock P.M. we crossed the Pa. line and our Raid for the first time was on abolition soil. The characteristic difference between the true Southrons and Abolitionists is so completely graduated as you approach the line of their territories from either side, that no very palpable difference is noticeable just at the boundary. Even in Burkley county Va. We passed many houses with closed doors and windows, where the ropes and pump handles had been removed, and all possible pains taken to prevent giving aid and comfort to the "rebels." At Williamsport, which contains probably 1500 or 200 inhabitants, the ladies at some half dozen houses cheered us on, while most of the citizens wore frowning countenances. We are now twelve miles from Williamsport, three miles from the Maryland line, and four miles from Gettysburg, Pa., and in this neighborhood are several gentlemen so intensely strong in their war sentiments, and so decidedly opposed to abolitionism as to make them strong sympathisers to the Confederate cause.

Gen. Rhodes's division is said to be at Greencastle. Nearly all the horses and beef cattle about here had been captured by him and driven south before we came. Our orders are very strict not to disturb citizens or private property except such as the army needs, and this is pressed by Quartermasters or other officers especially detailed for that purpose. We find here a very decided reduction in the price of articles of food from what it is in Virginia. For instance first rate bacon is sold here at from 15 to 20 cents per pound—butter, 12 ½—cents—Flour 3 cents; and what is still more strange, I have not heard of any refusing to take Confederate money, though several have refused pay, from soldiers, for milk, vegetables and perhaps a few pounds of meat.

If this division is not completely *mobilized* there never was one in that condition. We have marched, in the last twelve days, one hundred and seventy miles, and while our brigade forded the Shenandoah five times the whole Division forded it two or three times, and all the Potomac. And, afterall, it may be that our grand tour is now only commenced. This morning we had the luxury of sleeping till sun rise, and we are ordered to march at 7 o'clock. It is forty-six miles to Harrisburg, the capital of Pa., but whether we are to go there or not probably only Gen. Lee and a few of his junior Generals know. We hear of no organized force of the enemy except Pennsylvania Militia, in this vicinity, but we will probably raise a clatter before long.

SUNDAY MORNING, June 28.

Yesterday the march was continued on through Greencastle and Chambersburg, eleven miles from the former place, and are now bivouacked for the day two miles from the latter. Since leaving Williamsport our route has lain through one of the richest sections of country I have ever seen. Clover, wheat and corn are the chief and almost entire productions, and there is comparatively little corn growing, but the growth is very large and heavy. One is surprised to see so many large fine barns; some of them built of brick, others of stone and still others of wood and painted. They look as fine as churches and are twice as large.

Greencastle is a place of some fifteen hundred or two thousand inhabitants of neat and rather pleasant aspect. Few men, but a large number of ladies showed themselves, as we marched through, and there was such a strong expression of dread and apprehension on the countenances of all as to easily excite emotions of pity, I only saw two or three persons there even smile, and this was at some drollery of the soldiers that would have "made a horse laugh," while several were seen weeping.

Chambersburg is the county site of Franklin county, contains 5000 or 6000 inhabitants, is on the Railroad running from Hagerstown to Harrisburg, is rather a pretty town and has the appearance of considerable business. The stores and most of the dwellings here, as well as at Greencastle, were closed when we marched through. The Quartermasters of Roads' Division had pressed nearly all the boots, shoes, hats and other articles suitable to the army, before we came up.

We are stopping here today to rest, wash our clothes, and cook three days rations. If we go that way, and are not interrupted, we can easily march to Harrisburg in three days, it being fifty miles. The Flag of the Light Guards was carried yesterday at the head of the Regiment and received considerable attention as we passed through the town. The very best of spirits prevail and the Boys have their own fun as they "plod their weary way" through the land of suppressed public speech, a slave press and free negroes.

MONDAY MORNING. All is quiet yet and no orders to move. Is thought we will remain here today.

Bivouac 8th Ga. Regiment,
Wednesday morn. July 1, '63.

**Dear Courier:** Last Sunday morning I handed the mail carrier some account of our movements during the three days previous. Don't know whether the letter is sent off yet, and now write few additional lines, so that if an opportunity is offered the latest date possible may be sent you. Sunday and Monday our Division remained near Chambersburg, little occurring of interest. Our commissaries and Quartermasters issued some flour and bacon but nothing else of any considerable value, unless it was for their own use, or that of some few favorites. I do not suppose they got much though for anybody. The stores were all closed and their owners hid out many of their goods, but the aforesaid officers had orders to enter them forcibly if need be and press such articles as were of prime necessity for the army. The Railroad track was taken up for two or three miles and forty two barrels of whisky was destroyed near camp: but not a building has been burnt, not even the depot and court house, tho' some little depredations have been committed yet, private property has been respected quite as much as it would have been in our own territory.

Ewell's corps, or at least a portion of it, has been as far as Carlisle—twenty two miles from Harrisburg—but it is said that they have now turned back. Yesterday morning we left the vicinity of Chambersburg, and taking the Baltimore Pike marched to Fayetteville—six miles from C.—where we now are. A ridge of mountains lie between us and Hagerstown. A very large force is now massed in this vicinity. It is reported that Hooker is coming on and if so we will meet him in a day or two. It is now 8 o'clock, the men are cooking rations, and ordered to be ready to move as soon as possible.

THURSDAY MORNING. Yesterday at 4 o'clock P.M. we moved out to the Baltimore Pike twelve miles passing through a gap of the South mountains and by the Caledonia Iron Works that have been burned.[5] Halted at midnight and resumed the march again at 3 o'clock this morning, having proceeded six miles we are now in line of battle one mile from Gettysburg. A severe battle was fought here yesterday. A portion of Pender's and Hill's Divisions were engaged on our side. Archer's Brigade suffered very severely he and some five hundred or more of his men were taken prisoners. Maj. Gen. Heth was slightly wounded.[6] The enemy were driven back some three miles through the town which our forces now occupy. Nearly three thousand of the enemy were captured, including a number of officers but I hear of none ranking above colonel.

July 7, 1863

**Dear Courier:** While resting for a short time on the wayside the opportunity is embraced to say a few things in regard to the recent awful, bloody and hard fought battle at Gettysburg, Pa. The carnage was greater probably than on any other field since the commencement of this wicked war. The fight commenced on Wednesday, July the 1st; on that day only two Divisions and those of A. P. Hill's corps were generally engaged. The enemy at the commencement of that day had their line out some mile or more to the west of town but they were driven back with great slaughter through the town and our line at night established on the east side of the place. That day our forces captured about three thousand prisoners. The losses on both sides, considering the relatively small numbers engaged were heavy.

Hood's division arrived from Fayetteville Thursday morning, and McLaws' division arrived also. Until noon our army was engaged in finding the location of the enemy and in getting into position. Arrangements were made for Hood's Division to charge a strong position opposite to our right. We moved down to the right and commenced to fire about three o'clock. Our march to the right was continued until the force was opposite to the desired point when the order to move by the left flank was promptly obeyed and a more splendid line of brave men never moved on to deadly combat than this on that occasion. The line of battle was carried forward about a half mile under the most dreadful cannonading the Abolitionists have ever been able to bear upon our forces, in perfect order; the men were in good spirits and bravely determined

Confederate dead near the center of battlefield, Gettysburg. Library of Congress.

to carry all obstacles before them; on, on they moved in firm and steady line through wheat fields and woods, over rocks and fences, not wavering even when the lines were opened by the shell and cannon shot of the enemy and though the deadly missiles were almost constantly whizzing over their heads. At last coming up to within about a hundred yards of a heavy rock breast work the foe opened a most deadly fire of musketry. Still, undaunted, our brave men never flinched, but moved on to within about 75 yards of the enemy's line, they were ordered halt. Being in the woods the men took such protection as was afforded by the trees and poured a most deadly fire upon the Abolitionist hordes. After a short time our Brigade was ordered to fall back a short distance, about twenty or thirty yards—after resting a very few minutes they again charged forward with great spirit and determination; again they fell back, and again charged forward but after all they were reluctantly compelled to give up and so they returned in good order.

The other Brigades of our division all fought and suffered in a similar manner. Our Brigade lost in killed, wounded and missing 900 out of 2900 carried into the fight.

Friday the battle was resumed on the same lines as the day before, and ended in about the same way, after hard fighting, heavy losing and no permanent gaining on our side.

There were three days of the most severe fighting of the entire war during some part of the time and at some point nearly every Brigade of Longstreet's,

A. P. Hill's and Ewell's were engaged. At some points the enemy were temporarily driven back, but the strength of their position and their facilities for reinforcing such were such as to enable the enemy to soon again retake their lost ground.

Our loss has been very heavy. At present the only expression of number must be vague, say 30,000 killed, mamed and missing.

Saturday our wounded were ordered to move off towards Winchester, Va., all that could walk and also such as could be carried in the ambulances, and as my wound is in the arm I was sent off with a walking squad, and am now, Wednesday evening, at Winchester, having walked nearly the whole distance from Gettysburg, about 90 miles in five days.

The Potomac has been so swollen by the recent rains that it was not fordable, and as the Yanks had dashed in and destroyed our Pontoon Bridge below Williamsport. It has been a very tedious job to get some twenty miles of wagons and several thousand wounded men over that stream in one small ferry boat. Since Sunday morning they have been crossing as rapidly as the nature of the case would admit, but they are not nearly all over yet.

The Yanks made an attack on our wagon train and ambulances at Williamsport Monday evening, but they were repulsed, with a loss of most of their artillery, 3 or 4 pieces, and some two hundred men. No loss on our side of any amount. Between Gettysburg and W. they twice attacked our train and each time captured a few wagons say forty or fifty in all—though the accounts are much at variance to numbers.

Probably before this reaches your full list of the killed and wounded in our regiment will have come to hand. Out of the 36 officers that went into the fight 30 were either killed or wounded. Of the three companies from Floyd county I give below all that I know of—though the list is very defective except as far as the Light Guards are concerned.

Light Guards—Killed, W. S. Booten, Joseph J. Aycock and W. J. Leaser.[7] Wounded, Capt. Hall (very slight), Lieut. Dwinell (flesh wound in left arm) Wm. McCay, John R. Payne, Marion Payne, Wm. A. Barron, R. J. Franks, R. J. Mann, W. L. Morefield, Serg. J. F. Felton.[8]

Miller Rifles—I am not able to give any of the names in this company expect Lieuts. Harper and Huntington, both very slight, and W. H. Jones, also slight.[9]

Floyd Infantry—Capt. Yarborough was killed and Lieut. Echols died from the amputation of this leg the next day. Of the others I cannot say as I could not get about to gather particulars.[10]

Camp 8th GA. Regiment,
Near Charleston, S.C.,
Sept. 28th, 1863.

**Dear Courier:** Though camp life is embittered by many privations and sufferings, yet there is a pleasure of the highest order in rejoining here, the companion in arms who have made glorious, many a blood stained field in the cause of justice and human rights. There is evidence of this in the fact that soldiers, not unfrequently, when away, call camp *home*; thus showing by the sweetness of the *name* some love for the place.

The Regiment is encamped for the present on James Island, south of the city, and within a mile and a half of the wharf on Ashly river.[11] It is hoped that we may move in a few days. The camp is in an open field, with no shade, deep sandy soil, very little wood at hand or convenient, and water is obtained by digging a hole some 8 or 10 feet in the ground. We are on the bank of a bayou and about 20 feet above tide water. Neither musquitoes nor sand flies annoy us very much, but the common house flies are in such abundance as to be a great nuisance.

No tents have as yet been issued here, except one tent fly to the company which is generally occupied by the officers. The men have their little Yankee flies stretched, which makes a very good protection from dew and rain, but they are too small and close to be comfortable as a screen from the sun. The rations are fresh beef, corn meal, rice, peas, sugar, salt and soap. This does very well, yet bacon or lard is very much needed, for shortening and cooking the few fish, some of the boys occasionally get. Crabs are tolerably plentiful and a few poor oysters have been obtained. The water used, tho' warm, is not as unpalatable as might be supposed. On the whole we are getting along very well in the eating line, but yet would like very well to get a few vegetables, say sweet or Irish potatoes, and some vinegar or other anti-scorbutic, and flour would now be esteemed a great luxury. This part of the Island is proverbially sickly but our Regiment has not yet suffered, except by many cases of slight indisposition. We now have 312 men reported present of these about 40 are on the sick list—mostly chills and fever and many cases of cholic. There is an almost constant firing from our batteries on the enemy on Morris Island. I suppose the average, since Saturday evening, would be a gun every 30 minutes. The enemy do not reply to the firing but are reported to be very busy in perfecting their works. It is rumored today that quite a large number of their tents on that Island disappeared last night, and, of course, some movement is suspected.

Regular drilling was resumed to-day—company drill in the morning and Battallion Drill in the afternoon.

Camp 8th GA. Regiment,
Near Charleston, S.C.,
October 2nd, 1863.

**Dear Courier:** The dull monotony of passing events still goes on with but little change, so far as an absence from this position can see. The heavy booming of cannon, both from the enemy's Batteries on Morris Island and our own on James and Sullivan's islands, is heard at all hours of the day and night some times as rapidly as one every five minutes, and at others no more than two in an hour. A negro was killed two days since at Fort Sumter, and a man wounded at Fort Johnson yesterday: these are the only casualties reported on our side in several days past. The enemy, so far, have burned a vast amount of powder to very little purpose. Their great activity and extensive preparations still going on indicate that they will make a desperate attack before long. Great confidence is felt in our ability to repel any and all attacks that may be made. There is little doubt but that the enemy may set the city on fire, perhaps in many places by means of shells loaded with combusitble materials and fired from their long range guns on Morris Island. But if this is done the vigilant Fire department will probably suppress the flames and prevent an extensive conflagration; but even if this should not be done and the place should be reduced to ashes, still it is possible for Gen. Beauregard to hold the harbor and the site of the once proud city. It is not probable that Charleston will ever be of any value to our implacable foe.

The sickness in our Regiment is, at least, not on the increase, and nearly all the cases readily yield to the ordinary treatment. There are a considerable number of cases of slight cholic nearly every day, but the prevailing sickness is chills and fever.

Of the Light Guards thirty-one members are in camp. Of these there are on the sick list, Shelton, Stinson, G. W. Hutchings, DeJournett, J. R. Payne, Boggs and A. R. Johnson.[12] All have chills and fever.

The Floyd Infantry have thirty one men present, of whom Frank Bean, D. H. Hufford, T. H. Richardson and W. H. Drenon, are on the sick list, all having chills except the last who has dysentary.[13]

The Miller Rifles have twenty-eight men in camp and only two report on the sick list. Wilkins and Simpkins—these are very slightly indisposed.[14]

The apprehensions of severe sickness here, are not, I am happy to state, being realized.

Below is a tabular statement of the losses of the various companies of our Regiment since entering the service. Besides those stated 25 or 28 men from the ranks have been commissioned and assigned to duty in other commands and 17 have been transferred.

| Company | Killed | Died | Disch'd from wounds | Discharged from disability | Deserters |
|---|---|---|---|---|---|
| A – Rome Lt. G'rds, | 17 | 6 | 3 | 16 | 1 |
| B – Oglethorpe Lt In, | 16 | 6 | 13 | 17 | 6 |
| C – Macon Guards, | 16 | 10 | 8 | 25 | 2 |
| D – Echols Guards, | 14 | 20 | 4 | 20 | 3 |
| E – Miller Rifles, | 18 | 28 | | 21 | |
| F – Atlanta Grays, | 20 | 6 | | 34 | 4 |
| G – Pulaski Vol'ers, | 29 | 25 | 3 | 9 | 1 |
| H – Floyd Infantry, | 18 | 25 | | 13 | |
| I – Stephens Lt G'ds, | 24 | 10 | 9 | 11 | 6 |
| K – Oglethorpe Rifls | 11 | 29 | 10 | 19 | |
| | 183 | 165 | 50 | 185 | 23 |

Companies E, F, and H, did not make a distinction, in their reports, between those discharged from wounds and by reason of other disability.

There are a considerable number of men at present, belonging to the Regiment, who are disabled from wounds, but not yet discharged. M. D.

Camp 8th Ga. Reg. Near Charleston, S. C.,
Oct. 5th, 1863.

**Dear Courier:** There is nothing of interest to communicate from this camp except the gratifying intelligence that the amount of sickness is gradually yet surely on the decrease. Last Wednesday and Friday night we had rain and we now have a delightful atmosphere at an agreeable temperature. The siege presents no new phases. The firing has been perhaps a little less during the past two days, than previously. Lieut. Marshall, Adj. of the 59th Reg. died suddenly last Saturday morning, as is supposed, from taking an over dose of Laudanum. He had Diarrhea and the Surgeon had given him a bottle of that medicine to use at his discretion. On the morning of Saturday he could not be awakened.

Since writing the above, intelligence of a reliable character has been received that we are to leave here in a day or two, probably to rejoin our old division.

Chicamauga Station, Oct. 10

**Dear Courier:** Our command, small it is true, but in a fight "O scissors," arrived at this place last night. Nothing of particular interest occurred on our way here, except the voting on the cars. To vote is a civil privilege that has been very properly bestowed on troops from home, and with great apparent pleasure it was exercised. The evening before the election the camps resounded with hurrahs for Brown and hurrahs for Furlow, and an occasional one for Hill, and it really seemed like old times at home. Considerable earnestness was exhibited in some groups by the ardent advocates of various candidates, but in one sense the discussions were less *spirited* than, at old time elections. The order to move did not debar the men, the inestimable right of a voice in selecting the civil officers of the State, but arrangements were made to vote on the train. So at every wood or water station, or wherever else the train stopped the polls were opened, and some ten, twenty or thirty men voted. There never was, perhaps, a more orderly election than this, or one in which the elective franchise was exercised by every man, more completely without bias.

The men who were scattered away from their companies, failed in many instances to get a chance to vote, and hence the small number of votes polled.

As yet we have had no opportunity to "survey the landscape o'er" in this neighborhood, and even if we had all the news has already been made public that is not contraband. This morning it was thought that the enemy were about to bring on a battle. Their pickets were doubled a little before day, and some other fighting signs were noticed, but no serious demonstrations have been made to day—it has been, so far as firing is concerned, completely quiet all day. Quite a number of our Regiment took "French leave" at Kingston and some other points along the road. This was very wrong, but most of those who did this will be apt to plead in extenuation that they had never been home since the commencement of the war. At all events they should make all haste to return to their commands. Unless they intend to desert, surely they will hardly remain at home longer than two days at most.

Sunday Morning. Notice has been given that we will remain here until Tuesday. All quiet this morning. Communications for our Regiment should be directed to Chattanooga, Tenn. M. D.

Camp 8th Ga. Regiment,
Near Chattanooga,
October 10, 1863.

**Dear Courier:** After almost continuous raining for three day and nights, it ceased yesterday evening, and to-day we are enjoying the first sunshine we have had since last Monday. We are here in perhaps the muddiest little coop hole that mortals ever lived in. We have mud to stand in and mud to walk in, mud to sit in and mud to lie in, mud to eat in and mud to sleep in; we are in mud when we lie down and in mud when we get up; we eat mud and drink mud, and all who see us have unmistakeable evidence that we wear mud. This is no place to *define* "the *powers* of mud" for it seems to be endless; and besides it is quite weak in its effects, else we would all be completely "muddled."

Two or three of the temporary railroad bridges—put up in place of the good, substantial ones burned by that loving government, to whose affectionate embraces the "wayward sisters" are invited to return—have been washed away between here and Dalton. The train now comes by way of Cleveland. The creek between here and Lookout Point is swimming, and so we cannot get to our position in the line until it runs down.

Saturday Morning—All quiet in front as far as we can either see or hear, or get news from.

Camp 8th Ga. Regiment,
Near Chattanooga,
October 12, 1863.

**Dear Courier:** The plot thickens, and stirring events may soon be expected in this vicinity. It is reported that Rosencrans is receiving reinforcements daily, and new camps are seen nearly every morning, within the enemy's line.[15] Bragg's position on Missionary Ridge is a very strong one naturally, and made still more so by fortifications.[16] This position is said to be a much better one than that occupied by the enemy in Chattanooga. But both armies are as well situated for defensive operations that it is not probable that either will attack the other by a direct movement. An effort to flank, however, may be undertaken by one or the other at an early day.

Since ten o'clock last night, at, irregular intervals, cannonading has been heard in the rear of Chattanooga, probably some five or eight miles beyond the river. The occasion of this fire is a mere matter of conjecture among all except our principal officers. The general impression, however, is that a portion of our cavalry are attempting to cut off Rosencranz's communication with his base of supplies. Several little incidents have occurred within the past few days, tending to show that the enemy are already short of rations. One was that, today, to meet a flag of truce, the Yankee officers came out on foot, thus leaving the inference that their horses had been sent off for want of forage. A Yankee picket, yesterday, came out towards our line, and laying down his blanket—a very good one by the way—said to one, of our pickets, "if you will bring and leave at this place a pone of bread, you may have the blanket," and returned to his post. Our man carried the bread and took the blanket. Another, in a similar manner, gave a canteen full of whiskey for a pone of bread.

Good health and good spirits prevail within our lines. M. D.

Camp at Chattanooga Station,
Oct. 14, 1863.

**Dear Courier:** No satisfactory account has been yet given of the firing on the other side of the river last Monday. "The "situation" of both armies remains essentially the same as it was two days since; the almost constant rain, even if there was no other reason, having prevented general movements. Our Brigade still remains at this place and we are in a complete slosh of mud. We now expect to move out on the front-line to morrow. We will then probably have a chance to see something and will perhaps before many days "see sights." But there is no disposition on the part of the troops generally to put off the day of active operations. Appearances indicated that as soon as the necessary arrangement for rations, transportation, &c., can be made our Generals are resolved "to do something." A considerable portion of all the Georgians in the Confederate army are now on this border, and, when the time comes, if they do not strike rapid and heavy blows for all that is dear to noble men, then liberty and independence are no longer worth the price of manly effort. M. D.

Camp 8th GA. Regiment,
Near Chattanooga,
October 24, 1863.

**Dear Courier:** We are now encamped on the South side and just at the foot of Lookout Point. Left Chickamauga Station the 20th and arrived here on the 21st. The creeks—Chickamauga and Chattanooga—had then run down so as to be passable over the bridges. But yesterday it rained all day and the creeks are now so high as to prevent wagons crossing the bottoms of either side. The rations and forage due here yesterday have not yet arrived; the men are now either entirely without, or on short rations, while the horses and mules are becoming very weak from the short allowances they have had for several days past. Why the roads are not made passable, puzzles subordinates and privates, who are not supposed to be able to comprehend the plans of great big Generals, so high in command as to be seldom seen.

Several thousand troops in this vicinity are said to have subsisted on beef alone, for three days last week, just because the high water prevented the transportation of meal and flour from Chickamauga Station. And now, although a little work has been done on the road, the same suffering is likely to be endured again, by the same troops and others. It is not at all probable that Gen. Bragg is directly to blame for this and similar outages practiced on this army, but all must admit that the Quartermaster's department is grossly direlect in the performance of their important duties. Unless the animals are fed better, in two weeks there will not be a dozen horses or mules in our division fit for service and nearly or quite a third of the present number will be dead. Whose fault is it that a full supply of corn is not at Chickamauga Station is not apparent to the writer, but that same one is in fault no one can doubt, and it is not the flood that swept away the railroad bridges, for these ought to have been replaced at least a week ago. A hungry army is sure to be down on the Quarter Masters. It is said that *they* "live well, drink much and do little." There is certainly a great lack of energy in their department.

Since arriving at our present camp, many of the Regiment have visited Lookout Point, where an excellent view of both armies can be obtained.[17] The scene is grand and intensely exciting. But natural beauties here exhibited—the towering mountain and numerous hills, the meandering valleys and sloping plains, the winding river and gently flowing streams, and the forest, now so beautiful in its gorgeous autumnal colors—all these fail to hold the attention of the beholder, and his is at once absorbed in contemplation of the two great armies. A hundred and fifty thousand men here await but a word from the commander of either army, before they raise with deadly aim as many muskets, and send swift messengers of death into the midst of their opponents.

Nearly all the enemy's forces are encamped in a very compact body in and around Chattanooga. The river makes a curve to the North, and the town is in this bend, and as the Federal line curves from the river above round to the river below the town, their encampment is nearly circular. Their picket lines strikes the river some two miles below the town, near a steam tannery. They have two batteries on Moccasin Point, which is nearly opposite Lookout Point, on the other side of the river, and a few troops opposite the town where the Pontoon Bridge crosses.

Our forces are encamped in full view of the enemy, along the Northern slope of Missionary Ridge, and occupy a line some six or eight miles long, striking the river at Lookout Point and then again a little above the town. Our army is so much more scattered than that of the enemy, it is difficult to tell which army even appears to be the larger.

The enemy pickets in a continuous line of rifle pits, while our pickets are in holes dug in the ground, each large enough for four men. The picket lines are at distances from each other varying from 100 to 800 yards according to the nature of this ground. It is against orders, yet it is said that the pickets not unfrequently talk to each other.

It has generally been entirely quiet on the front line during the past few days, yet there has been some firing from the enemy's batteries on Moccasin

Point. It seems almost incredible, yet is a well attested fact, that they have thrown a few shells to the very summit of Lookout. Last Thursday morning we were offered to fall in immediately, and move down to the front line, is being reported that the enemy were advancing in heavy force. This proved to be a mistake and we soon returned to quarters. The Yankees threw five or six shells at the Brigade as it came in range of one of the batteries, but did no damage.

To-day it is quite cool with a North wind. Good health generally prevails, and, if we can get any wholesome food to eat, there is a prospect of a very good time here, for several days at least must elapse before general fighting will commence, and it is not probable that it will be here when it does occur. M. D.

Camp 8th GA. Regiment,
Near Chattanooga,
October 28, 1863.

DEAR COURIER: At a little before day break yesterday morning a force of the enemy, said by prisoners taken from that command, to be two thousand strong, crossed the Tennessee river at Kelly's old Ford at the head of Williams' Island, about five or six miles below Chattanooga, and attacked eight companies of the 15th Alabama Regiment on Picket at that place. The morning was very foggy and the Yankees got within less than fifty yards of our men before they were discovered; our men made a gallant little fight, but were soon forced to give back before the overwhelming force of the enemy. The Feds pursued them about a mile and took possession of hill a little to the right of the railroad and below Lookout Point. Our loss is reported to be five killed and seventeen wounded, among the latter Col. Oats severely in the thigh.[18] The 4th Alabama regiment was on Picket some four miles below at the time of the attack and two companies of the 15th were on Raccoon mountain. These troops soon came to the relief of their comrades and a line of battle was formed just above the bridge and the creek on the dirt road, and a little below Lookout Point.

The Yanks crossed the river in Pontoon Boats but at noon they were very busy in putting down a Pontoon Bridge and had it about two thirds completed. The other regiments of Laws' Brigade, also Jenkins' and Anderson's started in the morning for the scene of action, Laws' command went on immediately, but the other two Brigades lay on the road just below and in front of Lookout Point until about three o'clock P.M. They were heavily shelled by the Yanks from Moccasin Point but no casualties were reported. Great activity prevails all along the left of our line this morning, yet it does not seem probable that a general engagement will be brought on quite yet by either party. It may be thought that Rosecrans is getting so short of rations that he is obliged to fight or retreat, and the most probable of all is that he is now making a little demonstration for the purpose of covering his evacuation of Chattanooga.[19]

Tolerably heavy connonading is going on this morning in the vicinity of Lookout Point.

# Epilogue

After arriving in Rome, Melvin Dwinell did not remain home for long. He soon departed for Milledgeville, the state capital, and took his seat as one of the two new representatives from Floyd County. Almost immediately, he resumed his correspondence with the *Courier*, reporting on the activities of the Georgia legislature and still signing his letters "M. D." In his absence, B. G. Salvage continued to edit the *Courier*.[1]

The legislature adjourned for the year in early December, and Dwinell returned to Rome. He helped put out the newspaper and wrote many of the news items and editorials. He also continued to deal with the struggling finances of the *Courier*. As 1864 began, Floyd County's economy was in shambles, just like the rest of the Confederacy. The president of the Rome Female College abruptly closed and sold the school. The town's last remaining bank shut its doors. H. A. Gartrell, owner of the *Rome Southerner*, the *Courier's* longtime competitor, announced that he was enlisting in the army and that the newspaper was for sale. Inflation was rampant, and the market prices were "so fickle it [was almost] impossible to locate them," according to one story. Many of the county's leading families were selling their property and moving south. There also were several reports of slaves from the county escaping. "These are dark and gloomy days," the *Courier* declared in an editorial. "As a nation we are undergoing the severest ordeal to which any people in modern times have been subjected."[2]

Floyd County's units continued to battle through losses. In February, the *Courier* published the news that Capt. Sydney Hall, one of the original members of the Light Guards, died from wounds he received at the Battle of Knoxville. The loss was no doubt particularly hard on Dwinell. The two men had served together as lieutenants before Hall was promoted in 1862. Dwinell also had mentioned Hall regularly in his correspondence. In his first letter to the *Courier*, he noted that the two men were the first to stand guard at Camp Brown. In all, thirty-three members of the Eighth Georgia were killed, wounded, or captured in what was another shattering defeat for the Confederacy. For the first time in its history, desertion became a problem for the regiment. Only a handful of men had left the ranks in the first two and a half years of the war. However, during the winter of 1863–64 it was a regular occurrence for demoralized men to walk away from the regiment.[3]

In early March, the legislature reconvened and Dwinell traveled to Milledgeville, where he resumed his correspondence from the capital. That same month, news of Union army activities in north Georgia began reaching Rome on a regular basis. Then on May 7, Gen. William T. Sherman began his campaign against Georgia. Sherman's first goal was the strategically important city of Atlanta, and Union troops advanced relatively quickly against the outnumbered Confederate troops commanded by Gen. Joseph E. Johnston. On May 13, Rome residents heard the sounds of artillery fire "from noon until night." Two days later, a force of about twenty-three hundred Union troops were repulsed a few miles from the town. However, that news apparently was enough for Dwinell to decide it was no longer safe for a former Confederate officer to remain in Rome. He published the last issue of the *Courier* on May 16 and then joined the exodus of citizens from town.[4]

The next day, the Federal army's Second Division, Fourteenth Corps, under the command of Gen. Jefferson C. Davis, was sighted about two and a half miles away. Gen. Samuel G. French, who directed the Confederate troops

Gen. William T. Sherman.
Library of Congress.

at Rome, sent several brigades across the Oostanaula River. They managed to push back some of the Federals before the fear of being flanked forced them to withdraw. Later that evening, French was ordered to abandon Rome. He left behind a small detail to prevent the Union army from pursuing. Then on the morning of May 18, the remaining Confederate troops left Rome and burned the bridge over the Oostanaula. Federal troops crossed the river at about midday. As was customary, one of the first things the soldiers did was raise an American flag over the courthouse. A pontoon bridge soon was laid across the river, and within two days the remaining troops had moved into the city.[5]

It is not clear where Dwinell immediately went after he fled Rome. However, a week later, the editor of the *Atlanta Southern Confederacy* announced that Dwinell had visited the newspaper's office and described how he was forced to leave quickly with only a few supplies. Dwinell told the editor about his intentions to resume publishing the *Courier* as soon as he was able to return home. He eventually moved to Augusta, Georgia, where he served as adjutant for Brig. Gen. A. R. Wright, who was in command of state troops in the city.[6]

Federal troops continued to occupy Rome during the summer-long campaign against Atlanta. The town was part of the Union army's District of Etowah under the command of Maj. Gen. James B. Steedman. He set up his headquarters in Chattanooga and created garrisons in several towns including Rome, where four infantry regiments and one cavalry regiment were based. They guarded the railroad lines, bridges, and other strategic points. While occupying Rome, the Union army turned many of the largest homes and churches into hospitals. Train cars full of wounded soldiers arrived regularly from the front. The army also seized the abandoned office of the *Courier*, and a soldier with the Ninth Iowa Infantry put out an army publication called the *Union Flag* using the printing press and supplies left behind.[7]

After the capture of Atlanta, General Sherman and his staff briefly visited Rome on October 28, staying at the home of Charles H. Smith. A few days later, the Union evacuation of the town began. On the orders of Sherman, the last Federal troops leaving Rome on November 10 burned public property, army supplies, and any industries that might be of use to the Confederate army. Although no private residences were to be destroyed, a number were set afire by departing troops. One soldier said of the conflagration, "[T]he country is light with the burning of Rome. . . . It is against orders—but the soldiers want to see it burn." Marauding Confederate renegade deserters soon entered and plundered much of what had been left behind. "We are afraid to trust anyone now," one resident wrote. "It is so different from what we expected, that we almost wish for the Yankees again. . . . the Yankees never came into our houses

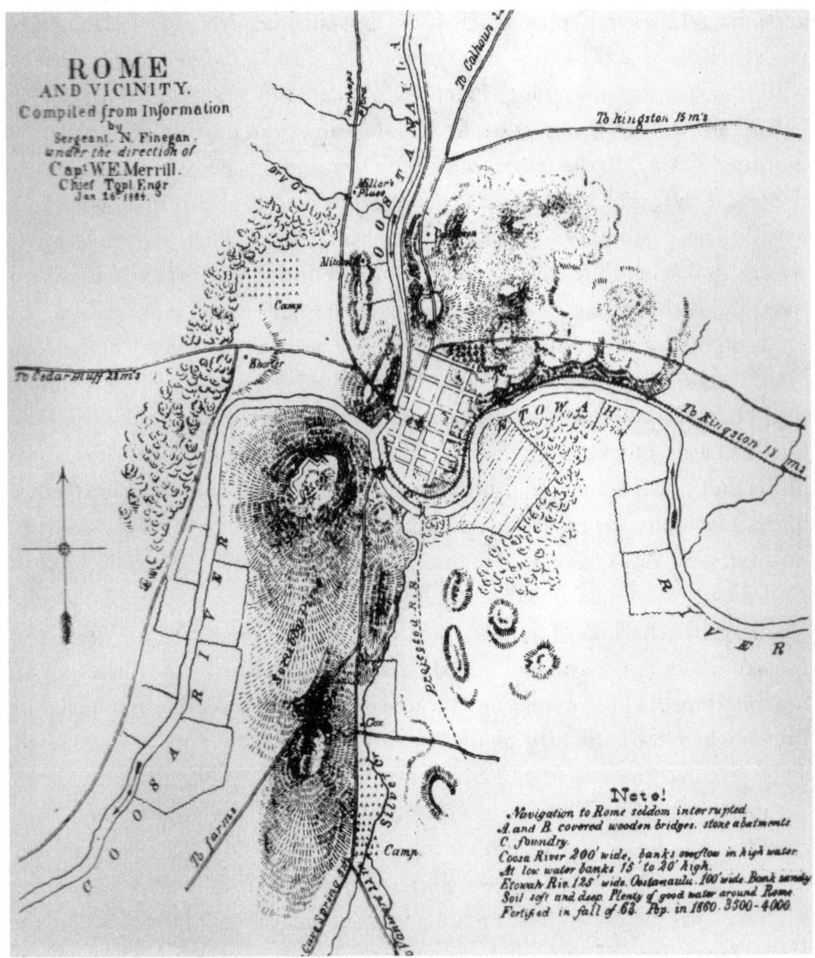


Map of Rome. Floyd County Public Library.

to trouble us." The city's remaining men organized a volunteer police patrol, but it could do little to stop the raids.[8]

With the Federal army gone, some residents who had fled began returning to Rome. However, Dwinell did not return until May 25, 1865, some six weeks after the surrender at Appomattox Courthouse and a year after he had fled. When he arrived, the editor found the *Courier's* office wrecked and some of the presses gone. Dwinell later described how he found the office "in great confusion," remarking, "Stands, tables, cases, presses, stores and stove pipe, imposing stone, cabinets, racks and everything else all turned 'topsy-turvey.'" The office, he wrote, had been "beaten to pieces with sledge-hammers and crow-bars until [it] looked like the Demons from the Infernal Region had been holding high carnival here." Dwinell said that the value of the *Courier's* office, once estimated at $10,000, was only worth $300 after being wrecked. That, and $22.50 in gold he had in his pocket, was the entirety of his assets when the war ended.[9]

Dwinell spent the next three months rebuilding the *Courier*. Without a press, he printed small circulars and handbills using a planer and mallet. With borrowed money Dwinell eventually procured a small press, and on August 31, he published the first issue of what was dubbed the "new" *Courier*. In that issue Dwinell addressed readers: "On the 16 of May, 1864, the last number of this paper was published. Federal forces occupied Rome the next day . . . and it was not deemed safe for such a 'Reb' as we *have been* to engage in any permanent business in Rome." The first issue of the *Courier* upon resuming publication was labeled "No. One, New Series." It also carried the Georgia state motto —"Wisdom, Justice, Moderation"—on its front page. Dwinell told readers, "It is our determination to publish a first rate family *News* Paper, giving the subscriber as much reliable Commercial, Political and Miscellaneous subjects as the columns will contain." Yet he recognized that it would take time to get the *Courier* back financially to where it had been before the war, and he appealed to readers to support the newspaper in any way they could. One announcement said: "Wanted. One thousand subscribers to this paper. Our Rates are low. . . . We will take in payment, Currency or Produce, any thing we can eat or drink or wear, at market price."[10]

One of Dwinell's first acts after returning home was to take the oath of allegiance to the United States. Upon doing this, he told readers that he "felt like the keeper of a cheap boarding house" who had to eat crow after losing a wager. He said he "could eat crow, but he 'didn't hanker after it.'" Still, the editor encouraged all citizens to take the oath as well. "It is as little as could possibly be asked of us after four years [of] most determined and earnest effort to disrupt the Federal Nation." He also pledged that the *Courier* would "do all in [its] power" to support the president and governor in restoring Georgia to "its once proud position in the great family of States."[11]

Privately and to his family in Vermont, Dwinell remained the defiant Southerner. In a letter to his brother Albert, he wrote, "Well we Rebs, 'so-called' have been 'crushed out,' 'subdued,' 'defeated,' or by whatever name you please to call it except disgraced. In the face of the civilized world the honor of the South stands untarnished and her sons will live in the world's memory as a chivalrous, gallant and brave people." Dwinell also expressed anger at the great destruction leveled against the South during the war. He told his brother,

"I wish you could go through the south, *wherever your army went,* see the destruction, hear of all the suffering, and learn what were the *real* and *effective* means used to 'crush the rebellion.' It is enough the make the blood of Angels boil." He recounted the fact that the *Courier*'s office had been destroyed by Union troops, saying that it was done "under circumstances that would disgrace any other than savages."[12]

Dwinell apparently had trouble finding suitable help in publishing the *Courier.* In a letter to his sister Irene written in 1866, he apologized for not writing sooner but said he was staying so busy that he had time to do little more than work. "I have no assistance in the editorial or financial department of my office and hence my inability to write as many letters to my friends as I would like to," he wrote. "It may be that I now owe a letter to each one of my brothers. I wish you would ask them to forgive the debt and write again." Dwinell also recalled with fondness his childhood in Vermont, which he told his sister was "still dear to [him]." He said he hoped the "bitter curses that some in his hometown had "wrongfully heaped upon [him]" for fighting had been forgotten. "I often think of you all up there in Vt. and try to Imagine how you all look and what the scenery now is, with as I suppose, 2 or 3 feet of snow on the ground," he wrote. "I have not seen the ground White yet this winter. . . . I would like a good sleigh ride and a skating frolick or two but will hardly be able to get them this winter."[13]

Business gradually improved, and Dwinell continued publishing the *Courier* for the next twenty years. Salvage remained on the staff for many years to help get out the newspaper. Eventually, the *Courier* became a daily and helped make Dwinell a prosperous man. He took some of the newspaper's profits and invested in a local iron works and in real estate. He traveled regularly, including a trip to the western United States and another to Europe and the Middle East. He published an account of his travels overseas, *Common Sense Views of Foreign Lands.* He also visited his family in Vermont on numerous occasions, likely seeking to rebuild some of the relationships that had been damaged during the war. In later letters, Dwinell described to one brother his growing business affairs. And in a letter to his sister, the longtime bachelor described his sour grapes in seeing his "little duck of a sweetheart" now married to another man. Dwinell continued to live in a downtown hotel from which he could walk to the *Courier's* office. Although the hotel changed ownership several times, he always kept his same room, No. 10.[14]

Thirty-one years after he had become owner of the *Courier,* Dwinell sold the newspaper to W. H. Hidell on January 15, 1885. Hiddell soon turned around and sold the *Courier* to a group of residents who eventually changed its name to the *Tribune of Rome*. Dwinell lived out his remaining years quietly. Toward the end of 1887 he became gravely ill, and on December 28, he died. An obituary in his old newspaper mourned the editor who had "been thoroughly identified with Rome and all her enterprises." A funeral was held for Dwinell at the Methodist Church in Rome, and afterward two family members brought his remains back to Vermont. The editor and prolific war correspondent was buried near other family members in East Calais, less than a mile from where he was born.[15]

# *Notes*

## *Prologue*

1. Ford Risley, "'Dear Courier': The Civil War Correspondence of Editor Melvin Dwinell," *Journalism History* 31, no. 3 (2005): 162–70.
2. J. Cutler Andrews, *The South Reports the Civil War* (Princeton, NJ: Princeton University Press, 1970); Patricia G. McNeely, Debra Reddin van Tuyll, and Henry H. Schulte, *Knights of the Quill: Confederate Correspondents and their Civil War Reporting* (West Lafayette, IN: Purdue University Press, 2010).
3. An overview of Dwinell's life can be found in Harold A. Dwinell, "Vermonter in Gray: The Story of Melvin Dwinell," *Vermont History* 30, no. 3 (1962): 220–23. Brief sketches of Dwinell's journalistic work in the context of Rome history can be found in Roger D. Aycock, *All Roads to Rome* (Rome, GA: Rome Area Historical Foundation, 1982) and Margaret Nola Burkley, "Floyd County, Georgia, During the Civil War Era" (PhD diss., Florida State University, 1998). In some accounts, Dwinell's first name is incorrectly spelled as *Melville* and his last name as *Dwinnell.*
4. George Magruder Battey, *A History of Rome and Floyd County, State of Georgia, United States of America: Including Numerous Incidents of More Than Local Interest, 1540–1922* (Atlanta: Webb and Vary, 1922), 1:1–17; Wade B. Gassman, "A History of Rome and Floyd County, Georgia, in the Civil War" (master's thesis, Emory University, 1966), 1–9; Aycock, *All Roads to Rome*, 1–12; Burkley, "Floyd County, Georgia," 9–13, 48–52.
5. Burkley, "Floyd County, Georgia," 29–33, 37–38.
6. Donald E. Reynolds, *Editors Make War: Southern Newspapers in the Secession Crisis* (Nashville: Vanderbilt University Press, 1966); Rabun Lee Brantley, *Georgia Journalism of the Civil War Period* (Nashville: George Peabody College, 1929), 32; Burkley, "Floyd County, Georgia," 19.
7. For editorials supporting slavery, see *Weekly Courier*, February 23, April 7, August 21, September 1, 1860; for editorials supporting Bell, see *Weekly Courier*, July 14, 21, 1860. See also Burkley, "Floyd County, Georgia," 57–71. The division over the future of Georgia even erupted in the office of the *Courier.* Associate Editor George T. Stovall advocated immediate secession, and his disagreement with Dwinell led Stovall to leave the newspaper. He promptly became editor of the *Rome Southerner & Advertiser* and dropped *Advertiser*

from the newspaper's name. There apparently were no hard feelings between the two men, as Dwinell warmly welcomed Stovall back into the newspaper business. *Rome Weekly Courier*, December 25, 1860, March 1, 1861.

8. *Tri-Weekly Courier*, February 9, 21, March 2, 9, 1861.
9. *Tri-Weekly Courier*, April 16, 23, 1861.
10. George S. Barnsley Diary, George Scarborough Barnsley Papers, Southern Historical Collection, University of North Carolina Library, p. 6. (Hereafter, this source is cited as Barnsley Diary.)
11. *Tri-Weekly Courier*, April 20, 23, 30, 1861. A story in the *Courier* said the Light Guards were comprised "almost entirely of young men—only five married, and, with two exceptions, those quite recently. The story continued, "Most of the members have lived in the city or in the immediate vicinity; they are connected with the best families, and are, of course, greatly beloved." Some of the men in the company took their slaves to serve as cooks and valets. The slaves soon became too much trouble to the army, and they were sent home. The Wartime Diary of Reuben S. Norton, hereafter cited as Norton Diary), Special Collections, Rome-Floyd County Library, Rome, GA; Barnsley Diary, p. 8.
12. *Tri-Weekly Courier*, May 13, 21, 1861. Dr. H. V. V. Miller (named Homer Virgil Milton Miller by his father, who was a student of classical literature) became a regimental surgeon. Aycock, *All Roads to Rome*, 480–81.
13. Warren Wilkinson and Steven E. Woodworth, *A Scythe of Fire: A Civil War Story of the Eighth Georgia Infantry Regiment* (New York: William Morrow, 2002), 10–12; *Tri-Weekly Courier*, May 25, 28, 1861. Floyd County averaged sending more than one company a month into service during the first year of the war, and at least eighteen companies from the county saw some service. Gassman, "History of Rome and Floyd County," 35–36. The other companies that made up the 8th Georgia were the Oglethorpe Light Infantry, Macon Guards, Echols Guards, Atlanta Grays, Pulaski Volunteers, Stephens Guards, and Oglethorpe Rifles.
14. *Tri-Weekly Courier*, June 8, 1861.
15. *Tri-Weekly Courier*, July 4, 1861.
16. A note in the July 16, 1861, issue read: "We received a letter from Mr. Dwinell on Saturday evening last, dated July 3rd, having been ten days on the way. As the items he sends have all been given from other sources, we think it unnecessary to publish the letter. There were no items in reference to the members of the companies."
17. Dwinell initially signed his letters "D" or "M" before settling on "M. D."
18. *Tri-Weekly Courier*, February 14, 1863; Burkley, "Floyd County, Georgia," 117. The *Courier* also published letters from other soldier correspondents with the Confederate army who were from Floyd County. They included men who wrote under the bylines "Floyd," "P," "H," and "Ino." However, none of the other correspondents wrote as frequently or for as long as Dwinell.
19. Albert Burton Moore, *Conscription and Conflict in the Confederacy* (New York: MacMillan, 1924); Debra Reddin van Tuyll, "The Rebels Yell: Conscription

and Freedom of Expression in the Civil War South," *American Journalism* 17, no. 2 (2000): 15–29.

## *Chapter 1*

1. Located on the Western & Atlantic Railroad, the camp had been a popular site for religious gatherings. Officers from more than twenty military companies from across the state trained at the camp. Wilkinson and Woodworth, *Scythe of Fire*, 7.
2. Sidney H. Hall was first lieutenant of the Light Guards. (Unless otherwise noted, information about members of the Floyd County units is taken from Lillian Henderson, ed., *Roster of the Confederate Soldiers of Georgia, 1861–1865*, vol. 1 [Hapeville, GA: Longino & Porter, 1959].)
3. Brig. Gen. William Phillips and Maj. F. W. Capers.
4. Marcellus A. Stovall went on to become a Confederate general. Mark M. Boatner III, *The Civil War Dictionary* (New York: Vintage Books, 1991), 811.
5. Brown's remarks portended the struggle that he and the Confederate government would engage in throughout the war over Brown's insistence that Georgia have a strong defensive force to serve at the pleasure of the governor. See, generally, William R. Scaife and William Harris Bragg, *Joe Brown's Pets: The Georgia Militia, 1861–1865* (Macon, GA: Mercer University Press, 2004).
6. Capt. George Hillyer.
7. Francis S. Bartow was one of the most prominent Georgians to serve in the Confederate army when the war began. Born into an affluent Savannah family, he graduated from the University of Georgia and attended Yale Law School. Subsequently, he served in his native state's house of representatives and senate. Bartow campaigned actively for secession and was on the committee that drew up Georgia's ordinance of secession. He was elected to the Confederacy's Provisional Congress but resigned to lead the Oglethorpe Light Infantry. In the summer of 1861, Bartow was elected colonel of the 8th Georgia Regiment. Kenneth Coleman and Charles Stephen Gurr, eds., *Dictionary of Georgia Biography* (Athens: University of Georgia Press, 1983), 64–65.
8. Edward J. Magruder had graduated from the Virginia Military Institute and moved to Rome before the war. On May 14, he married Florence Fouche, the daughter of one of the county's largest plantation owners, at Rome's First Baptist Church. During the ceremony the bride and groom walked through an archway formed by the sabers of the Light Guards. Roger Aycock, *All Roads to Rome* (Roswell, GA: W. H. Wolfe, 1981), 72.
9. This became a controversy after the company arrived in Richmond and the troops learned that the limited supply of rifles had been given out. Fifteen of the men could not get rifles and refused to carry older muskets. Apparently embarrassed by their "pluck" being questioned, several of the men later rejoined the regiment. Wilkinson and Woodworth, *Scythe of Fire*, 33.
10. This is the name Dwinell frequently used in referring to Union troops.

11. Hutchings was known as "Fred." This probably was a typographical error.
12. Ayre was a farmer and slave owner in the county. Pvt. George Norton was a clerk in his father's store.
13. Brig. Gen. Pierre G. T. Beauregard led the Confederate forces that attacked Fort Sumter, and he accepted the surrender of the Federal troops guarding the fort. During the summer, Beauregard was given command of the troops at Manassas Junction and led the line at the Battle of First Manassas. Boatner, *Civil War Dictionary*, 54–55.
14. In all likelihood this was a typographical error, and the correct date should be July 11.
15. The Stephens Light Guards were named in honor of Confederate vice president Alexander H. Stephens of Georgia.
16. Lucius Gartrell was a US congressman from Georgia. He resigned from Congress when the war began and organized the 7th Georgia Infantry Regiment. His regiment fought at First Manassas, and his sixteen-year-old son was killed there. Gartrell was elected to the Confederate House of Representatives later in 1861 and resigned from the army. He was reappointed brigadier general in 1864 and organized four regiments of Georgia reserves, which he commanded until the end of the war. Coleman and Gurr, *Dictionary of Georgia Biography*, 338.
17. Gen. Joseph E. Johnston had commanded troops in the Shenandoah Valley and took command at Manassas on July 21, 1861, by virtue of seniority.
18. Cpl. William S. Skidmore and Sgt. James T. Moore.
19. Dwinell was referring to Point of Rocks.
20. 2nd Lt. George R. Lumpkin returned to the regiment but resigned from the army in August. Pvt. George K. Sanford also returned.
21. Newport News, VA.
22. Dr. J. M. Gregory was the company's physician and surgeon.
23. Washington, DC, was commonly referred to as "Washington City" during this time. The rumor that the Federal army evacuated and burned the city was false.
24. Lt. Col. William M. Gardner was a former US Army major, a Mexican War veteran, and an 1846 graduate of the US Military Academy. Thomas L. Cooper, an attorney in Atlanta, was captain of the Atlanta Grays and the older brother of Capt. John F. Cooper of the Floyd Infantry.
25. Gen. Robert Patterson.
26. Although he misspelled the last name, Dwinell was referring to Maj. Gen. George B. McClellan, who commanded the Union's Department of the Ohio. McClellan would be given command of the Army of the Potomac later in the year. Boatner, *Civil War Dictionary*, 524.
27. Norton was from a prominent family in Rome. His father was one of the city's leading merchants and an alderman. Aycock, *All Roads to Rome*, 109–10.
28. Salmon P. Chase was the US secretary of the treasury.
29. Pvt. John L. Pinson; Pvt. Hugh McCullough; Pvt. J. L. Brodie; Pvt. William L. Payne; Pvt. Zachariah B. Hargrove.

30. The Shenandoah Army was one of several names the Confederate force in Virginia went by before it became known as the Army of Northern Virginia.
31. Lt. Dunlap S. Scott of the Miller Rifles was an attorney and farmer.

## *Chapter 2*

1. Dwinell no doubt was referring to Capt. J. E. B. Stuart. He frequently misspelled Stuart's name in his letters to the *Courier.*
2. Charles H. Smith, an attorney in Rome, was a member of Bartow's staff and later became a judge advocate. Early in the war, he began writing satirical essays for the *Courier* and other Southern newspapers under the pen name "Bill Arp." His humorous tales were popular with the troops, and for many years after the war he continued writing "Bill Arp" letters that appeared regularly in southern newspapers. Smith, who was mayor of Rome and a state senator after the war, wrote of his military stint that he had "joined the army and had succeeded in killing about as many of them as they had of me." Aycock, *All Roads to Rome*, 117–23; Jon L. Wakelyn, *Biographical Dictionary of the Confederacy* (Westport, CT: Greenwood Press, 1977): 388.
3. "To Our Boys" was a summary of news from Floyd County written for the soldiers. It appeared in the *Courier* regularly during the summer of 1861 but then stopped with no notice. "Jackson" was not identified.
4. Pvt. Wesley Rush suffered from tuberculosis.
5. Dwinell was referring to the fighting at Blackburn's Ford, where both sides suffered substantial casualties. It was the last engagement before the Battle of First Manassas. Boatner, *Civil War Dictionary*, 507.
6. It is not clear why the artillery commander's name was left out.
7. Brig. Gen. Barnard E. Bee commanded a Confederate brigade at First Manassas. He was wounded in the fighting and died the next day. Boatner, *Civil War Dictionary*, 56.
8. Bartow led his own regiment and several others at the battle. He was wounded in the leg and his horse was shot from under him, but he rallied his men for an assault on Henry House Hill. There, he was shot in the chest and killed instantly. Coleman and Gurr, *Dictionary of Georgia Biography*, 136–38.
9. Lt. Col. William M. Gardner, who was second in command of the 8th Georgia, was wounded early in the fighting. He crawled to a tree stump and continued shouting encouragement to the men. Gardner later was taken to the rear, but his leg was so badly injured that the regiment had to leave him behind. He and several others were captured, and they received medical attention from the Union army. When the Federals retreated, Gardner and others were left behind. Wilkinson and Woodworth, *Scythe of Fire*, 71–72, 81–82, 85–86.
10. John Branch was the regimental adjutant. After he was hit, his brother Sanford and others carried him to the rear. He later died. Wilkinson and Woodworth, *Scythe of Fire*, 74.

11. Pvt. Charles B. Norton; Pvt. George T. Stovall; Pvt. James B. Stark; Pvt. J T. Duane; Pvt. D. C. Hargrove.
12. Pvt. J. A. Anderson Jr. later was assigned to the Quartermaster Department due to his disability. Pvt. M. D. McOsker was discharged due to his wounds, but he subsequently rejoined another regiment and was wounded during the fighting at Vicksburg. Pvt. Jett T. Howard was discharged due to his disability and then joined an artillery battalion; he surrendered with Confederate troops at Greensboro, NC, in April 1865.
13. Pvt. A. J. Bearden rejoined the Light Guards but then was discharged due to his disability. Pvt. Richard W. Boggs rejoined the company and was appointed corporal; he surrendered at Appomattox. Pvt. James Dunwoody Jones rejoined the army and became a conscription officer in Georgia. Pvt. G. L. Aycock rejoined the Light Guards and later was appointed sergeant. Pvt. J. T. Shackelford returned to the army but deserted in late 1864; he took the oath of allegiance in Washington, DC, and was sent to Newark, NJ.
14. Pvt. William A. Barron was taken to Fortress Monroe but later released; he surrendered at Appomattox. Privates T. H. McGrath and M. A. Ross returned to the company. Pvt. John R. Payne was later exchanged, and he rejoined the army.
15. Pvt. Thomas Mobley; Col. Frank Lathrop.
16. Sgt. Oswell B. Eve, Pvt. William A. King, and Pvt. Lewis G. Yarborough died from their wounds.
17. Pvt. William A. Ware returned to his company and later was elected 2d lieutenant. He was captured during the fighting at Malvern Hill in 1864 and released after the war ended.
18. Pvt. A. W. Harshaw; Pvt. J. F. Madry; Pvt. Alfred F. Wamack; Pvt. J. W. Chastain.
19. Capt. John F. Cooper and Sgt. George G. Martin died from their wounds. Cpl. O. M. Porter and Pvt. J. T. Holbrook were discharged due to their disabilities.
20. The Confederate army lost about 1,900 men in the battle. Boatner, *Civil War Dictionary*, 101. An account of the regiment's fighting at First Manassas is in Wilkinson and Woodworth, *Scythe of Fire*, 62–86. For George S. Barnsley's description of the fighting, see Barnsley Diary, p. 10–22.
21. Norton's father, Reuben, a cotton merchant and one of Rome's best-known citizens, had just returned from visiting his son in Virginia when he learned that the young man had been killed. He immediately traveled back to the state to bring the body to Rome. Norton Diary, July 24, 1861; Wilkinson and Woodworth, *Scythe of Fire*, 96.
22. The amount of equipment captured by the Confederates, especially the number of cannons, was a wildly exaggerated rumor.
23. Rev. John Jones was the pastor of the First Presbyterian Church in Rome, and he had preached the farewell sermon for the Light Guards. He traveled to Virginia to learn the condition of his son, Dunwoody Jones. The younger Jones

had been slightly wounded. Robert Manson Myers, ed., *The Children of Pride: A True Story of Georgia and the Civil War* (New Haven, CT: Yale University Press, 1972), 690, 718, 726.

24. George S. Barnsley contracted pneumonia after First Manassas and was sent home. The physician later was appointed a hospital steward and eventually became an assistant surgeon. Wilkinson and Woodworth, *Scythe of Fire*, 102.
25. Pvt. John H. Dunn.
26. Sgt. Isaac "Ike" Donkle was a blacksmith before the war.
27. Noble Brothers & Co. was an iron foundry started by James Noble in 1855. Before the war, it manufactured steam engines and boilers, as well as pipes, grates, iron castings, and other products. After the fighting began, Noble Brothers secured a contract with the Confederate government to supply field cannons and battery equipment. Although the plant filled many orders, it suffered from shortages of materials and labor. The plant was destroyed when Federal troops captured Rome in 1864. Larry J. Daniel and Riley W. Gunter, *Confederate Cannon Foundries* (Union City, TN: Pioneer Press, 1977), 40–46.
28. Pvt. W. S. Booton recovered from his illness. Privates Adolphus R. Johnson and T. W. Swank also recovered from their illnesses; both were captured during the fighting at the Wilderness and later exchanged. Pvt. D. H. Miller recovered; he surrendered at Appomattox. Pvt. George W. Milam recovered, and he later was captured.
29. Pvt. W. J. Barrett was discharged due to a disability later in the year. Henry Smith, one of the regimental musicians, recovered.
30. Pvt. John Hill recovered; he was killed at Farmville, VA, in 1865. Pvt. Harvey A. Brice recovered and surrendered at Appomattox. Pvt. Thomas W. Asbury recovered. Pvt. Andrew G. Bobo recovered, and he later was wounded at Gettysburg. Pvt. John L. Pyles recovered, and he was reported absent without leave in 1862.
31. Pvt. Marcus L. Funderburk died from his wounds. Pvt. Newton S. Fain was discharged due to his disability.
32. Pvt. J. L. Callahan recovered; he was reported absent without leave in 1862. Privates L. J. Farmer and Joel Bagwell were discharged due to disabilities. Pvt. William H. Henderson recovered and subsequently was elected 2d lieutenant.
33. Privates J. M. Burns and Thomas Wright were discharged in 1862 due to disabilities.
34. The white marble obelisk was the first monument erected at the battlefield. The battlefield still contains what is believed to be the remains of the monument, but a tree has grown up around the ruins. A new marker later was erected a short distance away. The Joan M. Zenzen, *Battling for Manassas: The Fifty-Year Preservation Struggle at Manassas National Battlefield Park* (University Park: Pennsylvania State University Press, 1998), 2.
35. Many in the regiment believed that Maj. Thomas L. Cooper was unqualified for the position. Some of the commissioned officers approached Cooper about handing over the top leadership, but he refused. Then some of the enlisted

soldiers signed a petition calling on Cooper to resign, but he again refused. Thereafter the matter was dropped. Wilkinson and Woodworth, *Scythe of Fire*, 107–8.

36. Pvt. Thomas M. Barna.

## *Chapter 3*

1. Pvt. J. H. Johnson was officially discharged on September 4 because of a disability.
2. Pvt. Willis F. Rice died of disease.
3. Pvt. Charles M. Hooper later was elected 2d lieutenant of the Miller Rifles. He was wounded at Gettysburg and later appointed adjutant. He surrendered at Appomattox.
4. Pvt. John J. Stinson.
5. Pvt. William H. Skinner; Capt. B. F. Price; "McNutt" likely was Pvt. William S. McNall.
6. Privates Charles W. Hooper, John O. Oswalt, William J. Cannon, and Robert F. Wimpey did not return to the army. Pvt. M. M. Wright reenlisted with the Light Guards in 1862 and later was appointed sergeant.
7. It is not clear what Dwinell was referring to with respect to Towers. He was not killed in the fighting, nor did he resign.
8. Pvt. W. J. Barrett and Cpl. William S. Skidmore.
9. Pvt. Virgil A. Stewart.
10. Pvt. George Sanford later was elected 2d lieutenant. He was killed during the fighting at Darbytown Road, VA, in 1864.
11. Pvt. William J. Shockley later joined the Georgia state militia and was elected 2d lieutenant.
12. Sgt. Fred Hutchings later was elected 2d lieutenant. He was still in the company when the Confederate army surrendered at Appomattox. Sgt. James T. Moore later was elected 2d lieutenant, following the resignation of G. R. Lumpkin. Moore eventually became captain of Company A, a position he held until he was wounded at Darbytown Road and furloughed.
13. "Manassa" was a common spelling of the place in the mid-1800s.
14. Gen. Albert Sidney Johnston.
15. Pvt. S. A. Swilling.
16. Beecher was the well-known New York pastor and abolitionist speaker. His sister, Harriet Beecher Stowe, wrote the best-selling book *Uncle Tom's Cabin*.
17. Privates William A. Choice and S. S. Clayton.
18. Pvt. F. M. Ezzle of the Light Guards was discharged due to a disability.
19. William T. Wilson later became colonel of the 7th Georgia; he was killed at the Battle of Second Manassas.

## Chapter 4

1. Lamar had been a captain with Company C (Macon Guards). Towers had been captain of the Miller Rifles.
2. The three companies advertised for recruits in the *Courier*. The notice for the Light Guards read: "Under an order from the War Department, the undersigned are now in Rome for the purpose of Recruits for this company. We want 60 able-bodied men for the war. . . . Recruits get $50 Bounty, and $50 per anum for clothing—rations and pay commencing from the day of enlistment. . . . The Rome Light Guards is a Rifle Company, armed with Mississippi Rifles. . . . Applications must be made to either of the undersigned, or A. E. Ross. One of us will be found at Turnley's Drug Store."

   S. H. Hall,
   Capt. Rome Light Guards
   R. F. Hutchings, Serg.
3. Dwinell was referring to his election as first lieutenant of the Light Guards.
4. James M. Montgomery had enlisted as a private and risen steadily through the ranks. Augustus M. Boyd also had enlisted as a private; he left the army later in the year for unknown reasons.
5. Camp Jones likely was named for Brig. Gen. David R. Jones, the brigade's new commander.
6. Privates J. A. Stevenson Jr.; George McGuire; and Monroe Phelps.
7. George Yarborough was elected captain of the Floyd Infantry following the death of Capt. John Cooper.
8. Montpelier is the plantation estate of the Madison family that included President James Madison.
9. Dwinell was referring to the reports of the first day of fighting at the Battle of Pittsburg Landing, or Shiloh, where Union troops initially were surprised and routed by the attacking Confederates. Boatner, *Civil War Dictionary*, 754–55.

## Chapter 5

1. It is not clear to whom Dwinell was referring.
2. Dwinell was referring to Maj. John C. Mounger.
3. Pvt. Tom McKay later deserted the army.
4. The soldier's actual name was Frank Cone Jr.
5. Dwinell was describing the Battle of Seven Pines, or Fair Oaks, that was fought from May 31 to June 1.
6. An artillery shell wounded Johnston on the second day of the battle. He recovered from the wounds and was appointed commander of the Department of the West later in the year. He took command of the Army of Tennessee in late 1863. Boatner, *Civil War Dictionary*, 441.
7. Privates John Estes and James Perry.

8. Secretary of the Navy Stephen R. Mallory.
9. Pvt. John T. S. Johnson died from his wound; Pvt. G. W. Hutchings recovered.
10. Pvt. Marion Payne recovered and was wounded again at the Battle of Cold Harbor.
11. Pvt. R. D. DeJournett returned to the army; he deserted in 1863 and took the oath of allegiance to the US government. Pvt. William McKay also returned to army; he was discharged in 1864 due to a disability.
12. Pvt. J. M. Martin; Pvt. Simeon B. Asbury; Pvt. William A. Hardin; Pvt. Simon B. Wimpey.
13. Lt. James M. Montgomery died the day after being wounded. Pvt. Francis M. Reynolds died from disease later in the year. Pvt. J. A. Frix recovered from his wound.
14. Pvt. T. C. Estes recovered but was wounded again later in the year and discharged.
15. Pvt. William H. May returned; he was killed at Cold Harbor.
16. Charles Harper was released.
17. Pvt. J. R. Manning recovered and returned to the regiment; he deserted the army in 1864 and took the oath of allegiance.
18. Pvt. G. W. Pinson returned. Pvt. John M. Green also returned; he was killed in fighting later in the year.
19. Privates Hugh McCullough and Monroe Phelps.
20. Pvt. Samuel A. Chambers.
21. Capt. G. Oscar Dawson was with Company I. Wilkinson and Woodworth, *Scythe of Fire*, 145.
22. Dwinell was referring to the Battle of Frayser's Farm, fought on June 30.

## *Chapter 6*

1. Pvt. C. L. Johnson later was appointed 2d sergeant of the Light Guards. He was one of the members of the company still in the regiment when it surrendered at Appomattox.
2. Capt. George H. Carmichael.
3. Robert Wade had enlisted as a private; he was wounded in fighting at Fort Harrison, VA, in 1864.
4. Pvt. John T. S. Johnson.
5. Dwinell was referring to the War of 1812, fought between the United States and Great Britain.
6. Dwinell was referring to Maj. Jesse H. Pickett of the 17th Georgia Infantry.
7. The Richmond Hussars were Company B of Cobb's Legion Cavalry.
8. Pvt. William McKay.
9. Dwinell was referring to what became popularly known as the Battle of Cedar Mountain. Federal troops under the command of Gen. Nathaniel Banks attacked Gen. Stonewall Jackson's large corps. The Union army suffered 2,381

casualties, while the Confederate army lost 1,341 men. E. B. Long with Barbara Long, *The Civil War Day by Day: An Almanac, 1861–1865* (Garden City, NY: Doubleday, 1971), 249–50.

10. Pvt. M. Kaufman was discharged due to his disability.
11. Pvt. William F. Omberg.
12. Pvt. William A. Choice was appointed as a clerk at division headquarters. He surrendered at Appomattox. Pvt. Thomas M. Barna later was appointed a hospital steward.
13. R. T. Fouche had enlisted as a private and was later elected 2d lieutenant. Pvt. Frank Bean recovered from his wound and was captured at Deep Bottom, VA, in 1864. Pvt. Francis W. Quarles's badly wounded arm required amputation above the elbow; he remained in the army until being discharged in February 1863.
14. Dwinell was referring to the Battle of Rappahannock Station.
15. Pvt. J. M. Jack.
16. Pvt. David C. Harper.
17. Capt. Jake Phinizy of Company K was killed after most of the regiment's fighting had ended. He and his friend Lt. John C. Reed were exalting in their triumph when a bullet flew through the trees and hit him in the throat. Phinizy fell backward and died instantly, according to Reed. Capt. J. M. C. Hulsey of Company F lost his leg from an exploding shell; he died the next day. Wilkinson and Woodworth, *Scythe of Fire*, 175–76.
18. Pvt. W. F. Leigh died from his wound.
19. Maj. Gen. Richard S. Ewell.
20. Gen. William E. Starke.
21. Lt. Robert Wade; Pvt. James Davis.
22. Secretary of War George W. Randolph.

## *Chapter 7*

1. Pvt. John A. Hardin.
2. Pvt. W. F. Leigh.
3. Corp. Lewis L. Floyd had enlisted as a private and was later appointed corporal; he deserted the army early in 1865 and took the oath of allegiance.
4. John P. Duke had enlisted as a 2d corporal and was appointed captain in 1863. He was captured at Richmond on April 3, 1865.
5. Pvt. R. P. Watters.
6. Gen. John C. Fremont.
7. Anderson, known as "Tige," was a native of Covington, GA. He studied at Emory University but left to enlist as a cavalryman in the Mexican War. Afterward, he served as a captain in the 1st US Cavalry. Anderson was commissioned as a colonel in the Confederate army and rose through the ranks. Boatner, *Civil War Dictionary*, 13.
8. Francis H. Little.

9. The battery was Lane's Georgia Battery, a unit of the Sumter Artillery Battalion.
10. No military record of either man could be found.
11. Spotsylvania Courthouse was a small crossroads community ten miles southwest of Fredericksburg.
12. Dwinell was referring to the previous commanders of the Army of the Potomac—Winfield Scott, Irvin McDowell, George McClellan, and Henry Halleck—although Scott and Halleck never exercised direct field command of the army.
13. Gen. Ambrose E. Burnside.
14. Lt. A. C. A. Huntington was not discharged.
15. Pvt. J. L. Phillips was not discharged; he was last reported on sick leave in October 1864.
16. Dwinell was referring to A. P. Hill.
17. Sgt. G. L. Aycock died from his wounds in February 1863.
18. The Union army suffered 12,653 casualties at Fredericksburg, and the Confederate army lost 5,309 troops. Long, *Civil War Day by Day*, 296.

## Chapter 8

1. Dwinell was referring to the results of the US midterm elections of 1862. Democrats gained thirty-five seats in the House of Representatives. However, Republicans maintained control of both houses of Congress and earned a net gain of five seats in the Senate.
2. Horace W. Greeley was the influential editor of the *New York Tribune*.
3. Macon, GA.
4. Maj. Gen. Samuel G. French.
5. Dwinell was referring to Law's Brigade.
6. Dwinell was referring to Robertson's Brigade.
7. Maj. John E. Rylander.
8. Pvt. Thomas J. Glenn.

## Chapter 9

1. Lt. Gen. A. P. Hill.
2. Brown had continued warring with the Davis administration over military conscription by the Confederacy and the use of Georgia troops. Joseph H. Parks, *Joseph E. Brown of Georgia* (Baton Rouge: Louisiana State University Press, 1977), 198–219.
3. Gen. Richard S. Ewell.
4. Franklin County is in Pennsylvania.
5. Republican congressman Thaddeus Stevens owned the Caledonia Iron Works. He was an outspoken abolitionist and advocate for vigorously prosecuting the war. To punish Stevens, Confederate troops burned Caledonia. Wilkinson and Woodworth, *Scythe of Fire*, 227.

6. Maj. Gen. Henry Heth commanded the division that unexpectedly engaged Union forces on July 1 and precipitated the Battle of Gettysburg. Heth was wounded, and his division was transferred to the command of Brig. Gen. James Pettigrew. The division took part in Pickett's Charge on July 3. Boatner, *Civil War Dictionary*, 398.
7. Lt. William S. Booton.
8. Pvt. William McKay. Privates John Payne and William Payne recovered from their wounds. John was killed at the Battle of Cold Harbor, and William was wounded in the fighting. Pvt. Reuben Mann recovered and was captured at Knoxville, TN, later in the year. He then took the oath of allegiance and enlisted in the US Army. Pvt. W. L. Morefield recovered and was wounded again at the Battle of Spotsylvania in 1864.
9. Lt. Armistead R. Harper recovered but was wounded in subsequent fighting. His injuries were fatal. Lt. A. C. A. Huntington recovered and deserted to the Union army later in the year; he was captured at Chattanooga.
10. A detailed account of the 8th Georgia's fighting on July 2 can be found in Wilkinson and Woodworth, *Scythe of Fire*, 231–52.
11. Ashley River.
12. Sgt. J. F. Shelton; Pvt. John J. Stinson; Pvt. G. W. Hutchings; Pvt. R. D. DeJournett; Cpl. Richard W. Boggs; Pvt. Adolphus R. Johnson.
13. Pvt. Frank Bean; Pvt. Daniel H. Hufford; Pvt. Thomas H. Richardson; Pvt. W. J. Drennons.
14. Pvt. Andrew J. Wilkins.
15. Maj. Gen. William S. Rosencrans was commander of the Army of the Cumberland.
16. Brig. Gen. Braxton Bragg was commander of the Army of Tennessee.
17. Lookout Point is atop Lookout Mountain, the highest point in the Chattanooga area.
18. Col. William C. Oates.
19. Dwinell was referring to a daring operation by Union forces to throw a pontoon bridge across the Tennessee River. Within a few days, badly needed supplies were getting through to the Federal army, and the siege of Chattanooga was being loosened. Long, *Civil War Day by Day*, 426.

## *Epilogue*

1. *Tri-Weekly Courier*, October 29, November 10, 1863.
2. *Tri-Weekly Courier*, December 7, 15, 20, 1863; January 5, February 2, 1864; Burkley, "Floyd County Georgia," 257–67.
3. *Tri-Weekly Courier*, February 23, 1864; Wilkinson and Woodworth, *Scythe of Fire*, 280–82; James M. McPherson, *Battle Cry of Freedom: The Civil War Era* (New York: Ballantine, 1989), 670–71.
4. *Tri-Weekly Courier*, March 10, 16, 1864; *Weekly Courier*, August 31, 1865; Norton Diary, May 17–18, 1864. The last extant issue of the *Courier* is dated April 30, 1864. No issue of the *Courier* from May 16 is known to exist.

5. United States War Department, *The War of the Rebellion: A Compilation of the Official Records of the Union and Confederate Armies*, series 1, vol. 38, pt. 4 (Washington, DC: US Government Printing Office, 1880), 235–37.
6. *Atlanta Southern Confederacy*, May 24, 1864; Risley, "'Dear Courier,'" 167.
7. Norton Diary, May 18–June 8, 1864; Gassman, "History of Rome and Floyd County," 117–20; Lee Kennett, *Marching Through Georgia: The Story of Soldiers and Civilians During Sherman's Campaign* (New York: Harper Collins, 1995), 96, 104. No copies of the *Union Flag* are known to exist.
8. United States War Department, *The War of the Rebellion: A Compilation of the Official Records of the Union and Confederate Armies*, series 1, vol. 39, pt. 3 (Washington, DC: US Government Printing Office, 1880), 729–30; Norton Diary, October 29, 30, November 7, 11, 1864; Kennett, *Marching Through Georgia*, 232.
9. *Rome Courier*, August 31, 1865.
10. Ibid.
11. Ibid.
12. Melvin Dwinell to Albert Dwinell, 30 September 1865, Melvin Dwinell Letters, Georgia Department of Archives and History, Atlanta, GA. Underlining appears in the letter.
13. Melvin Dwinell to Irene Dwinell, 25 February 1866, Melvin Dwinell Letters.
14. Dwinell, "Vermonter in Gray," 231–35; Aycock, *All Roads to Rome*, 476–80.
15. Dwinell, "Vermonter in Gray," 235; *Tribune of Rome*, December 29, 1887.

# Bibliography


## Primary Sources

Papers

Barnsley, George S., Diary. George Scarborough Barnsley Papers, Southern Historical Collection, University of North Carolina Library, Chapel Hill, NC.

Dwinell, Melvin, Letters. Georgia Department of Archives and History, Atlanta, GA.

Norton, Reuben S. "The Wartime Diary of Reuben S. Norton, A Civilian of Rome." Special Collections, Rome-Floyd County Library, Rome, GA.

Government Documents

Bureau of the Census. Eighth Census of the United States, 1860. Washington, DC: National Archives, 1860.

———. Eighth Census of the United States, 1860, Slave Schedule. Washington, DC: National Archives, 1860.

National Archives and Records Administration. *Compiled Service Records of Confederate Soldiers Who Served in Organizations from the State of Georgia,* Roll 227, Eighth Infantry. Washington, DC: National Archives, 1959. CD.

United States War Department. *War of the Rebellion: A Compilation of the Official Records of the Union and Confederate Armies.* 128 vols. Washington, DC: US Government Printing Office, 1880–1901.

Newspapers

*Atlanta Southern Confederacy*

*Augusta Chronicle & Sentinel*

*Rome Courier*

*Tribune of Rome*

## Secondary Sources

Books

Andrews, J. Cutler. *The South Reports the Civil War.* Princeton, NJ: Princeton University Press, 1970.

Ash, Stephen V. *When the Yankees Came: Conflict and Chaos in the Occupied South, 1861–1865.* Chapel Hill: University of North Carolina Press, 1995.

Aycock, Roger D. *All Roads to Rome.* Roswell, GA: W. H. Wolfe Associates, 1981.

Bailey, Anne J. *The Chessboard of War: Sherman and Hood in the Autumn Campaigns of 1864.* Lincoln: University of Nebraska Press, 2000.

Battey, George Magruder. *A History of Rome and Floyd County, State of Georgia, United States of America: Including Numerous Incidents of More Than Local Interest, 1540–1922.* Vol. 1. Atlanta: Webb and Vary, 1922.

Boatner, Mark M., III. *The Civil War Dictionary.* New York: Vintage Books, 1991.

Brantley, Rabun Lee. *Georgia Journalism of the Civil War Period.* Nashville: George Peabody College, 1929.

Bryan, Thomas Conn. *Confederate Georgia.* Athens: University of Georgia Press, 1953.

Castel, Albert. *Decision in the West: The Atlanta Campaign of 1864.* Lawrence: University of Kansas Press, 1992.

Coleman, Kenneth, ed. *A History of Georgia.* Athens: University of Georgia Press, 1977.

Coleman, Kenneth, and Charles Stephen Gurr, eds. *Dictionary of Georgia Biography.* Athens: University of Georgia, Press, 1983.

Corley, Florence Fleming. *Confederate City: Augusta, Georgia, 1861–1865.* Columbia: University of South Carolina Press, 1960.

Craven, Avery. *The Growth of Southern Nationalism, 1848–1861.* Baton Rouge: Louisiana State University Press and the Littlefield Fund for Southern History of the University of Texas, 1953.

Crute, Joseph H., Jr. *Units of the Confederate States Army.* Midlothian, VA: Derwent Books, 1987.

Current, Richard N., ed. *Encyclopedia of the Confederacy.* 4 vols. New York: Simon & Schuster, 1993.

Daniel, Larry J., and Riley W. Gunter. *Confederate Cannon Foundries.* Union City, TN: Pioneer Press, 1977.

Dicken-Garcia, Hazel. *Journalistic Standards in Nineteenth-Century America.* Madison: University of Wisconsin Press, 1989.

Eaton, Clement. *The Growth of Southern Civilization: 1790–1860.* New York: Harper & Row, 1961.

Faust, Patricia L., ed. *Historical Times Illustrated Encyclopedia of the Civil War.* New York: Harper & Row, 1986.

Griffith, Louis Turner, and John Erwin Talmadge. *Georgia Journalism, 1763–1950.* Athens: University of Georgia Press, 1951.

Henderson, Lillian, ed. *Roster of the Confederate Soldiers of Georgia, 1861–1865.* Vol. 1. Hapeville, GA.: Longino & Porter, 1959.

Hewett, Janet. B., ed. *The Roster of Confederate Soldiers, 1861–1865.* Wilmington, NC: Broadfoot Publishing, 1995.

Krick, Robert K. *Lee's Colonels: A Biographical Register of the Field Officers of the Army of Northern Virginia.* Dayton, OH: Morningside Bookshop, 1979.

Long, E. B., with Barbara Long. *The Civil War Day by Day: An Almanac, 1861–1865.* Garden City, NY: Doubleday, 1971.

Massey, Mary Elizabeth. *Refugee Life in the Confederacy*. Baton Rouge: Louisiana State University Press, 1964.

McNeely, Patricia G., Debra Reddin van Tuyll, and Henry H. Schulte. *Knights of the Quill: Confederate Correspondents and their Civil War Reporting*. West Lafayette, IN: Purdue University Press, 2010.

McPherson, James M. *Battle Cry of Freedom: The Civil War Era*. New York: Oxford University Press, 1988.

Mitchell, Reid. *Civil War Soldiers: Their Expectations and Their Experiences*. New York: Viking, 1988.

Moore, Albert Burton. *Conscription and Conflict in the Confederacy*. New York: MacMillan, 1924.

Myers, Robert Manson, ed. *The Children of Pride: A True Story of Georgia and the Civil War*. New Haven, CT: Yale University Press, 1972.

Osthaus, Carl R. *Partisans of the Southern Press: Editorial Spokesmen of the Nineteenth Century*. Lexington: University Press of Kentucky, 1994.

Parks, Joseph H. *Joseph E. Brown of Georgia*. Baton Rouge: Louisiana State University Press, 1977.

Reynolds, Donald E. *Editors Make War: Southern Newspapers in the Secession Crisis*. Nashville: Vanderbilt University Press, 1966.

Risley, Ford. *Civil War Journalism*. Santa Barbara, CA: Praeger, 2012.

Robertson, James I., Jr. *Soldiers Blue and Gray*. Columbia: University of South Carolina Press, 1988.

Scaife, William R., and William Harris Bragg. *Joe Brown's Pets: The Georgia Militia, 1861–1865*. Macon, GA: Mercer University Press, 2004.

Wakelyn, Jon L. *Biographical Dictionary of the Confederacy*. Westport, CT: Greenwood Press, 1977.

Weitz, Mark A. *A Higher Duty: Desertion among Georgia Troops during the Civil War*. Lincoln: University of Nebraska Press, 2000.

Wiley, Bell Irvin. *The Life of Johnny Reb: The Common Soldier of the Confederacy*. Indianapolis: Bobbs-Merrill, 1943.

Wilkinson, Warren, and Steven E. Woodworth. *A Scythe of Fire: A Civil War Story of the Eighth Georgia Infantry Regiment*. New York: William Morrow, 2002.

Zenzen, Joan M. *Battling for Manassas: The Fifty-Year Preservation Struggle at Manassas National Battlefield Park*. University Park: Pennsylvania State University Press, 1998.

## Articles, Essays, and Theses

Bailey, Virginia Griffin. "Letters of Melvin Dwinnell, Yankee Rebel." *Georgia Historical Quarterly* 47, no. 2 (1963): 193–203.

Burkley, Margaret Nola. "Floyd County, Georgia, During the Civil War Era." PhD diss., Florida State University, 1998.

Dwinell, Harold A. "Vermonter in Gray: The Story of Melvin Dwinell." *Vermont History* 30, no. 3 (1962): 220–23.

Gassman, Wade B. "A History of Rome and Floyd County, Georgia in the Civil War." Master's thesis, Emory University, 1966.

Reynolds, Clark G. "Confederate Romans and Bedford Forrest: The Civil War Roots of the Towers-Norton Family." *Georgia Historical Quarterly* 77, no. 1 (1993): 20–40.

Risley, Ford. "'Dear Courier': The Civil War Correspondence of Editor Melvin Dwinell." *Journalism History* 31, no. 3 (2005): 162–70.

van Tuyll, Debra Reddin. "The Rebels Yell: Conscription and Freedom of Expression in the Civil War South." *American Journalism* 17, no. 2 (2000): 15–29.

# Index